PROFILES IN HUMAN DEVELOPMENT

GEORGE KALUGER, Ph.D.

Professor, Department of Psychology,
Shippensburg State College,
Shippensburg, Pennsylvania

MERIEM FAIR KALUGER, Litt.M.

Psycho/Educational Consultant,
Shippensburg, Pennsylvania

Saint Louis

The C. V. Mosby Company

1976

Cover photo courtesy Flint Laboratories, Division of
Baxter/Travenol, Deerfield, Illinois.

Library of Congress Cataloging in Publication Data

Main entry under title:

Profiles in human development.

   Includes bibliographies.
    1. Development psychology—Case studies.
2. Human behavior—Case studies. I. Kaluger, George.
II. Kaluger, Meriem Fair, 1921-   [DNLM: 1. Child
development. 2. Aging. 3. Psychology. BF713 K14p]
BF713.P76   155.2′5   75-37505
ISBN 0-8016-2607-2

E/M/M 9 8 7 6 5 4 3 2 1

To our wonderful
students, colleagues, and friends,
who graciously shared with us
their joys, their sorrows,
and their love

Preface

A lifetime of human experiences is difficult to put into one small volume. Indeed, a library of volumes would not be sufficient to touch upon all the experiences that a person could have in a lifetime. Yet, we are seeking, in a small way, to give a sampling of human experiences in development and behavior so that the content of life science, behavioral science, health science, and social science courses may be made more meaningful to students and their teachers.

The concept of profiles, as we view them, developed quite innocuously several years ago when we attempted to practice what we preached. We said, in effect, that if we truly believed in the existence of significant individual differences in the various abilities, characteristics, and systems that make up people, then, as teachers, we should be intellectually honest and offer students a variety of options, including their own innovative suggestions, to meet a writing and study requirement of the course. Profiles, or vignettes, of a narrow segment of a life experience were suggested as one of the options. It quickly became evident that those who chose to do the profiles were more enthusiastic than others about their writing projects and were able to relate better to the principles under discussion. The profiles approach, as a supplement to teaching, was used successfully in undergraduate and graduate courses related to the psychology of human development at all age levels and to courses in the psychology of human behavior.

Specifically, a profile is a short narrative that relates to a meaningful event, experience, or aspect of human development or human behavior. It is a cameo, a vignette, a sharp look at someone or something. The goal of a profile is to present an in-depth account of some event or experience of life that would give the writer and the reader a deeper insight into the nature of development, behavior, and emotional feelings of life. Several profiles, each dealing with a different stage of development, were required during the semester from those who chose this option. The profile could be written either about people they knew or about themselves.

The response and results were tremendous. The profiles touched on a large variety of aspects of life. Many were intensely insightful and creative in their presentation. The profiles that were permitted to be shared with the class proved to be exceedingly effective and useful in making content come alive. Of course, some of the best profiles were never presented since they were personal, private, and sometimes too revealing. Thus came the impetus for this book. The suggestion was made: "If you do not mind sharing your profile with others in such a way that your identity and the identity of the person in the profile are concealed, I would appreciate having your profile to keep for consideration for inclusion in a book of profiles."

The profiles in this book were selected from at least a thousand papers. The earliest date included is one written in 1968 and the latest are several written in 1975. Many considerations went into the selection of the profiles. The basic criterion was: "Is this topic related to what is generally studied in courses in human development and human behavior, and, if so, can it be used for teaching and discussion purposes?" In a general way, another criterion was: "Does this profile say anything meaningful?" A special effort was made to select a wide variety of topics at each of eleven age levels. An interesting element that emerged was sort of a historical time-line relating to important events in the lives of students from different generations.

All of the profiles were edited, some rather severely. All names, dates, locations, occupations, and identifying descriptions were carefully disguised or changed in order to preserve the privacy of each profile character and the writer. The students who wrote the profiles came from a wide spectrum of life. Because of its location, the college attracts a number of students from the military and from foreign service families, people who have traveled the country and the world. A good third of the student population comes from large cosmopolitan areas, about a third from rural and small town areas, and the rest from cities in between. What all the students have in common is that they came to college. A limitation of this book is that only a few of the profiles have been written by noncollege individuals. The socioeconomic spread, however, is from economically disadvantaged, subsidized students to students from families in the upper income bracket.

We made the initial selection of profiles. This set was then read by a colleague and dear friend, Margaret Gruver Hogg, who taught, in part, a creative writing course. The third set was read and partly edited by another dear friend and English teacher, Kathy Katz Aberman. Our deepest thanks go to these two individuals for their help. We made the final selection of profiles and did the final editing. A general introduction is presented before each chapter to provide an orientation as to the nature of the development and behavior presented in that set of profiles. Each chapter ends with "Things to Think About and Do" and a list of appropriate readings.

Our very special thanks go to Norma Strassburger, who has helped type the manuscripts of four of our books. She was helped by two particularly fine students, Susan Barton and Mary Luebbe. A special reading of the galley proofs was done by Dr. James S. Steck, a close friend and colleague. The photographs were taken by David S. Strickler of Newville, Pennsylvania.

Finally, our deepest and sincerest appreciation goes to the many students, undergraduates and graduates, who wrote and submitted profiles. Over a hundred of their papers were used. We feel humble that they were willing to share their personal human experiences with us and others.

George Kaluger

Meriem Fair Kaluger

Contents

Part three

THE ADOLESCENT YEARS

Part four

PERSONHOOD: MATURITY IN THE OFFING

PROFILES IN HUMAN DEVELOPMENT

Introduction

The way of life is one of involvement, experience, and change. Involvement, in this context, means to engage in activities that are significant to one's total growth and development. An experience is an act of participation and of experiencing by which intellectual and emotional responses are internalized. The element of change results as one uses what has been experienced to attain a higher level of competent, independent living. Learning, emotions, and psychophysical needs will initiate, direct, and control the nature of one's involvement, experience, and change throughout the span of life. Ultimately, feelings and emotions will color life and its adventures with shades of warmth or coolness, acceptance or rejection, love or hatred, and enthusiasm or apathy.

Environmental variables and bodily functions are pertinent, of course. The body and the mind function within an environmental framework that consists of people and objects, all of which, in one way or another, reflect an atmosphere of feelings and emotions. As children try to find out about themselves, as adolescents seek to relate to places and things at home, at school, and in the community, as adults interact with each other, they do so through feelings and value judgments. Feelings, emotions, and values are interwoven in all areas of development—social, intellectual, and physical. Within these elements, the individual develops a highly diverse and complex pattern of inner dynamics that will eventually be integrated into a unique identity. A total being, the psychologically mature individual, results from interaction in a total way, in a total life-field.

The experiential backgrounds of individuals are as varied and as numerous as the birds of the air. Individual differences abound. Yet, underneath it all, there exists a commonality in mankind, a thread that runs through every man, woman, and child in the world and ties them together in a pattern of sameness. Only the outer vestiges of manmade civilization, such as clothing, customs, and culture, give the impression of differences in man.

People are more alike than they are different. They are conceived the same way, born the same way, grow the same way, have the same basic needs, hopes, and desires for themselves and their families, and ultimately die. The profiles in this book speak of experiences that relate to all people. The "birds of a feather" simile will be noted if one but looks beneath the words, circumstances, and descriptions used in the vignettes. In some cases, you will identify completely with the character in the profile. In other cases, you will wonder: "How can that be?" In all cases, however, you will say; "But that is life."

Hope

Look to this day!
For it is life, the very life of life.
In its brief course lie all the varieties and
   realities of your existence:
The bliss of growth;
The glory of action;
The splendor of beauty;
The yesterday is already a dream,
   and tomorrow is only a vision;
But today, well lived, makes every yesterday
   a dream of happiness and every tomorrow
   a vision of hope.

From the Sanskrit

Part one

THE FIRST FIVE YEARS

CHAPTER 1

Thus it begins . . .

The miracle of growth and development of a child is more perfectly illustrated during the nine months prior to birth than at any other stage of life. Conception, the coming together and union of the female ovum and the male sperm, takes place within one to three days after the act of copulation. At the very moment that conception occurs, the baby's hereditary characteristics and sex are firmly established. Within twelve hours, the single, fertilized ovum begins to divide into multiples of cells and a new germinal identity is being created. For six to ten days after conception, cell division continues to take place while the zygote (the fertilized egg) makes its way to the wall of the uterus where it will implant itself in order to draw nourishment from the mother and to grow.

It is at this point that the multicellular fertilized ovum begins to form the amniotic sac, the chorion, and the germinal disk that will become the child. Growth and development progress at a fantastic pace to change the zygote from a collection of apparently undifferentiated cells into a recognizable human creature. By the time the new mother misses her first menstrual period, about two to three weeks after the act of intercourse, the baby's nervous system, digestive system, circulatory system, and heart have already begun to form. Indeed, by seven to eight weeks after copulation, the fertilized ovum has developed into an identifiable human being, albeit very minute in size, with all the characteristics, physical appendages, and functions of a human organism. Mother may not even know she is pregnant. Yet, the state of her physical and mental health, as well as the biochemical condition of her blood, can profoundly affect the development of the embryo during this crucial, critical period. The last seven months of prenatal development are devoted mainly to a strengthening, refinement, and growth of the systems, organs, and body developed during the

second to eighth weeks. The fetus is preparing itself for its next adventure—birth and the initiation of a self-sustaining life.

For the mother and father, the nine months preceding the birth of the child are filled with anticipation, preparation, anxieties, uncertainties, joy, love, concern, bewilderment—the entire spectrum of emotions, expectations, and experiences. It is difficult to imagine that the reactions and behaviors of any two sets of parents could be exactly alike. And yet there are some common thoughts and activities. Baby is coming, ready or not, wanted or not. How baby will affect the lives of others can only be surmised. In all probability, the main thought of the parents is simply the birth of the baby and the hope that baby will be all right. Anything else done up to that time is mostly window-dressing. The show begins when baby arrives. The profile "On Becoming a Father" tells of father's anxieties concerning the birth of his first child. The play "From Motherhood to Parenthood" presents the elated feelings of a woman who very much wants a child. In both cases, it's what happens afterward that makes a difference.

A couple waits six years to get married, then decides to start a family immediately in "A New Life—and a New Life." The modern motif in this profile is rather interesting. Father gives a high recommendation to the Lamaze technique in "Joys of Natural Childbirth." The young girl in "Ten Short Minutes," however, does not contemplate how she wants her baby born; her main concern is how to tell her boyfriend. In "A Way Out" another unmarried girl makes a decision that does not even consider how the baby is to be born.

Some babies are born under very difficult circumstances for their mothers. A young woman has physical problems resulting in an ileostomy; yet the desire for child is great and she becomes pregnant. Complications set in but are finally resolved in "That Baby was Born

Too Darn Soon." Problems of another sort occur in "My Second Child—Wanted and Unwanted." The mother wonders if the behavior of her second child might not have been caused by circumstances that occurred during her pregnancy.

On becoming a father

"Rusty, I think it's time to go to the hospital." This statement is not involved or explosive, but it served as the catalyst that got me started on the most apprehensive day of my life.

The morning of November 7 did not begin much differently from most other days. I had gotten out of bed at six o'clock to prepare to go to work. As I was sitting at the breakfast table, Marge came into the kitchen. "Rusty, I think it's time to go to the hospital," she said. "What! Oh my God, what should I do?" All of a sudden my appetite left. I could not finish my breakfast; I found that my knees were weak when I tried to stand, and I was in such a nervous state I could not even tie my necktie.

My wife sensed how I was reacting to her statement. She tried to calm me. She called the doctor and, after their conversation, assured me that all was well and said that we were to go to the doctor's office. "The doctor's office! Why there? Why not the hospital?" Marge had started to labor and we were going to the doctor's office! I did not clearly understand the labor process and its length; I really thought that there would not be enough time to go to the doctor's office and then to the hospital before the baby was born.

From this point on, my thoughts and emotions were those of near-panic. Hurry! Hurry! Hurry! I did not want anything to go wrong. The whole way to the doctor's offce, a fifteen minute drive, I was tense. I could not hold a conversation; I cussed out other drivers for being in *my* way, and I grew so nervous I could not even depress the clutch pedal properly. Through all of this action, my wife remained calm and tried to assure me that all was well.

Finally we arrived at the doctor's office. After a quick examination, which I was not able to attend, Dr. Dunlap opened the door. "Rusty, take Marge to the hospital. You're going to become a father today." These were his only words. He, of course, did not appear apprehensive and my wife was still calm, but my anxiety level was increasing.

From the doctor's office, Marge and I headed for the hospital. She told me not to hurry because the baby would not arrive until that afternoon. However, I was still tense and in a hurry. When we arrived at the hospital, I started to calm down because Marge was, at last, where the delivery could safely take place. What a relief for me that we made it before the baby was born!

Marge was admitted to the hospital, and Dr. Dunlap arrived soon after. He spoke to me for quite a while this time. Then he gave Marge another examination. "The baby won't arrive until two o'clock. You may as well go to work," he said to me after the exam.

By now my anxiety had subsided quite a bit. My wife was in the hospital and in good hands, so I went to work. I tried not to be nervous at work, but, as the day progressed, my attempts were not very good. My boss finally asked me if I wouldn't like to go back to the hospital. For some reason I refused. I wanted to do something to get my mind off the impending birth, but I could not do it. Finally my boss pointed out that I was anxiously pacing the room and was making the other workers nervous. He convinced me to go to the hospital. Just as I was leaving the shop, I got a phone call from Dr. Dunlap. "Rusty," he said, "the time is near. You had better come to the hospital now."

Birth is near! The tenseness grew worse. I hurried to the hospital; a lot of bad thoughts were going through my head. I really believe, now, that I did not want to be at the hospital when the baby was born. I was afraid something might happen. Maybe I would have to make a decision concerning a life. "Please, Baby, arrive before I get there!"

The baby did not hear my plea. However, when I did arrive at the hospital my wife was already in the delivery room. I tried to present a picture of calmness to the nurses and the other men who were expecting to become fathers. I did not want to pace the floor.

"Well, it must be close now! I can't just sit

here in the waiting room. Maybe there's something I can do." With these thoughts I left the waiting room and headed down the hall toward the delivery room. As I got nearer to the delivery room, I grew tense. "What are you doing down here?" said a voice. "Me? Why, I couldn't wait any longer. Please check and see if my wife's okay!" Fortunately, the nurse was understanding. She had me sit on a chair outside the delivery room and she entered. Only a few minutes passed before she came back into the hall. "Mr. Adams, your wife just had a beautiful girl. Congratulations."

"A girl! What the hell am I going to do with a girl?" I said to myself as I felt a rush of mixed emotions hit me. I was glad it was over but I was disappointed in the outcome. Then a nurse emerged carrying a bloody mess. The mess was my daughter. Before I had an opportunity to really look at her, Dr. Dunlap came to me. "Rusty, your wife had a fine daughter, and she and the baby are both fine. Congratulations!" "Thanks, Doc."

I waited in the hall hoping that I could see Marge as the attendants were taking her to the recovery room. Even though the doctor said that she was okay, I was still concerned. But I certainly did not want her to see my disappointment at having a girl. When the attendants wheeled my wife out of the delivery room she smiled and took my hand. I knew then that she was okay and I felt much better.

After a short visit with Marge, I went home. The next day at work one of the fellows who knew I had wanted a boy said: "Rusty, you'll never know what love really is until you hold your daughter." When I went to the hospital that night I discovered what he meant. Marge had "rooming in," and I held the new Baby Adams from the time I arrived until visiting hours were over. Without a doubt, I was the stereotyped proud father.

Now, just for contrast, I would like to relate some of the events which surrounded the birth of our second child some six years later. Once again I was eating my breakfast, but this time I had company, daughter Cheryl. As we began to eat, Marge got a severe pain. This one severe pain was her only indication that the baby was on its way. As soon as she recovered from it she told me to follow a plan of action that we had

laid ahead of time. As I calmly took Cheryl to a neighbor's house Marge called the doctor to make certain that someone would be at the hospital to take care of her, and then we left. This time I had some anxiety in the form of butterflies in the stomach but I had much more concern for my wife. She was having severe pain and, although she was trying to be brave, I realized that she was in trouble and that I would have to be the calm one this time.

As we rapidly progressed toward the hospital, I tried to review the delivery process. The possibility existed that the birth might take place in the car. I was hoping beyond hope that it wouldn't.

Fortunately, the trip to the hospital only took about eight minutes. I pulled the car up to the emergency entrance; an attendant got Marge and took her to the maternity floor. The time was 7:40 A.M. I felt some relief that we had arrived on time and I proceeded to go through the process of having Marge formally admitted. By 8:00 A.M. this process was completed and I headed for the maternity floor. As I arrived there, a nurse gave me Marge's clothes and told me that the baby would not be born until later in the morning. I decided to go to work but, as I walked down the hall, this same nurse yelled: "Mr. Adams, your wife just had a nine and one-half pound boy. They both are fine."

What a feeling! The birth process was so short, Marge was okay, and we had a boy. I had never experienced a feeling of relief quite like the one I experienced then. I remained at the hospital until I saw my son and my wife, and then I headed to work to share my joy with anyone who was willing to share it with me. Once again I was the stereotyped proud father!

A play: motherhood to parenthood

The point of this play may seem vague at first, but the "real" world associated with a newborn baby should become evident by the end of the play. Before giving birth there is no work involved; after giving birth the baby becomes an occupation in itself. As the reader progresses in this story of life, he or she will notice the incidents that cause the woman to realize that the wonderful bundle of joy, referred to as her baby, may bring some disappointing and depressing, not to mention fretful, moments. By the time the new life has developed and blossomed, the woman becomes a mother/parent and begins to see the "sugar-coated" world in a realistic manner.

The woman in the play may seem very corny, but she *is* real and everything that she says, she really said at one time. She is yours truly; that is why I know she is real.

CHARACTERS

Man (later becomes Father)
Woman (later becomes Mother)
Baby (later just becomes)
Doctor
Nurse A
Nurse B
Narrator

ACT I   THE INNOCENT BEGINNING

SCENE 1   Setting—Early in September, on a bench beside the tennis courts. A man and a woman are discussing marriage plans, children, etc.

Man: I love you.
Woman: And I love you.
Man: Will you marry me?
Woman: Oh, yes! As soon as you want! I love you. I want you to be the father of my children. Someday I want to have many fat babies. You know, little "mes" and "yous" running all over the house, crying and screaming and pulling each other's hair.
Man: Oh, no! (man beginning to get sarcastic)
Woman: (still serious) What do you mean? Honey, you will be a fantastic father. I think I'll be a good mother. Both of us are intelligent, educated, and well-adjusted people. What could be better than having us joined together forever? Our children will have children— they'll be part of us. Then their children will have children— they'll be part of us.
Man: That's great, but why *many* "fat" babies? I'll settle for one—two at the most.

Woman: Okay, you win. At least we have settled for one. The rest we can discuss later.
Man: Personally I think we can forget "the rest."
Woman: We can talk about that after we discuss the wedding. I want a big one. That will make my mother very happy. I want two bridesmaids, a ring bearer, and a flower girl.

Fade out as they discuss wedding plans for October.

Narrator: As you can see, the woman definitely wants to bear children. She is prepared to have children no matter how many arguments her husband can think of against having them.

SCENE 2   Setting—Seven months later, in April. The dinner dishes are being cleared away. Man and woman are discussing the events of the day.

Woman: Honey, you remember I had an appointment with the doctor today because I haven't felt well lately?
Man: Yes.
Woman: He told me what was wrong.
Man: What was wrong and how much did your prescription cost?
Woman: Oh, come on. He said I was okay, but I'd feel better in about nine months.
Man: What do you mean? (sitting up and paying attention for the first time in the discussion)
Woman: I think you know what I mean, silly. You are going to be a father and I am going to be a mother. Our first little fat baby. A little me and you.
Man: (still in complete shock) Are you sure?
Woman: Of course I'm sure. Just think how great it will be. A lot of our friends can't have children, but look at us. We weren't even trying, and we're well over a month on our way. I guess a couple should just concentrate on loving each other rather than trying to have a baby. Oh Honey, I'm so

happy! What do you want—a boy or a girl? I want a boy first because I always wanted a big brother—there always should be a big brother in every family.

Man: Are you really sure? Did the doctor do that frog test? Did you really kill a frog? I mean, we should really be positive about things like this before we do a lot of planning.

Woman: Yes, of course I'm sure. The test was positive. I don't think they used a frog. I don't think they do that anymore, but I was in the office while they did the test. Honey, aren't you happy? Gosh, I already bought some things for the baby and asked my sister to get out all of her old baby clothes for me. Wait and I'll show you. You will not believe how little they are.

Fade out as Woman leaves the kitchen to produce various articles of baby clothing.

ACT II   PREPARATION FOR THE UNEXPECTED—RATHER, EXPECTED

SCENE 1   Setting—In the attic of the Woman's Parents' house, in June.

Man: I still can't understand why we are here.
Woman: Oh come on. We are here looking through all of the toys that I had when I was a kid so I can fix them and clean them for our little baby.
Man: But the baby isn't due until December. It's only June now. We have plenty of time.
Woman: There is so much to do and so much to get ready before then. I want to fix up the baby's room with the toys before December.

Fade out as they begin to go through another box of toys.

SCENE 2   Setting—In the Baby's room-to-be, in August.

Man: What happened to my desk?
Woman: It's in the dining room. There was no more room in here for it since I put up the crib.

Man: (a little irritated and very sarcastic) We could have left the desk in here a little longer—it's only August. I work so well in here, Hon. Why does the crib have to be put up so soon? No one will be sleeping in it yet.
Woman: I just want the room to be right. It has to be a baby's room, so I want the crib up now. I won't bother you in the dining room while you are working. Is this picture in the right place? ...

Fade out as the Woman puts up pictures.

SCENE 3   Setting—In the living room one evening watching television, in September.

Man: Why aren't you in the baby's room? There are only three more months until the baby is due. Do you think the room will be ready?
Woman: (ignoring sarcasm) The baby's room was finished last week.
Man: What? You mean you're done decorating the walls with Winnie-the-Pooh pals, putting up circus curtains, and hanging mobiles?
Woman: Honey, don't make fun. Children need lots of things to look at when they are in their cribs with nothing else to do—it helps to give them a vast background of experience. I learned that in Child Development.
Man: Sometimes I wonder about the value of the courses colleges offer in Elementary Education. Soon we'll have a sandbox in the baby's room.
Woman: Honey, no! Don't make fun of elementary teachers now. Besides that, I know better than to get a sandbox already. That would only frustrate the baby because he wouldn't be ready for it. Honey, I'm bored. I'm done getting ready. Now I need the baby, but there is none. I'll go crazy here all day with nothing to do.
Man: Why not try the hospital? You can work there during the day.
Woman: Okay. I'll call tomorrow. I'll even look up the number now.

Fade out as Woman goes into room for the telephone book.

Narrator: The woman began to work at a private nursery school. She thought that would be better than working in the hospital because she could have a chance to be with young children. Besides the road to work went right by the hospital. Since she and her husband were new to the area it seemed wise to learn the route to the hospital and figure out the time needed to get to it.

ACT III　　THE BIG EVENT UNFOLDS

SCENE 1　Setting—In bed very early in the morning, in late November.

Woman: Will you pull me out of bed, Honey? (During the past week it had been difficult to navigate around the house. The baby shifted its weight and position from what seemed to be under the ribs to very low in the pelvic region. The older women at work advised her to quit work because they said the baby had "dropped" and it was soon going to be time to go to the hospital. Although the doctors had advised her to not listen to the "advice" and "old wives' tales" she would definitely hear, she quit anyway.)

Man: Is it time to get up already?

Woman: No, but I feel a little funny. I think I'd better go to the bathroom.

Man: What do you mean funny? It's not time for the baby yet, is it?

Woman: No, the doctor said the sixth, but he figured since it's just the first baby it will be due about a week or two later. I just feel uncomfortable.

Man: Do you want me to come with you?

Woman: No.

Man: Sure? Will you be okay?

Woman: (from the hall) Yes, I'll be fine. Go back to sleep.

Woman reenters and says: I think we will have the baby sooner than we thought.

Man: (now wide awake) Are you sure? How do you know? When will it happen?

Woman: (very calmly) The doctor said you'd be nervous. I'm supposed to keep you calm, so calm down. I just noticed a bloody discharge. I think the doctors call it "show." That's a sign that the labor may soon start. He said to call him when it happened. It's only 6:30 and Sunday, so I'll wait till later to call.

Man: Call now.

Woman: No. Just relax. Nothing will happen for quite a while. My water sac didn't break yet and I have no contractions. Just relax and go to sleep. That's what I'm going to do.

Fade out as Man and Woman pretend to sleep.

SCENE 2　Setting—Later that same day. About 11:00 A.M. In the living room trying to read the Sunday paper.

Woman: I think I am starting into labor.

Man: How do you know?

Woman: I just do. It feels like I have cramps.

Man: Call the doctor, please?

Woman: Okay. I hope I get him since it's Sunday.

Fade out while Woman is on telephone. Man in the foreground acting calm, but straining his ears to listen.

Woman comes into focus and says: The doctor said to come in to the hospital when my pains get closer together. He said they do not seem as if they are "real" yet. I don't think they are either, because they don't really hurt.

Man: Are you packed?

Woman: That's a silly question to ask. I'm packed and I have the baby's clothes ready for when we come home.

Man: How about something to eat while we wait? I'm starving.

Woman: The doctor said not to eat anything, but what can I get for you?

Man: Nothing. You go and start getting ready.

Fade out. Man to kitchen. Woman goes to bedroom.

SCENE 3 Setting—About 2:00 P.M. the same day. Man working on homework. Woman is just sitting.

Woman: Let's go. The pains are harder and about 15 minutes apart.

Man: I'll get the car ready and you meet me out front.

Fade out as the man goes out the door to the garage.

SCENE 4 Setting—At the hospital at 11:00 P.M. at night in the waiting room.

Woman: Go home, Honey. The pains stopped at six o'clock when they were about two minutes apart. They said it was false labor. They are keeping me though because they think the contractions will start again soon, possibly tomorrow.

Man: If they start, you'll call me, won't you?

Woman: Of course, I will. (They kiss and the camera fades out.)

SCENE 5 Setting—In the hospital about 2:00 P.M. Monday afternoon. The Woman is finally resting since the nurses made her walk all morning to help the labor cramps get stronger.

Woman: Nurse, I think I'm beginning to go into real labor. These pains aren't just cramps.

Nurse: Are they close or far apart?

Woman: Close.

Nurse: Lie on your back and let me time the contractions. (Nurse lays hand on Woman's stomach and feels the contractions.) They are a little over two minutes apart. Let's go back to the labor room. Do you want to see your husband first?

Woman: Is he still out there? Can he come in here? I don't think I can control my kidneys long enough to talk out there. (Since the baby had "dropped" to the pelvic re-

gion, the control of kidneys and bladder had been very difficult.)

Nurse: He can go back to the other waiting room. Only stay until you feel as though you can't sit anymore.

Fade out as Woman walks toward the back waiting room.

SCENE 6 Setting—In the back waiting room.

Man: How are you now? Do you hurt much? Don't look that way. Does it really hurt?

Woman: I'm sorry. It does hurt, but not that much. I think I'd feel better if I were lying down.

Man: Go back and lie down. I'll be here if you want me to come in later.

Woman: I'll stay a little while longer. From what I understand I'll be in there for quite a while.

Fade out as they continue talking about the baby.

SCENE 7 Setting—At the Nurse's desk.

Woman: (over intercom—*very* frantic) Nurse, why am I bleeding? Is the baby still all right?

Nurse: You are all right. So is the baby. Your birth canal is just widening to make room for the baby, and as it does there is bleeding. Don't worry about it.

SCENE 8 Setting—In the labor room.

Nurse: (Upon entering the room she sees the Woman sitting upon the edge of the bed, feet dangling, and humming to herself) Lie down please. We don't want you to fall. Are you "high" or what?

Woman: I feel pains I've never felt before, but I want the baby to know I am happy that it is coming. You know, make it welcome right away.

Nurse: I'm sure it knows, but now you'd better lie down so you don't fall and lose the baby.

Narrator: The reader may have doubts as to whether this really happened, but it *really* did!

SCENE 9   Setting—In the labor room.

Nurse: I am going to check you rectally to see how far along you are. You haven't made a sound, so you'll probably be quite a while yet.

Woman: Are you sure? I am getting so sleepy and so hungry.

Nurse: I'll check. Legs up! Oh! You are more than ready. Were you going to proceed without the Doctor? (She runs out of room. Soon there is a voice paging the Doctor over the loudspeaker. Nurse reappears and says:) We are taking you to delivery. It won't be long.

SCENE 10   Setting—In delivery room. Very bright lights.

Enter anesthesiologist; Nurse addresses him: She doesn't want any. This is going to be natural birth.

Enter Nurse B: Let's get on the delivery table. (Woman changes tables.) Feet up in stirrups. (To other nurse) Catheterization?

Nurse A: There is no time. Did the Doctor hear?

Nurse B: I hope.

Woman is becoming upset about the Doctor not arriving. Finally Doctor enters.

Doctor: Hi! What have we here? Did your little one finally decide to wake up? Okay, on with the pretty leggings.

Woman: Leggings?

Doctor: (after the leggings are put on Woman) Oh, how becoming! Okay, bear down and hold the contraction. Let up after the contraction is done, but not completely. Don't you ever moan or scream? What do you want, a boy or a girl?

Woman: At this point, just a baby with two eyes, a nose, two arms, two legs, (moan) two feet, fingers, the whole works in working condition.

Doctor: The head is out. Bear down with the contraction once again.

Nurse B: Hold the contraction.

Woman: Is that right?

Nurse B: Fine.

(The woman feels the most unusual sensation in the world—as if the baby "popped" out.)

Nurses: Oh, a girl! She is beautiful! At least six pounds, twelve ounces.

Woman: (up on elbows) I want to see. (From what seems to be two miles away the woman hears the most beautiful sound in the world—the "birth cry." From the Doctor's hands she sees hanging this little thing—skinny little arms and legs as compared with a huge head.)

Doctor: (to Nurse) Start cleaning this one. She is full of mucus. (to Mother) Lie back down. You are not finished yet. You'll feel more contractions. We have to get rid of the afterbirth.

Woman: This is the worst part. (moan) How long does it take?

Doctor: We have to make sure everything is cleaned out. (After a few more contractions) Let her hold her daughter now. She's finished.

Nurse: Here. She is six pounds, ten ounces, eighteen and one-half inches. She seems normal and is beautiful.

Mother: Hi, there, little one. You sure did make a lot of noise and got a lot of attention. We really have a lot to do together. Why is her head kind of caved in on one side, Nurse?

Nurse: That will soon smooth itself out. A baby's head is very pliable—the skull is not complete or very hard yet, so that it can take the shape of the birth canal, to get out without injuring the brain. That is normal. The next time you see her you won't notice it. You'd better go. Your husband is waiting.

Mother: Good-bye, little one.

SCENE 11   Setting—In the hall of the maternity ward. Enter Father.

Mother: Did you see her?

Father: Yes. She's something, isn't she? She's ours, but she still looks like a shriveled-up prune in a basket (teasingly).

Mother: She's beautiful. Hardly any wrinkles, like other babies.

Father: I guess she is. (still teasing)
Mother: I'll keep her. Say, look at my new figure. . . . .

Fade out from hall.

SCENE 12   Setting—In the hospital room.

Nurse: Wake up. Time to see little one.
Mother: (taking Baby) Hi! Did you rest well?
Baby: WaaHaa! WaaHaa!
Mother: Here, here. (rocking Baby in bed)
Nurse: You are nursing, right?
Mother: Yes.
Nurse: Let the baby nurse on each breast 5 minutes at first. This will help to get the milk flowing. There will be no milk for about 3 to 5 days, just a clear liquid. This is important for immunity. After that give the baby sugar water. This is very important. Your baby is full of mucus and the water will get it out.
Mother: Okay. (beginning to nurse Baby—Baby squirms and fights for the breast, but all is in vain.)

Nurse: Stroke the cheek gently. That tells her which direction to turn her head. Babies have to learn to find the breast. See—she turned her head the opposite way when I stroked this cheek. Be sure to get the baby's mouth completely around the dark part of the breast. This is where the milk glands are activated. Don't just put the nipple in the mouth. You'll hurt the nipple and the baby will not get milk.
Mother: (trying, but failing) But her mouth is too little.
Nurse: Don't try too hard. Relax. You'll get her upset, too. You've tried hard enough; give her some water.
Mother: (trying to forget failure) Here you go, sweetie. (Baby sucks hard. Nurse leaves. Soon baby regurgitates all of the water. To the woman in the next bed) What did I do? What should I do? Is she okay?

Baby immediately begins wailing: Waahaa! Waahaa!

Nurse comes in and takes Baby.

Narrator: The second feeding does not go very well either. The Nurse finally helped to make the feeding partially successful. It seems the baby had a hard time learning to suck. She put her tongue up instead of down. After much patience on the part of the Mother and the Nurse, the Baby finally learned. The third feeding was completely a failure. There was no Nurse around. The Mother was upset and the Baby was upset. The fourth feeding on the third day was terrible. Finally the Mother was so upset when the Baby left, she cried. This continued until it was time to go home. There was still no milk flowing. The Doctor told her to begin to bottle feed if she still met failure. Finally the Woman has to face the fact that she cannot continue in this way. She tells herself to relax and try less.

EPILOGUE   BABY IS HOME

SCENE 1   Setting—At Home

Woman: (upon entering the house) I'm so glad to be home again. I missed you.
Man: I missed you, too. Let's sit down for a while.

(They sit down and get comfortable. Soon the Baby cries. The Mother tries to nurse again but is unsuccessful. Ends up giving the baby a sample bottle of Similac.)

Man: Let's get something to eat.
Woman: You go and get it and bring it back. We all can't go. I have to boil some water for the Baby.

Man leaves.

SCENE 2   Second night at home
Baby crying. In fact, the Baby cries every twenty minutes. Mother cannot find out what is wrong. She changes the diaper. She rocks the Baby. She walks the Baby. The Baby still cries. Is the Baby thirsty? She thinks. She finally gets water for the Baby. The Baby nearly chokes to death. Tired, defeated, and upset, the Woman finally gets into bed as her husband is getting up to go to work.

Narrator: The next two nights the Mother walked the Baby from about 1:00 A.M. to 7:00 A.M. She is exhausted by the weekend. Finally her mother-in-law comes and makes her switch to bottles. She also brought with her a pacifier. Mother gets a much-needed rest while mother-in-law cleans the house and prepares the meals.

SCENE 3   Setting—One day in the life of Mother when Baby is about three weeks old.

7:00 A.M.   Baby crying. Puts on a bottle to warm. Changes Baby's diaper. Feeds the Baby. Changes the Baby's diaper. Talks a little to the Baby. Rocks Baby until Baby goes back to sleep.

8:00 A.M.   Begins to make formula. Cleans up the kitchen.

8:15 A.M.   Baby up again. (This baby does *not* like wet diapers!)

9:00 A.M.   Baby gets a sponge bath and clean clothes.

10:00 A.M.   Feeds Baby again. (This baby eats every three hours.) Baby sleeps.

1:00 P.M.   Feeds Baby again. Walks with Baby outside in the fresh air.

3:00 P.M.   Baby wakes. Mother talks to the Baby while she tries to clean up the living room.

4:00 P.M.   Feeds Baby. Begins to make new formula. (One package of formula only makes enough for six feedings.)

7:00 P.M.   Feeds Baby again. Goes to bed.

10:00 P.M.   Baby only wakes up for one feeding at 1:00 P.M. This is so unusual Mother lies awake because she thinks there must be something wrong since the Baby is sleeping so well.

Fade off as Narrator gives examples of the incidents that have happened to the Mother and Baby since Baby was brought home. Woman will never again be the same person as before!

A new life—and a new life

December 27 was the big day ... Amy L. Baker walked up the aisle and became my wife.

We had waited for this moment for six years, and now we were joined as one. We spent our honeymoon in the Poconos and arrived back home late on New Year's Day. Then it happened. On a beautiful, snow-covered winter evening in January, Amy and I decided to start a family. We thought everything would be beautiful, but it wasn't completely. You see, we live on a farm that my former college roommate and his father bought last summer. My friend, Reed, is a twenty-seven-year-old hippie who is a manic-depressive sort of person. To meet the mortgage payments on the farm every month, Reed decided to rent the two floors of the farm house. My wife and I rented the upstairs, and a social worker and his family rented the downstairs. Reed was really without a place to stay until he and his father could finish renovating the garage into a bachelor flat. So, only five weeks after we had returned from our honeymoon, Reed asked if he could move in with us for "only a couple of days." Things were fine the first two weeks, but during the third week, Amy thought she had the flu and was quite ill. At the same time, Reed was having emotional upheavals due to a strained relationship with his girlfriend. Although Amy refused to believe me, she was going through the first stages of pregnancy. Simultaneously, Reed's emotions over his girlfriend were getting the best of his ulcers. Since Amy was ill, she couldn't work, and since Reed was an upset hippie, he didn't believe in work. Therefore, a typical week day would start off like this:

Upon rising at 7:00 A.M., Amy would use all her strength getting me breakfast, while Reed was still fast asleep in the "odd room." I would leave for work at 7:45 A.M. and Amy would immediately go to the bathroom, still thinking that she had the flu. Around 9:30 A.M., Reed would wake up and knock on the bedroom door, waking Amy, who would listen to Reed relate and rerelate the problems that he was going through with his girlfriend. As the morning progressed, Amy's symptoms would become worse and Reed's ulcers would start to act up. The bathroom, therefore, soon became the most frequently visited room in the apartment. When I arrived home from work each day, Reed would talk to me about his girl-

A dreary place would be this earth
Were there no little people in it;
The song of life would lose its mirth
Were there no babies to begin it.

friend, which would make Amy mad because the same topics had been discussed with her earlier in the day.

And so it went, day after day. The days turned into weeks. Amy and I were getting quite upset but couldn't bring ourselves around to asking our landlord to move out because, underneath it all, we both really liked him. This continued until Reed had been living with us seven weeks out of our twelve weeks of married life. Then it happened.. I teased Amy one morning about living with two men for more than half her married life. She lost her temper

and went into a frenzied rage ... Reed moved out entirely within an hour.

March and April were a joyous time for Amy and me. She got an appointment with one of the obstetricians in town who confirmed that she was indeed pregnant. Of course, I had told her so all along. Baby books were obtained at the county library by the armloads and many nights were spent in diligent reading.

May was a beautiful month. Amy and I were so very happy. One night, around the twentieth of May, Amy and I went to the movies. It was very dark as we drove back to the farm. When we reached the driveway entrance, Amy let out a gasp. She thought she felt some movement within her but then dismissed the thought. However, around 3:00 A.M. the following morning I was awakened by the delighted shouts of: "Ted! Ted! He moved! He moved!" My response to this middle-of-the-night statement was: "Huh? Good, Honey. ZZZZZZZZZZZ" The little one had begun to make his presence felt as well as known.

Perhaps, at this point, I should discuss my wife's "magic belly," as we have come to call it. Most men, I presume, would say that their wives had good figures when they were first married. I am no exception. When we got married, my wife had a figure that would make any woman envious. As the months progressed, things happened and Amy's magic belly began doing magical things. The magic belly made Amy's skin very smooth and silky. The magic belly also made Amy's breasts swell and harden, which is a magic trick that I have thoroughly enjoyed. And the magic belly has even grown itself. Being a woman, Amy is quite upset with her figure these days. But, being her husband, I am quite proud of her physique and still think that she has a beautiful figure. In my estimation, she is the most beautiful pregnant woman in the world.

Meanwhile, back at the ranch . . . or perhaps I should say back in the womb, the little one is doing just fine, kicking about seventy-five to eighty percent of the time. It is such a joyous feeling to place my hand on the magic belly and feel those kicks of life. Amy and I have even obtained a stethoscope with which to hear the little one's heartbeat.

Amy is almost seven months pregnant now, and she and I are eagerly looking forward to the next two months. The doctor is very strict with Amy about her weight. Since my wife is a nurse, she does know better than to eat the wrong kinds of food and get overweight. Our big concern is that she has a small pelvis that was broken five years ago by a fall from a horse. Because of the doctor's strictness and very high professional competency, I am confident that my wife is receiving and will continue to receive the best of everything when the time comes to bring a new life into the world. Amy and I are both hoping and praying that we will have a healthy child. We are prepared, however, in case the baby is not in the best of health. And we have God.

Joys of natural childbirth

When my wife, Meg, became pregnant, we decided to look into the method of natural childbirth. We read as much information as we could find and took advantage of special films and lectures given in our city. We became very well acquainted with Dr. Lamaze's method, especially as explained by Margery Karmel in her book, *Painless Childbirth.*

Without too much trouble we found an obstetrician who had been using this method for some time. In her seventh month, Meg and I began private instructions on the Lamaze method from a registered nurse who was well trained in the use of this technique.

The first thing presented was a detailed description of the bodily functions during labor and delivery. We learned how and why the uterus contracted and the different positions of the baby during delivery. A basic concept of the method is that if the woman knows what is taking place, then she can cooperate with nature. The less the person knows about the prenatal process and delivery, the more apt she is to interfere with it. Interference with the natural processes causes pain. The patient, knowing what is happening, can usually relax and do specific breathings that help alleviate certain pain impulses. No anesthetics are used; therefore, the mother remains awake throughout labor and delivery. The gratifying moment comes when the mother sees her child being born. Since no drugs are used, the baby is born alert and ready for the oxygen that is needed to begin life.

Meg was x-rayed because there was a suspicion that she might be having twins. The x-ray revealed two fetuses in a vertical position. The next morning she was admitted to the hospital and, later that day, her labor was induced. During the long hours that she was in labor I stayed with her and helped her as I had been taught. I reminded her to stay relaxed, to do her breathing at the proper time, and to use the proper type breathing. I massaged her back and kept her alert and ready for her contractions. A problem developed in that the babies had intertwined themselves in such a manner that neither could give way to the other to be born. I overheard the doctors and nurses talking in the hallway about a cesarean. Immediately I got hold of a telephone and called the nurse who had trained us. I wanted to know if we would have to give up the Lamaze method at this point in view of what was happening. She wasn't very encouraging except to say that it should not be given up until it became absolutely necessary. Following that conversation I had a moment of prayer.

A number of hours into labor the doctor finally took Meg into the delivery room. I was asked to go with the doctor into the dressing room. There I was supplied with the proper garments for the delivery room. I was asked to scrub and out we went. Once in the delivery room I took my place next to Meg and continued to proceed with the instructions that I had been given for this phase of delivery.

At 5:20 P.M. my first son was born and 13 minutes later my second son arrived. They both were crying before they were completely born. This was the moment when I was most proud. While the doctor was delivering the babies, I felt a real part of the team.

It was the experience of a lifetime to have participated together with my wife in such an important event. It was exciting to see my children right from the start and to have been of moral support and encouragment for my wife. I would have missed a great deal had I been pacing the floor in the waiting room.

When the babies were taken to the incubators, a nurse, mistaking me for a doctor, asked me to come into the nursery to see the boys. I went in but when she asked me to pick up the babies, I was afraid to do so since I have never picked a baby up before. The nurse, noticing my hesitation, asked me if I was a doctor. When I said "No," she sent me packing.

I then took off my gown and cap and went to be with my wife until she was taken to her room. She and I paused to give thanks to God for such a wonderful experience. We cried with

happiness, not only because everything had gone all right but also because we were both there and able to be part of it all.

Ten short minutes

"Miss Ellison, your tests show positive. Will you be coming for monthly checkups?"

Positive! Oh, no! It is really happening. Don't kid yourself, Jean. I mean, weren't you expecting it? Isn't that why you came here in the first place?

"Miss Ellison, will you be coming back?"

"No! I don't think so. Thank you."

I wonder what my facial expression must be telling that nurse. I'm sure she has seen hundreds of such cases, so mine shouldn't upset her in the least. Don't gaze at me with that pathetic look either.

Me, simple little me! Here I was, waking each morning and sleeping each night, pretending to be busily attending to the duties of life, to give others the impression that I knew what life was all about. Here I am now, realizing what I didn't know before, that *this* is what sex is all about—the creation of new life.

Positive, it's still ringing in my ears like vibrating cymbals. Instead of fading, it's increasing in pitch and intensity as if to remind me of all the changes taking place within me at this very moment.

Jean, get out of this office. Be careful of those steps, little mother. Now, plant your feet firmly on the sidewalk and walk, one foot up while the other foot is down.

It almost seems mechanical. But the doctor said I was pregnant; he was positive of that. That makes me something more than a machine. I'm participating in one of the marvels of time and, for some reason, I want to tell the whole world about it.

Hey, Jean, you can't do that. It's wonderful, the creation of life and all that; but don't shout too loud. People might hear, turn away from you, and shake their righteous heads. You realize that you aren't married; so that makes the growing embryo somewhat taboo in the minds of some people.

I shouldn't have to think of a thing like that

now, not at such an eventful moment in my life. No one has the right to look upon me with pity or scorn for the joyous event happening. They should be envious that I am doing something that perhaps their age or circumstance will not permit. They should feel deep respect for this living being soon to become a part of their world.

A part of their world! How can you think a thing like that when you know your own moral parents will reject it, and you as well? How can you look into the eyes of your mother and say: "Mom, I'm fulfilling my role as a woman. I'm pregnant." Have you thought about the gossiping neighbors who will plague your grandmother? At least your proud sister will not have the honor of bearing the first grandchild. That will be a blow to her ego. And, Dave—what do you do about Dave? Certainly the father of the child should know so he can take his credit. Remember, dear one, you haven't met Dave's parents yet. You're going to make quite an impression on them by the time you see them in July. The crosswalk sign says: "Walk, Don't Run." Can you manage that, Jean?

Yes, I can. I can walk into the situation, but now I must be careful not to run through the solution. If only time could be slowed down to give me a chance to think it through. Instead, it rushes along like a babbling brook. While I was having fun at the shore a few short weeks ago, a fertilized egg implanted itself in the wall of my uterus. Already the embryo is differentiating the tissues to form all the major systems and organs of the body.

Chestnut Street, that's the wrong street. You turned the wrong corner. Retrace your steps, you silly girl—or is it woman now?

Retrace steps. If only I could retrace the past two months. That would be foolish too; Dave and I conceived that child in love, and I wouldn't want to blot out that moment. True, the conception was unintentional, but I'm not sorry for what we did.

I wonder if that man notices. I'd love to tell him, but he'd notice the missing wedding band. I don't even have an engagement ring. Dave and I discussed it and decided we both needed more time to get settled in life. His job means we would have to move around a lot and I'm not

sure I can cope with that. For a while it may be all right, but not after a family gets started.

It's started. It's here right now. Except I'm still not ready for marriage and, financially, not ready for a child. There are still so many things I want to do before worrying about washing diapers and warming bottles. My whole routine will have to change; regular meals, plenty of sleep, doctor appointments. All of this will require money.

Go straight on Vine, then two more blocks and you'll be in the privacy of your own car. Privacy, what privacy have I now? I can't expect to return to my teaching job in the fall and I'll have to move out of the house. It will make it easier on Mom and Dad if they don't have to look at my growing condition each day. Just bring the newborn infant to them and try to make your peace. But where to now, Jean?

I know Dave will marry me, but I'm not sure that it would be the right thing. We both agreed to wait a year to let our feelings solidify. I don't want the child to bring together a relationship that may not work. The environment, under the present conditions, may not be the best for the child; but why increase the problems?

It's not too late to have a miscarriage, Jean. You could involve yourself in active sports and try to dislodge the embryo from the uterus. It certainly seems like the easy way out of your predicament. How about an abortion? No one would know.

I'd know. And I do want that child. I want to see nature's handiwork in which I have been an instrument.

A telephone booth? I could call Dave at the plant; but that may upset the rest of his day, or cheer it up tremendously. I'd better wait till he gets up from Delaware this weekend.

Well, . . .327-555-7902. Hurry, before I chicken out!

"Hello."

"Hello, Dave?"

"Yes."

That baby was born too darn soon!

Pregnancy is supposed to be the easiest, most natural thing for a woman to go through.

Some pregnancies even survive through insurmountable obstacles. I would like to explain one of that type.

My older sister, Ann, at the age of twenty-five, became pregnant with her first child. Ann had to wait quite a while for this because, at the age of twenty-one, she had to have surgery to correct ulcerative colitis. This surgery, called an ileostomy, involved removal of the colon and large intestine. Therefore, Ann will always excrete wastes through the small intestine, which is on the surface of her lower abdomen. She wears a special bag to protect the stoma (which is what the exposed intestine is called).

At the beginning of her pregnancy, in fact up to the sixth month, there were no complications (women with ostomies can have children successfully) except the usual morning sickness, etc. The baby was very active, and the fetal heartbeat was strong.

At the beginning of the sixth month, trouble started. Ann began to feel pain, and her stoma was not excreting any waste. This can happen at any time with an ileostomy and is not considered serious. Either the intestine is just kinked or there may be adhesions around it. The kink may be corrected by liquid diet and, even if surgery is required, it is just a routine matter.

The only reason that this was complicated for Ann was that the baby needed nourishment and surgery is very dangerous during pregnancy. Ann tried liquids and ended up in the hospital for five days. At that time she was placed on a liquid diet with pills for pain, and irrigation of the stoma was performed. Baby was still very active. Luckily, this time no surgery was required. So Ann left the hospital, very weak, but with minimal pain. She was told, however, that it was very likely that the blockage would recur.

Two weeks later, Ann still was not functioning normally, and at six and one-half months pregnant, she weighed less than when she became pregnant—so it was back to the hospital. Ann still could not eat and the stoma was not functioning; she had to be irrigated every day. Poor baby was not getting nourishment, but it was still very active and the heartbeat was still very strong. Mother Nature is marvelous

with her provisions. Ann might have very easily lost faith at this point if it had not been for that moving, kicking baby that she felt inside of her. She could even lie in a certain position and feel that baby's foot against her rib.

Ann was on liquids including a special liquid called Vivanex, which was an awful tasting drink just *full* of vitamins for baby. Baby might have liked it, but mother was having a simply wretched time, trying to keep this ghastly stuff down.

Finally, surgery had to be considered. The doctors could only speculate on what was causing the blockage. Whatever it was, it was doing too much harm to Ann, baby or not. So, at seven months, Ann was to have abdominal surgery. Now the complications of anesthesia on the baby came into the picture. Ann had spinal anesthesia for her abdominal surgery. She had an incision from the navel straight down.

During surgery, it was discovered that a kink in the intestine caused the blockage and that the kink was caused by the pressure of the uterus on the bowel. All of this was corrected, with the obstetrician standing by in case the baby had to be taken during this surgery. The doctors thought the chances were pretty high that they would have to take the baby at this time, but everything went fine and Baby remained within Mama.

. . .Until two days later. Then, Baby decided that she had had enough of this nonsense. Time or not time, the contractions began. Since Ann had just had abdominal surgery, the nurses questioned whether she was in labor until her water broke. Then they whisked her off the tenth floor of the hospital and down to delivery. (Ann was not on the maternity floor because of her surgery.) Ann began labor early Sunday morning and went into hard labor on Sunday about 11:30 P.M.

Daughter Susan was born at 4:12 A.M. on Monday morning—after a grand total of almost twenty-four hours of labor (not to mention two days after surgery).

Susan, at birth, weighed four pounds, ten ounces and was seventeen inches long. It seems amazing that, even though Ann had weighed so little and Susan was eight weeks early, she still was born with reasonable weight.

At birth, there had been some problems. Ann had to be completely anesthetized because of all the pain, plus surgery, so she could not help with the birth. Besides that, the good doctor saw that the baby was having trouble passing through the pelvis—Ann's pelvis was too narrow, so doctor had to use the forceps and really help little Susan push her way out before she suffocated.

Of course, Susan went directly to the incubator. Mother Ann did not even know about her baby girl for five hours. Susan had jaundice and trouble with respiration, which is not unusual with premature babies. Her one lung was not fully expanded, so she had to have oxygen; intravenous glucose was given in the umbilicus and through a tube from the nose to the stomach. (She was too premature to even suck for very long.) Blood was taken from the heel, and antibiotics were given in the thigh. Things were really not as bad as they sound. She was a lively, spindly little thing, so thin that she looked almost like a plucked chicken. We liked to tease proud Mama and Dada about that.

Susan lost a lot of weight after birth. She went down to three pounds, fifteen ounces, but she never lost her activeness.

Susan spent almost four weeks in the incubator; her Mother spent two weeks in the hospital, recuperating from birth and surgery. She found the strength to go and peek at her baby about twenty-four hours after this whole confusing thing had occurred.

Susan was removed from the incubator at four pounds, six ounces, but she was still kept in the preemie nursery for about a week and a half. At five pounds, one-half ounce, Susan went home. Mom really had some adjusting to do!

Little Susan could not eat a lot at one time; her tiny little stomach would only hold so much, so Ann had to get used to giving small feedings—frequently!

Susan really began to gain weight after she got home. Every six weeks, at the doctor's office, she showed a gain of a couple of pounds. Susan's during-the-night feedings lasted about two months. Her stomach was still very small (as was the rest of her).

Susan is now almost seven months old. She is still small but very solid, very healthy, and very hungry. She talks and smiles and grabs at everything within her reach. Development is still slow, but this little fuzzy-headed preemie sure does look like things are going well. She has never had any serious health problems since birth, and it looks like, despite all the hassles, she really did do the right thing when she decided to be born! (Even if she was too darn early!)

My second child—wanted and unwanted

When I compare the pregnancies of my two sons, I find that they both were quite normal, physically. However, my emotional state of mind was vastly different, so much so that it seems to me to have had a decided effect upon the first year of my second son's life. My firstborn son, Ricky, entered this world in a most calm and relaxed way. The fact that I was in labor was difficult to believe. I can remember thinking at the time that I could not understand why women complained about the ordeal of childbirth if this was all there was to it. Ricky's first year of life was a happy, pleasant, and enjoyable one. This was not the story for my second son, Robbie, as the following paragraphs will reveal.

It is important to point out from the very beginning that Robbie was a "planned" and a "wanted" baby. My husband was quite proud of the fact that his firstborn child had been a boy, and he was confident that this event could be duplicated. Also, we both felt, since I was an only child and he was the first of five children, that our "only" child should know the companionship and the affection of a brother or sister. It was with a great deal of pleasure and pride that, after several months, I was able to confirm that I was once again pregnant.

As with my first pregnancy, this second one progressed quite normally. To be sure, I was not at my peak of physical fitness at times, and fatigue slowed down my work pace. But this did not really bother me, even though I was caring for my two-year-old son and doing most of my own housework. Fortunately I did have the help of a cleaning lady periodically to assist me with the heavier tasks of housecleaning. I was constantly busy at home, which I enjoyed immensely, and I was not without outside activities to lend variety and interest to what could have otherwise become a routine existence.

My relationship with my husband was, it seemed to me, what it had always been. For the most part our life together was quite congenial even though the two of us had few opportunities to spend time alone together. Let me quickly say that this was not because we had a two-year-old in the house. Ricky's daily schedule was unusually well regulated, and bedtime was always in the neighborhood of 6:30 P.M. The problem of little time together was caused by my husband's work schedule. His evening work schedule consumed what would have customarily been "our" time. This meant, of course, that my evenings generally were spent alone except for a sleeping son in a nearby room.

The truth of the matter was that I really had few chances to relax with my husband. It would have been reasonable to expect that we could have had some talk sessions when he completed his evening's work. But somehow the fact that his business closed at nine o'clock did not signify to him that it was time to come home. It was not unusual for him to arrive anywhere from 11 P.M. to 2 A.M. At first I tried waiting up for him. This only served to anger him because I suppose he thought that I was waiting to question him as to where he had been. And I must admit that I frequently did this, something which I have now learned never to do even though he maintains the same nightly schedule with consistency. Many were the times that we argued in the early morning hours about a husband's right to come and go as he pleases as long as he finally comes home to spend what remains of the night.

As time went on and I became obviously pregnant, I began to suspect that these late evening sessions were not entirely devoted to business. By the time that the holiday season had arrived (I was then a little more than four

months pregnant) I learned for a fact that he was spending the late evening hours with another woman. I can remember so vividly the morning that I went to market for Christmas greens. When I opened the trunk of his car to put in the greens, I discovered a large bottle of champagne and two glasses. To say that I was shocked is a gross understatement. I recalled immediately that the reason that we had not had the same beverage for our anniversary a month earlier was because it was too expensive. And yet here was a filled container to be shared with someone else. It seemed to me that our unborn child was in constant motion after that discovery and, as the days dragged by, this motion seemed to continue.

Although I had stopped discussing the whys and wherefores of my husband's late evening arrivals at home, I could not let this situation go without commenting about it. The inevitable discussion began. As might be expected, I was in tears before many words had been spoken. My only concern, or so I thought, was for our two-year-old son and our unborn child lest anything affect their innocent lives because of their father's indiscretion. In reality I was also fighting for my own marriage. But my husband assured me that I was completely wrong in my assumptions. However, as the days and months passed, I found lipstick marks on shirts and handkerchiefs and a decided slowdown in our sexual activities. True, I was pregnant, but this had not presented a problem during my first pregnancy and there was no medical reason, as far as my obstetrician was concerned, why there should be a problem now. Of course, I could only surmise and imagine what the true situation was. I made no attempt to gather evidence because I knew in my heart that I really did not want to be confronted with the facts.

It took every ounce of willpower that I possessed to force myself to make life seem pleasant and relaxed for my now three-year-old. To my knowledge he could not detect any outward change in me. But the inward turmoil that I felt constantly must have been speaking volumes to my unborn child. My husband's infidelity perhaps was not affecting our three-year-old, but it surely must have been keeping our unborn child in a state of general anxiety most of the time.

About two weeks before the estimated arrival of the baby, my husband was sent to one of the southern states on business. His anticipated length of stay was to extend two weeks past the date when the baby was due, but he assured me that he would come home the weekend closest to the time when the baby was scheduled to arrive. How can I describe the tremendous urgency I felt to have this baby on the very day that my husband came home for the weekend? As is so frequently the case, baby did not put in an appearance as desired. Each day of that long weekend the pressure mounted, and still nothing happened. Sunday came. Still no baby.

The time had come for my husband to return. To say the least I was tense, disappointed, and emotionally exhausted. But, being somewhat sentimental, I prepared a note for my husband to read at such time as our second child was born. As I attempted to hide this note in his suitcase, I accidentally uncovered several boxes of condoms. It seemed as though the whole bottom dropped out of the world for me. His explanation that he was taking them to a friend simply did not allay my deepest fears. Our parting was considerably strained. I can still see his car backing out of the driveway that beautiful, warm, sunny Mother's Day afternoon as my son and I watched in sadness.

Five days later I began to feel what I knew were the first pains of labor. But they did not increase in intensity as time passed. Finally I called my doctor, and he requested an immediate examination in his office. This check revealed that the baby would probably not be born for another day or two. Because he knew of my extreme anxiety over my personal problem with my husband, he insisted that I go right then to the hospital where he would, as he said, "get things started." A phone call from my husband the night before had informed me that he would be returning home sooner than he had expected, arriving in town some time the following Tuesday. I knew that I would not be able to hold off the birth of our child that long because I was having considerable physical discomfort due to the position of the baby. If only I could wait just two more days so that

our baby would be born when my husband was home. But the doctor's words were quite insistent: "Don't even go home. Just go to the hospital and I'll meet you there in a half hour." To obey these orders was really my only choice.

I knew almost immediately that the birth of my second child was not going to be like the birth of my first son. And it certainly was not. My labor, although it lasted only five hours, was extremely difficult, not the easy, comfortable, exciting experience that my first labor had been. It was almost as though this unborn child knew that I really did not want it to be born until later. My body was trying desperately to expel the baby which my mind did not want to let go. Finally our second son was born. He was a little slow in producing the birth cry, but my doctor assured me that he was all right.

The fact that the baby was healthy was of utmost importance, but of secondary importance was the fact that I had managed to produce another son. It was with a sense of satisfaction that I placed a long-distance call to my husband, only to learn that he could not be contacted. The old anxiety wound up again. Early the next morning I received a call from my husband, and I must admit that he sounded very happy about the fact that he was the father of another boy. I could not help thinking that maybe now he would finally see me in a different light.

As the time drew near for me to hold my new son for the first time, I could feel the excitement mounting. What a joyous meeting this was for me, even though he cried most of the time and absolutely refused to take any liquid whatsoever from the bottle. I can remember how dark his eyes were and how long his fingernails had grown. Little did I know that this was the only time that I would hold this little guy until I brought him home from the hospital five days later. Because he had spit up blood shortly after I had first seen him, my pediatrician ordered a complete round of tests to be made to determine what had caused this problem. The conclusion that was reached simply indicated that he had had a nosebleed because of excessive crying. Of course, I was extremely relieved that there was nothing organically wrong with my baby. I can't help remembering, however, how upset I had been as I looked through the nursery window at that pathetic little creature with zinc oxide covering his face where he had already scratched himself and how his arms were pinned down so that he could not scratch himself any more. It was all that I could do to keep from going in that room to pick him up and try to comfort him.

At the end of five days my husband took me and the baby home. From the moment that we left the hospital I could sense that I had a very unhappy baby, and this unhappiness continued for most of his first year of life. He did not eat well, he did not sleep well, he fussed and fretted continuously. For the first two weeks after we came home from the hospital, Robbie and I were alone together during the day since his brother was at his grandmother's home ill with a strep infection. Even though I could devote full time to the care of my newborn son, nothing seemed to make him comfortable. The pediatrician, a most respected man in his field, insisted that there was nothing wrong with the baby. I altered the feeding schedule, the bath schedule, sleeping positions, bed positions, anything and everything that might make a difference in Robbie's behavior. Nothing helped. I continued to try and he continued to fret. Eventually he did all of the things that babies do, such as grasping, cooing, sitting up, standing up, reaching for things, but none was really done with any degree of genuine happiness, or so I thought. After a year of this fussiness, he seemed to settle down somewhat to become a more pleasant little individual to have around.

I had not thought before about how the circumstances of my life could affect my baby during his prenatal development. But certainly there must be some connection between what I was thinking and feeling as I carried him and the way in which he responded to life after he was born and for the first year of his life.

A way out

Vicki, an attractive eighteen-year-old freshman, decided to have an abortion this year. Before the events leading to her action can be discussed, it is important to know something about her childhood and home life.

Vicki comes from an ideally sized family; she has a brother who is five years her senior and a sister five years her junior. Her father, a professional man, is in business for himself.

Because she is from a very small town, the inhabitants know all there is to know about one another. Understandably, it is quite a conservative town. Vicki's parents are very active in church and community organizations. They are not very close to Vicki, although she does regard them highly. She feels, however, that she cannot talk to them about important things.

Vicki had a happy childhood; she spent her grade school years as a tomboy. She was somewhat spoiled and always received more than her sister. When there were fights between them, it was Vicki with whom her parents always sided. The housework was never done by Vicki; she was expected only to clean her own room occasionally.

Even though Vicki hated piano lessons, her parents forced her to take them for three years. One of her major interests was her baton lessons, which she took for six years.

While she was in grade school and junior high, she was constantly reprimanded for talking in class. Her worst grades were in conduct. In high school, Vicki was very active. She was a cheerleader, a baton twirler, president of Girl's Club, on the Honor Roll, and a member of Student Council.

Vicki began dating in the eighth grade. She never went out with a number of different boys but always preferred to "go steady." The first time she dated Ron was in the eighth grade, and she has been dating him ever since. It was not until her sophomore year in high school, however, that they began to be really serious. By the time Vicki was a junior, she and Ron were having intimate relations quite frequently. Whenever they were alone, they just naturally fell into the pattern. When they first began having intercourse, Vicki always felt very upset the next day. She was sorry she had relented and found herself wondering whether or not she would become pregnant, since the only protections they used were the rhythm method and, at times, a condom. Sometimes she became pensive and wondered whether or not it was worth the uncertainty. However, Vicki convinced herself that the only reason she consented to Ron's requests was that she loved him and really believed she would marry him some day.

A few months ago, Vicki, now a college student, went to visit Ron at his college. They spent the entire weekend together and had relations a number of times during this period. Because they used no protection, Vicki was very concerned in the weeks that followed about her possible pregnancy.

After her menstrual cycle was a week late, she decided she had better take some action. She called an Abortion Referral Agency to find out all the intricacies involved in obtaining an abortion. She then made an appointment with a local doctor; it was on this day that she learned she was pregnant. The doctor was very concerned about her and asked her what she planned to do. Vicki replied that she had been thinking about having an abortion. The doctor then referred her to a clergyman who was a member of the Clergical Consultation Service. The pastor was very understanding; he gave her the name of a reputable clinic, where she made an appointment. They briefed her on the process over the phone.

By this time, she was six and a half weeks pregnant. Vicki called Ron and told him that she had decided to have an abortion and that it would cost $200. Ron felt this was the best thing to do. He even offered to help pay the expenses.

Neither Ron nor Vicki wanted to get married, even though they were both very much in love. They felt an abortion was the best course to take because both had three years of college remaining and felt they could not give the child everything it should have if they married so young. Vicki also did not want to tell her parents or to let her friends know about her premarital activities, something that could not be avoided if they were married.

Vicki's conscience did not really bother her about having an abortion; however, she did feel guilty in a sense when she thought about destroying something that she and Ron had created. She justified this destruction, however, by rationalizing that, as a baby, it could never

receive the attention it deserved and, frankly, by being unable to imagine it as a living being at this stage of development. She was not sorry about her decision because she never felt that a baby really existed at all.

There was one factor concerning the abortion that worried Vicki, however, and that was the fact that she might have to endure physical pain while having it. She was also afraid that somehow her parents would find out.

On the day of her appointment, she and Ron drove to New Orleans. They did not discuss the abortion at all on the way there. Ron did nothing to comfort Vicki. He seemed worried and irritable. Even though Vicki was upset, he aggravated her state of mind by telling her that he thought they should not date as much in the future. He was afraid the same thing would happen again and, although Vicki offered to take birth control pills, he felt his idea was the best possible solution.

When they arrived at the clinic, Vicki was told to go to the basement and have a urinalysis and blood test. Ron waited in the lounge. Vicki then went to the fifth floor and stayed in the waiting room. She filled out papers concerning her background and her relationship with Ron. Information explaining the abortion process was given to her.

While Vicki was filling out the papers, a young woman came in and told her that she would be with her throughout the entire process. Janet, as we will call her, took Vicki into a small office and talked with her about a number of relevant things. It was Janet who readied Vicki for the doctor.

The actual abortion took only five minutes. Vicki felt a pain similar to severe cramps during the process. After its completion, she rested and was given instructions to follow for the next two weeks. Vicki was very relieved that it was over and felt extremely happy.

Vicki has never regretted her decision to have an abortion. She feels that it was really the only possible solution to a terrifying situation. Because she does not want to ever have to go through the turmoil again, however, she is now taking birth control pills. Ron has relented, somewhat, and is now still enjoying his former privileges. Vicki thinks she is doing the right thing. After all, aren't they going to get married someday?

THINGS TO THINK ABOUT AND DO

1. Discuss the joys of parenthood. While you are at it, discuss the trials and tribulations as well. Which side of the discussion makes the better points?
2. Take a survey of your class on how many children make up an ideal family. Or change the question slightly and ask: "How many children would you like to have?"
3. Have an obstetrician come and lecture on any topic you and your group decide you would like to hear about.
4. Get information on the Lamaze natural childbirth technique. Does this procedure say anything to you? What are the pros and cons of other childbirth procedures?
5. You should never be embarrassed by anything that pertains to your body, your mind, or your well-being. If you have any questions or uncertainties about prenatal development, sexual functions, or the birth process, seek adequate, professional sex information.
6. Discuss the pros and cons of the birth control pill and other contraceptive devices. Perhaps you and your group should first decide whether or not this topic is one of personal privacy; if so, you may decide to approach the topic in another manner.
7. What effects do drugs, alcoholism, venereal disease, and poor nutrition have on unborn children? What about rubella or the German measles?
8. Do unhappy marriages—or an unhappy spouse—produce unhappy children?
9. What educational, social, economic, physical, and material preparations should a mother and a father make for the coming of a new baby?
10. Should mentally retarded adults, social criminals, or handicapped people have children?
11. We would suggest a debate on the morality of abortions or a discussion on the pros and cons of abortions, but this issue is too emotionally loaded to permit free interchange of ideas. Read what you can about the topic and make some decisions of your own. On a related issue, should a person's point of view on matters that cannot be explicitly delineated be respected even if it is an obviously biased point of view?
12. Is there a sexual revolution taking place? Is society more permissive than previously? Are people more promiscuous than twenty years ago? Fifty years ago? One hundred years ago? One thousand years ago?

READING SOURCES
Developmental psychology texts

Bernard, H. W.: Human development in western culture, Boston, 1975, Allyn and Bacon, Inc., chap. 2.

CRM: Developmental psychology today, ed. 2, New York, 1975, Random House, Inc., chaps. 4, 5.

Hurlock, E. B.: Developmental psychology, ed. 4, New York, 1974, McGraw-Hill Book Co., chap. 2.

Kaluger, G., and Kaluger, M.: Human development: the span of life, St. Louis, 1974, The C. V. Mosby Co., chaps. 1-3.

Mussen, P. H., Conger, J. J., and Kagan, J.: Child development and personality, ed. 4, New York, 1974, Harper & Row, Publishers, chaps. 2, 3.

Papalia, D. C., and Olds, S. W.: A child's world, New York, 1975, McGraw-Hill Book Co., chaps. 1, 2.

Related readings

Altman, L. K.: Physicians urge exercise of caution in prescribing drugs during pregnancies, The New York Times, June 26, 1970.

Carmichael, L.: The onset and early development of behavior. In Mussen, P. H. editor: Carmichael's manual of child psychology, ed. 3, New York, 1970, John Wiley & Sons, Inc., pp. 447-563.

Davids, A., and Holden, R. H.: Consistency of maternal attitudes and personality from pregnancy to eight months following childbirth, Dev. Psychol. 2:364-366, 1970.

Demarest, R. J., and Sciarra, J. J.: Conception, birth, contraceptives: a visual presentation, New York, 1969, McGraw-Hill Book Co.

Dubos, R.: Biological individuality, Columbia Forum 12(1):, 1969.

Ferdon, N. K.: Chromosomal abnormalities and antisocial behavior, J. Genet. Psychol. 118:281-292, 1971.

Hytten, F. E.: Smoking in pregnancy, Dev. Med. Child Neurol. 15:355-357, 1973.

Joesting, J., and Joesting, R.: Birth order and

desired family size, J. Indiv. Psychol. 29:34, 1973.

Reid, D. E., Ryan, K. J., and Benirschke, K., editors: Principles and management of human reproduction, Philadelphia, 1972, W. B. Saunders Co.

Scheinfeld, A.: Twins and supertwins, Philadelphia, 1967, J. B. Lippincott Co.

CHAPTER 2

Babyhood and infancy

The human individual probably learns more in the first twenty-four months of life than at any other time. Consider the almost total helplessness of the newborn child. There is very little that this neonate can do beyond responding with some survival reflexes and making a few random motor movements and oral sounds. By the time this infant is two years old he or she will be able to eat solid food, alone to some extent, walk about and show curiosity concerning the environment, communicate with and understand others, and have at least partial control of bladder and bowel movements. Compared to what an individual learns during any other stage of life, what the infant learns must be considered to be very impressive.

Social relationships and communication skills are prominent developmental areas during infancy. "Dear Diary" gives an account of the social world of a newborn to the age of one, at which time this particular child is joined by a new brother. A close social relationship of a different type is shown in "I'm Glad I was a Breast-Fed Baby." Language development is described in two very interesting profiles. "If You Pay Attention—You'll Hear Me" tells of how an eight-week-old infant communicates his needs; "Lordy, Lordy" presents interesting speech and language development of an infant between the twelfth and twenty-fourth months.

Many parents will identify with "Tom and his Corrective Shoes" as the story is told of how Tom's club feet were made normal. "The Adoption of Alan" will be meaningful to many children as well as to their adopted parents. This profile, however, not only speaks of adoption but also of the sadness of discovering that the husband and wife could not conceive children. Unusual teaching experiences are presented in "Behavior Modification with a One-Year-Old," in which a child is taught that there are certain things he may not touch. The impact of the admonition to keep medicine out of the reach of children is vividly portrayed in "Deadly Pills," where one diet pill causes a hyperactive nightmare.

There are some children born with defects, of course. "A Profile in Gratefulness" tells of a child with spina bifida and her battle to survive. After a series of operations, extensive care, and much love, she courageously overcomes the odds and begins to live a near normal life. At this writing, this girl is twelve years old and is enjoying seventh grade. The outlook for "Donnie" is still uncertain at this moment. Donnie is a hydrocephalic child who has also had a number of operations, including several to provide him with the ability to use his thumb. At fourteen months he was observed using his thumb for the first time. Will he ever mature to the stage where he can be self-sustaining?

Dear diary

FEBRUARY 22—It was a long, hard journey, but I made it. I really wasn't due until March 1, but I was anxious to see Mommy. Since I was so nice and big, I thought it was silly just to wait around for a calendar date. I was really worn out when I got here, but I didn't get to see Mommy right away. She was sound asleep. The nurse put me in a little bed in a room with a lot of other babies so I took a nap.

LATER—I don't know why the nurse put me in a bed called an Isolette. She said something about my needing oxygen, whatever that is. All I really need is my Mommy, but the doctor said I didn't breathe right. After all, I haven't had much practice yet. What do they expect?

I don't understand what is going on. Every few hours the nurses take the other babies to their Mommies for some milk, but they don't take me. The nurse feeds me. What's wrong with Mommy? Didn't she wake up? Doesn't she want to see me?

FEBRUARY 23—I don't know why I'm so tired and sleepy all the time. The doctors and nurses watch me a lot. A strange man peeped in the nursery window once; someone said it was my Daddy. He looked worried. I still haven't seen Mommy.

FEBRUARY 24—I saw Mommy today; she is alive and well—and awake. The nurse sneaked me to her for a few minutes, and Mommy loved me a lot. She thinks I look real healthy, but after a few minutes they rushed me back to my Isolette. They said something about my turning blue, but the doctor said I wasn't a blue baby. That doesn't make sense. I still sleep most of the time.

FEBRUARY 25—I must be better now because I am out of the Isolette and the nurses take me to Mommy. She holds me and hugs me and I like it. She says my name is Charles David. Charles is for my Daddy, and David is her favorite name for a boy. She calls me David. I like that name, too.

FEBRUARY 26—I came home today! The nurse dressed me up in the pretty little clothes that Mommy bought. Grandmother Boren bought a pretty fuzzy blanket to take me home in. Everyone is so proud of me. I am the first grandchild on my Daddy's side. The nurse carried me clear to the car and wouldn't give me up until Mommy was in. I guess she hated to see me leave. Home is nice. When I am downstairs I sleep in the little cradle that Daddy slept in when he was a baby. At night I sleep in a little bed in Mommy's and Daddy's room.

FEBRUARY 27—Grandma Burns and Aunt Julia came to see me today. Grandma made me a pretty little sweater. They thought I was nice, but I was too sleepy to enjoy their company.

FEBRUARY 28—Grandma is staying for a few days, to help Mommy. She rocks me a lot. She washes my clothes, too. I don't know why I have to have a bath and clean clothes every day, but I kind of like it.

MARCH 1—The little red marks on my face are beginning to clear up. Mommy said something about forceps, but I don't know what that means. I still sleep most of the time.

MARCH 5—Not much has happened the past few days. I had some company, and people brought me nice gifts. Today is Sunday, and I went to church with Mommy and Daddy. Daddy didn't sit with us, though. He stood up front and talked. Everybody sang some pretty songs. I guess they were trying to sing me to sleep like Mommy does. After church everybody crowded around me. They say I am cute.

MARCH 7—I've made a very important discovery—a thumb is good to suck! Of course, my bottle is better, but it isn't always handy.

I hope I don't get the colic tonight. I get it most every night, and Mommy has to hold me and walk with me for a long time. It really makes my tummy hurt.

MARCH 8—I had a terrible time last night. I hurt so bad and cried so hard that the doctor had to come. I tried to have a B.M. but I couldn't. He said my rectum was too tight so he put on a rubber glove and dilated me. I felt better after that. Mommy and Daddy and Grandma were all upset.

MARCH 10—I am growing right along. I am a nice, plump baby. I weighed eight pounds, nine and one-half ounces when I was born. But I still don't have any hair. Oh, well, you can't have everything. Maybe it's a maturational lag!

MARCH 15—Things are going smoothly and I have everything under control. I still get the colic so Mommy rocks me a lot. She rocks me to sleep every time I get sleepy, and we both like it. She doesn't get much sleep, though, because she has to be up with me so much at night. I guess Mommies don't really need to sleep, they are so big.

MARCH 30—Mommy is getting a little hard to handle. She forgets that I'm supposed to be in charge. When she cleans the house, she takes me into the other rooms and lays me down where she can watch me. I don't like that so I scream. I don't want Mommy to clean. I just want her to hold me. That sweeper makes more noise than I do, so I scream louder. Then Mommy gets provoked and scolds me. Can you imagine that?

APRIL 5—I wish I could see more of Daddy. Nearly every time he comes in the house I am asleep. Maybe if I stay awake he will take me on the tractor with him. But I know what Mommy will say!

APRIL 20—I don't sleep as much now, and I wake up too easily. I must have good ears because every little sound wakes me up. A dog barking off in the distance, a rooster crowing from far off—any little sound startles me. It's making Mommy nervous and she almost hates the telephone. Daddy has to be real quiet when he comes in so he won't wake me. When I wake up, I cry and am real cross.

APRIL 25—Mommy was worried for fear I had the palsy. I keep my arms going around and around in front of my chest, so she asked the doctor. He said it was normal, so she feels better now.

APRIL 28—I don't know why, but when Mommy goes where I can't see her, I get scared and cry. Now she tells me where she is going and that she will be right back; that helps a little.

MAY 1—I won the game last night! Mommy and Daddy took me to Bible Study at Lydia's house. Before the meeting started, the ladies passed me around and admired me. I really liked that a lot. Then when they started to sing, no one looked at me. I didn't like that. When Daddy started reading out of a little black book, it wasn't any better. After all, what was I there for? So I let them know I was there. I made more noise than Daddy, so Mommy took me to the kitchen. Then I really opened up and screamed. And do you know what? They thought I had the colic! So they made their excuses and left right away. As soon as we got in the car I lay back in Mommy's arms and smiled, 'cause I wanted to go home and sleep in my bed. Mommy and Daddy sort of laughed a little and called me a little dickens. But they took me home. I am learning how to condition their responses.

MAY 5—Mommy takes lots and lots of pictures of me, and everyone likes to hold me for a picture. Great-granddaddy is a real big man, and he likes to hold me. I have some aunts and uncles, too. This afternoon Mommy put a yellow overall outfit on me and put me outside in the stroller. It was pretty nice; Laddie came up once and licked me in the face. He is jealous of me sometimes, but he never hurts me. Mommy took a picture of Laddie and me. You should see my album!

JUNE 20—Life is pretty routine, but I get outside a lot now. Mommy swings with me on the porch swing nearly every morning and I miss it when we can't go out. I like to jump in my jumping chair and I like it when Mommy puts my playpen on the front porch. I can see a lot more there.

JULY 22—I am five months old and can sit alone now. I think I'm pretty smart.

JULY 29—We had our Sunday School picnic yesterday afternoon. It was so hot that I went topless. It was nice, but I always miss my bed. I got to eat some of the food; it was almost as good as my thumb!

AUGUST 22—Six months old and I can stand up in my playpen if I hold on to the side. It's better than sitting all the time; I can hardly wait to walk. When I see other kids walk, it looks so easy. I can crawl, though.

SEPTEMBER 12—I don't get held as much as I used to. Mommy has been busy canning all summer. I always play where I can see her, though.

OCTOBER 31—I went to Grandpa Burns' birthday dinner yesterday. He lives in West Virginia. I saw a lot of my aunts and uncles and cousins. My little cousin Joyce and I played kissing games. That made everybody laugh.

NOVEMBER 22—I made it! I took my first step, and I am only nine months old. I'm awfully clumsy, and I fall down a lot. But I just couldn't wait.

DECEMBER 12—I got my first haircut today. I didn't have much hair for a long time, but I needed a trim. Uncle Roy is a barber, so he cut it for me. I was real good, even when it tickled.

DECEMBER 20—You should see our pretty Christmas tree! I can't quite reach it, even when I stand on tiptoe. I wonder why Mommy put it up so high? I want those pretty balls.

DECEMBER 25—Christmas is a pretty nice day. Santa Claus brought me some new toys and we had a big dinner.

JANUARY 3—I just love books, so Mommy reads to me a lot. She has read to me as long as I can remember. My favorite book is about kittens. I always keep a book in my hand, and whenever Mommy sits down I put it in her hand. I don't talk very much, but I understand everything.

JANUARY 7—Mommy is so unreasonable at times. She won't let me play with the electrical outlets. I wouldn't hurt them, you know.

JANUARY 12—Everybody around here keeps talking about a new baby. That's funny, because I never see one around. I can't see that we need one either.

FEBRUARY 9—I'm so confused that I don't know what to do. Mommy went away and I am staying at Grandmother's. Everyone is real happy, and they keep saying! "It's another boy!" What do they mean?

FEBRUARY 11—I wish Mommy would come home. Why did she leave me? I want her to rock me to sleep. I want my own bed. I cry sometimes.

FEBRUARY 13—Daddy says we are going to get Mommy and my new baby brother tomorrow. What is a brother? I can't remember what Mommy looks like. I suck my thumb.

FEBRUARY 14—Grandmother and Daddy and I went to the hospital to get Mommy today. I felt bad about her leaving me, so I just pretended not to see her. She was carrying something wrapped up in a blanket; she seemed happy to see me, but I just ignored her. She gave the blanket to Grandmother and tried to take me, but I didn't make up.

When we got home she tried to show me what was in the blanket, but I wasn't interested. I just walked around by myself. They put the blanket in the cradle I used to use, and sometimes it made a noise. They say it's my baby brother, but I'm really not bothered.

FEBRUARY 15—Aunt Eva came to stay with Mommy for a few days. She rocks me and the new baby. Mommy rocks me, too. I guess I'll make up. I'll just pretend the baby isn't here.

FEBRUARY 22—Happy birthday to me! I am one year old and getting big. I can say some words now, and we are going to have a birthday dinner for me tonight. Mommy made a little cake and put a pretty pink candle in the middle of it. Maybe they will forget about that baby for a while!

I'm glad I was a breast-fed baby

I often hear my parents talk about how times have changed. Even I, a twenty-one-month-old baby girl, realize the truth in this observation, especially as it has to do with my being fed. At my age now, I become hungry at the same time as an adult—three times a day and sometimes more often. The snacks do not take long to prepare—a cracker or a pretzel. Regular mealtimes are the roughest for me because I must wait until my mother has the food prepared. Sometimes this seems like an eternity. But I wasn't always that way.

In the good old days, my meals were ready whenever I acted hungry. The milk was always the right temperature and especially delicious. Any bottle-fed baby will probably tell you that milk was not always this way, particularly at night. Most of us babies awakened during the nights of the first two months of our lives to have our stomachs filled again. The mothers of some of my bottle-fed peers were often too tired from cleaning bottles and washing diapers during the day to give their babies good tasting milk of just the right temperature. True, I have seen in the baby magazines that some makes of prepared formula boast that their milk is good at room temperature, right from the can. But how much thought and love is put into a can of milk? Some of the mothers were even too tired to hold the bottles for their babies.

Do you wonder why my milk was always the correct temperature? I was breast-fed. My mother nursed me almost as soon as I gave my hunger cry. She had no set feeding schedule with me, although I usually became hungry every four hours. I felt pretty important and very loved because my mother was giving of herself to help me feel full and secure.

Mommy did not need bottles for me except occasionally when she gave me water with white corn syrup. She did not have to take the time every day to wash six or more bottles and nipples like other mothers did. That meant she had more time to devote to me and to relax while reading me stories from magazines and books.

Are you wondering why my mother decided to breast feed me in the first place? She is very close to my Aunt Bonnie, who nursed all three of her daughters. Mommy saw the secure feeling my cousins had and decided to give of herself to help me feel secure, too. Also,

Mommy wanted a motherly feeling to grow inside her as much as possible.

Aunt Bonnie nursed each of my cousins only about five or six months. Luckily for me, Mommy met a lady who asked her if she knew about the nursing mothers' group called La-Leche League, the name being taken from the Spanish title of the Madonna (translated to be "Our Lady of Bountiful Milk and Easy Delivery"). Mommy had read about it in a baby magazine. The lady told her there was a chapter in my home town. She gave Mommy the phone number of the president and wished Mommy "good luck" with her nursing me. Mommy went to about four of the LaLeche League Meetings, and I profited as much as she did. She became acquainted with other nursing mothers who could answer her questions about our important activity. She also got to have a night out from home. But, most importantly, she learned that this kind of nursing can continue until the baby is weaned.

Mommy did not want to nurse me a whole year, but she *did* nurse me ten months. I had been drinking water from a training cup since I was six months old because the summer heat had made me extra thirsty. The last two months before I stopped nursing, I also drank milk from the training cup for at least one feeding, along with my high chair mealtimes.

Let me tell you some benefits of being breast-fed. The milk I received was always fresh, whereas my bottle-fed buddies had older milk that had been heated. Did you know that heat and storage are known to destroy many important nutrients? Mommy's milk digested quickly and easily compared to bottle milk. You have heard about colicky babies. Well, breast-fed babies are less likely to have digestive upsets and disorders. Breast feeding is also a natural method of spacing babies; Mommy had more time to spend with me since she was not preparing for a brother or sister for me. I read all the facts in this paragraph in a LaLeche League reprint from a book written by Niles Newton, *Family Book of Child Care*.

I believe one of the possibilities mentioned in the reprint is true, the idea that breast feeding may help build motherly love. It was said that a certain hormone is active in breast-feeding mothers. The hormone causes unmotherly animals to act motherly, and there is some evidence that it has the same effect on human beings. Mommy was almost right out of college when I came, and she really was not ready to stop working so soon. Nursing me settled her, because she *had* to sit and relax with me in her arms quite often.

Feeding time brought physical enjoyment to Mommy and me. Both of us wanted and needed each other physically and mentally. The satisfaction of our wants and needs helped to build a secure and loving relationship between Mommy and me. The nursing experience helped us to feel very close to each other, and this did not stop on the day Mommy stopped nursing me. It laid the groundwork for a very good relationship in which I was permitted to grow in independence confidently. Another important result was that Mommy did not feel as if she were simply carrying on her high school baby-sitting jobs with bottle feeding and changing a baby. She felt and still feels like a *real* mother!

If you pay attention, you'll hear me

My name is Beth and I am eight weeks old. I would like to tell you about my ability to communicate. I can't write yet, so my Daddy is taking care of that for me.

I said before that I can't write yet. Well, I can't talk yet either. You might say that, as an eight-week-old girl, I am pretty limited in my ways to communicate. It's true, but I think that I have some ways of letting others know what my needs are. After all, at eight weeks I have little more than needs.

I can't talk, but I do have a voice and I'm not afraid to use it. One way that I use my voice is to cry. I cry when I feel something serious is wrong. I can even communicate how serious my problem is by the way I cry. For instance, whenever Mommy is late in feeding me, I cry loudly and tears run down my face. Mommy is pretty good at telling when I'm hungry. However, when I'm wet, I don't cry so loudly and tears don't usually appear. Mommy usually figures me out on this problem, too.

Joy and dejection, pleasure and anger,
satisfactions and frustrations, the range of
feelings that a child has or experiences at home,
at school, at play—all these matter vitally in the
learning process and in the growth of the whole
child. What babies and young children need
most for their mental health is love and play.

Dorothy E. M. Gardner
FEELINGS AND LEARNING

There is one other time when I cry. I cry when I want to be with people. My crying then is not as loud as the other times, and tears don't appear. I'm very persistent, however, when I want to be with people. You see, I *can* communicate my needs to people, especially Mommy.

There is one special time when I really use my voice. That time comes when I get scared or feel pain. Let me give you two examples. One day Mommy went away, and clumsy Daddy had to change me after I told him I was wet. (Daddy is awfully slow.) Well, he changed me all right but he nearly broke my arm when he put my terry suit back on me. I told him about it, and he was very sorry. One other day Mommy was holding me and this terrible storm came. I was watching the wind play tag with the trees when this big bolt of lightning flashed. It scared me. Mommy closed the curtain and held me close. I felt better in a few minutes.

I use my voice in another way, too. I babble and coo. It's hard to describe. I do this when I'm happy being with people. I also do this sometimes when I'm doing what I like best, just looking around at various things.

That is about all the ways that I can use my voice except when I hiccough or cough. Daddy says those things are just physical reactions. He says I eat too fast.

There is another way in which I communicate. This way is an action. I use this action to tell Mommy and Daddy that I am hungry. All I do is find my thumb or fingers, put them in my mouth, and suck. I also make a little noise when I do this. I'm really good at this and, believe me, it gets results. I should be good at thumb sucking. I did it before I was even born.

Not too long ago, Mommy started feeding me certain vegetables. I tell her when I don't like them. I tell her in one of two ways. The first way is easy: if I don't like my food, I turn my head so Mommy can't put the spoon in my mouth. Even if she puts food in my mouth, I still have another way of telling her I don't like my food; I spit it out and it runs down my chin. Mommy gets upset when I do this, but she doesn't say anything. There is one other time when I spit my food. I spit my food when I'm full. This is the only way I have to tell Mommy when I'm full.

There is an action I use to tell people when I like something. I like to look around. When I look around at all the pretty things, I babble and smile. I smile at Daddy, too. He likes that. Sometimes I smile just for the sake of smiling. I'm hard to figure out then because nobody knows why I'm smiling. You won't tell my little secret, will you?

I frown, too. This action tells people that I don't like something or that I'm trying to relieve myself. I also practice frowning like I do smiling. Let's keep that a secret, too!

There is still another activity that I use to tell people things; really, it's several actions together. I kick my feet back and forth and up and down while I wave my arms all about. I do this for several reasons: I may only be playing and exercising; I may be angry; or I may be wet. I might also want to be picked up and loved. Mommy has to figure me out when I do this. It's not hard for her, though, because I usually do other things along with kicking and waving.

Some other actions I use to tell my needs are; pursing my lips tightly together when I don't like my food or when I'm full, and making awful faces. I make faces when I'm angry or when I don't want my food. This is how I communicate; if you really listen, you'll hear me!

The adoption of Alan

While Ted and I were engaged and when we were first married, we often talked of having children. We thought four boys would make a nice family. We both agreed that we would wait until Ted was out of college to begin our family, but in May, I conceived our first child. We were delighted from the time we first suspected, even though we had wanted to wait.

Ted was to graduate in January and the baby was to arrive then also. I had no problems during my pregnancy; I really felt fine. But during my third month Ted was awakened one night with excruciating pains in the genital area. He was never one to make a fuss over any physical discomfort, so when I was awakened by his screams and groans due to the pain, I knew something terrible was wrong. I was really frightened. On examination I saw that his testicles were swollen over two times their normal size. I immediately called the doctor and explained what was happening. He came over within minutes and, after examining Ted, said he had epididymitis, an infection in the tubes of the testicles, which usually occurs in men like Ted who have not had the mumps as a child. The doctor wanted Ted taken to the hospital immediately; he made arrangements with the local ambulance to take him there. It was a job getting him from our apartment down to the ambulance, for the slightest movement or bump made Ted wince with pain.

The swelling began to go down around the fourth week; once this began, Ted had less pain. By the end of six weeks he was feeling almost as good as new. He was anxious to leave the hospital and get back to school. The doctor released him from the hospital but restricted him in all activities for another month. The same day Ted was released from the hospital the doctor told us that, even though Ted was fine now, he would have after effects. We were told that one or both of Ted's testicles would atrophy. As time passed, the right testicle atrophied completely and the other one partially. We both knew before the doctor confirmed it that the possibility for having more children was not too good. The news was not easy to take, and so the fact that I was pregnant became more important to us than ever. Ted waited on me hand and foot. I really felt great the whole nine months and did everything I always had, but Ted was anxious.

Being laid up for six weeks really put Ted back in his studies, so he doubled his credits and worked harder than ever so he could graduate in January. Things worked out and he did graduate on January 8. The baby was due around the twenty-first, and on January 22 at 2:10 A.M. our son was born. What a wonderful glorious moment! It was not to remain so, however, for Steven didn't live more than a few hours due to respiratory complications. We were both totally crushed by the news and felt that life was cruel and unjust. It is still a part of our life that is difficult to think about. Time passed, and with it our grief lessened. We tried to have more children of our own, but to no

avail. Ted had test after test for sperm count and the results were always the same; the number of sperm was always so small that pregnancy was labeled as possible but not too probable. We finally accepted this fact and decided we could still have our four boys by adopting them. We talked it over and knew that it was something we both wanted, so in November of that year we talked to our doctor about adoption procedures.

He was pleased with our decision and suggested we go to three or four agencies in our county and neighboring counties. We soon learned that it was not as easy as we first thought to adopt a child. All the agencies we went to said they had more parents than babies. The waiting lists were long and we weren't given any real encouragement by any except the Family Children's Service. It was the only agency that took our name and said we would be called. Much to our surprise, about a month later we were called in for an interview. We were told from the beginning that they could make no guarantees as to when we could adopt a child, but they would do what they could. We both decided it didn't matter how long it took; we could wait.

It was four months after our interview in December before we heard anything from the agency. We received a call asking if one of their caseworkers, Mrs. O'Neal, could come to inspect our home and talk with us. We were delighted; maybe it would be sooner than we expected. Why else would they want to inspect our home? Needless to say, we were quite excited and a bit nervous about the visit. We were really looked over and asked a million questions before Mrs. O'Neal left, without giving us any encouragement about how long it would be. We found out later that the people we gave as references were really checked out and asked many questions about us.

It was now June, eight months since we had put in our name. Twice in one week we had unannounced visits from Mrs. O'Neal. One was early in the morning, a morning I had overslept and was dashing about getting ready to go to the local swimming pool to work as a swim instructor with the Red Cross Learn-to-Swim Program. She insisted I go while she visited with

Ted. All I could think of was what she would think of my unmade bed and dirty dishes in the sink. The second surprise visit was one evening when Ted happened to be away. We often wondered if these visits were planned, or if it was just a coincidence. We weren't given any indication about when we would get a child either of the times she visited. When we asked, she merely answered by telling us they had a long waiting list with everyone just as anxious as we were.

On June 22 we received a call asking us if Mrs. O'Neal could drop by that day. Our answer, of course, was yes. She arrived right after lunch and she had good news. She told us there was a little boy who was just perfect for us. Ted and I just sat there, unable to believe what we had heard. A baby, a boy baby, just right for us! I had always hoped for a child around six to nine months old (I knew none were released for adoption before the age of six months). I asked how old the baby was, and she said: "He was a year old on the ninth of this month (June)." I know I looked disappointed for the moment, but she kept talking about this darling little boy who was just perfect for us. "Come down to see him and then decide," she said. We both knew then and there that age didn't really matter; we also knew if we saw him, and he liked us, it wouldn't matter how old he was. Before Mrs. O'Neal left we had arranged to go down the next day to see him. His name, she said, was Andrew, or Andy as everyone called him.

Neither of us slept that night. We were going to be parents. We spent most of the evening on the telephone calling everyone to tell them the good news. We were up early the next morning to get our chores done so we could be at the agency at noon. Around 9:00 A.M. the phone rang; it was Mrs. O'Neal and my heart fell. She was calling to tell us we would have to postpone our visit because Andy was sick. He woke that morning with a high fever and couldn't be taken out. What a disappointment!

A week later we received word that Andy was fine and we should come down to see him on the twenty-eighth. Nothing went wrong this time and we got to meet our new son. What a

sweet little boy—blond, blue eyes, and a great big smile. I'll never forget that moment. Mrs. O'Neal was holding him when we entered the room. She left shortly so we could be alone. He wasn't a bit afraid of the two strangers in his midst, but he didn't take to me at all. He went straight to Ted and, whenever I offered to take him or would try to get near him, he backed off or went to Ted. I was hurt but not enough to give up the possibility that this fine happy little boy could be ours. The visit went well and he did wave "bye-bye" to me when we left. Ted felt bad that Andy didn't warm up to me, but he was pleased as punch that he seemed to like him.

After we left Andy, we were called in to see Mrs. Gleason, head of the agency, and Mrs. O'Neal. Arrangements were made for us to get Andy the following week. We hadn't done anything about getting ready for our new baby, so we spent the week making preparations and waiting impatiently for the "big day." We picked Andy up at 10:30 A.M. on July 7. He was all right until we drove away, and then he began to cry. He cried the whole way home. He kept crying "mommy, mommy, mommy," reaching out with his little hands as though he were looking for her. I was happy and sad; my heart went out to him, but no matter how I tried I couldn't comfort him.

When we finally arrived at the farm, Ted took him and he quieted right away. His foster mother, who had raised him since he was ten days old, had sent a big box of toys along with him including a "kiddie-car" and a riding steamroller that he had gotten for his first birthday. We put all these things down in the living room and put him down to begin to get used to his new surroundings. We had a pet dog that had been babied and spoiled. We were not too sure how she would take to Alan (this is what we renamed Andy). We worried needlessly, for when we set Alan on the floor, the dog went right over to him and began to lick his face. Alan squealed with delight and from that moment on they were inseparable.

We were not given any details about Alan's real parents except that the mother was a young girl whose husband had been killed in an automobile accident, and she was unable to keep him. We were not given any information about his foster parents either, except that they were older people who took him when he was ten days old and gave him much love and care. His foster mother sent pictures of him taken at his first birthday party and the ones showing the foster parents had the heads cut off to hide their identity. She must have been a wonderful mother to Alan. She wrote a six page letter telling me all about his habits, likes, dislikes, the age he sat up, crawled, walked, talked, first teeth, and just about anything else a mother would make note of during baby's first year. She ended her letter by saying: "God never made a better baby."

I have kept this letter and I have told Alan about it and her many times. We always let Alan know from the time we brought him home that he was adopted. He has never, in his twenty years of life, given us any reason to believe that he has not accepted it fully. In fact, his favorite bedtime story as a child and whenever he was sick was to be told the story "about when he was adopted." He never seemed to tire of hearing it. We never will know who his foster mother was, but I often think of her and hope that she somehow knows Alan is a fine young man today.

You might be interested in this one last note. When Alan was about two years old, he had an imaginary playmate. He came on the scene quite suddenly and left the same way. We went along with it but didn't overdo it. The interesting part is that the name of this imaginary playmate was Andy. We knew of no one by that name and none of our friends' children or his playmates was so named. We both assumed that subconsciously Alan never forgot his given name.

Tom and his corrective shoes

Mother Nature surely has done a marvelous job of planning and directing the development of an individual. It is exciting to realize that every individual develops in an orderly and sequential fashion.

My son, Tom, is a fine example of the fact that physical growth and development are continuous and sequential. He also demonstrates that there is that "something" within an individual that guides or directs him when the maturational processes within his body are ready for a new stage in physical development.

Tom had some difficulty being born. He was too large for my body structure. Thus, when it came time for his birth, Tom's shoulder presented instead of his head, and what would have been a short and easy labor was lengthened into seven hours. The obstetrician had to turn Tom so that he would be born head first and without any severe damage being done to him. This change was accomplished and all Tom had to show for his first adventure in life were black and blue bruises on his head, right shoulder, and right arm and club feet. His feet, because of his position in the uterus, were turned inward. Tom arrived two weeks early, and we sometimes wonder what might have happened had he met the obstetrician's deadline. As it was, he weighed eight pounds, fifteen ounces and measured twenty-two inches.

In spite of his bruises, which turned yellow and were assimilated by his system, Tom continued in a normal pattern of development. He cried, sucked, slept, and ate continually. At five weeks he delighted all the members of his family with a wide, toothless grin. He was aware of his family, he reacted to them, he was growing quickly, and all in all seemed a very happy and contented baby.

When I left the hospital with Tom, the pediatrician advised me to exercise Tom's feet in an effort to guide their growth, which we did. By the time Tom was two months old, we were sent to an orthopedic specialist who decided that Tom would have to have some orthopedic correction to ensure that his feet and legs would grow straight and strong. So it was that, at two months of age, Tom was prescribed a pair of shoes attached to each other by a long metal bar. He was destined to wear this device at all times—awake and asleep—except when he was being bathed. He cried for an hour when they were first put on him—the longest hour I ever knew—and then seemed to adjust to them. After that, he showed no more distress over the bar attached to his shoes.

My husband and I wondered if this orthopedic contraption would hinder Tom's motor development. Could he learn to turn over? Would he become frustrated? Would he be able to stand? Would he crawl? What about walking? Would it take longer for Tom to learn these skills than for a normal baby without this metal connection?

Development must be sequential, and it must result from some inner voice telling a baby what comes next! First of all, Tom learned to lift both of his legs at the same time. Over and over he did this. Up his feet would go; down they fell with a bang.

When Tom was physically ready to turn over, he turned over. True, he had to strain and strive a little harder, and a little more earnest effort had to be exerted, but he did it. Sometimes we would come into his room and find him in the oddest positions: half turned over, his feet caught on the bars of his bed, a wide grin on his face. It almost seemed that Tom compensated for this hindrance to normal development with an extra dose of determination.

When it became time to sit up, Tom learned to sit up, both feet stretched out in front of him connected one to the other by the metal crossbar. We were amazed! Around six or seven months of age Tom began to try to stand up. This was quite a feat for him with both feet still connected, but he never gave up. Tom also was able to crawl in his own peculiar fashion all over the house. He would pull his knees up together and go hippity-hopping to the regions beyond.

The one thing Tom couldn't do was walk. He would stand looking at first one foot, then the other, and try to separate them. He could not, however. When Tom was ten and a half months old the orthopedist said that all was proceeding well with the development of Tom's feet and legs and the crossbar could be removed. Tom would now be free to use his feet separately. What happened? At ten and one-half months of age Tom, with strong legs and feet, and an extra ounce of determination, walked. He walked everywhere.

Today my son is a strong, well-developed twelve-year-old. He has fine muscle coordination and as far as we can tell has had no disastrous effects to his personality as a result of the eight and one-half months he spent with his feet attached. When he walks on the sand without shoes, his footprints are well formed and straight. In spite of the confinement of a crossbar that kept his feet attached, he developed in a continuous, orderly, and sequential pattern. What a wonder!

A profile in gratefulness

My third pregnancy was not planned, as my previous two had been. Although I wanted another child, I had decided upon a time several years later. My two little daughters, then ages four years, six months, and one year, eight months, were the joys of my life. But, ready or not, I became pregnant! I truly had misgivings about this third pregnancy, and when Lisa was born, I remembered and wondered whether my earlier misgivings could have in any way affected my unborn child.

Sometime during the embryonic period of this third pregnancy, I contracted a severe case of intestinal virus. When I went to a physician for treatment, I explained to him that I was pregnant. I believed that the information might aid in determining the medication to be prescribed. An unthinking (or perhaps unknowing) young doctor dismissed this information as inconsequential since I had missed only one menstrual period and my pregnancy was not validated at such an early stage. Whether my sickness (with attendant spasms of severe nausea), the prescribed medication, or my generally weakened system (which lasted for about a month) had any effect on my baby during the embryonic stage cannot be determined. I do believe now that my baby could have been affected because my third little girl was born with a spinal defect.

Lisa Ann was born at 2:35 P.M. on July 16. Vital statistics concerning her birth were: weight—six pounds, two and one-half ounces; length—twenty inches; head measurement—twelve and one-half inches; chest measurement—twelve inches. Lisa was born with a birth defect which is medically described as a myelomeningocele, often referred to as spina bifida.

The degree of severity of the defect usually determines which term is used. The condition is medically defined as: "A severe birth defect in which there has been incomplete formation and fusion of the spinal cord. A rupture occurs in which the spinal cord and nerves protrude through the back and appear beneath the skin." The rupture which occurred at the base of Lisa's spine was a bulbous protrusion approximately three inches in diameter. When she was relaxed, the protrusion (which is best described as resembling half of a small, rubber ball attached to the spine) was soft and pliable, and the spinal fluid in the protrusion could be forced back into the spinal column. When she exerted or cried, the protrusion became firm and filled with fluid.

A severe meningocele is like an open wound in the spine with drainage of fluid, but such was not Lisa's case. The skin of the protrusion was strong and afforded good protection of the spinal cord. Shortly after Lisa's birth, a neurosurgeon was called for consultation. Her feet and lower extremities were pricked with pins, and she responded with the vigorous kicks and cries of a normal baby. All outward signs were good, but the attending physician did not hesitate to inform my husband and me of the many possible complications which could develop.

We were advised by the attending neurosurgeon that corrective surgery should be performed, but he advised waiting until Lisa was six months old and had a firm "hold on life."

Very anxious parents took Lisa home and began a long waiting period. Our only instructions were to avoid undue stress on the rupture and to be cognizant of Lisa's head development by continuing measurements at periodic intervals. Otherwise, Lisa was to receive the care of any newborn infant. We made regular visits to the pediatrician who kept us encouraged about her "normal" progress.

From the beginning, Lisa was a chubby, little baby with a full head of dark hair. She began immediately to hold her head erect and was aware of any movement around her, especially sudden noises. She increased at a standard rate in weight and size. She began to smile at the age of two months and laughed aloud by the age of three months. At the age of four months, she was able to turn over without assistance. Lying on her back never caused discomfort, and her apparently "normal development" was encouraging during the six months while awaiting surgery. However, we were unable to relax and enjoy Lisa's early infancy because of fear of the unknown. Would she exhibit symptoms associated with her defect? Would her development continue?

During the six month period, we located, by pure chance, a hospital in a neighboring state where two staff neurosurgeons had been performing corrective surgery for this type of defect on patients from all parts of the United States. They were particularly noted in medical circles for their work in such cases and, because of interest in advances to be made in such cases, they readily accepted Lisa as a patient. They were amazed that no complications had developed during Lisa's first six months of life and readily admitted a preference for performing surgery in these cases as soon as possible after birth. Corrective repair of the defect and the chances of recovery were statistically validated to be much better soon after birth, but of course we had no way of knowing this.

When the day of surgery arrived, we were called into conference by the doctors and given a realistic briefing of the corrective repair to be attempted. They explained that no exact operative procedure had been established since each case involved varying degrees of abnormality. While many advances were being made in this area of birth defects, no cause and effect relationship had been determined. A detailed description of the arrest of hydrocephalus and the lessening of its effects by a ceramic valving of excess fluid in the cranium into the kidneys for normal removal was reassuring, for we had been told that hydrocephalus might well occur. It was a constant fear for us. The corrective procedure to be attempted was explained as the overlapping of muscles along the spine to cover the opening caused when the tip of a bone in the spinal column had failed to form; thus the opening into the spinal column allowed fluid to escape into the sac-like protrusion.

The doctors were confident that, in view of her progress, and barring complications during surgery, Lisa had an excellent chance of full recovery. The very understanding surgeon assured us that we should be encouraged by the very fact that Lisa's case promised a chance for full recovery. The only payment asked in return was permission for use of photographs to be taken during all phases of her treatment. Our hopes of helping advance knowledge about such cases caused our ready agreement.

I shall never forget the picture of a black-haired, beautiful little baby disappearing behind the doors of an operating room. I suffered momentary misgivings, but I knew that I had to maintain confidence in the surgeons who were so much a part of my life at that time. The hours passed slowly for my husband and me, but at last we were given special permission to go to Lisa's crib in the intensive care unit for the rest of the day. During the recovery phase, Lisa slept peacefully. When she awakened, she began smiling as if nothing unusual had happened during her long sleep. She was immediately alert and curious enough to reach for a box of Kleenex which had been placed at the head of her bed.

The operation was declared to be very successful, but her doctors were surprised to discover some nerve involvement which had not previously been thought to exist. Fortunately, these nerves seemingly had no vital control function, although exact identity and function could not definitely be ascertained. We were encouraged to learn that the likelihood of additional adverse effects was remote but were advised to remember that in such cases unanticipated complications could always occur.

Several days after we took Lisa home from the hospital, we had some anxious moments. We had been advised to observe with care any unusual rise in body temperature. An abnormal rise would likely denote spinal meningitis, a disease which is easily contracted by a person whose spinal cavity has been exposed, even under the most sterile operative conditions. When Lisa's temperature rose suddenly and she became fretful, our first thoughts were of the possibility that she had meningitis. She was admitted to a local hospital, and we immediately began to make plans to travel back to her surgeons who would perform a spinal tap to accurately diagnose meningitis. Fortunately, our fears were unwarranted. The local doctor's diagnosis of a common virus precluded a more crucial testing. In a matter of days, no one would have ever suspected that Lisa had undergone surgery; she was the picture of health.

Lisa continued to thrive. When she was eight months old, she pulled to her feet. This event was recorded in her baby book as "a wonderful sight." Several days before her first birthday, she began to take steps and was walking soon thereafter. But as her feet developed, an inward roll was noted. The orthopedist prescribed corrective shoes, but having corrective shoes to wear and wearing them proved to be a different matter! To Lisa, the wearing of shoes was an unnecessary evil. I had a difficult time keeping them on her feet! In fact, clothing of any kind seemed to be a restriction as far as she was concerned. She certainly had no intentions of letting society dictate that she be decently dressed! Lisa was happiest when playing under sunshine, in sand, and wearing the barest of essential covering. She was strictly an individualist!

Lisa's language development was standard. By the age of fourteen months, she could say a few words. By the age of twenty months, her vocabulary was recorded as: Ma-ma, Da-da, Ka-thy, Gail, see, baby, puppy, bye, no, yes, car, shoes, socks, wet, dirty, eat, milk, night-night. By the age of two, she enjoyed story books, especially those with animal pictures. She would sit for long periods and look at pictures. Likewise, she would sit attentively as long as anyone would read to her from books. Lisa loved people and animals, and she readily captured the hearts of both. Even someone's cantankerous cat could be charmed by her kind and loving manner.

Lisa was a very untidy child. Even as she grew older, she managed to get more food on the outside than inside! She liked ice cream, but her unhurried movements allowed most of the treat to melt before she really had a good chance at it. I soon devised an arrangement which allowed Lisa to really enjoy her many messy treats as she saw fit. I put her in an empty bathtub; when she was finished, I could administer a much needed bath. We both were happy with the arrangement. I must admit that my patience was tested from time to time. Once Lisa placed a full bowl of spaghetti on her head like a happy little cherub with tomato sauce and spaghetti running down into her thick dark ringlets of hair.

During early childhood, Lisa seemed to be destined for many mishaps, like getting the crook of a coat hanger caught in her throat, jabbing a pencil in her throat, and swallowing a balloon which she tried to inflate by inhaling. Ask not how she came to possess these items, for such things seemed to magically appear in her hands! Lisa was physically active, but she was continually getting her feet tangled and taking hard spills. Her knees were usually skinned, and several times she had to have cuts under her chin stitched by the doctor. We began to realize, and the doctor confirmed, that Lisa had poor motor coordination. We could never be certain whether this lack was attributable to the nerve involvement of her birth defect, but very possibly it was. To be poorly coordinated is not desirable, but to think of less desirable alternatives which might have been in Lisa's case causes us to be thankful that Lisa can run, jump, and play. To us, her stumbling gait is as graceful as that of a prima ballerina.

It is very true that Lisa was not planned from the moment of conception, but before she came into our lives, we did not realize how much more meaningful life could be with a third little girl. To come to this realization, you need only to have a curly-haired little miss with a dirty face and hands crawl into your lap, have her put her arms around your neck, and say: "I love you."

Behavior modification of a one-year-old

Sammy, age one, was well versed in modifying behavior. Of course, he did not understand what it was all about when he modified my behavior three months earlier, but he had been responsible for an attitude which I had to adopt or suffer the consequences to my emotional health.

Most babies of nine months are adept at twisting, turning over, and grabbing for things. For parents, this is an exciting time—until it comes to changing a diaper. What used to be a simple task becomes a challenge. At first I rebelled against all this activity while removing and replacing the diaper. I had always been careful about putting the pins out of reach, strapping him on the table, and chatting with him during the diaper changes. Then Sammy began turning over and grabbing for things. Reaching for things did not bother me very much; the turning over was my main concern, since he could fall off the changing table so quickly. At first I would talk to him in a stern tone of voice, reminding him that I might stick the pin into him even though I tried to be very careful. I told him that he might fall and that I was worried that he might hurt himself. Still he persisted in kicking and wiggling and trying to turn over. I figured that I could get the message across with a quick pat on his bottom. He was startled the first time and cried. Subsequent changings produced the same cry after the paddling, but the fussing continued.

The changing routine occurred so often during the day that I felt frustrated much of the time. It did not take me long to realize that he was not being affected by the changing trauma since he had very few carry-over feelings once it was over. I was the one who was upset and angry, only my feelings held on longer than his did. In the middle of a diaper change, it finally dawned on me that my attitude was incongruent with what I value. Here I was, getting upset because Sam, who was acting like any normal nine-month-old child, would not conform to the way I thought he should behave. In a hierarchy of things to become upset over, lying on the changing table ranked very low. Yet I was about to get angry because Sam was acting curious and happy, completely oblivious to diapers and pins. It was then that I decided that I would intentionally decide when a situation was important enough to warrant anger. Once I came to this decision, diaper changing became enjoyable again. I learned how to change a diaper upside down, backwards, and sideways with little effort. Sammy certainly had much to do with modifying my behavior.

Within three months the tables were turned. Sammy was now crawling around very well. He was also pulling himself up to a standing position and walking as he held on to the furniture. It was at this point that we began to notice Sammy's fascination with the knobs and dials on the television set. This was our new piece of furniture and much of our entertainment. In the winter, only a few months away, static electricity built up in the nylon carpeting and a shock would be produced each time we touched the set. Knowing this, we felt that the television should be off limits to Sam. We began the discipline process. At first we said in a stern tone of voice: "No, Sammy, you may not touch that!" He persisted, so we picked him up and put him in a different location in the living room. He crawled back over to the television set immediately. Our next step was to say "NO" and give him a paddling. Soon he became immune to the paddling. He would cry and become upset for a few minutes, and then crawl right back to the set.

About this time my husband was taking a class in behavior modification, so we discussed using this technique on Sammy. We decided to institute a "time-out" procedure. One of the few things which Sammy disliked was to be confined and held when there was so much to explore. He would start crying to indicate to us that he had been held long enough and wanted to get down and explore. We decided that each time he touched the television set we would hold him for two minutes or until he stopped crying. The first day he was held about eight times. He looked surprised the first time we initiated our plan. He then began to cry and squirm, trying to get away. He looked confused about the silence on our part. There were no angry words or spankings, just neutral silence. During subsequent holdings he would cry very hard and push our hands, trying to force them open. After the first few times, he gave up the struggling but continued to cry. The second day he touched the television set only four times. The next two days he tried to get the knobs twice a day. The following three days he only attempted his feat once a day. For the next few weeks it was necessary only to hold him once a week. Then about once a month he would test

us to see if we were still emphatic about his boundary. We continued to enforce it.

We were happy that our system of "time-out" had worked. It was due to the conscious effort on our part and to the fact that it was consistently enforced, regardless of the inconvenience to us. This was perhaps one of the most efficient and effective ways for extinguishing a particular behavior that we had tried. It was a calm approach to what could have been a very trying and hectic experience for the three of us. Sammy learned rapidly that there were some areas in the house which he could not touch. This lesson was learned without the usual spanking and scolding which are often associated with the exploration stage of the one-year-old. One other side benefit for my husband and me was that we were able to keep our tempers, since there was no yelling involved. It was a beneficial experience for all of us.

Donnie

Throughout my nine months of pregnancy I felt no pain, suffered no diseases, encountered no accidents. All precautions were taken for a healthy baby, including vitamins, proper diet, plenty of rest, proper exercise, and avoidance of alcohol and cigarettes. Blood types were checked since my mother has the Rh-negative blood factor and because I received several transfusions as an Rh-negative baby; however, my blood proved to be O positive. The obstetrician informed me that my neonatal condition would have no effect whatsoever on my baby. There are no cases of deformity or mental deficiencies in either my family or my husband's family. During birth there were no complications, but the question then still remains: Why did I give birth to a hydrocephalic child?

The question was asked of me whether or not to permit the surgeon to perform a ventriculovenous shunt soon after my son Donnie was born. My only thought was that I wanted my baby alive, so I consented. Little did I know to what extent the "alive" would be.

Donnie is now fourteen months old and

very far behind the average child. The extent of brain damage has not yet been determined, but simple observation shows a noticeable degree of deficiency. Donnie has been further handicapped by the fact that his thumbs have never extended themselves from his palms.

For the first four months of Donnie's life there was no activity from him at all. He lived in an immobile and silent world. He ate, slept, and watched things, void of expression. He made no attempts at self-mobility or at expression. No object seemed familiar to him, yet he cried when he was hungry or uncomfortable. He jerked at loud sounds and sudden movements but showed no advancement from the neonatal stage. Donnie received special attention from everyone but was given no ray of hope from the doctors. He spent his first four months in and out of hospitals.

When Donnie was four months old, I had to resume my career. It was also the turning point in Donnie's behavior. Even though much of his first four months was spent away from his family, he seemed to object–to being separated again. His first discernible changes were facial. He seemed to cry with more feeling than before. For the first time, a smile was noticed. He grimaced at certain foods and began some bodily movements. It seemed that Donnie was acting like a newborn infant. His features took new form. His red hair seemed to look like hair, and his blue eyes began sparkling with recognition.

Within days Donnie was busy making funny noises and waving his arms around wildly. His enlarged head seemed, for the first time, cumbersome to him. He began noticing toys, colors, sounds, and people all at once. He was suddenly really alive and aware, and each new moment became precious for him and for us. On his next visit to the doctor, Donnie decided to show off. He kicked, cooed, cried, laughed, and pointed with his right forefinger extended for the first time. He seemed to be showing everyone that he really wanted to live and to learn. He seemed so fascinated with himself. Life had once again begun.

In the ensuing months many new things were noticed. He began trying to pick things up but could not because of the immobile thumbs.

Then the plans went into action for surgery to correct this situation by inserting muscles and tendons into the thumbs to provide movement. While in his playpen, he began to raise himself with his arms, never really getting very far. Most of his wasted effort seemed due to his heavy unbalanced weight, but some of the cause was his thumbs. Donnie began sitting with support and was then firmly placed into a high chair. In his chair he became aware of more objects and wanted a chance to feel them. Usually his attempts to grab things and pick them up were futile, since they fell to the floor. Then he began to enjoy pushing everything onto the floor. We actually encouraged such behavior, for it afforded him more and more exposure to his environment. When Donnie was ten months old, he worked his two hands together to pick up items. Some he could hold for quite a while, but others were too heavy for him.

At ten and one-half months Donnie's first thumb operation was performed. It failed to provide for him the proper use of his thumb and also seemed to set him back again emotionally. Soon after, a second attempt was made, with supposed success. Even though success was claimed, at thirteen months there was still no sign of movement in the thumb. Plans are now in the making for an operation on the second thumb.

At thirteen months Donnie's life had once again reached a lull. No new activities were observed, only an increase in nonsensical noise-making. He still could not sit by himself, nor stand, nor creep, all attributed to his head size and his thumbs. He had improved in picking things up; he managed to pick up objects, even small ones, by using both index fingers together. We were waiting for some true signs of communication to form but until this time none was made.

Last Tuesday Donnie was fourteen months old. On this same day two new and wonderful acquisitions were noticed. He was lying in his playpen when I got home. I went over to him and he, as usual, rolled over to his back and reached out to be held. After picking him up, I began to talk to him. When we went into the kitchen, I reached for a cup to get him some water. Donnie pointed and said: "Water." His pronunciation was clear; I was so stunned that I couldn't move. Donnie started squirming in my arms and insisted: "Water, Mommy." Needless to say, he got all the water he wanted. I think I sat and stared at this remarkable boy for some time. Despite all odds, he wanted to learn. Later, during his nap I approached his crib to discover him asleep. There was something different about him, but I didn't notice it at first. Then it hit me; he had his thumb in his mouth! It was his first self-extension of that thumb.

I know now that there are many new days of excitement ahead for Donnie. When the second thumb surgery is completed, we will have a son who may be able to really advance. We are also aware of the drawbacks that will continue to plague Donnie forever, but he seems happy now. For us that is the apex of life.

Lordy, lordy

The first word, if it was a word, that my daughter learned was "Lordy." One has to wonder how a child would ever learn such a word as her first word. I think it was probably due to the fact that I sang "la, la, la" to her when she was younger. That's the only word she said for quite a while: "Lordy, lordy." I thought for a long time that would be the only word she would ever say. But she was only one year old at the time and had plenty of time to learn other words.

My worries soon came to an end. After learning the motion of waving "bye-bye," she soon formed her lips to roll out the phoneme of "bye." It is interesting to note that she never said "bye-bye" as such. "Hi" was a word that was relatively easy for Stephanie to learn. When I added the motion to the word, however, she seemed to get "hi" and "bye" confused. She would say "hi" when she meant "bye" and vice versa.

Next in her vocabulary came the names of animals. Stephanie learned about animals from her books and from seeing the live animals. The latter seemed to be the more educational. The first animal word Stephanie tried to say was "cow," although it didn't sound like it was supposed to. It came out "keeeee" and sounded that way for nearly a month. I, as a first-time mother, was worried that that was the way she would say cow for the rest of her life.

Soon she came to call all four-legged creatures cows, or in her language, "kees." It wasn't until her grandmother got her a kitten that she learned the correct pronunciation of the word cow. I would say over and over to her: "nice kitty-cat." Soon she came out with "kitty-cat." The kitten had one sound of her own which, as everyone knows, is "meow." When rough treatment of the kitten takes place, naturally the kitten says "meow" and tries to get away. When saying "meow," this kitten really meant "ow"! Soon "meow" was added to the broadening vocabulary of my little one. And it was said as plain as day. Driving into the country one day gave me the opportunity to say to Stephanie: "Look at all the cows." And Stephanie said "cow" just as plain as could be. I was so proud of her that I almost ran off the road. I came to the conclusion that she rhymed "meow" and "cow" and ended with the correct pronunciation.

All parents want their children to learn good manners. Like some, I believe this should be taught while a child is young. So when my daughter wants anything, she has been taught to say "please." Of course, it doesn't quite come out like that; she says "peas." It sounds so cute and innocent that everybody makes a big thing out of it. I even heard an adult saying "peas" back to her. Now the problem is to get her to say "peas" meaning the vegetable and not "please." At the table when she says: "Peas, I want some," I always say: "Some what?" and then follow up with "peas?" Stephanie thinks I want her to say "please" and she says "peas." If only she would say: "Peas, some peas," I would be very happy. Of course, time works everything out. She does say "thank you," but it comes out "tank tu." Thank heavens there is no homonym for "tank tu"!

Then there are always those expressions I wish my child had never heard. When I once took liver out of the freezer to thaw for supper, my sister-in-law said: "Whew! are you having that for supper?" Of course, my two-year-old echoed: "Whew." I did not reprimand her for saying that word, but an incident soon occurred for her to use it.

We were shopping at the grocery store and one of my selections was a container of liver. Stephanie always places the grocery items in the cart. She put the liver in the cart without saying a word. When I took the liver out of the cart at the check-out counter, Stephanie said as loudly as she could: "Whew." She selected the exact moment when there was a line of customers waiting to be checked out. I was very embarrassed. The lady behind me said: "That's all right; I can't stand liver either."

I guess the word that touches most mothers' hearts is "Mommy" said for the first time. Stephanie says this with no trouble at all. There's one thing that puzzles me, however. I've tried to teach her the word "Grandma"; she always says: "Mom-Mom." I don't know what made her say this, but she calls both of the grandmothers Mom-Mom. So I call them Mom-Mom to her when talking about one or both of them.

No matter what she says, it's always interesting to observe her trying to say different sounds. Sometimes she tries so hard, but they just come out all wrong. I'm sure she thinks they're right. If they're right to her, they're right to me. I know from listening to her she'll soon acquire the correct pronunciation of words.

Deadly pills

Mark was twenty-two months old when a traumatic and nearly fatal event took place.

Mark is a sturdily built child who will surely be over six feet tall like his dad. He has brown eyes and light hair. He has two older brothers, ages eight and five. His parents are quite active in the establishment of a new business. As a result they often leave their children with other members of the family or with baby-sitters for varied periods of time, ranging from a few hours in the evening to two weeks away from home. Perhaps because of this uncertain schedule, Mark was late in talking and walking. Although the first two sons were toilet trained

and taught not to touch the usual "no-no's" at an early age, Mark has resisted these lessons. He has broken many knick-knacks and has cut and burned himself frequently. He became quite negative to outsiders at one year of age, expressing fear that he'd be left with them. Even now, he clings to his mother every opportunity he gets.

Mark's mother is from a large family who enjoy visiting each others' homes with their children. Consequently there is much going on when the family is together. On one such occasion, Mark's aunt and her two children dropped by around 7:30 P.M. While the others were in the kitchen, Mark found his aunt's pocketbook in the living room. With natural curiosity, he enjoyed to the fullest the challenge of opening such an item. Finally succeeding in his task, Mark discovered a wonderful array of gadgets, keys, money, and . . . pills. In what seemed not more than a minute from their arrival, his cousins found Mark happily playing with and swallowing the pills. A quick count of the newly filled prescription revealed just one diet pill missing and obviously consumed.

A consultation with a local physician ensued, resulting in the suggestion of having Mark's stomach pumped. He also stated that, if this was not done, the effect of taking one pill would be that Mark wouldn't sleep well that night. A "wait and see" attitude was decided upon by the parents in order to avoid the confusion of a rush trip to the hospital.

Shortly afterward, Mark went to bed and was asleep at 8:30 P.M., his usual bedtime. It took two and a half hours for the drug to digest and spread the high-powered stimulant through his bloodstream. At 10:30 P.M., Mark began screaming piercingly while he raced back and forth in his crib. His mother caught him but couldn't hold his thirty pounds as his body twitched and jumped in extreme hyperactivity. When she finally got him downstairs out of earshot of the other sleeping youngsters, he raced through the rooms, bumping into furniture and crashing into walls without seeming to notice. He showed no signs of recognizing either of his parents. Occasionally Mark cowered under the kitchen table in the manner of a wild animal, shrinking back from the parent who was trying to calm him. There seemed to be no way to constrain him.

Finally at 5:30 A.M. he fell asleep exhausted in his father's arms. When the father rose from his chair to put Mark into bed, the child resumed the hyperactivity at the same frantic level as before. However, now he was too hoarse to emit any sound. For two more hours he rampaged until he finally fell asleep once more in his father's arms. He slept barely an hour.

Not until 8:30 A.M. was the doctor able to administer phenobarbital to counteract the effect of the "pep" diet pill. Had it been given before, the countershock of the powerful depressant after the acute stimulation could have been fatal. The major threat to the child during the period of hyperactivity was possible heart arrest and bruising or breaking of bones.

After the depressant medication was administered, Mark slept for six hours. Upon awaking, he showed signs of thirst by licking his lips and puckering but refused to drink anything. It was several days before he would eat or drink significant amounts.

There are several developmental factors of importance in relation to this incident:

1. In the first year or so of life, the child needs consistent love and attention and discipline from just one or two significant persons in order to establish a feeling of security and also to define the limits of behavior. It's unfair to compare siblings, but the other two boys would never have touched the aunt's pocketbook at the same age. At that time in their lives, the mother had nothing to do but watch over and care for them.

2. Children at twenty-two months are quite explorative and curious. They have strong desires to find out about things by using their hands and taste. They will practice motor skills like opening pocketbooks and bottles until they have mastered the skill. Perhaps this is why Mark hadn't consumed more pills—he was too busy mastering the bottle cap. It's also possible that he didn't like the taste, but in that case he probably would have spit the pill out.

3. When the main, functioning part of the nervous system is affected by powerful drugs, the organism reverts to primitive behavior. It would seem that the sympathetic nervous system was in action during the stress period, shutting off all systems of the body not needed to release the excess "pep."

THINGS TO THINK ABOUT AND DO

1. Imagine a newborn baby before being brought home from the hospital. How helpless is this baby? Is there anything at all that this baby can do for or by himself or herself? Consider self-care, feeding, movements (motor), locomotion, communication, speech and language, bowel and bladder control, emotional responses, socializing gestures, intellectual responses, and personality characteristics.
   a. Make a chart and compare what the newborn can do alone in the areas listed above to what he or she can do at six months of age, twelve months of age, eighteen months of age, and twenty-four months of age.
   b. What areas of development appear to be maturing or developing the fastest? Speculate as to why these areas appear to be developing first.

2. The profiles on "If You Pay Attention, You'll Hear Me" and "Lordy, Lordy" are on communication and language development. Imagine a baby seeing a cat for the first time. Consider the intellectual understanding that this infant gains as various senses receive input (stimuli) concerning the cat. In other words, what does the child learn about the cat through the use of visual, auditory, tactile, olfactory, and taste senses? Could the infant learn as much about a cat if only one of these senses was used? What does all of this discussion tell you about how children learn?

3. Trace the stages that an infant goes through in learning to pick up an object with thumb and forefinger. Do the same for learning how to walk alone.

4. Survey several mothers of babies less than two years old on the question: What changes have you noticed in your baby between the time you brought him (her) home from the hospital and now? What surprises or amazes you about him (her)?

Survey the fathers of these same babies with the same questions. Are there any interesting contrasts or similarities between what the mothers and the fathers say?

5. Observe and record the behavior of several infants for a period of one to two hours. What impresses you about them?

6. Contact an adoption agency and find out what the procedures are for adoption. Also, ask if there is as much demand for babies to be adopted now as compared to five years ago or ten years ago. Are there as many babies available for adoption as previously?

7. Is it possible to spoil a one-year-old or a two-year-old? What would the parents have to do in order to spoil an infant? Would it really hurt the baby to spoil him?

READING SOURCES
Developmental psychology texts

Bernard, H. W.: Human development in western culture, ed. 4, Boston, 1975, Allyn and Bacon, Inc., chap. 7.

CRM: Developmental psychology today, ed. 2, New York, 1975, Random House, Inc., chaps. 6-9.

Hurlock, E. B.: Developmental psychology, ed. 4, New York, 1974, McGraw-Hill Book Co., chaps. 3, 4.

Kaluger, G., and Kaluger, M.: Human development: the span of life, St. Louis, 1974, The C. V. Mosby Co., chaps. 4, 5.

Mussen, P. H., Conger, J. J., and Kagan, J.: Child development and personality, ed. 4, New York, 1974, Harper & Row, Publishers, chaps. 5-7.

Newman, B. M., and Newman, P. R.: Development through life: a psychosocial approach, Homewood, Ill., 1975, The Dorsey Press, chap. 2.

Related readings

Bayley, N.: Development of mental abilities. In Mussen, P. H., editor: Carmichael's manual of child psychology, ed. 3, vol. 1, New York, 1970, John Wiley & Sons, Inc., pp. 1163-1209.

Bell, S. M., and Ainsworth, M. D. S.: Infant crying and maternal responsiveness, Child Dev. 43:1171-1190, 1972.

Brown, R.: Development of the first language in the human species, Am. Psychol. 28:97-106, 1973.

Coursin, D. B.: Nutrition and brain development in infants, Merrill-Palmer Quart. 18:172-202, 1972.

Dales, R. J.: Motor and language development of twins during the first three years, J. Genet. Psychol. 114:263-271, 1969.

Escalona, S.: Basic modes of social interaction: their emergence and patterning during the first two years of life, Merrill-Palmer Quart. 19:205-232, 1973.

Goldberg, S., and Lewis, W.: Play behavior in the year-old infant: early sex difference, Child Dev. 40:21-31, 1969.

Lewis, M., and Rosenblum, L. A.: The effect of the infant on its caregiver, New York, 1974, John Wiley & Sons, Inc.

Macnamara, J.: Cognitive basis of language learning in infants, Psychol. Rev. 79:1-13, 1972.

Scrimshaw, N. S.: Early malnutrition and central nervous system function, Merrill-Palmer Quart. 15:375-388, 1969.

Seth, G.: Eye-hand coordination and "handedness": a developmental study of visuo-motor behavior in infancy, Br. J. Ed. Psychol. 43:35-49, 1973.

Stone, L. J., Smith, H. T., and Murphy, L. B., editors: The competent infant: research and commentary, New York, 1973, Basic Books, Inc.

CHAPTER 3

Preschool childhood

Children at the ages of three to five seem so much alike the world over in their activities and growing up that it is easy to overlook the fact that within the boundaries of normal development individual differences can and do exist in children. The expressions "terrible twos," "trusting threes," "frustrating fours," and "fascinating fives" may serve to give some hint of the typical behavior patterns of children at these ages, but it is not true that all two-year-olds are "terrible" nor that the vast majority of five-year-olds are particularly fascinating. To say that most four-year-olds are very frustrating is both misleading and erroneous. All that characterizations of this sort do is to label children and put them into mental pigeonholes.

There are some dominant characteristics of children of the preschool years, however. Without question, preschoolers are extremely active. They are talking, moving, and playing all the time. They have reached the point where they can be relatively independent in seeking and reaching out for what they need and want. They are also becoming more aware of their individuality and they work at gaining mastery of their potentialities by practicing self-assertion. Children are not unmindful, however, of their interdependence on others; they are responsive to social influences. Yet they are not completely amenable individuals who will always do something simply because some adult tells them to do so. What occurs is a situation wherein children must learn ways and means, such as attitudes, self-ideals, and behavior mechanisms, by which they can respond to the directions and demands of adults while at the same time maintaining some degree of respect and dignity for their own self-esteem. In part, they are so active because they have so many social, communicative, physical, and cognitive skills to learn in order to live cooperatively with others and peacefully with themselves. Preschoolers have to work out these things for themselves.

"A Case Study of a Three-Year-Old" is an in-depth developmental study of a child and his family. The child has a palsy condition and a speech problem that he and the family must accept and deal with. The vivid, verbal imagination of a three-year-old is pleasantly revealed in "Imagine That," while the imaginary playmates of a four-year-old are delightfully portrayed in "The Imaginary World of Childhood." The energetic day-to-day activities of four-year-olds, as well as their unique characteristics, are presented in "From One Thing to Another" and "A Fun-Loving Four-Year-Old." Just as interesting are the experiences of a four-year-old in "Nursery School?"

Of a more unfortunate nature are the pathetic conditions surrounding the life of a young girl born to unwilling seventeen-year-old parents, making her "A Victim of Circumstances." As touching is "Life with Dale," a profile that describes a mentally retarded, hyperactive child in a kindergarten situation. Perhaps most moving of all, in a different sense, is the powerful, yet simply stated, recollection of "My Fear of Birds." On a different note is the story of "First Encounter," a five-year-old's first involvement and exposure to curiosity of a sexual nature.

Imagine that

To me, the imagination of a three-and-a-half-year-old boy is limitless. I have a son, Nino, who never ceases to amaze me with his imagination. At about the age of twenty-eight months, Nino was able to talk, using sentences with four to seven words. This was the time when his imagination began to blossom. At first he would carry on conversations between two of his trucks with which he usually played. Sometimes he would have the trucks talking, and sometimes the people who were supposed to be inside the cab talked.

As he grew older, he began to talk to all types of objects as if they were alive. Whenever we would go for a ride out in the country, he would say: "Hi, Mr. Cow." "Hi, Mr. Corn." "What are you doing, Mr. Silo?" The other day my wife bought some blueberries. She gave Nino a few of them to eat. He took one look at them and came running over to me, excitedly shouting: "Look, Daddy, Mr. Blueberry only has one eye. Can't he see?" I told him that Mr. Blueberry doesn't have to see because he just grows big so people can put him in a pie to eat. Nino accepted this explanation but examined each blueberry carefully before putting it into his mouth.

There is also an imaginary friend, a bug, with which he plays. He keeps him in his pocket and takes him out only to pet him, talk to him, or put him in his mouth. I am allowed to pet the bug only if I promise not to eat it.

All of the above experiences are not really out of the ordinary. However, he told me something a few weeks ago that really surprised me. He said he was going to build four buttons on the floor: when he would push a certain one, he would grow big; push another one and I would grow little; push a third one, and Maria, our second child, would grow big; push the last one and Mommy would grow little. I asked him how he was going to make the buttons and he said: "I will go to school with you and learn!"

A case study of a three-year-old

IDENTIFICATION AND SOURCE OF INFORMATION

Brad Harrington
Park Avenue
Pasalena, Oregon

Brad was born on October 4 to white American parents. At the time of his birth his mother was thirty-eight and his father was forty-one. He has a brother and a sister who were sixteen and thirteen respectively when Brad was born.

The following study is based on personal observation, facts from his mother, and comments made by a pediatrician and a speech therapist.

Date of case study: March and April, four years after birth.

HISTORY OF THE FAMILY

In Brad's family all members are slender and active. The family has a good health record. The only illnesses have been the usual childhood diseases, along with an occasional broken bone. His maternal grandparents are both living and are in their seventies. The paternal grandparents are both dead; the grandmother died at the age of fifty-nine and the grandfather at eighty-four. Brad's father was the last of seven children. He was born when his mother was thirty-five and his father forty-seven. Brad's mother was the fourth of five children, and both of her parents were in their early thirties when she was born.

Brad's parents are both high school graduates. The father was trained in radio and electronics while in the U. S. Coast Guard. He is now and has been employed for fifteen years as a production manager in a fairly large manufacturing plant. He has taken extension courses in management and production techniques. The mother has not worked since Brad was born, but prior to that she had worked as a part-time clerk in a local drug store. They live in a suburban area about six miles from the father's place of employment. They are about the same distance away from a large shopping center.

Brad's brother is now a sophomore in college and is majoring in engineering. His sister is a junior in high school and a very good student. There is an aunt (on his father's side) who is a school teacher and an uncle (on his mother's side) who is a graduate of an agriculture college. The family took an active part in the activities of the school while both siblings attended school. They agree that a good education is the basis for a full life.

This appears to be an average middle-class suburban family with two medium-priced cars and sufficient income to pay their bills promptly. They are genuinely friendly with their neighbors and invariably join in neighborhood picnics and other social gatherings. They belong to a Protestant Church group but have not attended services regularly since Brad was born.

Father was a Little League coach, a Boy Scout advisor, high school Band Parents' Association president, and Football Booster Club president. He is still treasurer for a local scout troop, a member of the local Industrial Management Club, and on the board of directors for the United Fund. Mother was a nursery helper, a den mother, and an active member of the Band Association. She plays bridge regularly with a women's bridge club. Both parents prefer an evening with one or two couples rather than hosting or attending a large party.

Their interests are varied and have changed somewhat with the two older children. They have taken two automobile trips to the east coast, both before Brad was born. Both siblings were members of the school band. Brother played football and baseball, and sister is cheerleader and class president. Mother and sister read a great deal, father and brother less often. All are interested in current events, however, and follow the news by television and newspapers. Father is a great "do-it-yourself" man and enjoys working on his home and lawn.

HISTORY OF THE CHILD

Brad was born a month ahead of the expected date. The doctors did not consider him premature because he weighed six pounds, fourteen ounces and was twenty-one inches long. His was a breech birth with his feet behind his head. The pediatrician examined him and announced that he appeared normal in all respects. The first two weeks of life were calm; he ate and slept well. Then he developed a severe case of diarrhea and was hospitalized at four weeks in order to bring it under control. From that time on he seemed to have digestive gas and was considered a "colicky" baby. When he was five months old, he was again hospitalized with severe croup. While he was in the hospital, a study was done of his upper digestive tract and all seemed well. The doctor attributed the digestive upsets to a nervous condition. He said Brad had a slight disturbance of the central nervous system. Brad moved his arms and legs much too rapidly when crying or when excited. He had poor muscular development but showed no sign of any serious disorder. He was given a mild tranquilizer for a time to slow him down, and it helped. By six and one-half months he was sitting up by himself. Brad continued to be overactive in

random movements but made no attempt to stand until he was past one year of age. He was crawling and investigating constantly but would not attempt to stand.

When Brad was fourteen months old, the pediatrician suggested a visit to an orthopedist. He checked Brad for all types of palsy and found nothing. However, he did discover that the tendons at the back of each heel were too long and that his hips were turned out. This was probably brought about by his breech-type birth. The pediatrician explained that Brad's lack of attempts at standing probably resulted from a feeling of insecurity by the child at this stage. His foot could stretch so far front and up that the toes would touch his shin. He found it impossible to balance himself. Brad was put in corrective braces and immediately began to stand. He walked in a straight direction in an unbelievably short time. His adjustment to these braces was good. He regarded them as something that he wore each day, such as any article of clothing. When the heel tendons strengthened, he changed to a "twister" type of brace. This change was made at the age of twenty months. The new braces consisted of a belt at the waist with spring tension cords leading to the shoes. The tension bars forced interior rotation to turn the hips to a "back-in" direction. He wore the twister type brace until age three. He is now wearing an orthopedic type corrective shoe.

When Brad was eighteen months old he was hospitalized for "acute dehydration," a condition following a severe bout with a virus.

Brad is a very slender child; his height is thirty-nine inches, which is slightly above the average for his age. He will probably always be slender, but his weight gains have been average for the periodic regular checkup times. At three and one-half years, he weighs twenty-seven pounds.

The boy's sleeping habits are very good. He has always been a child who needed and wanted regular sleeping hours and a great deal of rest. He often runs to the stairway leading to his room and is always ready to go to bed as soon as his mother mentions bedtime. He continued to take two naps a day until he was beyond two years of age. However, he would never fall asleep in a strange home or bed and never in a car. He seemed to require the security of his own sleeping surroundings. He developed a specific liking for a special blanket and cuddled up with it in order to get to sleep. He seldom seeks out the blanket during the day unless he is upset or feeling ill. At times he sucks two of his fingers but only just prior to falling asleep.

His nervousness continues to show in many ways. When very anxious or excited, Brad still waves his hands and arms very rapidly. It also shows in his speech efforts. He has in general made few attempts to speak. When he was two, he still was not saying anything that could be distinguished as words. A visit to a speech therapist was suggested. The following is an excerpt from the therapist's report to the pediatrician:

> Brad's speech is almost completely unintelligible. There are only a few single syllable words that are recognizable. Knowledge of his developmental history makes this easy to understand. I feel that his energies the last few months have been concentrated on physical development and adjustment to the leg braces. His speech development has necessarily been slowed also during this period. Although the p, b, m sounds are normally the first ones to appear in a child's speech efforts, Brad seems to have skipped them and is using more of the guttural sounds. I was able to get him to say "ka" for cat. He seems prone to omit the consonant sounds in a word and say just the vowel sound.

The following are the specific recommendations of the speech therapist:

> Brad must feel the need to speak. He should be made to feel that his desires and real needs can only be met when he has made an effort to express them by speech. He must be made aware of sounds of all kinds— animal, daily environmental, etc., as well as sounds created by speech. He should be encouraged to imitate the speech of others and enjoy the satisfaction of communication with other beings. Reading stories to him will be good for a listening exercise. Use of large crayons to color large single pictures will help develop muscle control and eye-hand coordination. All this is related to speech development. Use of records and toys that make speech sounds are very useful.

Brad's family began to work with him. He was encouraged to color pictures and play with clay. He enjoys the clay but still doesn't do very well with the crayons. He was read to frequently. At first, his attention span was very short but is gradually lengthening. He will now sit and hear a story to the very end. In the past month he has begun to pick up a book and pretend that he is reading it. He remembers the stories and repeats some of them. He has had a talking alphabet toy since he was two and one-half. Only recently has he pulled the string on the toy and then repeated what the toy says. He enjoys music and will dance to the records as they are played.

When he was about three, his family noticed he began stuttering. Mother thought it might be temporary but, due to his other problems, decided to again consult the speech therapist. At this time he was three and one-half. The therapist also feels the stuttering is a temporary condition that a good many children go through. If no attempt is made to stop him or make him aware that his speech is different, it should disappear. The stuttering is done mostly when he is excited. The family was instructed to just supply the word he was attempting to say and help him go on from there. For example, when he sees a bird fly away and starts "wh-wh-wh-" they know he is trying to say: "Where's the birdie?" So they just say; "Where did the bird go?" and he answers: "He flew away."

Brad will continue to see the speech therapist once a month—not for actual therapy at his age but just for observation. On these monthly visits, the mother will be instructed as to what sound to concentrate on and further ways to help him. The assumption is that these sounds will come to him and the therapist will lean toward that theory until it is proved incorrect. When Brad is in a responsive mood, he will make the sounds clearly, but at other times he is too hurried and careless. The p, b, m sounds are now clear most of the time. He has trouble with v, d, t, and l. For example, he "cakes" his coat off; a dog is a "gog"; and so on. At age three and one-half his average sentence consisted of four words.

Until recently Brad was very restless in his play. No toy could absorb his interest for more than a few minutes at a time. He went from one thing to another all day long. His favorite plaything is shoes. From the time he could crawl he just loved to put his hands in a pair of shoes and crawl around. Now that he is older he puts them on his feet, regardless of size, and clomps around. He notices the shoes of all guests and wants to remove them so he can play with them. His mother wonders if this developed because *his* shoes were so different from everyone else's.

Brad has had very few opportunities for play with other children. Most of his mother's friends and neighbors have children who are in the teenage period. Since children learn more quickly from other children, this probably accounts for some of his slowness in developing play habits. Mother has brought a boy aged four to the home several times in the last few months. Brad does a lot of watching and then repeats some of the play habits of his guest after the guest has gone.

Mother now realizes that Brad needs more social contacts and experiences with children of his own age. It was too easy to leave him with their teenage daughter when she went shopping or visiting. On his first trip to a shopping center recently, he just ran like a wild Indian. He was so excited with the lights and all the people. He didn't seem to notice a thing in the stores and made no attempt to touch or grab anything from the counters. Mother feels he is now ready to start to Sunday School and maybe a nursery school next winter if it can be arranged.

Brad's only noticeable fear is that of anyone dressed in white. This probably stems from his many trips to the doctor's office and to the hospital. He cries as soon as he enters the doctor's office and usually does not stop until he leaves. He had his first trip to the dentist recently and cried through the whole visit. Mother noticed his stuttering was much worse all that day and into the evening.

Brad has a good appetite. It varies, as it does with most people, but on the whole he eats well. He gets a midmorning and midafternoon snack, mainly because he does not eat large quantities of food at regular meal time. He has very few food dislikes and eats a great variety including pickles, cole slaw, tossed salad, potato salad, and lots of foods the older children would not have touched at his age. The only food he consistently refuses is mashed or boiled potatoes. Brad takes no vitamin supplements but gets orange juice and vitamin D milk every day. He drinks fluoridated water. Last winter he had no colds.

Once while I was a guest at Brad's home during dinner, a glass of water was accidentally spilled in my lap, but not by Brad. I instinctively jumped up and commenced to laugh about the whole incident. The sudden reaction to the little episode seemed to center within Brad; he was upset so much that he scrambled from his stool, almost unnoticed, and hid under the table. He seemed to feel that he had done something wrong and had to be immediately reassured that everything was all right.

Here, it seems, is a boy who is an interesting contrast. In some areas his development is about normal for his age, in other areas quite slow. He can dress himself except for tying his shoes. He puts simple puzzles together, uses his spoon very well, and is completely toilet trained. He stays dry all night and uses the toilet independently during the day. His eating and sleeping habits are regular. On the other hand, his speech is slow; he asks few questions and does not communicate easily. Emotionally he is retarded. A three-year-old is usually cooperative, sure of himself, anxious to please other individuals. Brad is just now in the negative stage. His contrariness and insistence on certain rituals at bed time are still evident. He goes to bed better for his father.

PROGNOSIS FOR THE INDIVIDUAL IN THE CASE STUDY

The outlook for Brad's future is optimistic. The physical handicap that is correctible is being successfully treated. The establishment of emotional stability will take time and patience, but strides are being made in that direction. The parents have no qualms about holding him out of school a year if he is not mature enough at five or six. With continued effort and an abundance of care and understanding, Brad should grow into a responsible, normal adult.

From one thing to another

Awakening before Mommy does is quite common for me, because I'm only four years old and have a lot to do in a day's time. This morning I awoke at six o'clock and sleepily stumbled over to Mommy and Daddy's bedroom. "Get up, Mommy, I want to go downstairs," I said. But, as usual, I was talked out of this by a very tired mother.

I then returned to my bedroom deciding to sleep longer. Actually it was Mommy's suggestion because I was very anxious to get in high gear. After an hour's nap, I heard Daddy taking a shower. I woke Mommy so I could get downstairs to see him. We met Daddy on the steps, and I couldn't resist pulling his towel away from his waist. He picked up the towel and then tickled me until my laughter woke Shauna, my four-month-old sister. This didn't go over too big with Mommy. When Daddy and I began clowning around in the hall, Mommy knew she had another one of those days ahead of her!

While Daddy finished getting ready for work, I decided to go see my sister. She always greets me with a smile; I tickle and talk to her until Mommy gets her out of the crib. Now the day really begins. Mommy likes me to help so I obliged and went to get a washcloth wet with warm water so she could wash the baby. I then kissed Daddy as he left, and now there were only three of us.

When I came downstairs, I turned my television on to watch the cartoons. Like most four-year-olds, my attention span is not very long, so I soon wanted breakfast. After three fourths of a bowl of cereal, a Pop-tart, and a glass of orange juice, I was ready to resume my television watching. After about five minutes I had to go to the potty. When I returned to the television room, I found my sister in her playpen, so I hopped in with her to assist in the playing. After this frolicking, Mommy called and told me to get dressed. Usually I'm quite uncooperative because I'm too interested in the objects around me. Mommy suggested we walk up to Janie's house so that I could play with her. I bundled up in my hooded coat and off we went. Much to my dismay she wasn't home; this made me mad. While walking back, I stamped my feet and said I was going to my bedroom. This mad mood never lasts for more than two or three minutes.

Returning downstairs, I asked Mommy to get my water paints ready. I then painted for a while and ate the charms out of my Lucky Charms cereal. During the artistic spree I listened to my Sesame Street record and pretended I had an audience while I followed the instructions of the record. I danced and sang until the record ended. You must remember at this point that I have already asked my Mommy many questions, such as: Where did Janie go? Which page can I paint? May I have a drink of water? Are we going bye-bye? Are Carol and Beth coming to my house? These are just a few of the questions I bore Mommy with all day. Sometimes I even ask my sister questions, but she never seems to understand.

Now my tummy began to growl, so as any normal person would, I asked for my lunch. Mommy fixed me a barbequed ham sandwich, a dill pickle, a bowl of chicken noodle soup, and a glass of milk. I usually eat all of my lunch and then seem to get very sleepy at this time of the day. Like most four-year-olds I hate nap time so I pretend not to be tired. Usually I give myself away by becoming very cranky. I tried to play with my sister, but by this time she is usually more miserable than I am. Mommy then feeds Shauna while I play my record player. After my sister is content, I watch her while Mommy goes downstairs to get the laundry out of the machine. Remember that the record player is still running and the television is still on.

My nap time was growing very close so I retired to the television to watch *Bewitched*. Usually if I'm quiet Mommy won't tell me to go up for a while, but I could fight it no longer. I went up to my room myself and decided to look at some of my books. Finally I lay down until I felt someone lie down beside me. I opened my eyes and there was my big Daddy. I don't know why it is, but every time we get

A careful man I ought to be;
A little fellow follows me;
I cannot once escape his eyes
Whate'er he sees me do he tries,
Like me, he says, he's going to be
The little guy who follows me.
I must remember as I go
Through summer's sun and winter's snow
I am building for the years to be
That little guy who follows me.

Author Unknown
ILLINOIS PARENT-TEACHER

together it is nothing but trouble for the both of us. After our fifteen minutes of bedlam, Mommy told us she had just put clean sheets on the bed. Well, that was a fine time to tell us that!

By that time *Sesame Street* was on television; I never miss it. Daddy says it is the only hour of the day I'm not active. After the program was over I told Daddy what I learned and we wrote our numbers.

It was now time for dinner, so I asked Mommy if I could help set the table. Of course, I had to have the orange glass. When dinner was ready, I sat down to my favorite meal: roast beef, mashed potatoes, and corn. After eating everything on my plate, I woke my sister and began playing with her. Soon Mommy was ready to feed Shauna so I decided to have some fun with Daddy. We played my bean bag game and guess who won—ME! By now Mommy summoned me to put on clean clothes and have my hands and face washed because we were going to visit my cousin Anne. When we arrived at Anne's house, she greeted me with a big: "Hi, Krissy." We started to play with her toys and then we decided to have a tea party. After a couple hours I began to get sleepy so Mommy put my coat on and I said good-bye to cousin Anne. I was so tired that I fell asleep on the back seat of the car. As we pulled into the garage, I opened my sleepy eyes and realized we were home. Daddy carried me and Mommy carried sister Shauna into the house.

Then it seemed I got my second wind and I was ready to play again. But to my dismay Daddy said it was now bath time. Of course, I love to play in the bathtub, but then I also know it's time for bed. As Daddy was running my bath water I decided to be a big girl and undress myself. I just love when Daddy gives me a bath—it's fun to splash water in his face. After my bath, I always brush my teeth; then Mommy brushes my hair and sometimes puts it up in pin curls.

I ran into my sister's bedroom to kiss her goodnight. Mommy was getting her ready for bed and soon she would be sound asleep.

Daddy said I could go downstairs and have a little snack. I leaped down the stairs and soon had some Tasty-kakes in my hand. While I was eating them, I had a big glass of chocolate milk. When I finished my snack, I kissed Mommy and Daddy good-night. I marched up the steps and climbed into bed. I said my prayer that I learned in Sunday School.

While closing my eyes, I realized I had to go to sleep fast so I could wake up bright and early tomorrow morning and begin another new day of fun.

The imaginary world of childhood

Imagination may be commonly defined as a creative experience of the mind which is not readily visible or perceivable. At the age of four, my world existed more in the imaginary realm than in the readily perceivable. Partially, this illusionary world can be attributed to my unique family situation, for I was raised in a home where my nearest sibling (my sister) was nine years my senior. In addition to the fact that strong sibling relationships were lacking, our neighborhood failed to supply adequate companionships, for the majority of the other children were in my older sister's age range; although at times they gave me an inordinate amount of attention, for the most part I left to my own resourcefulness in providing entertainment. How much of the following I actually remember and how much has been recounted by my sister, parents, and friends, I really cannot determine. But, in any event, here is (or was) my imaginary world.

Marie Kooterstein emerged one fine summer day close to my fourth birthday. I was having a marvelous time playing house in the living room utilizing all of my Mother's favorite knick-knacks to furnish my "lovely" home. Tragedy struck when I decided that what I really needed to complete my decor was the antique red Chinese vase from on top of the mantle. Being a well-skilled climber, I maneuvered a stool and a chair into position, finally managing to reach the vase. Down it came, but not as I had expected! Soon I was looking down upon the shattered pieces of ceramic glass and up at a very stern face which bore a strange resemblance to my mother. As I stared up with a most "angelic" expression (as my mother recounts the incident), I murmured in all innocence: "But Mommy, I didn't do it—Marie Kooterstein did." Perhaps my mother's reaction of laughter was the incentive, with a lack of punishment as an additional reward, but the emergence of my imaginary family began to develop rapidly from that point onward.

Soon Marie was joined by another good buddy named Albert and a rambunctious dog called Woof. The times to follow must have been frustrating and trying for my parents, who attempted to humor, cajole, coax, and convince me that "my friends" did not exist. But, of course, I knew that they were wrong, and I really couldn't understand why they failed to see and understand the existence of these little people. In addition, their attempts were further frustrated by the older children in the neighborhood who sat and listened for endless amounts of time while I recounted the trials and tribulations of Marie and Albert. All I really needed was an attentive and interested audience to permit my imagination to run to its wildest extremes.

Soon my parents gave up their futile attempts to find more "constructive" entertainment for me and decided to play along—after all, how long could this stage last? To cope with the family rituals that evolved, my parents must have needed the patience of Job coupled with a good sense of humor. Since my total recall on the subject is limited by the passage of time, only the most memorable incidents will be reiterated.

With the arrival of Albert and Marie, my family's dinner time habits took a drastic turn. No longer were only four places permitted to be set—after all, Albert and Marie had to take part in all family gatherings. So now there were six, and heaven help the individual who sat down in my friends' chairs! As I remember, the only person to protest was my sister—she totally lacked enthusiasm for doing the extra dishes involved. Her comments started with: "How long do we have to humor that kid?" But it really didn't bother me, for now I had almost as many friends as she did.

One prevailing ritual was long walks taken around our neighborhood with Albert and Marie. Of course, Woof went too, firmly at-tached to the long piece of clothesline which I had begged from my father—"What if Woof runs away!" As the "gang" trotted around the neighborhood, we would carry on the most fascinating conversations. Often the neighbors would invite me in to play with their dogs (I think they were slightly concerned about the poor child dangling the rope), but of course I refused—after all, I couldn't hurt Woof's feelings and I knew that he far surpassed their mangy animals.

At this time my favorite television program was *Bride and Groom.* I was far from content to just sit and watch, so another daily ritual soon became established. One of Mother's white dresser scarves quickly became transformed into a magnificent bridal veil, and freshly cut flowers from the garden made the perfect bouquet (when roses were out of season, the house plants made a good substitute). As the Bridal March sounded, I took Albert's arm and down the aisle we "two-stepped." Of course, Albert had to play a double role as we went through the entire ceremony from beginning to end.

Family excursions were a highlight of my childhood. Because I was an extravagant female, even at the age of three, the lure of a shopping trip to the "big city" was always a long antici-pated delight. However, much to my parents' chagrin and my adolescent sister's horrified dismay, we had to take Albert and Marie along. It took much heavy-handed persuasion to convince me that Woof would not be welcome in the department stores, but, finally, I gave in and my favorite canine friend (rope and all) re-mained at home. Once we arrived, we made quite a sight parading down the street, leaving room in between Mother, Dad, and me for Albert and Marie. Somehow my sister always managed to either lag behind or be fifty paces ahead—I don't think that she wanted to be associated with the rest of us! When we started out on one of our excursions one fine summer day, part of my imaginary world nearly came to an abrupt halt. As we all piled into the old green car, I shrieked with terror. Mother had sat on Albert! Soon order was restored, a badly crushed but amazingly unharmed Albert was planted in the back seat, and we were off for another exciting journey into the outside world.

Perhaps the proudest day of my life was when Albert went off to college. Eddie Ramer had long been my ideal within our neighborhood. Being almost eighteen and a senior in high school gave him a certain amount of prestige that my sister's friends lacked. Eddie and his friend Ben would sit for hours and talk and play with me and my friends; that gave them a big plus in my book! (Of course, as my sister so bluntly put it, they enjoyed adding fuel to my imaginary fire!) For months I had heard Eddie talking about his plans to go to college in September. I didn't really understand the meaning of all this, but I did know that it sounded very impressive and exciting and I was thoroughly convinced that whatever Eddie did would be just great.

One day as Albert and I were talking, I decided that what Albert really needed was to go to school. Where better to send him than with Eddie? After all, I was sure that Eddie would take good care of Albert, and that way neither of them would be lonely. Immediately I ran across to the Ramers' to discuss this with Eddie. After receiving numerous assurances that it would be fine with Eddie if Albert accompanied him, we discussed the fact that I might be lonely without Albert. Finally, however, I decided that my favorite friend should depart in September.

The preparations preceding the big event were extensive. I felt that what Albert really needed was a new suitcase like the one Eddie had, but Dad felt that Albert would be better off just borrowing his for the time being—then if Albert really liked the school, we could purchase a suitcase at a later date. The night before Eddie and Albert were to leave, the Ramers had a cookout to celebrate. As long as I live, I will never be allowed to forget the sign hanging from the back porch. In large lettering it read: "Good luck, Eddie" and in tiny red lettering underneath "and Albert." (Mother still has it tucked away with some of my childhood mementoes.) The following day was a sad occasion. Albert climbed into the back seat of the Ramers' car with Eddie and off they drove, but not until I made Eddie promise that he would bring Albert home with him on every vacation, so that I would be sure to see my good friend again.

How long my imaginary world would have continued, had it not been for the intervention of new next-door neighbors that fall, is a mystery. For months Marie and I had watched the construction work which transformed our beautiful field into a new modern home. Dad would take us next door and explain how all the equipment worked while Mother complained about the dust and dirt. Finally, the big day arrived, and Marie, Dad, and I were up early to watch the movers. About noon a shiny new car pulled into the driveway and out climbed two adults and one child—a little boy slightly younger than I. We went over and introduced ourselves and soon Punkie and I were exploring the sawed-off timbers left by the construction workers. As we returned, I heard multisyllabic phrases such as "imaginary playmates," "overactive imagination," "only child," "lack of companionship," and "well, I guess we have a similar problem!" Soon Marie and Woof began fading into the background (Albert, off at college, was quickly forgotten), and Punkie's friend "Harold" was usually sent off to play elsewhere. Oh, our imaginary friends were still around and easily came into focus when we needed them for about another year, but for the most part Punkie and I were content with our newfound friendship.

The imaginary world of children is an amazing thing; it can compensate for many things which are lacking in a child's own world. In this instance, I feel that my parents handled the situation in the best way possible; they showed an amazing amount of understanding and love even though I'm sure that the times were trying. Eventually, the child, if given the proper guidance and direction, will outgrow the imaginary world as he or she develops new interests and expands the environment, or, as in my case, discovers that a real live friend far surpasses anything that the mind can create.

Nursery school?

With anxious anticipation he awaited, patiently, the arrival of September 8. After all, he was four and the youngest child in a family of four children. Everyone else went to school; now he was old enough, too. The approaching thoughts were heightened as the school wardrobe began to take shape. With great pride he would show off his new "school shoes." He wanted the world to know he was going to school, more specifically, nursery school.

It became very obvious that he did not know what to expect or how to react to this new experience. He only knew this was the grownup thing to do. His peer group acceptance, his family position, and, most importantly, his self-esteem all said he should and must go to school. He accepted this decision with growing reluctance, however, as the first day of school came closer to being a reality.

The first day he was up early, eager to undergo an unforgettable experience. Washing, dressing, and even breakfast were all routine and very matter-of-fact. He was, at least mentally, ready for this new experience. His mother accompanied him for the first two hour session of getting acquainted. A new world of unknown faces, situations, and expectations took their toll on his eager, anticipating mind. Since he knew the letters that spelled his name, it was easy to find his seat. He could "read" his seat and name tag. He had learned the Pledge of Allegiance by watching television, so the beginning of school appeared to be a breeze. He was gaining a little confidence on entering this new world. Sometime during that first day a very special friend was found. Both little people were searching for some needed security, and he and Bud found that in each other. As the first session approached its end, confidence was achieved.

The school behavior appeared to be structured by his home and experiences of the past. He was very proud to announce, shortly after the beginning of school, that he had homework just like his brother. He diligently went to the encyclopedia and asked his mother to locate the ant for him. He proceeded to "read" all about this little insect for the next ten minutes, carefully taking notes as he read. He insisted that the teacher told them to "study" the ant. He put his paper away carefully after his lesson was finished, obviously content with the fact that he knew all about the ant. It is interesting to note that this homework was done at the table next to his ninth grade brother who was at the time researching a topic in the encyclopedia.

It was with great pride and complete sincerity that he announced after the first week of school that he had to stand in the corner for the greater part of the day. He gave a very detailed and gory description of punching a classmate in the nose and the teacher's punishing him. He delighted in recounting all of this to his older brother and sister, indicating that he had an apparent disregard for authority. When his mother checked the incident with his teacher, she learned that no such incident had ever occurred. His teacher recounted, quite to the contrary, that he was a model, cooperative student. He still delights, however, in retelling his bad acts the first week of school. His imagination is vivid, his comprehension complete, and his stories detailed.

To accompany his stories of male mischievousness, he could also recount the times he served as teacher for the entire class. All four-year-olds take their turns "teaching" some phase of the class for a period of time. His turn came early in the year and not only made him a big guy in the eyes of his peers but also raised his self-esteem. It was his job to teach colors. His teachers discovered early that he had a thorough knowledge of the different colors. He had to show the others which color was which, and where each was located. His teaching became an important factor in combining his experiences of learning at home with what he did in school.

Since that first week, school has become an accepted and enjoyable part of his life. There is no one who enters his home now without noticing his art work and other school work proudly displayed on the refrigerator door. His explanation must accompany the confused masses of color, but each and every person can easily see the "dog," the "airplane," or the "fire truck" that was the object of his crayon on that particular day. He will freely recount his trips to the orchard to pick apples or his ride on the fire truck the day he visited a real fire house. He is still so very proud of the times he has been the teacher. He can sing, without missing a word, a finger ballad or a safety song. However, he continually belittles himself in regard to his educational accomplishments. Whenever he is asked what he has learned in school, he replies the same, emotionless: "Nothing." Obviously, it is both big and necessary for him to be smug, since he really appears to be wearing his school learning on his sleeve. Already, one can sense the "I go to nursery school" attitude and a greater anticipation of "I'm going to kindergarten next year."

He is growing up rapidly and his world is becoming new, thrilling, and exciting with every new day. He appears to be living the fact that there is no fear about tomorrow, it must be better than today, because I'm learning. At age four, can there be a better thought?

A fun-loving four-year-old

Andy is a cute, blond-haired, brown-eyed four-year-old; he is nicely tanned from playing outdoors and seems to be in excellent health. This is probably partly due to the fact that his mother is a nurse and he is an only child, so he has constant care. Andy does have flat feet and, as a result, must sometimes wear corrective shoes, which noticeably hamper his otherwise quick movements.

Andy is very expressive in speech, body movement, and facial expression. He has a good command of language, shown best by the chants and stories he loves to make up. In fact, one of his favorite indoor activities is a "silly words" game. Although he seems quite content to play indoors, he would much rather be outside where he has a large expanse in which to move.

"Pretend" games are Andy's favorite, however, so it's not unusual to see him running and playing in a blue cape. This cape originally made him Robin, Batman's trusted friend; Andy has now advanced to the "big time," so the cape is now Batman's cape and Andy is no longer Robin but Batman himself. Perhaps Andy likes "pretend" games so well because he has such a fine sense of the dramatic. For instance, when he played service station attendant and the older neighborhood children drove their cars (bicycles) into the station for gas, Andy was not satisfied to merely give gas, he asked for credit cards, washed windows, and even gave green stamps.

Another of Andy's great enthusiasms is playing Tarzan. Trouble arose one day this summer when Andy wanted to play Tarzan but was not allowed to take off his shirt. (Whoever heard of playing Tarzan with your shirt on?) He could not comprehend the fact that, even though the season was summer, the weather was not summer weather so he became very angry at having to keep on his shirt. Andy does tend to become angry when he feels he is justified in a certain action but is not permitted to follow his own inclination. He doesn't actually sulk when reprimanded but will become less talkative.

Andy experiences doubt when he is not sure whether he is being kidded or not; he has reacted over a period of time in such a way that he will tease in return the person who kids him the most. In fact, he is very friendly and associates well with almost all adults. Because he is very independent, however, he does not usually seek adult company; he does like to know where people are in case he should want to find them. Being an independent fellow, he doesn't like adult help (or is it interference?) as a general rule. For instance, even when he was only two years old, he would not be helped down the stairs; but of course, he would gladly help anyone else down the stairs (same result).

Although Andy definitely avoids the bully type children, he is not otherwise especially particular with whom he plays. His favorite friend with whom to play the silly word games and to work jigsaw puzzles is a seven-year-old girl. On the other hand, I've seen him have a lot of fun playing with a thirteen-month-old baby—just pretending he was a robot and periodically moving (robot fashion, of course) a few feet while the baby tried to catch him. Depending upon which person or age group he is playing with, Andy can be a leader or a follower.

Andy seems to be a quite happy four-year-old. There are probably several basic reasons for this. For one thing, Andy is an only child in a stable home. He was wanted not only by his parents but also by his extended family; his grandparents are a considerable influence in his life. Andy visits them at least once a week, often staying with them for a few days (and sleeping in grandma's bed!). Also, in Andy's neighborhood, every house is a "block home"; he is welcome in all families.

Andy is enthusiastic about many things, both large and small—a bubble machine's "joker" ring, Batman, birch beer (much better than his three-year-old love of orange soda), and visits to the amusement park (in his blue cape, of course). He is curious, wondering about babies, how the garden grows, what different foods taste like, and so on. He watches and imitates (especially his daddy and grandpa) and is rapidly learning as he grows. Andy is a happy, "complete," and alert four-year-old.

A victim of circumstances

Robin's mother was eight and one-half months pregnant when she married. Both father and mother were only seventeen years old. The birth was very difficult for the young mother; she was unconscious or semiconscious for the next three days. Following Robin's birth her mother moved in with her in-laws. Soon afterward, her mother returned to high school and was gone most of the day. During school hours, Robin's paternal grandmother took care of her. Despite the circumstances of her birth, she received love from her mother and her paternal grandmother. At no time prior to Robin's birth were there thoughts of putting her up for adoption.

From the start, there were difficulties in the marriage of Robin's parents, resulting in a final split after three years of marriage. Her mother was quite emotionally upset at the time and was hospitalized as a result of an overdose of sleeping pills. After recovery, her mother took the three-year-old child and moved to a small town some ten miles away. Robin was happy about this move and told people that she and her mother had a new house. She adapted to a change of playmates quite easily and quickly found a new playmate, her cousin Alyce.

During her stay in this small town, Robin's mother worked the second shift in a factory and Robin was cared for by Alyce's mother.

Since Alyce was also in this home, Robin accepted the change with no fuss. Soon Robin's mother was entertaining other men in her home. This received little comment from Robin; however, she remembers it quite well and knows the names of all her mother's boyfriends.

After living there for about seven months, Robin's mother moved back to her home town. Since Robin's mother was now working days, an arrangement was made for Robin to stay with her maternal grandmother during the week. Robin did not greet this move with enthusiasm and showed overt disappointment.

Robin's mother is presently considering marrying a man named Dick. Robin is excited about the idea. In fact, Robin was the first to suggest the marriage. She insists on one thing, however: that she be allowed to live with them. Robin's play habits and language development seem quite advanced. She seems to ask the questions "Why?" and "How come?" a thousand times a day. Every Saturday and Sunday she goes with her mother and Dick to Dick's parents' farm. She accepted this new group of people as eagerly as they accepted her. By the second weekend, she was calling them "Pappy" and "Grandma." She quickly saw that these names elicited a favorable response and continued to use them.

Robin insists on being at the center of activity when she is at the farm, whether it is helping Dick hoe the garden, playing in the brook, or working in the hayfield. She enjoys Pappy's rides on the tractor and Dick's rides on the motorcycle. At the farm she also encountered a new experience in toilet training, an outside toilet. Her first question was why Pappy had two barns and why he didn't keep the hogs there. She has no fear of the toilet. Last week Alyce went to the farm with her and one of her first acts was to take Alyce out to the toilet just so she could smell it.

Robin has obviously experienced quite an emotional environment. She is somewhat self-centered and is a perfect child as long as she gets her way. During the last eight months, she has thrown temper tantrums if she is not allowed to exercise her own will. She appears at least normally intelligent and enjoys going places and meeting people. Her language development is good and she greets each new experience with enthusiasm. She is a pretty girl and is becoming increasingly aware of it. She enjoys looking in the mirror after she has taken a bath or has had her hair fixed a new way. Despite the large number of seemingly bad influences on her life, she appears to be happy and well adjusted.

Because at the present time she has several authority figures, she often approaches another adult if her mother tells her she can't do something. She seems a bit confused over what she can and cannot do. Her grandmother and her mother do not permit or discipline the same activities. Whatever effects these bad influences have had or will have are not yet visible. Unfortunately, they may manifest themselves in the future.

My fear of birds

Fear does strange things to people. Many of our childhood fears are forgotten when we grow up; we look back and laugh at how silly we were. However, these fears will never leave some people. This seems to be my problem. The fear is childish and I have tried to talk myself out of it. Over the years it has seemed to lessen, but then I'll find myself in a situation where it is suddenly thrown back at me full force. Strangely enough, the feeling I have at these times seems very familiar, and I almost imagine myself as a small child. It is hard to write about a fear that I don't even talk about. My research for this paper has taken me back to the age of five when I first remember any evidence of my fear of birds. Since it's difficult to start with any one incident I'll try to relate them as I remember them.

Many small children imagine seeing things in the dark, especially before falling asleep at night. Well, my imaginary monsters were chickens. Every night as I lay in bed, I remember feeling sure there were chickens all around my bed. The worst part was that I was certain one of them would jump up on the bed and start flapping its wings. Just when I knew one was getting ready to get on the bed, I would scream

for my mother. Thinking back now, I realize my mother remained quite patient through this stage. I would explain to her about the chickens surrounding my bed. It was funny that the chickens never seemed to be there when the light was turned on. After a thorough search on all sides of my bed and, of course, under it, I could finally fall asleep.

This fear did not limit itself to night-time experiences; it haunted me during the daylight hours, too. My aunt Betsy has always been my favorite aunt, and I loved to spend the weekend with her and my uncle and small cousin. For Easter one year my cousin got two baby chicks. It wasn't too bad while they were small because they stayed in a box. This enabled me to keep my distance without giving away my secret. Finally, as all peeps do, these two grew up. To my dismay, one of my cousin's favorite pastimes became chasing the chickens and catching them. I can remember being absolutely terrified but just as determined not to let my feelings show. The only thing I could do was pretend that I liked chasing them. Actually, I ran away from them and I made sure I didn't run fast enough to catch one. It was around this time that my fear became most intense. It reached the point that I would avoid doing things I enjoyed for fear of being touched by a bird.

My grandmother had a pet canary at this time. Often when we went to visit she would let it out of the cage to fly around in the house. This was usually to please my brothers, who were delighted when the bird would land on their heads. At first, I would make excuses to go outside or try to get the boys interested in something else so that my grandmother would put the bird back in the cage. After what seemed an eternity the canary died. To my relief, it was never replaced!

Even walking outside, I remember constantly keeping a lookout for birds that might be nearby. Everywhere I went there seemed to be birds that wanted to fly at me. I even suspected my mother of putting pieces of dead chicken in my food. Chocolate milk was my favorite drink, but for a while I could never finish the whole glass because I thought there was a piece of chicken floating in it.

When I decided to write about this fear, I wanted to find reasons that could possibly be the cause of this fear. There are several incidents that I remember that I'm sure helped to develop it.

One of these is being chased by my brothers with a dead sparrow. We had been outside playing when they found it. The first thing they did was throw it in my direction, and I jumped. This was their cue to have some fun. They picked it up and chased me with it until, sobbing and terrified, I ran to Mother.

During one summer our neighbor decided to kill his chickens for eating purposes. The kids of the area were all interested in seeing chickens beheaded. I was a little uneasy, but I didn't want to miss out on any fun. It turned out that I became petrified as one after another the chickens lost their heads. All the other kids darted back and forth, yelling and screaming, trying to catch the chickens as they flopped and ran about without any heads. I wanted to cover my eyes and ears and run. I didn't run. I was glued to the spot. It was like a horror movie and I was part of it. I don't think I'll ever forget the way I felt at that time!

There's another experience that I had that I feel certain had a part in creating my fear of birds. We lived in a small town, and our neighbor had a barn and several small sheds. During the summer we used the shed as a playhouse. There were windows in the building that didn't have glass but could be closed by a wooden shutter. Most of the time they were left open. Stored in the shed were bags of feed for the chickens. One day I went down to play with my friends and all of the windows were closed. The kids tricked me into going inside and then slammed the doot shut. It was very dark inside and this was enough to scare me at the age of five. What I didn't know was that pigeons had flown in and were feeding on some of the grain on the floor. I began crying and beating on the door for them to let me out. All this noise startled the birds. They began to flutter about trying to find a way out. One brushed against my face. My crying became hysterical. I could hear their wings flapping and hitting against the wall. By this time my mother heard the commotion and came to get me out. I

was so upset and completely unnerved that I had to be put to bed. I still shudder whenever I think about it.

Looking back on these things I still remember the thoughts and feelings I had. Even today I don't eat chicken or any other fowl. I try to tell myself that it is because I don't like the taste, although I'm sure it's a carryover from this fear. The worst part of having this fear was keeping it a secret. I was ashamed and dreaded the ridicule and teasing I would get if I admitted to being afraid of birds. I was a victim of fear that I created in my own mind. How long it took me to allow myself to forget about this, I can't remember. I haven't lost the fear but I now realize how it developed and can understand it. No longer does it completely overshadow everything I do. Perhaps the best part is now I can tell people about it. Will I ever be able to lose this fear entirely? I'm not sure, but I do know I'm better equipped to cope with it.

Life with Dale

I suppose that in every classroom there is one child who demands more time and attention than most of the other children but who literally steals the teacher's heart. Such was the case with Dale, a little boy in my kindergarten class this year.

Dale was a well-dressed little boy with light blond hair. In spite of his crossed eyes, he was an attractive, engaging child. Dale was beginning kindergarten for the second time, having attended my class for two weeks the previous September. Since his parents had moved to the area during the summer and he had not been enrolled in the usual manner, the teacher and school principal were not prepared for the special problems Dale would create.

On the first day of kindergarten, while the other little boys and girls were becoming acquainted with their new teacher and with each other, Dale reacted to the new situation as would a very curious two-year-old child. In a hyperactive manner, he raced around the room, ran out into the hall, and rolled on the floor. His speech was almost unintelligible, and I was not certain that Dale could understand even my simplest directions. In order to keep him within the room, I had to grab Dale and hold him while I instructed the others. I nearly collapsed with exhaustion that afternoon, but I was able to enlist the aid of the school psychologist to observe and test Dale.

The school psychologist came to observe Dale several days later. I was explaining a simple coloring activity to the class and at times encouraging Dale to join in. This is what he saw Dale do within thirty minutes: Opens the piano. Closes the piano. Opens the window. Closes the window. Opens the door. Closes the door. Opens the door. Checks to see that both classroom doors are open. Calls "Hey" to others. Uses the water fountain. Gets up, turns over his chair, and lies on the floor. Sits on the floor and plays with his chair. Closes the door. Opens the door and swings it. Turns the light switch off and on. Crawls on the desk. Stands on the desk, trying to reach the light. When the teacher puts him in his seat, he slaps the inside of his desk. After fifteen seconds, he gets up, turns over his chair, and lies on the floor. Disrupts another pupil. Draws with crayons on the back of the teacher's easel board. Says: "I want to go home." Opens the piano and plays it. Looks into the ventilator. Uses the toy telephone. Dials and says: "Good-bye." Turns on the toy stove as he grunts and grunts. Sits on the floor and says: "Ya, ya, ya." Goes outside and looks at the other children through the open window. Comes inside. Opens other windows. Gets a drink. Opens the classroom door. Stands at the door, drops his pants, and urinates on the pavement. After sixty-five seconds, he starts screaming and slapping his desk. Tries to give his crayons to his neighbor. When his neighbor ignores him, he drops them on the floor. Closes one window and the doors.

Needless to say, Dale's behavior indicated that he was not nearly ready for the experiences of kindergarten, so his admission was postponed for one year. The following September, when Dale arrived at school, I noticed some definite changes and progress, but he was still far from the level of a normal kindergarten age child. However, I was astounded at his progress in speech, and he did seem to comprehend much better when spoken to. Due to his hyperactivity and lack of inner discipline, he was again tested by the psychologist, who found him to be mentally retarded, of the trainable category. Since trainable classes were, unfortunately, filled to capacity for the year, I decided that, if I could keep my sanity in spite of Dale, we would try to have a profitable year together.

Often during free time, Dale would come up to my desk to talk to me. Our conversations consisted of his asking: "What is that?" I would turn the question on him and ask him to tell me, and he would. He continued this game all year with both the other kindergarteners and adults.

His vocabulary showed great gaps. At the beginning of the year, any animal he saw he identified as a "doggie," but as the year progressed, he began to discriminate somewhat. And, amazingly enough, he did have a great memory for some things. One game we played early in the year was "Fish Pond," in which the children had to "catch" paper fish by using a magnet on a string and identify the color of the fish. Several months after the game was put away and forgotten, some children were sitting on the rug in the place the pond had been, and Dale admonished them to "get out of the water."

After Christmas, Dale began to show improvement in social and academic abilities. He began to relate slightly better to the group, occasionally trying to play with them and attempting to converse with them. He also began to take an interest in shapes, numbers, and the letters of the alphabet. He exhibited this by constantly writing them at his desk. It was a joy to see that the learning had taken place in such a short period of time.

In May, the group took a field trip to a farm. He was half afraid of the pony that was taking the children for rides in a cart. Later Dale was persuaded to go for a ride. During the course of the ride, he asked the woman supervising the rides what a certain building was. When she, not knowing the game, answered, "a barn," Dale was thrilled and told the lady she was right. I guess he thought his teacher was terribly stupid for making him tell her all year what things were.

On the last day of school, I was reluctant to

leave Dale, for I doubted whether I would ever see him again. I wondered what Dale's future would be. I was sure that I would miss him, for he had become a part of my life.

First encounter

It was a pleasant day in June. My five-year-old son, Randy, and I were sitting at the kitchen table having lunch. Randy was chattering away about the things he and the kids across the street had been doing during the hour before lunch. He always talks with great enthusiasm and is very dramatic when describing the events of the day. He makes all kinds of faces and uses his hands to help express his thoughts. While I was listening very carefully and thinking how grownup he was becoming, Randy suddenly paused, wrinkled up his nose and mouth, and said: "Well, I better not tell you that." I was a little surprised and yet curious, so I tried to be casual and told him that he didn't have to tell me anything he didn't want to but that Mommy was always interested in what he did and would like to know. He paused for a few seconds. I could just see the wheels turning in his mind. He looked right at me. Then, with his hands turned out in a type of shrug, stated: "Well, it's bad. So will you smack me if I tell you?" Still trying to be casual and relaxed and trying to make the right decision, I told him I would not smack him if he was honest with me.

By this time Randy's face had lost some of its brightness, and it was considerably longer. He proceeded to tell me that Sharon had asked him to show her his—he stopped and pointed to his privates, not being able to use the word he always used so naturally before. He then tilted his head a little to the side and, looking at me with a pained expression, waited for me to reply.

Feeling as if someone had just struck me, I tried to think clearly. I asked him if he had shown Sharon and he said he had. I explained to him that he knew that that wasn't the thing to do and that just because Sharon had told him to do it, it didn't mean he had to do as she wanted. I reminded him he was getting to be a big boy now and that sometimes he was going

to have to decide what to do and what not to do on his own, even if it meant his friends would be mad at him. Randy looked down at his feet and said: "I know, Mommy, but she told me to show her, and then she showed me hers." Feeling terrible and half angry, I replied: "Sharon doesn't have a 'dingy.'" He said: "No, she showed me her hair." Then he stopped, looked at me, made a face, and very pathetically said: "It made me feel sick." I honestly don't know what I said next because Randy began to cry. I do remember him saying he didn't like Sharon and that he wouldn't do it again. After Randy stopped crying, he informed me he didn't want to talk about "that subject" again, and he found something to entertain himself.

As he played I tried to sort out my thoughts, wondering why it had happened. I know kids go through a stage of curiosity, but Sharon was in sixth grade and twelve years old. My husband and I were never happy about Randy's socializing with Sharon and her brothers because they were older. But they were the only children in the vicinity, and Randy loved to have company. There were three boys and one girl, ranging from eight to thirteen. Randy usually played with the boys; on this particular day they had invited him over to their yard to play on the swing their father had built for them. This particular incident happened right at the swing, which is in the middle of the yard and visible from my living room window. I can't help thinking Sharon was really curious. Even though she had brothers, they were not as young as Randy, and maybe she thought Randy was different. However, why did she show him herself?

Randy had always been very open with his feelings. When he felt sad, he said so and why. However, when he didn't want to talk about something, we didn't press him. A few days later, I asked Randy how he felt about what had happened with Sharon, and he stated he felt ashamed. Then he didn't want to talk about it. I didn't know he knew what "ashamed" meant until he used the word then. I'm sure he understood then. About two weeks later I asked him again, and he said he felt better. He also added that Popper, his imaginary friend who appears and disappears at Randy's convenience, didn't like Sharon for showing herself. My husband asked him if he told Popper what he had done and he said no, he was afraid Popper wouldn't like him if he did. We both explained that we had forgiven him and that we knew he was sorry and that we felt that, since Popper was his friend, he would forgive him too. He smiled and seemed to understand.

THINGS TO THINK ABOUT AND DO

1. Imagine yourself just having had your third birthday. As a three-year-old, how does the world (life) look to you? How capable are you in terms of competent, self-help skills and independent living? In other words, how much do you know and what will you have to learn in order to be capable of purposeful action and reasoning? After the above discussion, observe several three-year-olds to determine how correct your insights concerning this age level were.

2. How would you deal with a negative, somewhat headstrong child of preschool age? Would a spanking do any good? Can you "reason" with this age level?

3. Form a story-telling group, perhaps at a nearby library or day school nursery, and arrange to tell a story to a group of preschoolers once or twice a week for about six weeks. Record, mentally or graphically, the characteristics of the children.

4. With a pad, pencil, and stopwatch, follow the activities of a two-, three-, or four-year-old for two hours. Record type of behavior and length of time spent at each activity. Compare your notes with someone else's. What did you find in common?

5. Observe different age levels of preschool children at play. How much time does each age group spend in isolated play, parallel play, or socialized play? What do they play?

6. Some authorities claim that two- and three-year-olds can be taught to read. Discuss the pros and cons of teaching this age group to read.

7. What emotional impact would a broken home have on a child five years of age or younger?

8. "My Fear of Birds" was written by a freshman in a General Psychology class. She took on that project in order to learn why she was so afraid of birds. The work she did on the profile answered many questions for her and helped her to learn to cope with her fear. Have you any fears, concerns, behaviors, or ideas that you wonder about? Can you trace back through your life to learn how you got that way?

9. Do a developmental case study of a child up to the age of six.

10. Discussion: How much love should a preschool child be given? Does the child need anything else beyond tender loving care (TLC) in order to grow into a nice, likable, pleasant person?

11. How does a child learn how to learn?

READING SOURCES

Developmental psychology texts

Annual Editions readings in human development, Guilford, Conn., 1975, Dushkin Publishing Group, Inc.

Bernard, H. W.: Human development in western culture, ed. 4, Boston, 1975, Allyn and Bacon, chaps. 8, 13.

CRM: Developmental psychology today, ed. 2, New York, 1975, Random House Inc.

Hurlock, E.: Developmental psychology, ed. 4, New York, 1975, McGraw-Hill Book Co., chap. 5.

Kaluger, G., and Kaluger, M.: Human development: the span of life, St. Louis, 1974, The C. V. Mosby Co., chap. 6.

Mussen, P. H., Conger, J. J., and Kagan, J.: Child development and personality, ed. 4, New York, 1974, Harper & Row, Publishers, chaps. 8-10.

Newman, B. M., and Newman, P. R.: Development through life: a psychosocial approach, Homewood, Ill., 1975, The Dorsey Press, chap. 3.

Stone, L. J., and Church, J.: Childhood and adolescence: a psychology of the growing person, New York, 1969, Random House, Inc., chaps. 6, 7.

Related readings

Birnie, L., and Whitely, J. H.: The effects of acquired meaning on children's play behavior, Child Dev. 44:355-358, 1973.

Brainerd, C. J.: The origins of number concepts, Sci. Am. 228(3):101-109, 1973.

Denzin, N. K.: The genesis of self in early childhood, Soc. Quart. 13:291-315, 1972.

Eveloff, H. H.: Some cognitive and affective aspects of early language development, Child Dev. 42:1895-1907, 1971.

Hoffman, M. L.: Father absence and conscience development, Dev. Psychol. 4:400-406, 1971.

Jones, P. A., and McMallin, W. B.: Speech characteristics as a function of social class and situational factors, Child Dev. 44: 117-121-1973.

Langlois, J. H., Gottfried, N. W., and Seay, B.: The influence of sex of peer on the social behavior of preschool children, Dev. Psychol. 8:93-98, 1973.

Liebert, R. M., and Baron, R. A.: Some immediate effects of televised violence on children's behavior, Dev. Psychol. 6:469-475, 1972.

Manosevitz, M., Prentice, N. M., and Wilson, F.: Individual and family correlates of imaginary companions in preschool children, Dev. Psychol. 8:72-79, 1973.

Singer, J. L.: The child's world of make-believe, New York, 1973, Academic Press, Inc.

Part two

THE SCHOOL YEARS

CHAPTER 4

The transition from home to school

After five years of being under an all-encompassing, almost totally protective custody of parents, six-year-olds find themselves somewhat abruptly thrust into a new world where mother and dad are not there to tell them what to do, what to say, or what decisions to make. They are on their own. They are surrounded by other six-year-olds who, for the most part, are no more ready for this transition from the comforting security of the home to the relatively impersonal group atmosphere of the world. For the first time, a new authority figure enters life-space. Kindergarten may have helped soften the change from home to school, but there is something about all-day school that is unnerving. The uncertainty of what really happens in a class where you have to learn to read out of books, the imaginative fantasies about unknown, mysterious places away from home, and the tales that others tell about what to expect and what it was like "when I was there" are sources of great anxieties for these children. School will be the focus point of their lives, for better or for worse.

Children beginning school soon become acclimated to their new situation, only to discover that there are other things that they must learn and do. The sheer number of other boys and girls forces them to interact with others. The routines and rules of the classroom and the school make certain demands on them to learn to discipline and control themselves. Exposure to letters, words, and numbers compels them to extend into a world of adult concepts and symbolizations that they really never thought too much about before. As they grow to seven, eight, and nine years of age, their relationships with their peers take on new dimensions. To be able to play the games of the group, to be part of the gang, and to learn about styles of living and thinking other than that to which they were exposed at home become increasingly important. There is no question but that these are the years in which children build the intellectual, physical, social, emotional, and moral foundational structure that will be their identities and personalities and determine their level of competency for many years to come.

These are the years of learning, but not every child is ready to begin learning at the same time. Factors other than intelligence can deter learning, as revealed in "Too Young for First Grade." Even after a child has been in school and has enjoyed it, he or she may change, as did the boy in "Do I Have to Go to School?" Some children have handicaps that will make it more difficult than usual to respond to learning. "Markie" is the story of a partially deaf child who had a different type of adjustment problem, as did his teacher.

It is interesting to trace the development of children during this particular span of growth. "Development of Six-Year-Old Twins" traces their development from birth and presents a more than subtle suggestion that the parental treatment of the twins shows some favoritism; you wonder how that could be. The characteristics and development of an eight-year-old are presented in "Too Good to be True"; it does make you wonder whether this is a typical child. A not too uncommon condition, that of enuresis, is poignantly presented in "It's Always Been a Problem." On another note, "A Child's Fear of Death" describes how the death of a relative and pets and a hospital experience produce a dreadful concern of death in a child. But childhood is generally a happy time of life, and you can almost feel the excitement in a boy's "First Major League Baseball Game."

Too young for first grade

Up until the time I was five years old, my family lived in an apartment in what was considered to be a rural area. Since we were rather isolated, I had no playmates except my sister Denise, who is three and a half years my junior, and the children with whom I came in contact during a one hour Sunday School period each week. By nature I seemed to be a rather introverted child, preferring to play alone or sit and listen to an adult conversation rather than to seek playmates my own age.

My parents bought a home in Connecticut, and we moved there just two weeks before I began first grade. At that time there were no other children in the neighborhood where we lived, and in the two weeks before the start of school, I did not meet any children in the vicinity of our home.

When school began, I was an emotional wreck. I can recall vividly how much I hated to leave the house each morning and noon to head for the red brick school building three blocks away. For almost three months of that first year, Mother walked me to school twice a day. While in the classroom, I kept to myself almost completely, frightened of the other children. I used to come home quite frequently and complain that I didn't like school because the children made too much noise. From the beginning, I never had any academic problems. I caught on quickly to everything that was presented, including reading. I always loved the learning aspect of school, being eager to do well and to move on to something new, but I was definitely immature in social development.

An experience which stands out clearly in my mind as being one of the most frightening of my year in first grade was the Hallowe'en party. I feel fairly sure that I was probably the only child in the room who had never seen a Hallowe'en costume, much less worn one. After much coaxing, my parents convinced me that I should "dress up" to go to school that day. I really thought my Bugs Bunny costume was quite nice. I admired myself in the mirror at home before leaving for school, but without my mask in place. As usual, Mother walked me to the building. That afternoon, I insisted that she also accompany me to my room at the end of the hall. At the doorway to the room, she attempted to get me to put my mask on, but I would have no part of that. When I walked through the doorway and saw the room full of

children, all wearing costumes and masks, I was frightened to the point that I ran crying into the hall. Only after some of the children had removed the false faces could Mother and my teacher persuade me to enter the room.

As a result of having no exposure to childhood germs before entering school, I had little resistance to the diseases that circulate around the classroom continually. Even the common cold was a problem for me! During that first year, I missed thirty-five days of school. The worst episode involved chicken-pox, which I contracted in the spring of the year. By that time I had become somewhat accustomed to school life. After being home for two weeks, however, I went through a severe emotional setback when it came time to return to school.

In retrospect, it is obvious to me what some of my problems were. Naturally, I have discussed all of these occurrences with my parents through the years, sometimes in a joking way, but usually in a serious manner. Probably the biggest mistake for me was being sent to first grade at the age of five and a half. Had I been in contact with children from birth to that point, it would probably not have been as much of a social problem for me. But since I had almost no exposure to other children, I definitely needed another year in which to ready myself for what I was to face in the classroom. At that time there was no kindergarten where we lived. In any event, had I been able, in the first year we were in town, to become acquainted with the neighborhood and some of the children who would be my classmates, I'm sure that many of my fears would have been allayed. All in all, I guess I was too sheltered and socially inexperienced to be able to fit well into the classroom structure.

Do I have to go to school?

It was with a great deal of anticipation that Jeff looked forward to his first full day in school, that day when he would eat his lunch in the school cafeteria and come home on the bus with his older brother. He even went so far as to say that now he would not have to go look for someone to play with after morning kindergarten, as he did last year, since he would not be returning from school until the middle of the afternoon. I suspect, though, that he had thought about this business of going to all day school for the entire summer before he actually entered first grade.

Jeff asked many questions during the summer preceding first grade: What will the teacher make us do? Will we have any play periods? Will the teacher punish me if I do something wrong? How will we know when to go to lunch? What if I don't like the food that is served in the cafeteria? All of these questions, and many more which I cannot now remember, were asked by my six-year-old. It seemed that they were asked at the oddest times, especially when I would think that he was enjoying himself tremendously by being totally involved in his play activities. Perhaps some of the questions were formulated from the conversations that he had overheard his brother having with some of his friends as they anticipated the beginning of another school year. Perhaps others were an outgrowth of his kindergarten experience of the preceding year, although I must confess that I was under the impression that these had been pleasant days for him. Apparently some things had happened that I was not aware of, mainly because I returned to full-time work when Jeff entered kindergarten. I was able to spend only a half-hour at lunch time with him after his morning session in school. At any rate his little mind must have been frequently filled with thoughts of a whole day in school, which, in reality, must have meant to him a whole day away from home. Even today he is somewhat insecure after he decides to spend a night with a friend or a grandparent away from home. Almost always there is a telephone call from Jeff requesting that he be picked up earlier than the previously planned time.

I was not unduly concerned about the way in which Jeff was regarding the beginning of school. After all, he had attended half-day nursery school for two years, and he had had a reasonably successful experience in kindergarten. The readiness tests that he took at the end of his kindergarten year indicated that he was indeed ready to begin first grade, with the exception of the fact that the man that he was asked to draw was labeled by the teacher as "below average," which it was. The man had no arms and no ears, and he was not what one would call an average-looking man. At any rate, Jeff was recommended for first grade, and I was also convinced that he was ready. After all, his sixth birthday had been celebrated the preceding May.

When the first day of school arrived, Jeff and his brother eagerly left home for the bus stop, each audibly wondering if any friends would be in his room and if he would get the teacher that he was hoping for. For Jeff, however, it seemed to be more important that he have some friends in his room than having a particular teacher. When he returned from school that afternoon, I was not at home because my job required me to be away until four o'clock. By the time that I arrived home, he was contentedly playing with some friends. The only real conversation that we had about the first day of school took place at the dinner table. Of course, Jeff had to share this time with his brother, who had much to tell, and with me, for there were some interesting things that had happened to me that I wanted to report to the family. All in all there was really no way to detect any underlying tensions or reservations that Jeff might have had about school because there simply was not enough time to uncover any.

The next morning, the morning of the second day of school, he did not seem to be quite as eager to speed through the necessary morning chores—brushing teeth, washing face and hands, eating, and dressing. I was so busy getting myself ready to go to work and checking on his brother that I did not notice the hesitation with which he left the house to catch the school bus. His arrival home that afternoon was similar to that of the day before. Dinner followed the same pattern, and off to bed he went. However, after he had said his prayers, Jeff remarked that he really did not think that he liked school. My response to him was something to the effect that the next day was Friday, and that this was the last day of school for this week. This seemed to satisfy him, for he went right to sleep. I could not help observing that night that, as he slept, he was unusually restless.

On the third morning of school, chores went slowly, but Jeff and his brother left on time for the bus. In a matter of a few minutes I saw Jeff running back toward the house. As he drew nearer, I could see the tears streaming down his face. The reason for the tears was prompt in coming: "I don't want to go to school, Mommie." It took quite a bit of talking to stop the flow of tears. The only argument that I could think of at that time was the one that I had used the evening before. "Only today yet, and then you have the whole weekend to play before you must go back again." He managed to dry all his tears before the bus came, but it was a very forlorn-looking little boy who feebly waved good-bye to me from the bus window. By the time that I got home that afternoon, Jeff was his usual pleasant self, and no mention was made of the coming Monday morning.

When Sunday evening came, the storm broke. Jeff insisted in no uncertain terms that he simply was not going to go to school the next day, in fact not at all ever. Now what does one tell a six-year-old who has come to such a decision? My argument went something like this:

"Jeff, if you don't want to go to school, Daddy and I aren't going to make you go. But do you know what will happen to us if you don't go?"

"No," said a very tearful voice.

"Well, if you don't go to school, Mommie and Daddy will be put in jail."

The obvious question came. "Why?"

"You see, there is a law in our state that says that all boys and girls must go to school. If they do not go to school, then the mommies and daddies of these boys and girls must go to jail." These seemed like very strong words, but it was apparent that Jeff was beginning to think about things other than not wanting to go to school.

The next question from my six-year-old gave evidence to this fact. "Who will take care of Jon (his brother) and me when you and Daddy have to go to jail?"

"I don't know, Jeff."

"Why can't Grandpa and Grandma come out and stay here with us?"

"I'm sure that they would not be able to be away from their home that long because of all the things that they have to do."

Now came another tactic. "Who will take care of you when you are in jail? Who will give you something to eat?"

"I don't know, Jeff. But I do know that it won't be very pleasant eating my meals behind the bars of the jail cell and sleeping on those hard cots."

"I don't guess you'd be very happy there, would you?" said Jeff.

"No, I don't guess I would," I responded, feeling by now that he must be approaching a decision about the matter of going to school the next morning.

"Well," sighed Jeff, "I guess there's only one thing to do. I guess I have to go to school."

"Yes," I said very quietly, "I guess you do."

With that our conversation ended, and Jeff settled down to go to sleep. But somehow I was not convinced that this was the end of the matter, as indeed it was not.

It was a very unhappy looking six-year-old who came to the kitchen for breakfast that Monday morning. He had lost the sparkle that he usually had as we talked over each other's plans for the day. As is our custom, as each person finishes his meal, he excuses himself and goes on to do whatever else must be accomplished before it's time to leave for school. Jeff excused himself to go get dressed, but after he had gone to his room, I realized that he had eaten very little of his breakfast. Naturally, I called him back, but when he returned he simply stated that he had a pain in his stomach and could not eat any more. Soon I discovered that he was having bowel problems. Both of these manifestations quickly told me that I was looking at a little first grader with a great big problem about this business of going to school. When the time came for him to leave for the bus, Jeff trailed after his older brother without a complaint, but I could see a few tears welling up in his eyes when he said good-bye.

By this time I was greatly concerned about my unhappy six-year-old. My first attempt to make the situation easier was to telephone his principal and explain to her the events of the past several days. She was very understanding and suggested that she relay this information to Jeff's teacher. Perhaps the teacher could find something special for him to do in the morning as soon as he got to school. Apparently this is exactly what happened, because that afternoon Jeff called me at work to tell me that Mrs. Mailey had asked him to put a sheet of paper for the boys' and girls' morning work on each of the desks. This was to be his job each morning for the next two weeks. I began to feel a little better about this whole matter of Jeff and school.

But the next morning Jeff was again as unhappy as he had been the morning before. And the same complaints were registered—pains in the stomach and loose bowels. I thought perhaps it was time to talk again about his special job in school. As it turned out, he had already analyzed why his teacher had given it to him: "She just wants me to think that I like school." He might be little but he certainly was perceptive.

Needless to say I was becoming concerned about the stomach pains and the loose bowels which were present every morning. Jeff was now beginning to lose weight, and his sleeping habits were certainly not of the best. He had no trouble going to sleep, but he got up in the morning looking so very tired. And no wonder—he had tossed and turned all night. My next move was to call our pediatrician, who very quickly prescribed two types of tranquilizers, one to be taken before he ate in the morning and the other before he went to bed. Jeff did start to eat a little bit more in the morning, and the stomach pains came only now and then, as did the loose bowels. Gradually I could sense that he was quite a bit more relaxed about the whole matter of going to school, especially since he had been bringing home work papers with stars on them. I soon took him off the nighttime tranquilizer completely, but we agreed that if he had a pain in his stomach when he got up in the morning, then he would have to take a pill. This happened only once or twice a week for several weeks, and then after that only occasionally.

By the time that November came, Jeff seemed to be completely adjusted to the idea of going to school. Several times during those weeks since school had started, he had repeated our conversation about the "jail" matter. And each time that he did, he always came to the same conclusion that he just had to go to school. I stopped all pills, he stopped having pains in his stomach and loose bowels, and we all settled down to what turned out to be a very pleasant year in school.

I must quickly point out that Jeff certainly had his ups and downs during the first grade in school. Many were the times that he brought home papers with little messages written on them to the effect that he was sloppy and careless. This never seemed to bother him, and his only comment was that maybe he would do better the next day. He never seemed to remember to bring things home from school, however, until his teacher put his papers in a paper bag with a note on it and sent it home. I must admit that I was bothered by things like this, especially since Jeff's brother was such a well-organized and efficient third grader. In spite of these things, however, Jeff did progress well in arithmetic and reading. In fact, he quite astonished those of us at his seventh birthday party when he read every word on all of his cards. I know that he was pleased with himself because he remarked that nobody had to help him read anymore; he could do it himself.

All in all, Jeff's year in first grade proved to be a successful one. On his final report card he received all A's and B's, which certainly gave evidence of the fact that he had made a tremendous emotional adjustment during the year. How differently he ended the year from the way in which it had begun!

As a final report on Jeff, who is now in second grade, I must mention that we began this school year in the same manner as last year. We did not have any conversations about the fact that he must go to school. This he already knew. But Jeff did experience the same stomach pains and loose bowels once again. The interesting thing, though, was that as soon as these symptoms developed, it was Jeff himself who suggested that I give him some special pills to help him get rid of his problem. I did give him a few pills over a two week period. Then one morning he simply announced that he didn't need them anyone. His stomach was fine, and, as only Jeff can say it: "I don't even have to go to the bathroom very much anymore." With that he seemed to relax and settle down to what I think will be another good school year for him, considering the quality of work he has been bringing home since that time. But, you know, I never really did find out what caused his problems. I guess there are many things that mothers never find out about what their children do.

Markie

Markie was under the table. All of the other children were properly seated on this first day of school—all, that is, but Markie. And, as I said before, he was under the table.

Markie was a cute little rascal. He was small for his six years, padded with a little baby fat, and he had an innocent looking face. He wore a colorful harness-like piece of apparel over his shirt, in the pocket of which was tucked the battery for his double hearing aid. How proud he was of that!

No, he wasn't quite deaf—he had fifty percent hearing within ten feet—but he had not yet learned to pay attention, so he appeared to be totally deaf. He was smart, though—smart as a whip at anything that did not require oral language. HIs visual perception and motor coordination were superior, and his winning ways endeared him to everyone.

One day before school opened, when the teachers were preparing their classrooms, Markie's mother brought him in to get acquainted with his teacher and the room. While she and I talked, Markie studied me with solemn eyes and then disappeared behind his mother's skirt. He stayed there, too. Of course, I couldn't blame him much—with everything being so strange and all—so I left the room for a while so his mother could show him around.

The first day of school, his mother brought him in. We were all a little concerned about his reaction, but when he discovered some building blocks on the round table, he sat down to build. His mother slipped out, but that was all right. He didn't panic.

There weren't many children in that room—only eleven, for it was a newly appointed Specific Learning Disabilities class. Each child had a problem, and the problems were varied. Ages varied, too—from six to ten years. The interesting thing about such children is their complete acceptance of one another. In that room there were no oddballs. Everyone belonged.

As soon as the bell rang and the other children took their seats, I motioned for Markie to come to his seat; that's when it happened. He just slid down and under, and there he stayed. Not knowing what to do, I decided to do nothing for a while. So I went on with the first-day-of-school business and ignored Markie. He did look cute, though, and in a way it was funny. After a while I realized that Markie had to come out and join us before lunch time, because he couldn't eat under the table.

In the class was a ten-year-old boy who was extremely friendly. This boy, Todd, had played blocks with Markie before the bell rang, so I thought maybe he could help. I asked Todd to go to the table and play with the blocks, trying to lure Markie out. It worked! Soon Markie and Todd were happily playing together.

I still didn't know what would happen when we went to the cafeteria. When it was time for the children to wash their hands, Todd pantomimed the activity to Markie, and he washed his hands. Under Todd's guidance, he took his lunch box and got in line for lunch; he got along fine in the cafeteria. That afternoon he sat in his seat and became one of the group.

He was a very independent child. Since his parents were determined that he would not be spoiled, Markie waited on himself completely. One day when we were on the playground he came running up to me with his hands behind him, looking distressed. He ran inside and stayed in the bathroom for a long time. When he came out, he was patting himself on his backside and I heard crackling sounds. Later I asked his mother if he had had an accident, and she said yes. He pantomimed to her how he had cleaned himself up and padded himself with paper towels.

Markie could also be determined and stubborn. He had to be *made* to do some things, and he didn't mind telling his teacher "no" occasionally. A few power struggles ensued during the year, but we teachers were firm, fair, and consistent.

Although he didn't say many words, he could imitate any sound he heard. When I showed him a picture of an airplane and asked him what it was, he made airplane sounds and flew an imaginary airplane around. He did the same for any objects that made noises. When I showed him pictures of objects that did not make sounds, he pantomimed how they were used. When he was shown a picture of a fried egg, he cracked an imaginary egg over a skillet, salted it, fried it, put it on a plate, cut it up, and ate it. An adult working with him had to wait for all of this activity to be finished.

He did say a few words occasionally. Any four-legged animal was "puppy." He said "ball" and "outside play?" His most-used expression was "bad boy!" That was directed to anyone, child or adult, who crossed him. On a few occasions I used it on him, simply because he knew what I meant. During the latter part of the year he began to babble a lot, especially if upset. No one could understand the words, but everyone understood the meaning. His tone, inflection, expression, etc., were that of complaining.

For several weeks after school started, Markie was shy. On the playground he and a little girl with a slight neurological problem clung closely to my side. I was happy for them when they finally played freely with the group. Once he got started, Markie thought he was king of the hill, and he played anything that the larger ones played. He was good at kickball, and the children enjoyed having him on their team. They made a pet of him.

I loved Markie as though he were my own child, but I felt inadequate to the task of teaching him. I had no training whatever in any kind of special education and knew nothing about how to help a child with Markie's handicap. Having children with so many different difficulties gave me too little time to devote to any one kind. I did the best I could, knowing that the child was not receiving the

kind of help he needed. Each day I made him a worksheet with some simple seatwork. He could do the work easily, but he did not want to; sometimes he would put it away when I was busy with other children and sneak off to play. Toward the end of the year he enjoyed his work and even asked me to help him. He pulled his desk and chair up to mine and let me help him. Previously he had resisted help. He even tried to "read" like the others. Bringing a book to me, he made baby sounds as he "read" page after page. I believe that he really thought he was reading.

Markie was able to form his letters and numerals when he came to school, but math concepts were difficult for him to grasp. He drew very well and had excellent coordination. One time he used a ruler and drew "Pop-pop's house," complete with back porch, a light hanging from the porch ceiling, and a flight of steps. It would have been good work for an eight-year-old. When the older children in the room were learning to write, he used the writing chart and taught himself cursive writing.

Markie was fortunate to have the parents that he had. From the time that they discovered his problem, they did everything possible to help him. He was in preschool programs for hard-of-hearing children and came to our school in first grade to see whether he would be able to adjust to a regular school. His parents did not want to send him to the school for the deaf unless necessary. Until the end of the year we all feared that he wouldn't make it, but now we have hopes. The family has moved to a city where he will attend a special class for children like himself. He has so much intelligence, spunk, and charm that I believe he will make it now. He will always be one of my bright spots. I'm glad that I had the privilege of knowing him.

Development of six-year-old twins

The fraternal twins, both boys, were born five weeks prematurely. Mrs. James was only eighteen years, eleven months old at the time, and she had no warning from the doctors that she would have twins. The reason given by her pediatrician for the surprise occurrence was that the babies were positioned vertically in the womb, with one in front of the other. Because of this position, the separate heartbeats could not be detected. The larger and first-born twin, Donald, was placed in a regular nursery, but the small twin, Daniel, had to be placed in a premature nursery for three weeks. After four days passed, he was joined in the premature nursery by his older brother, who had lost too much weight to remain in the regular nursery. The parents came to the hospital each day for the next two and one-half weeks so that Mrs. James could nurse the boys. The following table will provide for a comparison of the early development statistics of the twins:

	DONALD	DANIEL
Time of birth	10:38 A.M.	10:40 A.M.
Length		
At birth	19 inches	18 inches
One year	31¼ inches	30½ inches
Two years	35 inches	34½ inches
Weight		
At birth	5 pounds, 5 ounces	4 pounds, 13 ounces
Four days (lowest point)	4 pounds, 11 ounces	4 pounds, 4 ounces
Six months	20 pounds	20 pounds
Three years	37 pounds	33½ pounds
Six years	49 pounds	47 pounds
Creeping	12 months	9 months
Walking	15 months	12 months
Simple words	18 months	18 months
Trained	2 years, 9 months	2 years, 9 months
Weaned from bottle	10 months	10 months
First tooth	10 months	8 months

Very soon after their birth, Mrs. James could tell that there was going to be a distinct personality difference between the boys. This was particularly noticeable to her while she was nursing them. Donald, who began nursing almost immediately, loved to nurse and got considerable nourishment this way. He never had to be coaxed. Daniel, on the other hand, was not permitted to begin nursing for one week since he was not yet ready to be held by his mother. When the doctors felt he was strong enough to nurse, he was completely uninterested and actually got very little nourishment from it. He paid very little attention to his mother. Both boys continued nursing for one month, at which time the doctor felt they should switch to a formula even though Mrs. James could have nursed them much longer. Both were fed on a demand schedule for the next four months, and both boys used pacifiers from age one and one-half months to four months. According to their mother, the pacifiers worked very well.

As far as Mrs. James could recall, all other aspects of physical development were normal. Daniel was given iron supplements for the first few years but no longer requires them. They had no serious diseases or injuries during infancy, and both boys today are healthy, energetic youngsters. They are facing the usual rash of diseases for all school children—chickenpox, mumps, measles, and colds—but seem to recover rapidly with no side effects. Both are of normal size for their present age and, according to their teachers, they show no signs of a developmental nature that would indicate that they should be held back in school. Their motor ability, visual and auditory perception, and speech seem to be on a level with those of their classmates. They both sleep well at night now, although Donald used to have difficulty with this at about age five. He would often have to get up two or three times each night while his brother slept continuously.

The twins entered kindergarten at age four years, ten months. Both boys are evidently very capable youngsters according to tests administered at the end of kindergarten by their principal. The Detroit Beginning First Grade Intelligence Test indicated that Donald has an I.Q. of approximately 120, and Daniel's is approximately 140. The boys had the same kindergarten teacher, but they are now separated for first grade. All three teachers were interviewed at length, and several differences in the personality characteristics of the twins were discovered as a result. Donald is a very happy youngster, always outgoing and friendly with everyone he meets. He likes to be a leader in school and wants to be first when anything new is suggested. He is not reading as well as his brother is now, and he requires more pressure to get his work done. When he is pushed, however, he can do very good work. He requires firmness and sincerity from the teacher, or else he will become careless and lose interest.

Daniel, on the other hand, is described by his teachers as being very quiet, withdrawn, and sensitive. He is without doubt a better student that his twin, but he is also far more difficult to handle. During his kindergarten year, he was quite stubborn at times and would often ignore his teacher's requests completely. One day he stood in the hallway and refused to come into the classroom. Reasoning with him brought no success, so the teacher had to drag him into the room, take his coat off, and put him at his desk. On another similar occasion, Daniel reacted by kicking his teacher very hard in the leg. She was quite shocked, since this had never before happened to her in eight years of kindergarten teaching. She did not spank him but simply took him to his seat and made him sit down. Later in the year, Daniel refused to take off his coat and leave the coat room. By now the teacher was aware of what he might do, so she let him stay there. He remained in the coat room for over two hours and would not even come out for the cookies and milk served during the middle of the morning. Donald then asked if he could take the food to his brother, but the teacher decided that Daniel would have to come out and eat with the rest of the children. The next day she received a note from Mrs. James saying that she had "punished" Daniel enough by letting him stay in the coat room and should not have denied him the milk and cookies.

The kindergarten teacher actually received many letters and visits from Mrs. James throughout the year. The letters, in general, were requests by Mrs. James for help. She feels she is a failure with the twins and cannot understand Daniel. She is very unsure of herself in dealing with the personalities of the boys and does not know how to discipline them. At the same time, the letters contained instructions as to how the twins were to be treated at school. She requested that the boys not be forced to do anything they did not want to do. During this same period, Mr. James visited the school without his wife's knowledge and told the kindergarten teacher how happy he was that she was being very firm with the boys. In the teacher's opinion Mr. James was indicating that if the boys were to receive firm, consistent discipline it must come from the school. Due to these very unusual circumstances, the teacher decided not to report the kicking incident to the parents, since she felt she would surely be in the wrong.

As mentioned previously both boys scored quite high on an intelligence test administered toward the end of kindergarten. The first grade started in normal fashion for Donald, but Daniel refused to come to school the first day. All three teachers and even the principal commented about the unusual way in which Mrs. James handled the situation. Rather than talking it over with the child for a while and then insisting that he come to class, Mrs. James put Daniel in the car and drove him around town trying to convince him that he should go to school. This continued for the entire morning. After lunch Daniel returned to school with his father, who had spanked him at home and insisted that he go to school. On another occasion Daniel, without his parents' knowledge, spent the morning at a younger child's home rather than going to school. His mother returned home in the afternoon to find him upstairs hiding under his bed.

Other than these incidents first grade has gone fairly well for the twins. Their teachers have not noticed any major personality problems, and they agree that the boys like each other and always look for each other when they leave their respective rooms. They get along well with their peers and do above average school work when they are motivated. One interesting developmental statistic should be noted, however. In spite of their high scores on the intelligence tests, both boys did poorly on the Sheldon Basic Reading Series Pre-Reading Test. Donald's percentile rank was ten and Daniel's was forty-three. The principal feels that while they could still improve considerably, these scores were definitely not good in the light of the I.Q. scores.

In their interactions with adults and other

children, the twins have again been distinct opposites. At age three, his mother notes that Donald seemed much more gregarious than Daniel. He was always more aggressive, more daring, and more talkative. He gets along very well with all children and is especially considerate of the younger ones. He has been observed helping a crying three-year-old while the other children his age ignored them. Once, when his mother repeatedly asked him if he liked her best, his reply was: "But Mommy, I love everybody!" Nevertheless, in the family structure Mrs. James notes that generally Donald is overly affectionate toward her. He has just recently begun letting his father do things for him. In his play Donald is very fond of drawing large, colorful pictures and building with Lincoln Logs, Tinker Toys, and blocks.

In contrast to Donald, Daniel at age three was described by his mother as unfriendly with doctors or any new people. He was very resistant to suggestion, extremely wary of new situations, and generally very stubborn. At the age of four and a half, Daniel was described as very short-tempered and easily embarrassed. According to his mother, he would become violent if his younger sister knocked down one of the block towers he built, or even if his mother called him to lunch while he was playing. At about this same time Daniel came very close to causing a major tragedy in the home. Mr. and Mrs. James had found some burned matches in the twins' bedroom. While they were reprimanding the boys and warning them of the danger of playing with matches, Daniel quietly left the room and went downstairs to the kitchen. He lit a newspaper on the gas stove and threw it in a cardboard box in the playroom. The blaze grew large enough to scorch the walls and ceiling while Daniel stood and watched. Donald came downstairs, discovered the fire, and screamed loud enough to warn the parents who were still upstairs. They were able to stop the blaze but were unable, in their minds, to convince Daniel of the seriousness of his act.

In his play Daniel was coloring all his pictures in black during kindergarten but has since begun to use all the colors. He loves to look at books and have stories read to him. He

studies the minute details very closely and is quick to answer questions on the reading. He is very good with all types of building materials. Often he prefers to play alone, refusing to join the other children even if his mother suggests it. On other occasions, however, he plays with his younger sister and has a lot of patience with her. His teachers also noted that he looks after Donald and often tries to help him improve his school work.

I think it is reasonable to say that neither of the twins has been able to formulate any kind of philosophy or life plan at this early age, yet I have tried to show throughout the study that they are quite different in their attitudes and approach to life in general. Donald is a very open child who greets people in a friendly and playful manner. He is afraid of no one and needs little prodding to try something new. Daniel is a very moody child who is afraid of strangers and unfamiliar circumstances. He is easily angered and will resort to violence if his domain is threatened.

At the present time, the greatest difficulty the twins face is their relative inability to meet the demands of the school environment. This gap in their adjustment stems from a lack of consistent, meaningful discipline in the home. Their teachers noted that it was impossible to use the words "can't" or "don't" when trying to tell them what to do. They would just shut themselves off and lose interest immediately. The feeling among the teachers was that there were too many negatives used at home and that the boys were conditioned to react to these words by withdrawal.

The problem of disciplinary inconsistency may be illustrated by a trip to a local Tastee-Freeze. Since the weather was very warm, Mrs. James told the boys that they could not have an ice cream cone because it would melt. Daniel violently insisted upon having one, and his mother left the car saying that he would get nothing because of his behavior. While she was out of the car, Donald told Daniel not to worry because he knew he would get a cone anyway. True to Donald's prediction, their mother returned to the car with a chocolate cone for Daniel. Obviously the boys knew that mother's "no" meant very little. Having been reinforced

True discipline is not something that is imposed from without. It is self-control—control which springs from within. Children being great imitators, the self-control which they will practice will depend largely on how conscientiously the elders try to discipline themselves.

for his temper tantrum, I feel sure that Daniel will resort to this kind of behavior in the future.

Mrs. James had a very traumatic childhood. Now, faced with the problem of raising her own children, she is unable to find a way to show them her love and discipline them at the same time. She makes meaningless demands of them to assert her authority, yet her threats of punishment are usually empty and are therefore ignored. The discipline is often left for the father, who sees no reason to spank his boys for something they did hours before.

Finally, there is one more situation which may affect the twins' future development. Because of the vast personality differences between the twins, Mr. and Mrs. James have begun to focus their attention upon Daniel in an attempt to make him feel more secure. In doing this, they are not intentionally ignoring Donald, but he is often left in the background while his more sensitive brother is catered to. It is my judgment that, if this present trend continues, considerable injury may be done to both boys. Daniel needs not only understanding but meaningful discipline which he can respect. He is not getting this, however, because his parents feel he is too sensitive. Donald, because he is clearly less able academically, needs continued encouragement and guidance lest his present overflowing personality turn to insecurity and envy.

Too good to be true

T. J. is an active, normal eight-year-old youngster. Although small for his age (weight forty-eight pounds, height forty-eight inches), he is very well coordinated and enjoys all types of physical activities. Due to immature motor development, however, T. J. sometimes walks and runs on his toes, a physical handicap which he will eventually outgrow.

T. J. is happiest when he has something to occupy his time. Last year was the beginning of camping away from home for him. After a week at Y Camp he was so enthused with the program that he begged to return for a second week. This past year he became eligible to join the Cub Scouts and to be a member of the Pony League baseball. These social activities have proved to be of great value to him; I believe this will be a most interesting year for him. He has learned the necessity of true sportsmanship and how to accept defeat.

Like all boys his age, he doesn't very often associate with members of the opposite sex. Occasionally he will invite the girl next door to join him in playing kickball, and he quite often practices his pitching style with our twelve-year-old daughter, who is physically well coordinated. The only social involvement T. J. has rebelled against was singing in the children's choir in church; this was because he was the only male participant, so we let him drop out of the choir. Socially, he seems to get along fine with all his friends in school and in the different organizations to which he belongs. At home there are the daily arguments, teasing, and bickering with his two older sisters, ages ten and twelve—arguments not uncommon in children of those ages.

T. J. seems to be well adjusted emotionally. He used to sulk when he didn't have anything to do and would also become upset if the girls didn't want him to join in one of their games. I believe he has become more stable emotionally because in the past year his extracurricular activities have kept him from being idle.

Of all my four children, T. J. is perhaps the most concerned about others. When I had a very serious back operation two years ago, he was always asking how I felt and if there was anything he could do for me. Some mornings he tells me to stay in bed and rest, and he'll fry his own egg. He is quite thoughtful and sentimental. Many nights before going to bed he'll come and give both his dad and me a kiss, and invariably he tells me he loves me. T. J. gets quite emotionally involved when playing baseball, football, or any other active sport. Just recently he has learned that he's not always right and that teamwork is more important than individualism.

Since he began kindergarten T. J. has been an above average student, maintaining all A's and B's on his report card. Until this year he found school life very stimulating, but, due to a very strict teacher and an embarrassing classroom experience, he no longer shows the desire or enthusiasm for school work that he had previously. The unfortunate situation took place in his third grade classroom where the teacher gives speed tests in arithmetic almost daily and always records the grades from the tests. T. J. was caught trying to change an answer after they were supposed to have put their pencils down (in order to obtain a better grade was his excuse). The teacher tore up his paper, gave him a zero, called him in front of the class, and spanked him. She then proceeded to tell the children in the class: "Here is a cheater—we all know you cheat now, T. J. Don't try it again because everyone will be watching you!"

I went to see her about this problem because I was quite shocked at the way the situation was handled. For weeks after this happened, I had to push T. J. out of the door each morning for school. This third grade teacher is basically an excellent teacher of subject matter, but I'm certain she will warp the personalities of young children during her teaching career. This teacher commented recently that T. J. is still doing fine work but he just doesn't seem to have the interest and initiative that he had at the beginning of third grade; well, no wonder!

Reading is one of T. J.'s favorite pastimes. He receives *Boy's Life* and the *Ranger Rick Wildlife* magazine each month. He mostly enjoys stories centered around sports, biographies, and autobiographies about important persons—past and present—and anything pertaining to wildlife. Presently at home he is working on a wildlife notebook, drawing pictures of the animals, birds, or fish and writing a short description of each.

As far as moral awareness is concerned T. J. is, of course, not old enough to express his opinions on those aspects of our society. He does realize when someone has done wrong. He has formed a concept of God; when I asked him what he thought of God, he said: "I respect Him; He helps me; He's good to me."

Perhaps this description appears "too good to be true." I don't wish to imply that T. J. is a perfect angel—far from it. He has his moods, has been disrespectful to the baby sitter, teases and provokes, has been caught playing with matches, and occasionally is insulting to his friends, but these things, I believe, are just a part of growing up. Perhaps I'm just prejudiced because he's my son!

It's always been a problem

Children have many problems. Some of the problems are apparent to everyone; other problems are known only to the child and his family. We learned that even those secret problems are embarrassing to children because they feel they have failed in some way. Sandy, our eight-year-old, has the problem of enuresis. It isn't a family secret any longer because it isn't just a night problem; it has become a problem 24 hours a day.

We always had this particular trouble with Sandy. When she was around four I was concerned, but other mothers frequently indicated that they had the same problems with their children. I was hoping that when Sandy started school she would correct the problem herself. There were times when I was hopeful because she seemed to improve. These times were few, however, and short-lived. We kept hoping she would outgrow her "wetting problem," as we called it.

This past year, when Sandy was in third grade, we decided it was time to do something. She was eight years old, and she was developing a very bad odor as a result of her problem. I took her to a medical doctor, who talked to her as I had. She should go to the bathroom just before going to school and at every recess. Her excuse was that the teachers wouldn't allow her to go out to the bathroom. This excuse was fine for school, but she had no excuse at home. The doctor also told both of us that Sandy should wash her soiled clothes every time. He said: "*All* of her soiled clothes and *every* time." We followed his "orders." Of course, Sandy got tired of this. She said: "If it doesn't help, why must I wash my clothes?" We did drift away from it, and I laundered all of her clothes again.

The doctor then gave me the names of several urologists, and we made an appointment with one. The urologist thought there might be something abnormal in the urinary canal and showed me on a model in his office what he thought the problem was. Since he couldn't really be sure of anything without an examination, we set up a time for Sandy to go to the hospital. I thought if this were something she could correct herself, maybe the thought of going to the hospital would snap her out of it. At first she said she didn't want to go to the hospital. She almost cried. I talked to her and did my best to tell her what it would be like. I related to her my experience in the hospital when I was ten and had a broken arm. I included the fact that I did get lonely, but I stressed the good parts. She grew to like the idea of going to the hospital; in fact, I think she felt like a celebrity. By the time Easter vacation came and she went to the hospital, she was actually eager.

While Sandy was resting after her examination, I talked to the doctor. He didn't find anything abnormal in her structure. He said he examined her very thoroughly because he really felt he would find something. He did, but not what he expected. She had an acute bladder infection. He said she had had it for so long that it could be called chronic instead of acute. He said her bladder was very red and sore looking. I asked him if this was a type of infection that wouldn't give discomfort. The doctor replied: "She should have had pain. She looked awful."

Sandy has been taking medicine since Easter. The infection is pretty well cleared up, although she must continue on the medicine for several months more. The enuresis has not cleared up. The doctor didn't give me much help in this area. I told him it was becoming more of a problem. She was old enough for camp this year and she has girlfriends asking her to stay overnight. His only suggestion was to let her stay overnight. Maybe she'll make it without an accident. She has stayed away, and sometimes has had an accident; other times she has not.

I am not overlooking the fact that this may be an emotional problem. I have done much soul-searching in this area, but I can't see its origin. Every time my mother-in-law and I see an article on enuresis, we read it. I do remember one article stated that we commonly think that emotional problems cause enuresis, but the writer believes the opposite to be true. His experience was that once the enuresis was cleared up, the emotional problems went away also.

I think the most interesting thing in all of this is Sandy's reaction. Does it affect her emotionally? For the most part I would have to say it doesn't. She accepts herself as having a problem, and her friends also accept her the way she is. When the odor was so bad, I pictured the other children making fun of her and her teacher trying to stay away from her. It wasn't this way at all, though. Naturally she doesn't like it when we say something about it to her or when her sisters say something. Her daddy asked her if she likes to have wet pants on. She said no, she doesn't. When she has an accident at night, she gets up and takes care of herself, and I don't even hear her. She just accepts it. I don't think the problem has an emotional basis because we can't say things like: "When her sister was born she started wetting her pants" or any similar statement. There is nothing we can point to because the problem has always been there.

First major league baseball game

The day that had been so anxiously awaited had finally arrived. My son was going to Baltimore to see his first major league baseball game. He had spent the previous days in a constant state of excitement as he eagerly anticipated all that he would see and do at the ball park. He had questioned me continually on the relative merits of all of the Baltimore players. His first act on the big morning was to check the sports section of the newspaper to determine who was scheduled to pitch in today's game.

Finally the moment arrived to board the bus. My son and I were going to the ball game with other members of his Little League baseball team and their fathers. As we began the two hour journey, the noise level started to intensify. As I looked at my son, I couldn't keep from remembering the day when I went to my first major league ball game and the excitement that I felt.

The two hour trip was spent with my answering, or I should say attempting to answer, the numerous questions my son asked: Would this particular player hit a home run? Who is the best player? Where would we sit? During one of the few moments of silence we experienced on the trip, I couldn't help thinking how a child believes that his father knows the answers to all questions.

Our arrival at the ball park was duly noted by all of the boys as the noise level reached a new peak. After my son had disembarked from the bus, he stood and stared at the stadium in fascination. The immensity of the structure was almost beyond his comprehension!

We purchased our tickets and entered the stadium; it was as if my son entered into a new world. We bought a program, and he acted as if it were the first material ever printed. He excitedly turned the pages, looking at the pictures of all of the ballplayers with awe. Although he had seen them on television, he gave the impression that he was seeing them for the first time.

We continued the walk to our seats with my son gaping at all of the sights found in a ball park. The vendors with their Baltimore Oriole souvenirs held the most attraction. Having brought some of his own money, he asked if he could purchase something. I gave him permission; he approached the booth and stared at the display of wares. Now he was faced with a most difficult decision. Of all of the various items for sale, he had narrowed his choice to three. Should he buy the baseball cap, the pennant, or the protective helmet? "What do you think, Dad? Which one should I buy?" he asked. This was one question I really couldn't answer, and knowing that a choice of mine might unfairly influence him, I said it would be better if he made his own decision. Finally, the protective helmet won, and with him wearing his newly purchased treasure, we made our way to our seats.

Here he found another delight. By checking the name and number in the program, he could recognize the ballplayer on the field. As he identified a player, he would turn to me and, with great pride, inform me that the one near the dugout was Powell or the next one to bat was Robinson.

The game began, and his state of excitement rose even higher. The apparent ease with which these men performed the mechanics of the game truly amazed him. As each and every play was made, he would ask if I saw that stop, or that catch, or that throw. The speed with which the pitcher threw the ball elicited the comment that they didn't throw the ball that fast in the Little League. The game progressed, and he was elated when one of his favorite players hit a home run. It was almost as if he had hit it himself! As the Orioles scored more runs, he seemed to cheer even louder. Finally the game was over, and he reached the crest of his happiness since his team had won.

The ride home was spent replaying the game in its entirety. All of the hits, catches, and throws were rehashed. The protective helmet was held, admired, and worn. Gradually calmness returned but the thrill of his first major league baseball game will remain always with this nine-year-old boy.

A child's fear of death

Betsy was a child of six when she learned about the tragedy of death, especially of a loved one. A first grader at the time, she was very fond of pets. That was an understatement, since she had four of her own: a puppy named Laddie, a parakeet named Tisa, a cat named Mitzi, and a fish who had no name.

Coming home from school one day, Betsy noticed that Laddie wasn't around to greet her. She asked her mother if she had seen Laddie, and her reply was: "God took him away." Betsy, not being too curious at the time, believed her mother and didn't ask too many questions. She even thought in her mind that if God took Laddie away, there was a possibility that God would bring him back. Her mother thought that Betsy wouldn't understand that the dog had to be put to sleep because of a terminal disease. Soon Laddie was replaced but never forgotten. The word "death" wasn't actually used in an explanation to Betsy, although this experience was the start of a buildup of Betsy's fear of death.

Two years later, death came into Betsy's family. She remembers her aunts and uncles crying and saying: "She's dead." They were speaking about Betsy's own grandparent, her maternal grandmother. She remembers seeing her grandmother lying in the casket. She said to her aunt at the funeral: "Why is Grandma in that box?" The reply was: "God decided it was time to take Grandma to join His family in the sky." Betsy now came to the conclusion that when God took someone away, He never brought him back. She had been hearing about God in Sunday School. Not until much later did she learn that her grandmother had died of cancer. Betsy decided she didn't want God to take her away. She wanted to remain with her mother and two younger brothers. An apprehension of hospitals emerged in her mind because that was the place from which God took her grandma.

A year later Betsy became quite ill with a strep throat and a bad cold. Her mother told her her tonsils would have to come out. The answer to Betsy's question "Why?" was that the tonsils were causing her to have colds and sore throats and after they were removed she would no longer catch colds. Of course, Betsy thought this to be a little exaggerated but she accepted the explanation.

It was necessary for Betsy to go to the hospital to have her tonsils removed. This fact didn't really bother her too much, for it was a new experience for which she had been prepared. Activity in the operating room scared Betsy, however. A mask of some sort was attached to her face and she was asked to count to twenty. After she had counted to eighteen, the doctor asked: "Are you sleeping?" Of course, Betsy said: "Yes."

The first thing that she noticed when she awoke was that she still had a sore throat. "And Mother said I wouldn't get any more sore throats," she thought. It also felt as if something was stuck in her throat. Her feeling was correct; an object had been placed in her throat to stop the flow of blood caused by a broken blood vessel.

The night following the operation, Betsy awakened and heard a nurse in the corridor saying: "She's going to die." Of course, Betsy thought this person was talking about her. To this day Betsy doesn't know whom the nurse was talking about. It did put a great fear in her, though.

Betsy didn't have an occasion to go into the hospital until two years later. She was admitted for a severe brain concussion and loss of consciousness caused by a knock on the head. It was customary for Betsy to take swimming lessons every Saturday afternoon at the local YMCA. She was in the beginners' class and doing quite well. One particular Saturday the instructor told her that if she could sit on the bottom of the pool at the three feet depth, she could advance to the intermediate class. This gave her much determination. After that, she doesn't remember much except that the instructor held her hand on top of Betsy's head to help her remain underwater while trying to sit on the bottom. As Betsy came up from underneath the water, she hit her head along the concrete edge of the pool and was knocked unconscious. She was taken to the hospital and remained there for the next month. The first thing she asked when she came to and realized she was in the hospital was: "Am I going to die?"

No, Betsy didn't die, but this incident put a fear of swimming and the possibility of dying in her. She didn't resume her swimming lessons until a year later but she could never learn how to dive. She was afraid of going head first into the water. The following summer Betsy was involved with another ordeal just by being in the wrong place at the wrong time.

Betsy, her two brothers, and the babysitter were visiting a nearby park whose main attraction was the stream that flowed through it. Betsy stood on the stream's edge just looking at the water ripple by. All of a sudden she felt someone lift her under the arms and throw her into the water, which was about five feet deep. She looked up and saw a strange girl standing there laughing like a crazy person. Betsy felt herself going up and down and knew that she was drowning. She started yelling that she didn't know how to swim. Finally, the stranger jumped in and pulled her out of the water. Betsy was so frightened that she ran out of the park and down the street without giving thought to her brothers or the babysitter. While running and crossing the street, she barely missed being hit by a car. The experience has made an indelible impression on her mind.

Every child probably has a certain fear of dying when he or she learns about it. Betsy has an exaggerated fear of it. This concern was imprinted in her mind by the experiences she had and the specific details she remembers about them. Now, as an adult, she understands death and the reasons why she had this strange fear of dying.

But she is still upset by the idea of it. It is interesting, however, that she sometimes thinks death doesn't always mean dying. But that's another profile!

THINGS TO THINK ABOUT AND DO

1. Can you recall your first day of school in kindergarten and compare it to your first day in first grade? What were your feelings or experiences? If you can't remember those days, ask your parents. They'll be pleased to have you help them relive the days when you were a small child.

2. Discussion: What developmental characteristics must a child have in order to be ready to meet the demands of first grade? What are the demands of first grade?

3. In a number of European countries, children do not begin the equivalent of first grade until they are seven years old. Does this seem like a good idea to you? Explain your answer.

4. Of all the elementary grades, we believe that second grade is one of the nicest grade levels of children to teach. Why do you

suppose we believe that? Think about it. Do you agree or disagree with our statement?

5. Visit an elementary school playground, with permission of the principal, of course. Observe the children. What kind of games do they play? What kind of activity do they engage in? Talk to some of the children. Do they seem different from what you were expecting them to be like? If you have time and permission, do a little survey, just so you can get to talk to them. Ask questions like: What is your favorite TV program? (or favorite game, food, television star, etc.) How old are you? How many brothers and sisters do you have? How do you like school—a whole lot, some, a little, not at all? Make up your own list of four or five questions.

6. How are eight-year-olds different from six-year-olds? Consider physical, social, emotional, mental, and moral characteristics. How do you imagine it would be to be an eight-year-old as compared to a six-year-old?

7. Talk to teachers and ask what content they teach in first, second, third, and fourth grades.

8. How do you imagine it would feel to be an exceptional child in school, that is, one who is mentally retarded, partially deaf, partially seeing, orthopedically handicapped, or learning disabled?

9. Talk to parents of first or second graders. Ask them what differences they see in their children now as compared to before they went to school.

10. Should children have pets? Discuss and maybe do a survey on how many have pets.

11. Are children who go to school in urban areas, perhaps inner city, any different from those who go to school in a suburban area? A rural area? Do they have different types of experiences? Does it matter? Would it make a difference?

READING SOURCES
Developmental psychology texts

Bernard, H.W.: Human development in western culture, ed. 4, Boston, 1975, Allyn & Bacon, Inc., chaps. 9, 14, 15.

CRM: Developmental psychology today, ed. 2., New York, 1975, CRM/Random House, Inc., chaps. 14, 15.

Hurlock, E.: Developmental psychology, New York, 1975, McGraw-Hill Book Co., chap. 6.

Kaluger, G., and Kaluger, M.: Human development: the span of life, St. Louis, 1974, The C. V. Mosby Co., chap. 7.

Medennus, G. R., and Johnson, R. C.: Child and adolescent psychology, New York, 1969, John Wiley & Sons, Inc.

Mussen, P. H., Conger, J. J., and Kagan, J.: Child development and personality, ed. 4, New York, 1975, Harper & Row, Publishers, chap. 11.

Stone, L. J., and Church, J.: Childhood and adolescence: a psychology of the growing person, New York, 1968, Random House, Inc., chaps. 8, 9.

Related readings

Adams, R. L., and Phillips, B. N.: Motivational and achievement differences among children of various ordinal birth positions, Child Dev. 43:155-164, 1972.

Boshier, R.: Self-esteem and first names in childhood, Psychol. Rep. 22:762, 1968.

Clifford, M. M., and Walster, E.: The effect of physical attractiveness on teacher expectations, Soc. Ed. 46: 248-258, 1973.

Hindelang, M. J.: Educational and occupational aspirations among working class Negro, Mexican-American and white elementary school children, J. Negro Ed. 39:351-353, 1970.

Kaspar, J. C., and Lowenstein, R.: The effect of social interaction on activity levels in six-to eight-year-old boys, Child Dev. 42:1294-1298, 1971.

Levinson, B. M.: Pets and human behavior, Springfield, Ill., 1972, Charles C Thomas, Publisher.

Meredith, H. V.: Body size of contemporary groups of eight-year-old children studied in different parts of the world, Monogr. Soc. Res. Child Dev. 34(1):1969.

Palermo, D. S., and Molfese, D. L.: Language acquisition from age five onward, Psychol. Bull. 78:409-428, 1972.

Steward, M. A.: Hyperactive children, Sci. Am. 222(4):94-98, 1970.

Werry, J. S., and Quay, H. C.: The prevalence of behavior symptoms in younger elementary school children, Am. J. Orthopsychiatr. 41:136-143, 1971.

CHAPTER 5

Preadolescence: the peak of childhood

Perhaps no other stage of development in life has been as deeply affected by changes in society than has the preadolescent or late childhood period. The adults of today, thinking back to when they were nine to twelve years of age, merely shake their heads in disbelief and bewilderment as they contemplate the preadolescents of today. "Whatever happened to kids?" is the cry. "We sure were never like that . . ." Then there is usually a discourse on "what it used to be like" in a childhood paradise, now lost.

That childhood paradise probably never really was as adults now depict it, but it is true that in many cultural and social ways preadolescents are different today compared to youngsters of the same age of as recently as ten to fifteen years ago. The preadolescents of today are more knowledgeable about the world in which they live, they operate on a higher level of sophistication in thinking and living, and they are much more involved and concerned with society than in the past. It is interesting to speculate as to why and how these changes have come about. Probably the greatest instigator of cultural and social changes in late childhood has been the attention and homage paid to television. The constant impingement of mass media in general into the life-space of individuals makes a tremendous impact on their minds and behavior. We believe that all of society has been affected by these intrusions into our living rooms and lives, but it is the preadolescent who has been influenced the most.

Typically, late childhood is a period of great freedom and few responsibilities, a time when children are avid, active seekers of knowledge that they want to learn about, a phase when they are both willing spectators and aspiring participants in the affairs and activities of slightly older contemporaries. Children of this age are everywhere. They form a society of children. They travel on their bikes, they talk on their walkie-talkies, they are found at all community affairs and events, and they always seem to be where the action is. When you put together the typical, active, searching nature of this age level with mass media exposure to concepts, ideas, and behaviors of a more accepting, adult society that is in the midst of change itself, some worldly-wise influences are bound to be picked up by those who have reached the zenith of childhood and are ready for bigger and better ways of living their lives.

"That First Cigarette" will bring a touch of nostalgia to many readers. "Thoughts on Baseball" tells of how the Little League player views a baseball game, as compared to what his sister, father, and mother think about at the same time. A sadder picture is presented of a rejected baseball player in "It Means a Lot." Somewhat typical of this age level are "Stagefright" and "No Girls for David."

Not all children are fortunate in their circumstances of living, but "A Little Bit of Heaven" tells how one boy was made happier by a couple who took an interest in him. Also resulting in a happy ending is the story of "The Effect a Brain Tumor had on My Development." Not so fortunate is a fifth grader who still reads on a second grade level in "Sam Can't Read." More typical are the diary comments of a girl in "Who Says Fat is Beautiful?" "A Profile in Wonderment" is a sequel to "A Profile in Gratefulness," presented in the section on infancy. It tells of the development and creativeness of a girl who had spina bifida. Finally, "A Mother's Thoughts" is a touching letter written by a mother to her son on his last day in elementary school.

That first cigarette

All through elementary school, my best girlfriend lived across the street from me. Sally was a year younger than I, but we were inseparable. We played Cowboys and Indians, played marbles, rode our bikes, spent nights at each other's houses, and walked to school together. We both had vivid imaginations and, because of this, we were quite active and experimental in trying new experiences. We would try things out just for fun even though we knew we might get punished for doing them. On might say we were very curious.

On this particular Saturday my parents and sister had gone away. My neighbor was baby-sitting for me, but Sally and I were out playing. While we were playing, Sally suggested smoking a cigarette to see what it was like. So we decided to try it. We knew it was wrong and that if we were caught we would be punished, but my parents were out of town and we decided to hide from her parents. I do not remember where we got the money, but we bought the cigarettes at the grocery store two doors away from her house. The lady thought nothing about a third and fourth grader buying cigarettes because Sally often bought them for her father. I got the matches from my father's pipe stand, and we were ready for a new experience.

The junior high school was on a hill a block from our houses. Behind the school was a dense growth of trees, bushes, and shrubs, so we decided to go there and hide while we smoked. We were pretty brave after a while, so we moved to a small clearing on the hill where we could look down at the cars going by on the street. A few people saw us, but that was all right because we didn't know them. But the next thing we knew, Sally's father went by and happened to look up. We thought he saw us but when he didn't stop, we assumed he didn't see us after all. As it turned out he *did* see us. At the time we didn't know that, so, feeling quite brave, we decided to stop hiding and walk along the street. We were laughing, talking, showing off, and feeling very grownup. We were completely pleased with ourselves.

After we had smoked all we wanted, we discarded the rest of the pack and went to my house where we gargled with mouthwash to get rid of the cigarette smell. Then we decided to go over to Sally's house. When we got there, her mother informed us that her father had seen us

smoking and that Sally was not allowed to play anymore. She also said that she was going to tell my parents. Feeling very safe, I thought to myself "ha-ha," then I told her my parents were out of town and would not be back until time for supper. But she said she would come over then. When I left, I began to worry—should I tell my parents when they got home or should I just wait? I knew it was better to tell them myself but I just could not do it, so I waited, hoping Sally's mother would forget.

It was not long before my parents and sister came home; by then I was really worried. Just as we were ready to sit down to eat, the doorbell rang. When Mother answered the door and I saw who it was, I started to go upstairs to my room. Mother knew something must be pretty important to have a visitor at mealtime. I got halfway upstairs when I heard: "Mary Anne, I think you ought to stay and hear this." My parents shot a startled, shocked look at me, and I sat down with my head bowed, waiting for the lead ball to fall. Then it came. I knew by my parents' expressions that they could not believe I would do such a thing. Then they sent me to bed without any supper! And I was so hungry! I could not believe it. I had never been punished like this before.

After what seemed to be hours, actually only about fifteen minutes, my parents came up to my room and, sitting down on my bed, asked me why I did it. When I said I had smoked just to see what it was like and promised never to do it again, I was allowed to go downstairs and finish eating my meal with them.

I will never forget how ashamed I was! I sat at the end of the table, with my sister at the other end and our parents in between us. While I ate, there were three pairs of eyes just staring at me, and no one said a word. I just looked at my plate and tried to eat between tears. I was ashamed because I had disappointed my parents, but I was especially ashamed for my sister to know what I had done. She was eighteen, in college, and she did not smoke. I tried very hard to imitate her—she was my ideal.

I don't smoke today because I don't want to smoke. I tried once again in college because it seemed to be the thing to do, but I remembered my mother telling me that if I started to smoke, then she would also (and I detested the thought of my mother smoking). I also felt as if three pairs of eyes were watching me every time I puffed a cigarette, and I decided it was not worth feeling guilty about!

A little bit of heaven

Joe Martin, a part-time policeman, was patrolling his small community one cold November night. As he was driving through the intersection, he noticed a dark figure riding a bicycle. He pulled the police car aside to question the rider. Much to his surprise, the rider was a ten-year-old boy. Upon questioning the lad, Officer Martin learned that the boy's name was Amos. Officer Martin explained to Amos that he would have to take him to police headquarters because of curfew violation. This incident opened the door to a new life for Amos because from this point on Joe Martin and his wife, Beth, took a special interest in Amos. Beth and Joe had no children of their own, although they were very fond of children.

Several weeks after the bicycle incident, Amos stopped by the Martin house to talk to them. In the ensuing conversation with Amos, the Martins were able to learn some of his family background. Amos is next to the youngest child in a family of eight. Seven of the children are living at home, and one is married. The parents live together sometimes. To quote Amos: "Daddy only comes home when he needs money for beer." His mother works in a factory.

More and more Amos came to visit the Martins. On occasion, he was so terribly dirty that Joe and Beth decided to try to help him. Amos was not visibly dirty, but he had a terrific odor. It appeared that he slept in his clothes. He also wore the same outfit for many days at a time. When Amos undressed he wore no underwear. He had on three shirts: one was used as an undershirt, one was a regular shirt, and the top one served as a coat. The Martins bought him new underwear, a shirt, and trousers. Amos showered and put on his new clothes. The next day when he came back to the Martins, he was

dressed in his old clothes. Upon questioning him, they learned that one of his brothers had taken the new clothing. This time the Martins bought several new outfits for Amos and kept the new clothes at their home. Each evening Amos would go to the Martins, take a shower, and put on clean clothes. He was given a drawer of his own.

Amos has curly brown hair. He had no idea how to keep it clean. In fact, it seemed as though it was seldom, if ever, washed. It was quite long and unkempt. Joe took Amos to the barber shop and had his hair cut. He also taught him how to wash it and to do it frequently. Amos said that his father cut his hair, but it got long because his father didn't come home very often.

Amos used to constantly keep his head down. He looked up to say "Hi" and immediately put his head back down. He has made much progress in this respect. Now he talks with his head up. No doubt he had some very insecure feelings. He was literally thrown around at home. One incident which he described is horrible to me. He refused to get an older brother a cup of coffee one evening. As a result, this brother threw Amos against a wall and then slammed him into a chair. Amos still carries the scars from this incident above his right eye.

Amos had many problems in school. His problems were not only academic in nature, but social as well. Children did not like Amos because he "smelled bad." His teacher mentioned that children refused to sit beside him, play with him, or include him in their activities because of the odor. At their home, Mr. and Mrs. Martin helped Amos with homework. Before this time it rarely was done. After two marking periods Amos came up one letter grade in each subject. The teacher said he had improved vastly, not only in academic work but also in being accepted by peers and in his overall outlook or attitude.

It is interesting to see how much Amos has changed in such a short period of time. He does not resent the idea of cleanliness; in fact, he looks forward to a daily bath and clean clothes. He has become aware of clothing and how he looks. He is always asking if certain shirts and trousers look all right together. Just recently he said a little boy in his class came to school with holes in his socks. Amos said: "I really felt sorry for that boy because I had enough of that."

Since summer has arrived Amos practically lives with the Martins, who have a camping trailer which they take to the mountains each weekend. Amos has been going along and is thrilled with fishing. He gets up at 6:30 A.M. each day to go fishing. The only thing he has caught is a small fish, but to him this fish was the same as a large one. The first weekend, when returning from camping, Joe and Beth asked Amos how he liked it. His answer was: "Oh man! It's like a little bit of heaven."

The effect a brain tumor had on my development

A brain tumor will have different effects on different people. The effect it will have will depend largely upon the location and severity of the tumor, the success of the operation, and, of course, the type of person who has the tumor. It is also important to remember that the person's home environment will influence development after the operation.

I was born into a middle class family of four and lived in a small home directly across from the school which I attended. I enjoyed school tremendously. One might almost say that I lived for every new day in school. One particular part of school that I enjoyed the most was the competitiveness. I had always enjoyed competing with my peers, both in and out of school. I believe that this competitive spirit kept me at the top of my class in both subject matter and sports.

I had many friends and spent much time with them after school and on the weekends. Some of the things which I enjoyed doing with my friends included bicycle riding, hiking, playing games such as tag and baseball, and bowling. It must seem rather strange to think of an eight- or nine-year-old girl bowling, but this was a sport which I had started with my older brother when I was seven years old. I kept myself quite busy as a child, as most children of that age must do.

Unfortunately, at the age of nine, I developed a brain tumor after being very ill with a virus. The first signs which indicated that there was something wrong with my health were a series of headaches which increased in intensity and number. Up until that winter I had never been ill, except with the common childhood diseases such as the measles and the mumps.

Soon after I started complaining of these headaches, my parents took me to see several doctors. It was discovered that I had a brain tumor which had to be removed immediately. This tumor was located very close to my optic nerve center.

I can remember how upset I was when my parents walked into my hospital room and told me that I was quite ill and would need an operation in order to feel better and be able to do all those things that I loved so much. Of course, at that age I had no idea of the seriousness of a brain tumor; I only knew that I had terrific pain, and I agreed that I should have an operation.

In preparation for the operation, I was sent to the Presbyterian Medical Center in New York City. I was placed in a private room and was not allowed any visitors except on Sunday. My head was shaved completely, and I was sedated very soon after my arrival to decrease the severity of the pain.

After the operation was completed, I stayed at the hospital for five weeks. During this time I found that my eyesight had been impaired quite considerably. It was impossible for me to read a book or comics; I could not even see the numbers on cards well enough to play solitaire. At this time I also discovered that I had lost the ability to balance myself in simple tasks such as walking, climbing, and hopping.

When I was officially released from the hospital, I really did not want to go home. There were many reasons for my fear of returning home, but the greatest was that I felt I would not be accepted among my peers. I was completely bald, except for a small amount of peach fuzz on the top and sides of my head. I had a seven inch scar on the back of my head which reached down to the bottom of my neck, and I definitely resembled a boy from every possible angle.

Since my balance and eyesight had been impaired, I found that I had quite an adjustment to make as I returned to school. At the time I did not realize what a lucky girl I was. All I understood were the difficulties I had with my subjects and the tears I felt when I tried to play some of my favorite games and fell flat on my face.

Instead of school being enjoyable, it had now become a dreaded chore. It was a place that I was forced to go every day, a place where I encountered a great deal of embarrassment continually. My reading had become so poor that I just stumbled through sentences, praying that the teacher would soon let me sit down.

My brain tumor operation had really left me discouraged with and uninterested in life. At this age when a child should be full of life and enthusiasm, I had none. I was ashamed of my appearance and my inefficiency.

I was very fortunate, however, in that I had wonderful parents who were both good and patient. They spent a great deal of their time talking to me and trying to encourage me. They helped me to see how other children, not realizing the experience I had been through, could say things which caused me many tears. They encouraged me to keep trying my best in school. They had told me that it was going to be a hard road to travel for a while, but in time my eyes would improve and I would be able to read again, just as I had before. When I got frustrated and was ready to give up completely, they would be standing at my side to give me a hand.

Both of my parents worked with me daily to help me improve my balance. One day we would practice riding my bike, and the next we would work with my roller skates. We also spent a great deal of time tossing balls back and forth to improve my eyesight.

It took approximately two years for my hair to grow to a length which would permit me to comb it in an attractive hair style. It had also gotten long enough to cover my lengthy scar. I'm not sure whether the improvement of my appearance or the constant work of my parents to encourage me had a greater effect, but I finally started coming out of my invisible shell. I became much more courageous and attempted to try even harder in both my school work and my social life. In due time I started to see where my academic achievements began to improve tremendously. At the same time that my academic achievements started to improve, my social life took a turn for the better.

My balance had improved to the point that people would never have known that I suffered so much difficulty just a few years back if they had not been told. I also had developed my eyes to the point that glasses were not needed. They will never be perfect, but I'm not complaining any more.

The beginning of the ninth grade was the beginning of a new era for me. I had finally achieved that burning desire for competition again. It was at this point in my life that I started making my upward progress again. I started to take a sincere interest in school, extracurricular activities, clubs, peers, and, of course, life.

It was not easy to catch up on all the knowledge that I had let slip by, and heaven knows, I may never catch up, but I've caught up enough to give me the desire to keep learning!

___

Sam can't read

Sam is a student of average intelligence, with an I.Q. of 101. His reading achievement, however, is around grade 2.3. This score is too high, for Sam has problems reading first grade material. Nevertheless, because of his age, he is in a fifth grade class. Needless to say, his day at school is filled with frustrations.

The first class of the day is reading. Even though the school makes an attempt to minimize the frustration that these children experience by grouping procedures, Sam has problems. Three days a week he participates in a low reading group that uses a basal series. The books are classified as being on a fourth grade level. With the gap between the reading level of the book and the level at which Sam can achieve, he does not function well.

This class period is really a frustration to

Sam. Usually he tries to find a way out of reading. He does such things as moving about for a long period of time so that the class does not start, approaching the teacher with problems or conversation that hold her up, or lingering at the book cart under the pretense of getting a new library book. Once the class has started, Sam feels a good bit of pressure. He likes to follow along as the teacher or another child reads but after a time he loses his place (he must point to words that he does not know until he comes to familiar words to tell him where the other person is reading) and he must look on other children's books for clues as to the place.

One might think he would be content just to listen, but since the reading material is the source of the frustration, he shuns everything pertaining to reading. Sometimes he is called upon to read. The result is enough to make anyone feel his frustration. He has trouble reading three or four words together. This inability leads to a disregard for punctuation and further confusion on his part. After about four or five lines, his reading no longer makes sense and the frustration mounts. Now he has trouble with easy words, mispronouncing even those he knows. Finally, he gives up and tries to get out of further reading.

Silent reading presents more problems. Just as Sam has trouble with oral reading, he cannot identify the words in a story he is to read to himself. After a few minutes of trying to identify the words and put them together in some meaningful fashion, he feels the pain of defeat. Now he lets his attention wander to daydreams or to things that are going on outside. However, the job is not finished for him. Even though he cannot read the selection, he must answer the questions that follow the reading material. His efforts to gain the answers lead to more frustration. Since it is against the rules to get these answers from others, he tries to do it without getting caught. Usually the teacher catches him and this again leads to frustration. His final out is bad temper, misconduct, or an attitude of defeat.

Two days a week the reading is individualized. Here Sam feels a little more at home, for the difficulty of the material is closer to his reading level. He will stay with a book for quite a while, even finishing some books. The frustration here comes from the activities associated with the book. Sam's writing vocabulary presents a problem to him, for even when he wishes to express himself about what he has read, he cannot do it. Even the activity cards present problems to him, for he cannot always comprehend what he is to do. Another problem is the peer group pressure. Those who can read the more advanced books are quick to point out their superiority. At times this renews Sam's dislike for books and causes him to shun even the books he can read. In his frustration, he forgets the accomplishments he had made. He feels that trying to read only creates bad feelings.

Even on a one-to-one basis with a teacher when problems are kept to a minimum, Sam gets frustrated. Most of the books he works with are on the first grade level. The rest of this class are working on different levels, all of them higher than Sam's. He receives a lot of the teacher's attention. When he is working with the teacher, he seems to feel somewhat at ease, but he does react physically to mistakes or new words. He will toss his head and pull back from the desk, only to plead that he does not want to be told. If he misses the same word many times, he becomes angry with himself and will do things such as hit his head with his hand or lean back with a gesture of disgust. When the teacher moves away to check on other students' progress or to offer assistance to others, any confidence he seemed to have fades. He becomes restless, often talking to the teacher across the room, or doing things to attract his friends. If the teacher is gone too long, he begins to make verbal attacks such as: "Why do I have to read?" or "I hate to read; I'd rather be out of here." Yet he is always ready to resume the one-to-one relationship. It is almost as if he fears the frustration that his own efforts bring.

Recently he took part in a testing program. The first test was a speed and accuracy test. Even though the students were told that they were not expected to finish and that they were only required to do their best, when the time was up he responded by rubbing his hand across

They disregard authority,
Respect for age they lack,
They follow pleasure most often
And duties they do slack.
You think I mean the kids and so
I do, those of fifty years ago.

Irving Leibowitz
INDIANAPOLIS TIMES

his head, symbolizing his inability to do as much as he felt he should and the pressure it seemed to bring. The second part of the test was vocabulary. Sam seemed to be able to attack the first few questions with some comfort, but he soon hit a wall. At first he just looked at the test as if it would tell him the answers if he looked long enough. After a while, he began to make faces, showing that he felt the frustration building. Then he began marking the answers without even reading, or attempting to read, the questions. Even when

he was told he did not need to answer those he didn't know, he continued until he had marked them all. He was very happy to get out of the room when he had finished.

Frustration can have a serious effect on an individual. Sam and others like him have problems that will not go away. The frustration of one day is not forgotten by the next. It is just added to it. Tomorrow is not going to bring success to the person who has reading problems. No one can learn to read for us, and we cannot turn our backs on its necessity. Thus

Sam's frustration may be the director of his activity and may be the factor that will determine his success or failure in meeting the world and its challenges.

It means a lot

To me, children in the early adolescent stage of development are very cruel. Around the ages of eleven, twelve, and thirteen, boys especially can be mean to other boys in their peer group. This cruelty can easily be seen at any Little League baseball game.

About one month ago I decided to go see a Little League baseball game in my community. The game was important for both teams because the winner would be in first place. When I arrived, I could feel the tenseness present within all the players. I was sitting directly behind one of the teams' benches and could hear the various conversations that were going on. "We have to win this one! We can beat them any day of the week!" There was one boy in particular who apparently took the role of captain of the team. He was very easy to pick out from the rest of the players on the team. He was taller, heavier, more confident of his actions, and he moved about from player to player, giving them instructions.

When the team took the field, I noticed that there was a boy, whom I shall call Joe, who did not seem as excited as the others. He was not shouting and moving about as the other players were. In fact, he looked very timid and shy. Joe's physical appearance was also noticeably different. Although he was as tall as or even taller than the other boys, he was fat. As I observed him, he had trouble running or even walking because of his obesity.

When the inning was over and the team came off the field, some of the boys began moaning at Joe because he was not "hustling" off the field. He did not respond to them verbally but just sat down on the end of the bench. As I suspected, Joe was the last batter, and he struck out. When this happened, the entire team began calling him "stupid," "fatso," "tub-of-lard," etc.

The next time his team took the field, there was a fly ball in his direction. Joe tried to get in position to catch the ball, but he fell down in the process. The ball bounded past him, and the other team scored a run. The other eight players all looked disgustedly at Joe but did not really have much to say to him at that time. When the inning was over and the team was once again on the bench, the coach came over to Joe and told him that another player was going to take his place. The captain of the team came over and told Joe that he should quit the team, because he couldn't hit and couldn't even catch a ball. He said this so loudly that everybody in the stands heard what was going on.

Joe just sat there by himself for a few minutes, motionless. There were big tears forming in his eyes, and he soon began to cry. He got up and sat under a tree about one hundred yards away and watched the rest of the game from there. The coach reprimanded the other boys for yelling at Joe, but they all responded by saying: "We don't need him. He stinks anyway."

When the game was over, it turned out that Joe's team won, and everyone was very happy. The manager told the boys that he was going to buy everyone an ice cream cone. Joe just stood around with his head bowed. One boy said that the manager should not buy Joe an ice cream cone because he almost lost the game for their team. Joe once again began crying and this time ran away from his teammates.

The following week, I attended another Little League game between the same teams. When I got there I looked around for Joe, but he was not present. After the game, I asked one of the team members where Joe was, and he answered: "Who cares!"

Stagefright

It seems as if it happened in another lifetime, but it was only about fifteen years ago when an incident occurred which had a profound influence on my life. I was in the fifth grade when this event took place, and I can still remember it vividly. It was certainly one of the most traumatic occurrences of my life, and to this day it affects my behavior.

It was early in the day during my home-room class. We had just finished our section on current events and were moving on to a new section. Toward the end of this section, the teacher asked if anyone had an unusual hobby. I had begun to take guitar lessons, and I felt that this could be considered an unusual hobby. I didn't know many other kids who played the guitar at the age of ten. Raising my hand, I answered that I had an unusual hobby. To my later chagrin, she asked if I might like to demonstrate my musical ability to the class. My music teacher had recently said that I was definitely beginning to learn how to handle the guitar, and I was beginning to feel as if I was becoming rather good. "Why shouldn't I play for the class?" I thought to myself. Without hesitation, I volunteered to play a few songs the next time the class met. I was pretty excited about playing for the group and really felt confident. I had been playing the guitar for six months and didn't feel as if there would be any trouble. If only I had known what was in store! What transpired the next day, I'm sure, had a tremendous effect on my life even till this day.

Arriving at class a few minutes early, I quickly made my way to my seat. I had a big guitar case by my side and felt very proud. Sitting at my seat, I felt somewhat anxious, but I cannot say that I was nervous. After the usual class trivia was done, it was time. The teacher made the announcement, and I simultaneously picked up my case. Proudly I strolled to the front of the room and seated myself on a large stool. Slinging the strap over my shoulder, I faced my audience. I had picked a certain song to play, because I had done this particular song many times with my teacher. I knew it so well that I didn't even need to use the music. When I felt the moment was propitious, I started to strum. Everything was okay, and I was doing fine.

Now came the vocal part, and I raised my head to look at the audience. As I looked at the thirty pair of eyes centered on me, I realized for the first time what I was doing. Here I was, at the front of the room, with everybody staring at me. As if hit by a hidden paralysis, my body tensed. I felt a sharp pain run the length of my spine, and a vertigo hit me. I felt as if I was going to topple off the stool. As if these symptoms weren't enough, my mouth felt dry and my heart felt like it was going to pound right through my chest. I wanted to run, but I knew I couldn't. Everyone was expecting a performance, and I had to perform. It seemed like an interminable length of time had lapsed since the point when the vocal part was to begin, but it was only a few seconds. My mouth opened to sing but nothing came out—I couldn't speak! No matter how hard I tried, I couldn't speak. My neck muscles were so tight, and I was so dizzy that I felt sure that I was going to faint.

The expressions on my peers' faces began to change. Everybody was smiling, and soon I was able to detect laughter. There was only one thing left to do, and I did it—I ran like hell out of that room into the hallway. Instead of the applause that I had expected to receive before this debacle had started, I heard a loud derisive laughter. The teacher tried to quiet the class and explain that I had tried and shouldn't be laughed at. No matter what happened now, I knew that I was an ignominious fool. How could I face my classmates again? Suddenly I started to cry, which only made matters worse because some of my friends saw this. Now, in addition to being a coward, I was also a crybaby. The teacher tried to comfort me, but all I wanted to do was go home to my room. The teacher had enough empathy to call my father and ask him to take me home.

When I arrived home, my father showered me with platitude after platitude, trying his best to make me feel better. I didn't speak to anyone that night and tried to think of some way for me to stay home from school the next day. For some unknown reason, the next day my father took me to school an hour late. In retrospect, I think the teacher instructed him to bring me to class late so that she could have time to talk to the class. She must have really been emphatic with the class because nobody said a word to me about the incident. I approached the class with the most trepidation I had ever experienced. Somehow I got to my seat, and I was shaking like a bowl of gelatin.

I never did continue with my guitar lessons. Actually, a strange hysterical reaction occurred whenever I tried to play the guitar. After a few strummings, my hand would become stiff and I couldn't continue. About two weeks after the fiasco in school, I sold my guitar. I was really glad to get rid of the instrument, hoping that time would heal the wounds. It never happened. I never did forget what transpired; and until this day, some fifteen years later, I can still remember the incident vividly.

Thoughts on baseball
A PLAYER'S THOUGHTS

Woke up this morning feeling pretty good. Should be a good game tonight. Let's see, their record is 0-8. This should be a pushover. My batting average will probably go up to at least .450. What must I do today—cut the grass and go swimming. Coach said I shouldn't tire myself. Will have to watch what I eat before the game. Don't want to eat too much and not feel well.

The grass is finished. Will go for a short swim. Can only stay until 2:30. Have to be home to rest for a while.

Mom is always rushing me and making sure I have the cleanest uniform on the field. Where did Mom put my socks? Oh, here they are in my drawer. Wonder where she put my belt when she washed my pants.

Dog-gone-it! I told her I didn't want to eat too much. Come on, I want to be at the field before everyone else to get a little practice in on batting. Well, I'm late again. Everyone else has their shoes on and are throwing. Darn shoelaces—have to remember to tell Mom to get me new ones.

I start tonight—thought I would. This pitcher looks like a piece of cake. My throws to home are a little off tonight. Will have to remember that. Greg is pitching tonight—probably won't have too many hits and those who do hit will be swinging late.

This pitcher has more than what it looks like. Two strikes, one ball. He will probably waste one, a curve. It is, and what a hit! The coach says to hold up. Bunt signal is on. Good bunt. Both safe. Pitch and go for third. Ha, ha, another stolen base. Jimmy just hit a home run.

That will bring three of us across. Good lead to start the game with.

If things go right, I will get up in the second inning. I hope I get the bunt signal. Look where the third baseman is playing.

Dog-gone-it! Mr. Mack is taking us all out and letting the others play. Well, I guess he knows what he is doing, but it sure is disgusting sitting here waiting for these guys to do something.

Well, next week is another game. It will be much tougher so we will probably play the whole game. Have to go over and shake those guys' hands.

A SISTER'S THOUGHTS

Oh, no, we have to go home early again today because of baseball. Why do we always have to go home early because of a dumb baseball game? Guess I'll jump in the pool one more time before it's time to leave.

Okay, I'm coming now. Why do we always have to go home because of baseball! Always when it's nice—we have to go home! Sure will be glad when baseball season is over.

Yes, I'm hurrying to get the table set. The milk is poured. Don't see why we always have to go to the baseball game. It's no fun! Just go and sit there! Can't see why Natalie and I just can't stay at home. Well, better get something to drink and our Barbies. Then we can just sit in the car. . . . Well, might just as well watch the game for a little while. Keith is up to bat. Hope he hits it. He didn't even hit it. Why is he going to the base? Now, what's that kid's name? I think it's Davey. Boy, he hit the ball way out to the fence. Keith can run fast.

Wonder how much longer until this game is over. I'm going to the car.

A FATHER'S THOUGHTS (AS A COACH)

Won't be able to finish this tonight. Keith has a baseball game tonight and I must get home in time to line the field.

Hope dinner is ready on time. I want to get to the field early and rake it out and line it.

Keith will have to leave when I do. I will need some help lining up the foul lines and setting up the batting boxes.

I want to get the boys together before the

game and give them a little pep talk. This other team's record is not too good, but they are the type of team that will really put one on you if given half the chance.

George, you take third tonight. I'll go on first. Ray, you warm up with Bob while we are on the field. I want you to be good and warm. Randy hasn't pitched that much this year and he may tire.

These kids just are not watching for the signals tonight. They can steal the catcher anytime—especially when the pitcher looks only once.

George, I don't think you should make these changes with only a three run lead. Bob feels the same. I realize you want to get everyone into the game but let's not do it at the team's expense.

Well, we lucked out on this one. Tomorrow is the big one. Let's get these things packed up and go get them tomorrow.

A MOTHER'S THOUGHTS

Guess I'd better get the kids over to the pool for a little bit. Won't have much time because we have a game tonight. Better get the potatoes pared while they're getting their suits on. Really should stay home and run the sweeper, but then I haven't been to the pool with them this week.

Why can't they remember their own towels and pool cards? If only they'd put them away so they'd know where they are. Someone is always forgetting something!

It hardly seems worthwhile. Seems like we just got here and it's time to go home. The girls are going to be complaining again. It will be nice when baseball season is over, but I sure will miss it.

Hope that meat is about done. It's a good thing I got the potatoes ready before we left.

Keith's suit is washed and hanging in the basement. His belt is in the drawer. Hope he remembers to put on clean socks. Oh, no, I forgot to get some new shoelaces.

It hardly seems worthwhile rushing around cooking. Seems like we just had lunch. With all this rushing around, no one is even hungry. It sure will be nice getting back on schedule and eating at a decent time instead of the middle of the afternoon.

Only missed the first half of the inning. Our team is up to bat. We should win tonight. The opponents don't have a very good record. Hope Gene doesn't holler too much tonight. Hope the coach didn't tell them the game was a pushover. That's why they lost the last time.

Oh, no, Keith is at bat. This sure makes me nervous. Hope he doesn't strike out. Now why did George tell him to bunt? Well, at least, he got on base. Maybe he'll score a run. Wish he wouldn't take such a long lead off the base. Oh, good! Jim got a home run. That gives us a three run lead. If Ed had only called time before he got off the base, we'd have four runs. Wish Gene hadn't hollered so at him. I know he should have known better but . . .

Thank goodness, they won that game! They almost lost it by putting in the second team. Oh well, it's just another game.

Who says fat is beautiful?

In this society much emphasis is placed upon the appearance of the female. A female must be pretty and have a stunning figure. Fashions are designed for the woman who has the hip size of a teenage boy. Television and motion picture screens emphasize facial beauty. The mass media rarely suggest that the "Plain Jane" exists, and if they do suggest such existence they never picture a successful one.

This paper is being written to describe a girl named Cindy who is between twelve and thirteen years of age. She has a problem suffered by many people in America; she is overweight. She is not the beautiful woman shown on the television screen. She has plain, ordinary brown hair. Her eyes are hazel and are functional. They do not, however, glow in the dark or seduce helpless men. As a matter of fact, she resembles her father, who definitely does not resemble Elizabeth Taylor.

More of her appearance will be described in the pages that follow, but it will be described by Cindy—in her own words—from her diary.

• • •

Dear Diary,

I'm glad you cannot see me when I write in you. Otherwise you would probably lose your key so I couldn't open you. I would understand, though. I looked into the mirror and saw that horror my parents say they love. How can they? I've disappointed them. My sister is so pretty, and my parents can be proud of her, but me! Just look at me. Why do *I* have to look this way? I do not have a waist. I think if I could be about eight inches taller I'd be fine. Then all of the fat would stretch out.

The school nurse said not to eat bread and potatoes for a while. She measured and weighed us yesterday. I am four feet, eight inches tall and weigh 142 pounds. At least I'm not like my friends Carol and Nancy. Carol weighs 175 and Nancy weighs 190. What does that nurse know anyway? I have starved myself, and still nothing happened.

Dear Diary,

I wish I were Susan. She is so pretty and her clothes are all so *little*. I'll bet my Mom hates me. She had to drive thirty miles to Sioux Falls to buy me some "Chubby Size" dresses. I take a 14½. It wouldn't be so bad, but the dresses are so ugly and old looking. At least I'm not like Nancy. She takes a 16½. Her mother must really hate her. My dress was $26, and the bigger they are the more expensive they are. All the kids in Susan's gang are so skinny, too. All of my friends are fat like me. Someday I'll be skinny. By the way, I started another diet today.

Dear Diary,

Tonight at the school dance the kids started to call me the "vitamin pill." At least that's not as bad as "the ugly dumpling." I'll never go to a school dance again. I was so insulted that I cried. I might go see a doctor without my Mom knowing about it. But how would I pay?

Dear Diary,

I've started a new hobby after school. I'm reading all the books I can. I love Nancy Drew, but my favorite is Trixie Belden. Trixie is just who I want to be. She's pretty and skinny, but she is nice. If I read after school, then I do not have to go out with the rest of the kids and play games.

Dear Diary,

It's Saturday night and I'm up at my Uncle Ben's. I've been coming up here every weekend since that dance. I've decided the kids aren't worth it. I'd rather be around Uncle Ben, Aunt Ann, and Aunt Jenny. Aunt Jenny is crippled, and I like to help take care of her. She likes it when I put puzzles together with her. She couldn't care less about how fat I am.

Dear Diary,

I don't know if you feel this way, but every time I go out I feel like everyone is saying something about me or looking at me and laughing. I don't know why I can't be accepted for myself rather than the way I look. That's what we talked about in history class today. I really like my teacher. I really cannot understand why people don't like me. I can't help it if I'm fat. The boys can't stand me. They don't like other girls either, but they hate me. The skinny girls won't talk to me. At least I've got Carol and Nancy, Patti and Peg. They are all fat and they like me. I think I am a little better than they are. I'm a little thinner than all of them. They make me feel smaller since they are so big. That is a good feeling. I'll never be mean to any of them the way Susan is to me, though.

• • •

These are a few excerpts from my diary of how I felt when I was twelve. I only described enough incidents to explain how I looked physically and how I felt emotionally, socially, and mentally. I had a problem and it was starting to affect me. My self-concept was suffering.

Socially I was withdrawing to avoid more threats to my self-concept. I still had a partially positive self-concept, reinforced by my position in my group. My aunts and uncle helped my self-image too. I needed to prove my worth to my parents, but I felt I could not because of my appearance. My mother could not be proud of me as she was of my sister. My sister was in many activities and was very pretty.

Emotionally I felt very inferior because I considered myself unattractive. I strove to maintain as much of a positive self-concept as possible by avoiding further detrimental comments.

Intellectually I gained. This was possible because of the hobby I acquired. I did read. I read everything I could and began to identify with many different characters and visualize many different concepts about many things. I found reward in this area. I achieved scholastically, which helped to reinforce my positive self-esteem.

A little more explanation of my self-image, I feel, is necessary because the reader will notice a relationship between my self-concept at the age of twelve and my perception of myself now.

I was very close to the point of actually hating myself. I disliked my body and was very concerned about it. I feel now that my appearance was just a phase that happened about the time of puberty, so-called adolescent fat that some girls acquire. The emphasis that was placed upon it by the other boys and girls, however, had a deep and lasting effect. The other boys and girls helped to make me feel very "low on the totem pole." I was not as "good" simply because I was fat.

By the age of sixteen, I had a completely changed physical appearance, however. My body had filled out differently. I finally had a waist. But my self-concept had not changed. I still felt ugly and I never tried to change that idea. I never went places where other people were—especially those my own age. I never wanted to hear those names like "Fats," "Tubby," "Skinny," or "Fatso" again. In order not to hear them, I avoided people. I usually stayed with my friends who were just like me. I felt secure and safe there.

To this day, I still have some lasting effects. When I see a pretty girl, I feel very inferior. I very seldom make friends easily with attractive girls. I like to be around unattractive girls, especially ones who are overweight. Then I feel secure and sure of myself, just as I did when I was with the girls in my gang. I am able to have that feeling that I am a little better than they are.

Gradually I have been changing this concept of myself. I have a tiny-featured body, but at times I feel bigger than my husband and bigger than many people who are much bigger than I. I am constantly comparing myself with other people. I compare my legs to theirs, my hips with theirs, and my weight to theirs.

I still dislike the insults directed toward overweight people. I still get that dull pain in the pit of my stomach. I still do not feel as though I brought happiness to my parents. I needed to show my worth when I was twelve, but I did not. I cannot do it now.

I still have my hobby of reading and, believe it or not, I still think of the heroine Trixie Belden. She was an idol I identified with, and I think I still try to identify with her characteristics. Intellectually, I think that all of the reading that I did at that time still guides much of my learning. I read many things and they extended my background. I still know how to entertain myself in my leisure time, which some people cannot do. I did, however, neglect learning many social habits. Most of all, I sympathize with anyone who is overweight.

A mother's thoughts

Dear Son,

In a few minutes you will be coming home from your last day in sixth grade. Next month you will be twelve years old and ready to begin junior high school. Do you find it as difficult to believe as I do that you are now half way through your public school days?

You and your bedroom—what bridges from the past to the future you both are! Each is anchored in yesteryear and reaches for a destination planned for, yet not clearly visible. Your bedroom has a firm foundation—sturdy steel beams in the basement, a sturdy floor, rising walls, two sparkling windows, and a brightly lit ceiling. Within it are your treasures, your delights, your fears, and your aspirations.

Yes, you are very much like your bedroom. Dad and I have supplied the foundation by giving you life, guiding, loving, and nourishing you so that you are becoming more firm. Together, we have all laid the sturdy floor. A few boards were difficult to nail down, but most seemed to fit easily into place when we all worked together.

Your eyes are your windows—clear, revealing, allowing the light of knowledge to enter, and occasionally needing the sprinkle of tears to be blotted away.

Your body, "growing into your legs," rises as do your bedroom walls. And what a bright light your mind is—perhaps not brilliant, but certainly illuminating your world and ours.

Your room has changed as you have. Where your crib used to be, there is now a full sized bed. Remember how hard you tried to stretch out to reach from one end to the other? I'm glad you reach out, son, and are eager to be a man.

Your closet no longer contains snowsuits and diapers. Instead, I see your Boy Scout and Little League uniforms. Next to them is your old yellow slicker and rain hat. I remember the day I said you looked like a little yellow duckling and off you went, quacking, to kindergarten. Beside that I see a pair of bell bottoms, just like your older brother's. In many ways he has become more of a model for you than Dad. Also on the floor are the socks I told you three times to pick up!

Your rocking horse has been replaced by a drum set. With the former I worried for your safety; with the latter, I'm concerned for *my* sanity. Your record collection, here, is a "now" thing, but I think your interest in music will last. How proud I was of you at your band concert, your head barely visible above the others, but your "flam taps" coming through loud and clear.

Your bookcase and desk reflect your whole life. Your very first books are there, including several well-worn ones by Dr. Seuss. How you loved to "read" before you started to school! You have always been a great one for classifying things. Here is your third grade bird scrapbook, and, next to it, a notebook you kept on states and birds you counted when we went to California four years ago. Baseball cards, again classified by league and position, will soon need a larger box. Beside the books on baseball are a few mysteries you enjoyed. I think you must have every "Happy Hollister" book ever written. You quickly outgrew these and room was made for history books and encyclopedias. Do you still want to be an historian? With your love of searching for answers, I know you'd be a good one. Maybe your reluctance to part with things from the past reflects your love of history?

On the edge of the unmade bed is your newspaper bag. I never thought anything would get you up that early! I had reservations about your taking a paper route but I recognize your need to earn some money on your own besides what you earn mowing the lawn for Dad.

On the wall, almost as good as new, is the .410 you got for Christmas. Again, I think this was your brother's influence. Your compassion for animals and love of nature prevent you from enjoying hunting. Grandma was so pleased when I told her how you had rescued a bird from the creek and had used the first aid methods you learned in school. You checked its breathing, looked for broken bones or bleeding—but how do you give a bird artificial respiration?

Life will always be interesting and challenging to you. You make learning relevant by applying what you have learned to everyday situations. Remember using fractions to make fudge the other night?

You have also learned early in life that you can't excel in everything. Track was a disappointment to you. Because of your size, you weren't able to keep up to the larger boys. So, you competed with yourself and were pleased when each day you were able to run a few seconds faster than you could the day before.

Size is only one thing you've had to compensate for. Being left-handed has never seemed to be a drawback because you haven't allowed it to be. You seem to take pride in the accomplishments of other left-handers. Playing the drums was more difficult because the major parts are written for the right hand. But look how that has helped in baseball. You're a switch hitter. You've said you're not a big hitter, but the team can always count on you to steal when you do get on base. This is perhaps the greatest thing I admire about you. You recognize your limitations and your capabilities. You are always able to rechannel your efforts and to think positively.

Some children find it a disadvantage in school if their parents are teachers. You have not yet reached the point where you are embarrassed or ashamed of them, as some are. You love to learn, and you dislike a situation where no learning takes place. You prefer a strict teacher with high standards. Remember how proud you were that you could spell so well when you were in first grade? We used to take long walks and you'd spell any word I'd give you. I'm proud of your scholastic record and the fact that you can appreciate learning for its own sake. You have always been so highly self-motivated that we never had to prod you.

Being a younger child can also present problems, but you seem to have taken it in stride. You are naturally envious because your brother is bigger and can do more things than you can. The other day I saw you trying on his old sixth grade gym suit to see if you are as big as he was. You seemed quite disappointed that the suit was too large. But we talked this over, and I think you understand now that all children don't grow at the same rate. You laugh now and seem so disgusted over the fact that he has a girl friend. I hope you will be able to laugh about it when you get to be his age and become interested in girls.

As I turn to leave your room, the last thing I see is the bureau with pictures of your best friends on it. They have become quite an influence on your life and I'm pleased to see you've made wise choices. I would put some things away but I know you have a "private drawer," and I wouldn't destroy the trust you have placed in me.

I hear the school bus coming, so I'll close the door. It's almost like closing the door to elementary school and waiting to see what awaits as it again opens—this time to junior high school, puberty, and, sadly, probably a very, very different boy.

A profile in wonderment

Mona was born with a spinal defect and underwent corrective surgery when she was six months old. The surgery was termed successful, and the attending neurosurgeons stated that the likelihood of adverse effects was remote, but always a possibility. As Mona grew and developed, her motor coordination was poor, but otherwise she developed in much the same way as our two older daughters. She had more than her share of cuts and bruises caused by her stumbling and falling. Nevertheless, she took most adversities in stride and was cheerful and happy. Her most frustrating moments came when she was learning to dress herself. She could never get her shoes on the correct feet,

nor did her clothes go on the right way. But Mona decided that life was too enjoyable to worry about trivialities, so most of the time she was satisfied to dress only to meet the minimum rules of propriety.

Mona's physical growth was in accordance with "standard norms," although over the years she has never lost her "baby fat"; currently she is somewhat overweight. She is now twelve years old and in seventh grade. Her poor motor coordination has always been a hindrance to learning some physical skills. Mona can skate, swim, and ride a bicycle, but she lacks the dexterity to fully master skills such as jumping rope, playing team sports, and gymnastics. Because of skill deficiencies and a lack of aggressiveness, she often found herself not included in many playground activities. I have always been grateful for one of her teachers who insisted that every child participate in all play activities, regardless of proficiency.

Because of physical inadequacies, Mona has directed her leisure time to listening to her favorite recordings, reading, imaginative play, bike riding, skating, swimming, and watching television. Most study activities proved less difficult for Mona than organizing herself for study. Pencils are never on hand—the dictionary is always in another place—clean paper is not available. Mona was never able to tear a page neatly from a notebook, keep her desk or herself organized in an orderly manner, or keep track of her personal belongings. By the end of each school day, she had usually lost or spilled something or fallen down—sometimes all three activities had occurred. These happenings have not changed from year to year.

Corrective shoes were prescribed for Mona soon after she began to walk. She continued to wear them until no more benefit was derived. As her feet developed, each grew somewhat differently. Currently, her right foot is flat and two sizes larger than the left foot, which has a very high arch. An orthopedist has indicated that surgery should possibly be performed on her left foot after she attains optimum growth. Mona has worn glasses from the time she first entered school; she is markedly near-sighted. She also has a slight hearing loss in each ear, but not to the extent that any corrective device is required.

When Mona was eleven years old, her physical mechanism indicated that she was entering puberty. This by no means meant that her mental and emotional processes were in agreement, for Mona was definitely not ready to put away childish things! However, she took in stride the transformations which were taking place, much as she had previously accepted and tolerated other facts in life. She attempted to carry on as usual despite new body proportions and monthly indispositions. She has become the envy of her two older sisters who have not attained her body proportions, and they stand in amazement that she is not more concerned about becoming a young lady. She very openly and honestly indicates that she likes certain boys, but she is amused at many of her girl friends who proclaim that they are "going steady" even before they are allowed to have dates.

Mona's unpretentious spirit, helpfulness, loving kindness, and genuine concern for her classmates have allowed her a comfortable relationship with boys and girls alike. She will probably never become the high school beauty queen or be elected "most popular," but unless her personality changes drastically, she will be able to accept without disparagement the role which is designated for her. I would not imply that Mona always remains passive or is a mere conformist; she is definitely a nonconformist. She is never regulated by what her peer group is wearing or by what their moralistic values happen to be at the time. She remains staunch in what she believes. If the group is participating in something that she thinks is wrong, she is not swayed. Neither will she tattle on those who are. Fair play is very important to her.

One would surmise that Mona's slow, patient mobility indicates a none too expansive thought process. Yet at times, she amazes one with profound wisdom far beyond her age level. For a fleeting moment, one will see her playing patiently and happily with her younger brother and his friends, tending them and seeing to their needs like an awkward "mother hen." The next moment one may find her reading a book of fiction intended for those far beyond her years.

She enjoys a creative writing hobby as long as she is not required to give heed to penmanship or spelling. (You may enjoy reading some of her writings which I have included at the end of this profile, though greatest appreciation comes only from reading the original manuscript.) She has the patience to write stories for her younger brother to read, and recently she wrote the script for our annual family Christmas play.

Each day I yearn for Mona as she makes her way to meet the challenges of her first year in junior high. I worry about the three flights of steep stairs which must be conquered as crowds of more aggressive children rush down the halls with intentions only of reaching the next classroom in minimum time. Not too many problems await Mona within the classroom, but rather the challenge comes when she changes classes or during lunch periods.

How does one solve an equation like Mona? I wish that I knew! There are too many unknowns which lie deep behind dark, brown eyes and a tousled appearance. One is undecided when to give a helping hand or insist that she stand independently. Mona very seldom asks for or wants help with her school work as such, but I am sure that too often I have answered a telephoned plea of: "Mommy, I left my assignment at home, and I will be in trouble if I don't have it." As recently as last week, Mona lost all of her gym clothes, but I can see some progress in her organizational makeup. She even stops to look in the mirror occasionally when she is getting dressed! Who knows, this untidy young girl with skinned knees and rundown shoes may gain a measure of grace and poise and become a young lady. The wonderment of it all!

SAMPLES OF MONA'S CREATIVE WRITINGS

Note Mona's trouble with "ie" and "ei." She had the "i before e, except after c rule." To her the rule was absolute—she can't remember to make allowances for the exceptions: example, their is always spelled thier.

Age nine:

Spring Springs!

Spring springs with flowers. And with the green grass that springs up. And the little birds spring from thier eggs and sing. When bears spring from thier caves. Butterflys spring from cacoons with thier lovely wings. I love the spring because it springs. "Spring Springs!"

by Mona B.

Age ten:

Morning Flowers

Early in the morning 'bout the break of day. I see the morning flowers reaching up to say. Good morning sun! And when the breezes pass through them. It seems as if they are yawning and a streching for this new bright day. Then they open up thier petals and put on thier dresses of many colors, for a new lovely day.

by Mona B.

Age ten:

The Wind is a Funny Fellow

The wind is a funny fellow. Sometimes he's tall and sometimes he's small. And sometimes he's not even there at all. Sometimes he's nice and sometimes he's mean. Sometimes he's inbetween. He'll romp and play and be so gay. Then sometimes gentle and mild like a child. He's mean and mischeivous, and nice and fearless. He's like a big terrible tiger and then a playful little pup. The wind is a funny fellow!

by Mona B.

Age eleven:

America, as I See It!

America is our country. Our land has beautiful mountain tops and sparkling waters. It has things to be proud of! We have fought and won many a great battle and have had many great men. This is surely something to be proud of. America is a *free* country.

Yet how many of us really think of this? We mostly take these things for granted, but we *shouldn't*. We should be proud and stand up for our country!

Think of how many sorrows we would have, living in a communist or socialist nation. We would not have much happiness, having someone telling you what to do, and having someone higher than yourself.

Another thing which we don't think about much is our own flag. Every day in school you say the "Pledge of the Allegience to the Flag." Do you think of what your saying, or do you say it just to get it over with? Do you *really* mean what you say? What do you think the colors of the flag mean? What I think they mean is this: the red stands for the blood shed in great wars, the blue means the blue skies above and blue seas below, the stars mean each state and our space program. America is a place of beauty, happiness, love, knowledge, and great men. Be proud of your country "America."

Age eleven:

Look Out Upon the Lonely Night

Look out upon a lonely night. What does that darkness hold? See the little points of light up in the sky in the night. They are just stars shinning in the night. See the creepy, scary shape. It is just my front gate. Hear the lonely distant sound. That is just a lonely distant hound. Hear the whistle of that far away train. Hear the roar of that overhead plane. With lonely people aboard, I can see. Look out upon the pitch black night. Who is there and Why? For my answer all I hear is the sigh of the wind passing by. Then before I climb into bed I bow my head and pray "Thank you God that I am home in bed, instead. Instead of in that pitch black night, boundlessly seeking light."

Age twelve:

The Magic of Christmas

Some people say there is magic in Christmas. What is the magic of Christmas? My magic of Christmas is when you go shopping and people rush about while Christmas music is playing and the cashier lady is not quite as cranky today. Or when the whole family decorates the tree and you are not even scolded for breaking a ball and yelling your head off. Or when you get in a lot of trouble for shaking your presents. Or when you present a Christmas play for your family and your little brother trips on his robe and upsets the manger and your dog carries away the doll that was supposed to be Jesus. Or when you go caroling and your hands freeze and the person next to you sings off-key. Or when you ask Santa (ha) for something you want and do not need and you get something you do not want, but do need! Still, all these tiny wrongs add to the one big right that Christmas is, the celebrating of the birth of the Christ child. That's what really makes the magic of Christmas real.

No girls for David

David was in sixth grade. He was very good in sports, well liked, a good student, and involved in his first romance. Of course, like most boys this age, he didn't like girls. But this one particular girl? That was different. He could like her, and everyone knew it, but he wouldn't dare admit it. His Christmas gift to her was hidden in his locker until the time came when he could slip it into her desk so that no one would notice.

Naturally, this romance ran its course and evaporated for some reason, but within two months a strange transformation occurred in David. He got so that he couldn't stand the sight, sound, touch, or thought of anything to do with girls. He would wipe off his desk if a girl would happen to sit in it, and he would practically want to give up basketball if a girl would want to play with him. When we would talk about problems with blacks and other races, he would agree that we shouldn't be prejudiced for superficial reasons, but being a girl was not in the same category. To him, being a girl was an unpardonable sin!

This situation caused several unhappy moments for both David and the girls in my class. Only a few months earlier the girls had been able to talk to him, tease him, and enjoy being friends with him. But all of a sudden he no longer wanted to have anything to do with them. At times he would talk to them and be fairly pleasant, but usually he ignored them or complained about them. In fact, he developed a prejudice against Italians because the girl sitting next to him was an Italian.

I believe that David is presently going through a normal stage of development that most boys go through. At this stage, boys are trying to show everyone that they are grown up, that they have developed into men, not just boys. To do this, they turn away from girls and

anything connected with femininity. To like flowers, for example, would question the fact that they were as grown up as John Wayne or Hank Aaron. But in David's case, he went beyond the point most boys do in rejecting the feminine world.

There are two major reasons why I feel that David went to the extreme point that he did. The first was his best friend, Glenn. The two of them had much in common and were together much of the time. Since both boys seemed to have started into this state of disliking girls at about the same time, they influenced each other greatly. It was something like a contest between them to see who was the most grown up; that is, who disliked girls the most. If one did or said something against girls, the other had to outdo him. The second influence is the fact that neither boy has a father living at home. Because of this they are subjected to more of a female-dominated world than most are, so when they began this rebellion they rebelled that much harder. Their reaction was intensified by their situation. Also, since they both had no father to identify with, they seemed to identify with each other's facade of grownup adult men, trying that much harder to conform to their image of a man. David was just the more aggressive and outspoken of the two, the one who reacted more severely. I feel that there is no real problem here. It is a normal reaction and, although this is more intensified than usual, he will grow out of it in an average way.

THINGS TO THINK ABOUT AND DO

1. Do you agree or disagree with the paragraphs that state that preadolescent children of today are different from what they were a decade ago? Are they any different from you and your peers at that age?

2. Visit an elementary school or middle school playground. Watch the children at their games. Do you notice any difference in the behavior, games, and talking of the older and younger children? Perhaps you could do a short survey or poll to learn something about their interests or preferences of today.

3. How grown up is a twelve-year-old of today? Are they as grown up or more grown up than you were at that age?

4. Talk to several teachers of nine- to twelve-year-olds. How do they see their traits and characteristics? What do they say about the desire for learning that their pupils have?

5. Invite some eleven- and twelve-year-olds to your class and carry on an interview or discussion about their ideas and activities.

6. Children of this age have a great interest in prehistoric animals, monsters, and ghosts. Why do you suppose this is so? Are they superstitious? Do they talk about haunted houses, being scared in the dark, and of evil forces?

7. The humor of eleven- to thirteen-year-olds is often harsh, brutal, and sometimes even sick. Do you agree with this statement? Why do you think this is so?

8. Do a study to determine what kind of stories or books preadolescents like to read. Do you find stories similar to Jack Armstrong, the All-American boy, the Hardy Boys, or the Ruth Fielding series? How do adventure stories hold up?

9. Talk to some adults over the age of forty-five or fifty and ask them to reminisce about their childhood. What age level do they mostly talk about: preschool, ages six to nine, preadolescence, or adolescence?

10. Would you mind being ten, eleven, or twelve years old again? Why or why not? If you were that age again, knowing what you know now, what changes would you make in your life?

READING SOURCES
Developmental psychology texts

Bernard, H.W.: Human development in western culture, Boston, 1975, Allyn & Bacon, Inc., chap 10.

CRM: Developmental psychology today, ed. 2, New York, 1975, CRM/Random House, Inc., chap. 16.

Kaluger, G., and Kaluger, M.: Human development: the span of life, St. Louis, 1974, The C. V. Mosby Co., chap. 8.

Mussen, P.H., Conger, J.J., and Kagan, J.: Child development and personality, ed. 4, New York, 1975, Harper & Row, Publishers, chaps. 12, 13.

Stone, L.J., and Church, J.: Childhood and adolescence: a psychology of the growing person, ed. 3, New York, 1975, Random House, Inc., chap. 8.

Related readings

Berlyne, D.E.: Children's reasoning and thinking. In Mussen, P.H., editor: Carmichael's manual of child psychology, ed. 3, New York, 1970, John Wiley & Sons, Inc., pp. 939-981.

Emans, R.: What do children in the inner city like to read? Elem. School J. 69:118-122, 1968.

Gesell, A., Ilg, F.L., and Ames, L.B.: Youth: the years from ten to sixteen, New York, 1956, Harper & Row, Publishers.

Keasey, C.B.: Social participation as a factor in the moral development of preadolescents, Dev. Psychol. 5:216-220, 1971.

Liebert, R.M., and Baron, R.A.: Some immediate effects of televised violence on children's behavior, Dev. Psychol. 6:469-475, 1972.

Maw, W.H., and Mageon, A.J.: The curiosity dimension of fifth-grade children: a factorial discriminant analysis, Child Dev. 42:2023-2031, 1971.

McGhee, P.E.: Development of the humor response: a review of the literature, Psychol. Bull. 76:328-348, 1971.

Mussen, P.H., Rutherford, E., Harris, S., and Keasey, C.B.: Honesty and altruism among preadolescents, Dev. Psychol. 3:169-194, 1970.

Nelson, M.O.: The concept of God and feelings toward parents, J. Indiv. Psychol. 27:46-49, 1971.

Reese, H.W.: Attitudes toward the opposite sex in late childhood, Merrill-Palmer Quart. 14(4):157-163, 1966.

Part three

THE ADOLESCENT YEARS

CHAPTER 6

The transitional world of early adolescence

Of all the age levels the years of early adolescence surely must be the most complex and trying for the youngster involved. Just to recognize the physical and emotional changes that take place within an individual in a relatively few short years is enough to cause one to wonder how anybody could pass through these years quietly, unobtrusively, and without turmoil. The signs are all misleading. The appearance of adult-like features and a developing interest in the opposite sex are not enough to indicate maturity or capability of dealing with the world of grownups. The nine- to eleven-year-old is more stable than is the twelve- to fourteen-year-old simply because the younger child has reached a high level of competency of dealing with the childhood world. The early adolescent has to learn a completely new repertoire of communication skills, social skills, and adjustive skills, in addition to recognizing and accepting an entirely new concept of self.

For many children the first overt sign of entering early adolescence is entrance to a junior high school. "A Giant Step" describes one girl's experience on such a day. Since self-concept and identity are so nebulous at this age, it is interesting to read how a mother views her daughter, how the mother thinks the daughter views herself, and, finally, how the daughter says she sees herself; all this is in "Three Views of Kim." A pathetic situation, but not as uncommon as one might think, is presented in "On Experiencing Puberty."

The junior high school years are years of fads and the extreme in fashions. A nostalgic look at fads of the "nifty fifties" is presented in "Fads Come—and Fads Go." What is interesting is that many of the junior high students of the fifties now have children of their own in junior high! The loyalty and intenseness of the junior high youngster are vividly portrayed in an even older flashback in "A Papertrooper in WW II" (World War II). What is fascinating to observe is

that the time, place, circumstances, and clothing styles may differ but the characteristics of the age level remain the same.

Problems of this age level are usually intense because emotional stress cannot be kept under control. Emotions appear to vacillate and to bound to extremes. "Growing Up—Too Fast" combines rapid physical growth with very sad home and family conditions to produce a child "beyond her years." The drug culture, as one teacher indicates in "You Can Get Anything You Want," was totally unexpected on the junior high school level. Now it is known that drug usage knows no age limits. Another serious situation occurs when the parent of a young teenager dies. Difficulty in expressing feelings at such a time is indicated in "A Sad Christmas." Note how vividly the writer can now tell about that period in his life. Not being able to identify the seriousness of a teenager's problems and not being able to relate to the youth and his or her needs may have tragic consequences, as revealed in "What Can You Do?"

A giant step

When you're twelve years old and filled with a desire to learn all there is to learn, entrance to junior high school can be an exciting experience. My daughter, Sandy, is just such a person. Twelve is a marvelous age of mixed fantasy and reality, an emerging sense of responsibility, physical development, and mental curiosity. It's a roller-coaster ride, a cuddle-up spin, and a dodgem-bump from waking hour to bedtime! Sometimes one would think the mind, at this age, was a vacuum cleaner trying to sweep all the knowledge of the universe into its possession.

Early morning sunshine shimmered through the soft pink curtains and mixed with the reflections from the subtle pink carpet to give the bedroom and its occupant a rosy glow of youthful femininity. Sunbeams danced happily and played with an assortment of dolls, stuffed toys, and treasured odds and ends gathered during the lazy summer months. They seemed to follow Sandy as she headed for the bathroom to begin a now-established morning ritual. The day was not routine, however, since it was to be her first day of classes in junior high school.

"Morning at last!" she thought. "I was beginning to believe it would never come. I don't know why, but I just couldn't seem to sleep last night. Time seemed to move about as fast as a lazy turtle: I had so much time to think! I wonder if school will be like I thought?"

It seemed forever until the family was up and ready for breakfast. "I don't want any breakfast," Sandy said, expecting a quick reproach from Mother for such a suggestion.

"O.K., but be sure to eat lunch," was the surprising reply.

Finally, it was time to leave for the bus. The ringing of the door chimes from the front door was followed almost immediately by a less impressive single "bong" from the doorbell at the back door. Instantly the house was filled with the jubilant chatter of eager young girls.

"Who didya get for homeroom?"

"You look cool!"

"We have history together!"

As the girls drifted out the front door and up the walk, the chatter continued until it became just a murmur to Mother, who remained in the doorway, watching her daughter go off to school. The house had lost its vitality, giving way to an all-consuming world of education.

"Here comes the bus," Sandy called out, as the happy, yellow mammoth bounced its way toward the group of noisy children. She wondered: "Who will be on it? What if they don't remember me? After all, I've been gone all summer to be with my grandmother. By now they're probably all settled with new friends and with kids they will be having classes with." A funny feeling gripped her. More than anything she wanted to be one of the crowd.

"Hi, Sandy!" a friendly voice reassured her. It was Bonnie. Now she knew that once again she was part of the group. Happily she settled into her seat and added her voice to the tumult that filled the joyful bus.

As the bus labored up the hill toward the junior high school, a different feeling took command of her senses. It was that feeling of uncertainty that comes with an approach to something unknown. What was it like inside that big building? She wondered if she would be able to meet the challenges and responsibilities of junior high. After all, she'd only been in an elementary school. A desire to flee came over her. But where could she go? No, now was the time to face it.

There she stood, face to face with the building that would be her home away from home for the next nine months. Standing at the door, she felt all alone. Remembering an earlier visit to the school with Dad, it had not been this way. At that time, everything seemed friendly and comfortable. Hadn't they joked and laughed as they walked the maze of halls joining newly carpeted classrooms? The halls that rang with voices of anxious, happy children then were now menacing to a frightened, sensitive girl.

As she stepped inside, a new reassurance gave her courage. There to greet new students were a teacher and a member of the student council.

"What's your name?"

"Sandy," was the timid reply.

"Sandy, all students are to report to the gym. In a while your homeroom teacher will come and take you to your room. Do you know who your homeroom teacher is?"

"Yes."

The gym was bursting with activity. Hundreds of children were bouncing around, meeting old friends, making new ones, and trying to make their voices heard over the crowd. In a moment Sandy was engulfed by the excitement of this new experience. However, being shy and unfamiliar with the surroundings and the people, she limited herself to a vicarious type of participation. Soon it was time to be taken to her homeroom.

Junior high school began with a disappointment. The room to which she was assigned was by far the worst-looking room in the school. The tile showed the years of wear that had prompted the laying of carpet in the other rooms. Old, wooden chair-arm desks stood in five neat rows, beginning at the back wall and encroaching on the area occupied by the teacher's desk. Surrounding them were pale green walls lighted by sturdy ancestors of the fluorescent tubes. Even the sun seemed unable or unwilling to enter the room through the windows that resembled heavy-lidded eyes. All in all, it was a dismal letdown for one enthusiastic youngster!

The next few hours were long but busy ones. An endless supply of cards passed onto Sandy's desk requiring many repetitions of her name, address, and phone number, making her restless and unable to grasp the full meaning of what was going on. After all, hadn't she come here to learn? Well, why doesn't it start?

Just when things seemed to be getting more than she could bear, the bell rang to signal the passing to another room. With her guide book in hand and her schedule inside, Sandy moved off to seek her next station. How nice it was to leave that dismal room! She felt lifted. However, her new feeling of ease was soon erased by a new emotion—frustration.

"Where is that dumb room?" she asked herself. "These stupid numbers are so hard to follow. I'll be late for class on the very first day."

Quickly she glanced from room to room as she moved rapidly down the hall. The bell rang again, and the halls were almost cleared of people. A few pupils in the same predicament as she was hastened through the halls, frantic in their effort to find their place. A feeling of futility enveloped her and a tear began to form at the corner of her eye. She wished that someone, anyone, would help her.

"Hello, can I help you?" a voice asked, almost as if in response to her mental pleas. It was the voice of one of the teachers. Unable to reply, Sandy handed him her schedule and guidebook. Her goal wasn't far away, and the teacher assured her that there was no penalty for being late on the first day; in fact, he assured her, people get lost for the first three or four weeks. It was comforting, but walking into class late was not a very acceptable idea to a sensitive young girl.

The rest of the day passed without incident. No classes were held. Instead, it was a time to get to know the teacher and to find out what the expectations were for students in the classes.

Sandy began to feel more a part of the gang as she joined her friends on the way home. Now the bus was even more active with excitement than it had been in the morning. It was fun to analyze the teachers and the school, tell stories of the day's adventures, and share the glee of others' adventures or misadventures. Joy reigned.

It was a busy evening for Sandy. The girls in the neighborhood had to compare notes. Each time a new thought came to mind they would rush to one house or the other and share their information. During the brief intermissions, the telephone was used to communicate the latest scoop to distant friends. Even the dinner table reverberated with enthusiastic stories of that first day!

Finally, it was a tired twelve-year-old who crawled into bed. Physically, emotionally, and mentally, she was drained. As I looked in on her, she wore a smile of contentment. She was still one of the gang, she was settled in her schedule, she had an idea of what was ahead, and she was eager to see where the school year would lead. "Goodnight, young lady. It *was* a big step, wasn't it?"

Three views of Kim
HOW KIM'S MOTHER THINKS
KIM SEES HERSELF

My name is Kim and I'm thirteen years old. I'll try to describe myself and tell what I like and what I don't like. It will be hard to do, but I'll also try to explain how I feel about things. I guess I should tell something about my family, too.

I'll start with my family. I live in a red brick ranch house with my mother and grandmother. My dad died when I was only five years old. I remember him, and I still miss him. Sometimes I cry when I'm lonely for him but Mom doesn't know that. Mom says he was sick and died. I don't ask her about it much. I don't think she likes to talk about it.

We have a small family, even if you count my dog and cat. We had seven gerbils at one time. I'm glad I have lots of aunts and uncles and cousins. I wish my mother would get married again. I'd like to have a father. Mostly I want brothers and sisters.

I think I'm kind of homely. One time I asked Mother to look at me but not as a mother. When I asked if she didn't think I was ugly, she smiled and said I'm cute. She just wanted to make me feel good.

I'm about four feet, ten inches tall and my brown hair is long and straight. My eyes are blue, but I wish they were brown. I have to wear braces and I need to wear glasses.

For my birthday Mom let me get contacts. I was surprised because it wasn't even time for my glasses to be changed! But I lost the contacts one time. Mom sure was upset but so was I. We got them replaced. Last week I lost my right lens. I sure hated to tell Mom about losing it. Mom didn't fuss much, but she says I have to call the eye doctor and pay for the replacement myself. I didn't call yet. I'm embarrassed to have the doctor know.

I'm kind of thin, but I'm proud that finally I'm starting to get a figure. I like to wear real short shorts and skirts and tight tops. Mom makes me change when we go anyplace. She doesn't understand.

I wish I'd start my periods. All my friends started a year ago. I feel like a little kid.

There are lots of things I like. I really like boys. I think about them more than Mom knows. Alan liked me for a long time. I felt great about that. Lots of girls like Alan, but he liked me best. Sometimes he'd call me on the phone. Then one day he started liking another girl. I don't know why. I pretend I can't stand him. Really I still like him. Mom says it's okay for me to like boys, but she won't even consider letting me date until I'm sixteen. I think that's really dumb. She keeps telling me she understands how I feel about boys and things, but I know she really doesn't! Sometimes I wish my mother were young like our neighbor. She's twenty-five and seems just like me.

I like to mess around in the kitchen. I make real good brownies. But I don't like to clean up afterward. In fact I don't like to do *any* work anymore. I always feel tired if I have to clean

my room. It's funny, but I'm not tired when I ride bikes!

Mom says I should be an actress because I can show lots of emotion. She's only kidding, but I really do fool her sometimes. I can cry or get insulted or be mad if I just *want* to. Sometimes people do what I want when I act a certain way.

I really would like to be an actress. I'd like to have lots of people looking at me. That's another funny thing. Sometimes I think people are staring at me at the pool and places like that. I don't like that at all. Mom says they really aren't staring. She thinks I have an overactive imagination. There's a lot she doesn't understand about me.

I like school. Mostly I get good grades but I'm not so good in math. I don't like math. It never makes sense to me.

Thirteen is a good age to be because I'm allowed to babysit. I have lots of regular customers. They all tell Mom how dependable I am. I really like little kids. I like being thirteen because I'm a teenager, but I can't do things some teenagers do. I wish I could go to see rock groups when they come to town. I can't get Mom to change her mind. Being thirteen is strange in a way. I'm not a little kid anymore so I can't do some things I'd really like to do. I'd feel silly. And there are things I'm not old enough to do. I think it will be neat to be grown up and be my own boss.

I like men, I guess, like the fathers of my friends. But I never know how to act around them. I'm a little afraid of them. I'm not sure when they are kidding or when they're serious.

Since it's summer, I can usually stay up until I want to go to bed. That's something I really like. Once in a while Mom and Grandma go to bed before me. When that happens, I pretend I am the grownup in the house. I fix myself tea and drink it as I watch TV. Mom gets up long before I do because she goes to work.

I like to wear eye makeup like my friends. Mom lets me wear it around the house and when I play, but she won't let me wear it away from home. She doesn't understand that all the kids are allowed. I bet she won't let me wear makeup because she never wears it. I don't think that's fair. She keeps telling me if she wanted a seventeen-year-old she'd adopt one. I think that's a dumb thing to say!

I take piano lessons. I don't like to practice my lessons very much, but I do like to play songs for people. I'm pretty good. I like to read, ride bikes, listen to tapes, talk on the phone, swim, watch TV, go on trips, and have family reunions. I eat all the time. I laugh every time Mom says my stomach is a bottomless pit.

There are things I don't like. I get mad if I have to come in at night when other kids are still out. I tell my mother she isn't fair, and I go in my room by myself to show her! But usually I come out before long. I don't want Mom to know this, but I am glad she makes me do some things when I say I don't want to do them. I act grumpy to fool her.

I don't like to be lectured because Mom lectures too long. She keeps talking even after she makes her point. You'd think she'd know I'm not a little kid.

I forgot something I really like to do. I like to have friends sleep at my house, and I like to sleep at their houses. I feel popular if I get invited to slumber parties. For my thirteenth birthday, I had twelve friends spend the night with me. Mom tells everyone we went through food like a cloud of locusts!

I'm happy when people talk to me like a grownup. When they do, I can tell them how I feel about drugs, the Middle East, and the death penalty. Lots of people think kids my age don't have opinions about serious problems.

That's about all I can tell you about myself. I hope it helps you to know me.

This, then, is how I believe my daughter sees herself and would express her feelings.

I recognize that many of Kim's ideas refer to me. That's natural, considering our situation. While I'm neither overly protective nor overly permissive, her behavior and attitudes are considerably attuned to my approval and disapproval.

From the readings I've been doing I realize Kim is, for the most part, a "typical" thirteen-year-old. She has always been a child to push for limits, but never to the extent she does now! Her thoughts are very much preoccupied with boys and being grown up.

I'm sure Kim feels I don't understand her, but she does talk things over with me.

KIM WRITES ABOUT KIM

Dear Dr. Kaluger,

I'm thirteen years old and my name is Kim. I am five feet tall and weigh eighty-three pounds. I have blue eyes and light brown hair. I have contacts and braces.

I like boys. I also like to travel. Traveling around the U.S. is lots of fun. I also like all winter sports and swimming in the summer. I really like listening to my 8 track tapes (especially 3 Dog Night). I like to sketch houses, too.

But I absolutely *hate* to clean my room. My Mom bugs me about it a lot. I don't blame her though; it *is* a wreck! I also hate to go to the dentist. I haven't liked it since I was a little kid. I hate to get nagged!

There's not a whole lot that I'm good at. I'm pretty good at babysitting, though (that's coz' I love little kids). I've been taking piano lessons for four years, so I'm getting good at that.

What I most need to improve in is math and history. It seems to go in one ear and out the other. I need to improve in handwriting (guess you can tell). I also put a lot of things off till the last minute. I guess everyone needs a little improvement in personality. No one is completely perfect.

There are so many things I would like to do. So many I couldn't put them all down on paper. For one, I'd like to come to one of *your* classes and see what they're like. My Mom talks about them a lot. She says you make them so interesting. I'd like to attend one of your classes. I'd also like to go somewhere this summer. With my Mom going to school every day, we can't go anywhere this summer. I would also like to be sixteen, then I could drive and date. Boy, I can hardly wait! But I guess my wildest dream is to become an actress in Broadway plays. I'd like to have a southern accent (my neighbor does). Well, that's about it.

Kim

KIM AS HER MOTHER SEES HER

Kim is a peppy, cute thirteen-year-old girl. She's about four feet, ten inches tall and weighs about eighty pounds. Kim's brown hair is long and straight. She looks nicest when she wears it in two ponytails. Kim has big blue eyes. She is wearing braces now and they are really helping to straighten her teeth.

There are so many things Kim likes that I can only put part of them in a list. The list has no particular order of preference! Kim likes babysitting, listening to stereo tapes, swimming, boys, riding bikes, and talking on the phone. She also likes baking "goodies," slumber parties, pets, taking trips, reading, telling jokes, shopping, talking to grownups, eating, having her picture taken, and getting mail.

Among the things that Kim doesn't like are: being told what to do, being lectured, cleaning her room, going to bed early, practicing piano, doing homework, and having people stare at her.

Kim is very good in many activities. She is a good piano player and a very good babysitter. She has talent in drawing, singing, and writing creative stories and poems. She will be a good actress for school plays. Kim is very good in her school work. Two of Kim's strongest traits are reliability and honesty.

Like everyone, Kim has areas that need improvement. She needs to develop patience and better math skills. She needs to be a more willing worker. Kim should wear the headgear for her braces more hours each day.

I believe Kim would like: to have brothers and sisters, to learn to sew, to be popular, to have a great figure, to wear makeup, to be grown up, and to be an actress or a teacher.

On experiencing puberty

The onset of puberty can have various effects on the adolescent, ranging from fear to elation. This paper is an attempt to relate the feelings that I had when experiencing puberty about ten years ago.

When I was in the third grade I heard some other girls talking about menstruation and had no idea what they were talking about. Since they wouldn't tell me about it, I asked my mother. She gave me a basic description, but I felt it was very incomplete; in turn I felt some fear because I really didn't understand what was going to happen to me or why.

The health nurse explained menstruation to us when we were fifth graders. I grasped the intellectual part but was concerned about the other factors. Would I really change inside? Would my feelings and actions be strange to me? Would it mean I was an adult? Did it really mean I could have a baby?

My mother found it difficult to talk to me about these things, so I didn't bother her. I kept everything inside of me except for some discussions with classmates which usually resulted in misinformation.

The big question was: "When will I start?" Most of my classmates had already reached puberty by the eighth grade, but so far I had not. I really wondered if my body was normal. Any questions I asked my mother got the response that really I was lucky because menstruation was like a "plague" and the longer I went without it the luckier I was! As a result, I really wondered whether I wanted to grow up.

Childhood seemed like a good place to stay. I had few responsibilities and could do just about what I wanted. But growing up was appealing, too. Someday I could date, there were school activities, and there was freedom to make decisions. Yes, I thought I would like to grow up.

During the eighth grade I became involved in the political campaign for our mock elections. We worked diligently to win. It was while I was giving a speech for my candidate that menstruation began. The upset stomach and nervousness I had felt were attributed to the campaign and not to puberty. I had completely forgotten about it. In fact, I thought I had sat in Coke or something; it just never dawned on me what was happening. Truthfully, I guess I had a defense mechanism built up because of fear.

The following morning I realized what had happened and called to my mother to come to the bathroom. Her reply was: "I don't have time. What do you want?" Since I had two brothers, I could not yell downstairs to tell her;

after some bickering she finally came to see what was the trouble.

Mom's reaction was that it was just another pain for her. In her defense, let me say she was pregnant and was also suffering from arthritis. Even though I knew she felt bad, I could not really forgive her reactions to me. I needed help, but she didn't have the time. I felt totally rejected, unwanted, and unloved. I suppose I really felt a hate for her—hate, yet love, mixed with a plea for acceptance and understanding.

I wanted to escape, to find someone who would want to help me: my parents never had time. Since I couldn't leave, I had to divert the energies. I put all I had into school work and graduated at the top of my class. Negatively, I became easily upset and intolerant of others; I became a perfectionist. The pattern has stayed with me to a certain degree, but I now have control over it. It is a horrible experience to verbally lash someone, know you are doing it, and yet have no control to stop.

The things I experienced at puberty have had long-lasting effects. I feel I have the battle partially won because I see these things and can try to overcome them. By understanding the cause and effect of the above, I have greater human understanding. I sincerely hope I can do better with my daughter if I am fortunate enough to have one.

Fads come—and fads go

Each year finds junior high school students strongly influenced by new fads. Fads that change the most frequently are those associated with clothing styles. I would like to recall some of the fads that were followed by girls during my early adolescent years in the latter part of the "nifty fifties."

A leading hairstyle of the 1950's was the "twist." Girls pulled their hair back, rolled it around their fingers, and inserted bobby pins. If someone looked at the back of this hairdo, it looked like a twister. A girl never wore a hat for fear of messing her hair. No one ever heard of teasing hair.

As far as hair color goes, rinses were used. Anybody could buy cheap capsules in the local dime store. After I used these, no one really could see a change in the color of my hair. One time, however, a group of us sprayed gray in our hair. We all got called down to the principal's office. He threatened to kick us out of school if we did it again! You notice I have said "a group of girls." No one would ever have the nerve to do anything as an individual. If my friends didn't buy lunch, I didn't buy lunch. Everything was done in groups.

When I was in junior high, I usually identified with movie or TV stars. Tab Hunter was my ideal guy. Pinups of him were scattered on my bedroom wall. Dr. Casey and Dr. Kildare were other idols of mine and my friends. This attraction introduced us to a type of blouse I frequently wore. It was the Ben Casey blouse, which looked like the orderly's shirt of today. They came in all colors, but white was the color usually worn. We girls wore them with much pride. To think back about the blouses that we girls wore is really funny. Of course, it wasn't funny at the time. We were right in style. Another kind we wore was the fancy blouse that came way below the waist. It was usually decorated with lace, ruffles, and frills. I should have saved those blouses to use as a latter-day fashionable mini dress!

I remember the fad of skirts. We usually wore pleated or A-line skirts. The skirts were as wide as possible. The reason for the width was that we girls used to wear crinolines, as many as six or seven of them, to see how far our skirts could stick out. The only problem we had was when we'd sit down, our skirts would stick out in front. It used to drive the teachers mad! Usually these skirts were made of loud colors and prints. Wrap-around skirts were also popular. I always hoped that there wasn't a strong wind blowing the day I wore that skirt. Hemlines were below the knees while necklines were at the neck.

After wearing all types of ankle socks or "bobby sox" for years, wearing hose really made an impact. I began to wear nylons just like my mother. Of course I didn't wear them everyday because they were too expensive, and I always got too many runners in them. When I didn't wear nylons, I wore tights which came in all colors. I usually wore tights the color of the

All of the young adolescent's emotions are intense; many new interests are opening up to him and prove to be absorbing at the moment ... There are moments when we as educators might conclude, along with parents, that early adolescence is a period of constant problems to the older generation. But the size of the problem to elders is as nothing as compared to the size of the problems the young adolescent is to himself.

Elizabeth Lee Vincent
PHI DELTA KAPPAN

sweater I was wearing that particular day. The styles of sweaters were very much as they are today—V-neck, turtleneck, and cardigan.

The nylons were always held up by garters, a garter belt, or a girdle. I had only one experience with garters. Apparently the garters weren't as tight as I thought them to be, and my nylons kept falling down at school. Then I switched to a garter belt. Only the fat girls wore girdles. They said the only reason they wore them was to keep their nylons up. I think the weirdest thing I ever saw was girls wearing nylons, as dark as you could buy them, with sneakers!

Shoe styles were basically loafers, saddles, and sneakers. When I dressed for a prom or formal dance, however, I always wore the highest heels I could find or buy. They were called "spikes." Sneakers became very popular for daytime, not only for gym. But they couldn't be brand new white sneakers. They had to be dirty, worn out, and usually with writing all over them.

As for accessories, we girls always carried pocketbooks called "bucket bags." If I was going steady, I wore my boyfriend's ring on a chain around my neck.

All of the girls ran around in a group. We went everywhere together. The boys did likewise. The activities frequented by us were "Y" dances, football games, and the downtown movies. The dances popular at the time were the jitterbug and the twist. Rock and roll music became popular in the late fifties. Opinions of kids were often expressed in "slam books." Autograph books were also popular at this time.

Fads are always a part of junior high life. It's interesting to look back and think of all the fun we had trying to look like each other, but different from adults. We went to extremes with our fads because we didn't really know enough to be able to tell what looked best on us. It was more important to us to be just like our friends.

A papertrooper in WW II

It puzzles me when people ask how I can stand the junior high age group. I'm tempted to ask why *they* can't stand them! I honestly believe they must envy the enthusiasm, the vitality, the honesty, and, most of all, the youth of this group.

As each school year begins, I find myself wondering whether these kids are any different, basically, than when I was their age. Times were different, but were the people any different?

A native Washingtonian, I attended junior high school during World War II. I like to think we were very patriotic in helping with the war effort. I can remember being a Papertrooper. The competitive spirit has always existed, I guess. Each homeroom competed to see which could collect the most newspapers. On the wall of the cafeteria was a picture of an airplane which was paid for from the sale of papers from our school. Tin cans were duly flattened and brought in also. I wonder whatever became of the gigantic balls of tinfoil we rolled. Bacon grease was strained and taken to the grocery store where we snickered over the sign: "Please do not put your fat cans on the counter."

In addition to being a Papertrooper, I was an Air Raid Messenger—complete with helmet and arm band. Our job was to accompany the Air Raid Wardens through the neighborhood during an air raid test to make sure all blackout curtains were pulled and all cars had the top half of their headlights blackened. We held regular meetings and had the responsibility of memorizing the location of every fire alarm and police call box in our neighborhood. One of my classmates was Ed White, the late astronaut. Little did we know when he and I used to spot airplanes that one day he would be the first American to walk in space. It was a marvelous game; we had complete faith that no enemy airplanes would ever get through.

One of our unofficial assignments involved an imagined espionage case. Convinced that the new neighbors were enemy spies because they wore sandals in the winter and spoke with a strange accent, we kids studied their every move. No one entered or left the house without someone writing down the time and description of all visitors. Our parents became suspicious after a while and tried to explain that they just seemed different to us because they were from Massachusetts. Then we began to wonder about our parents!

Rationing didn't have any direct influence on me, except for shoes. I wanted to disown my brother when I discovered that he had bought some gasoline for his car on the black market. I even accused my mother of hoarding and of having black market friends.

Our school savings plan involved the purchase of war stamps which could be converted to a war bond when enough had been saved. We stood in line to buy them, foregoing ice cream. Signs were posted in the school, such as: "A slip of the lip will sink a ship." At about this time an uncle of mine went on a mission for the Navy to explore the possibility of air bases in Alaska. Before he left, he told me it was a military secret and that I wasn't to tell anyone. Well, I wasn't about to contribute to the murder of Uncle Paul, so many nights I fought sleep, for fear I would talk in my sleep. It was a terrible burden to carry. I knew that if anything happened to him I would be shot to death as a spy. After all, didn't "loose lips sink ships"?

So fiercely patriotic were we that we stamped upon "Jap Boxes" with a real frenzy. This must have been a local thing—no one my age remembers such a thing. Actually they were some sort of four-pronged surveyor's marks placed in the cement on the sidewalk—as many as ten on one city block.

Another city pastime was riding the bus free on Sundays. Anyone who bought a weekly bus or streetcar pass was entitled to take an unlimited number of persons along, free, on Sundays. We used to ride to Union Station and page each other over the public address system. I suspect we may have been a little interested in watching the uniforms go by, too!

School was really bad. Most of the men had been called into the service; consequently, many of our teachers were women who were called back from retirement. My favorite teacher was our eighth grade Latin teacher who taught us to sing "Beer Barrel Polka" and "Let Me Call You Sweetheart" in Latin. When she began knitting things, we knew she would be leaving us soon.

We were taught social dancing in gym classes. What a disaster! We were always lined up wrong. Being the shortest girl, I always got the tallest boy, who used to delight in lifting me off the ground. Later we learned to jitterbug and "cat."

Not fun was Miss White, my sewing teacher. She accused me of stealing a pin of some sort from her and badgered me for months about it. I could never convince her that I didn't even know she owned a pin. One day I burst into tears over her accusations. When she took me into the faculty lounge I thought I had at last convinced her. But she concluded that tears were proof of guilt! To this day I've never touched a sewing machine. More than that, I've never accused a student or my own children of stealing.

We used to take advantage of our teachers as often as we could. We delighted hearing them speak in hushed, secret tones about a "stink bomb" one of the boys had put in the bathroom. The girls' favorite trick was to remove a bobby pin from their pompadours and twang it inside their desks.

As I look at old pictures, what terrible hairdos! Plaid shoelaces on saddle shoes?! Snoods?! Peasant blouses were ruled out in my school because they were too revealing.

We had slam books, too, but no one signed his or her name. Some were very cruel. The worst thing a girl could be called was "cheap" or "A.K." if she was a good student.

We had our heroes then, too. I guess the greatest moment in my life as an early teenager came when I was caught in a revolving door with Alan Ladd. We were great movie fans; we carried on lengthy correspondence and requests for photos for imaginary fan clubs. Ronald Reagan was my idol—how he suffered in "King's Row." I guess he was always conservative—all I have left of our correspondence is a post card he sent, urging me to check with Uncle Sam if I didn't get the third picture he sent. We spent hours outside local hotels, hoping for a glimpse of our favorite stars. War Bond drives were big and they were also great publicity for many stars. FDR's birthday balls brought many more big names to town.

Gold stars in the windows reminded us that life wasn't all fun and games. Brothers returning with injuries were a reminder that war was more than movies and newsreels. V-J Day in Washington was not like any other day I have known. Since the father of one of my friends had a law office downtown, we decided to watch the celebration from there. Our first stop was at church, though, for a prayer of thanksgiving.

Where does all this rambling lead? How are kids of today like those of the past? How do they differ? Whole-hearted support of what they believe in, fads, heroes, a little mischief in school, love of togetherness, searching for values, analyzing values of parents and other adults—it seems to me there are far more similarities than differences.

Growing up—too fast

At age thirteen, Shirley truly feels she has lived a long time. Her appearance, her actions, and her demeanor all reflect her formative years. Shirley is at one time the typical teenager and at other times either a mature young lady or an immature child. Shirley is constantly in quest of her place and identity in the worlds in which she lives and moves.

Shirley, as an early maturer, is a very attractive, well-developed young lady. As a result of a broken home, she lives with foster parents whom she both loves and yet violently dislikes. Following the divorce of her parents, Shirley lived with her natural mother. In a series of unforgettable and impressionable events, the court declared Shirley's mother unfit and placed Shirley in a foster home. The foster home provided competent and understanding parents, along with a favorable environment in which to grow. What was missing was a comprehension on Shirley's part of what had happened and why. All of this took place when Shirley was only seven years of age. Her personality was already being shaped, and perhaps distorted, by many worldly matters. With great remorse Shirley recounts stories of her real mother. She respects her mother, maybe even loves her, but she cannot forgive her for not being able to continue to be her mother.

Shirley considers a foster mother a poor substitute for reality. She knows her foster parents are paid to care for and love her. She finds this contrary to the genuine family feelings and devotion she sees in many of her friends' homes or hears about in the school classroom. A resentment has festered within her and, as a budding human being, Shirley often, quite honestly, questions her existence and place. She recounts with feeling how her "brothers and sisters" living in her foster home have three different last names.

Shirley appears, by all physical measures, to be much older than her thirteen years. As a result, she is often the object of much attention from males older than herself. One outcome has been a rapid social maturity that was almost a necessity for her survival. As a child she lived in a very "loose" environment and even now finds the lines of right and wrong very blurred. Her imagination and self-image propel her to social encounters not usually thought of at age thirteen. She delights in telling of her two proposals of marriage. She vividly relives torrid lovemaking sessions with a countless number of males, named and unnamed. She revels in the promises of older guys who find her quite enticing. A recent amorous episode involved an eighteen-year-old Marine. According to Shirley, he had only her to live for. He repeatedly begged her to quit school and marry him. She, displaying "remarkable wisdom," would always reply in the negative, using her schooling as an excuse. For a short time, she proudly displayed a ring that was a token of his feeling and a hint of the future. Much to her chagrin, he married a childhood sweetheart!

Nevertheless, Shirley never seems to be without male companionship or escort whenever or wherever she desires it. Every story Shirley tells holds the name of at least one beau who is the latest object of her affection.

Not only male friends but friendships in general are a prime requisite for Shirley's existence. Often she comments that she cannot walk down the hall at school, walk down her own street, or even visit the local hamburger stand without people noticing and talking to her. Shirley needs friends and the feeling of security they generate in her. She is always very quick to point out that she has "many, many" friends. Actually, Shirley's personality is such that she has no problem making or keeping friends. Her background, her boldness, her experiences, and her knowledge make her a natural leader and, usually, the center of happenings.

Shirley tolerates but does not like school. She balks at formal learning and most particularly at learning insignificant materials. She was constantly referred to the guidance office during the last two years because of academic difficulties. Shirley honestly feels her teachers misunderstand, misinterpret, and pick on her unfairly. Schooling, other than for social purposes, has always been a bore and a waste of time. She proclaims that in the world of dating and love she knew what it was all about by the time she was eleven. Shirley has no reservation about playing hooky, even for a very invalid reason. She does not have a sharp academic mind but rather an inquisitive and searching curiosity.

Shirley is not proud of, but will talk about, her habit of smoking cigarettes. She is forbidden to smoke by her foster parents, but she continues to sneak to do so. She tells of many instances of close calls when she was almost caught by either a parent or some other threatening adult. Because her real mother and related early experiences not only condone smoking but also foster it as well, she encounters a conflict of values. Shirley has withstood many punishments, but she insistently goes on smoking. In this regard, her older foster sisters also defy their parents, and Shirley condones their behavior, even though she believes it is wrong.

Alcohol also enters into Shirley's growing up. Perhaps as an outgrowth of her acceptance by older males, she has been introduced to, and, for all appearances, taught to enjoy alcohol. Shirley has frequently recounted how she was going to quit drinking. But if a boy would suggest a drive, a date, and a drink, eventually they would turn up at a dance or a social affair very much under the influence of alcohol. Once, because of alcohol, Shirley had to be escorted home by the police. Of course, this created greater difficulties than ever in a home where alcohol, as well as tobacco, is frowned upon. The punishment, however, appeared to only heighten the desire to defy authority. Shirley knows she is wrong in disobeying, but it offers her still another avenue of fast maturation and of peer group attention.

The foster home situation places some domestic demands on her. Shirley is directly responsible for her four-year-old foster brother. She is expected to care for him whenever it is physically possible to do so. This presents some problems in what she would like to consider her "whirlwind social life." Amorous situations are often curtailed because of her brother and the fact that he must accompany her. She is highly competent and capable of taking care of the boy, but her resentment of the situation is being imprinted upon his impressionable mind. To hear her talk about it, one can detect her honest concern for the boy but one also detects a sense of obligation on her part to rebel against the imposed responsibility. Despite all this, she is really loved by her foster family. Shirley knows this, but she still has her doubts and reservations about her place in the family unit.

She continually demonstrates a need to be accepted and heard. Her cries for self-identity and direction constantly go out to anyone who will lend her an ear. She feels incapable of dealing with many decisions, even though she vehemently asserts her right to make them. In some ways she really does not lack self-confidence as such, but rather self-direction and skills in handling a new situation or putting up with a deplorable old one. At this age, she definitely fits the description of thirteen-year-old going on nineteen. She wants to be so much older than she is and she acts as if she is older, but she fails to see that what is happening is not leading to a more secure, stable, and happy life than she is now experiencing.

You can get anything you want (1970)

My interest in drugs at the junior high school level came into focus as a result of a comment made by a relative who is attending a junior high school in my home town. The relative, an eighth-grade girl, casually commented: "You can get anything you want—just let the right person know." This was her matter-of-fact answer to a group consisting of young adolescents and adults, between the ages of twelve and twenty-three, at a family gathering. Everyone there seemed hesitant to comment on this statement about drug usage.

After the others left, I talked with Miss X about the real drug problem of young adolescents. I had quite a few questions that I wanted her to answer before I would be ready to concede that drug use was as widespread as was earlier intimated. Some of my questions were: Where are the students in the junior high getting these drugs? What kind of drugs are they getting? How are the students who are taking these drugs paying for them? Is the drug usage limited to any one age, sex, social, or economic group? How widespread is the usage? Lastly, how long has the group, or persons, who have been taking these drugs experimented with the drugs?

At first Miss X seemed rather offended with my disbelief of the widespread use of drugs, but as I continued to question her and ask her for concrete facts she was unable to answer many of my questions to my satisfaction. I was able to ascertain that there were pills of some type and marijuana being circulated for sale. Miss X had been offered some pills but was not sure where they had come from. It was rumored that the drugs were coming from a larger city nearby, but Miss X seemed uncertain as to who was bringing them or how pupils might be getting them at the junior high.

The conversation then turned to Miss X and her refusal to take the pills that were offered to her. Why had Miss X refused when other students were experimenting with drug use? I would now like to give you some background on Miss X before citing her reasons for not using or experimenting with drugs.

Miss X is an eighth-grade student. She is in the top section of students, most of whom are planning to go on to college after graduation from high school. Miss X is doing well in school and seems rather secure in the academic aspects.

Socially, Miss X is less secure. She is an only child. Both of her parents have worked since she was two and she has stayed with a relative while her parents were working. When Miss X started to school she had an extremely hard time adjusting to the other students and gaining their friendship. She has been quite self-conscious of her height and weight throughout her years in school but particularly since she started junior high. This self-consciousness has made her overly sensitive about her posture. She is quite sensitive about the fact that she is slightly overweight. Thus Miss X tries to compensate by wearing all the latest "in" fashions and hair styles in order to gain acceptance in her group. This has worked to some extent, but Miss X still does not feel totally secure socially, especially where students of the opposite sex are involved. Much of her insecurity with the opposite sex is probably common with this age group.

Miss X gives the following explanation and reason for deciding not to take the drugs that were offered to her, when she admits that one or more of the students in her class are experimenting with the use of drugs.

"I could have taken the pills, but I was afraid that someone would catch me and then I'd get arrested. Also, most of my friends don't see anything that great about those pills. Most of the kids that I know who are taking pills are the ones who come from rich families. Those kids don't care if they get caught, because they think their parents' money will get them off. Besides getting caught, I'm kind of scared about what those pills do to your body. I've seen a lot of ads on television, and I've been reading articles about drugs. Sometimes I wonder if the articles and T.V. commercials are just to scare people. Maybe drugs aren't as bad as these people want us to believe. I didn't take any pills this time but I'm not so sure that I wouldn't if I knew I wouldn't get caught. I really don't know what I'll do the next time."

When I talked to Miss X about the drug use I was rather skeptical about the actual widespread use of drugs in the junior high school, but today as I drove home from school I heard on the radio that three students from the junior high school in the district where I teach had been arrested in school for possession of marijuana and other drugs.

A sad Christmas

I wish to discuss an event that happened to me when I was fourteen years old. It was not a pleasant experience, and the effect it had on my life was catastrophic; but the inner feelings I had at the time still puzzle me.

On November 19 my father passed away. I was at football practice doing calisthenics when I saw my brother's car come speeding toward the practice field. My father had been sick, and the first thing that entered my mind was that something had happened to him. My brother jumped from his car and raced to the coach. After talking to my brother for a few minutes, the coach called me to the side. He told me to go take my shower because there was trouble at home. My suspicions seemed confirmed.

As I ran toward the shower room, I started to cry. While I was getting undressed and taking my shower, I asked my brother what was wrong. He said he did not know, except something had happened to Dad, and we were to hurry and get home. When I had finished dressing, we got into my brother's car and raced home with tears of fear in our eyes.

When we reached home, we sprinted into the house. On the way in, I saw my father's brothers standing around outside the house, thus embedding my previous fear even deeper throughout my body. When I entered the kitchen, I saw my mother sitting at the table with my oldest brother and his wife. My mother told us to sit down. She then said that our father had died at 3:30 that afternoon. Then everything broke loose, and everyone started crying, myself included. However, this is one of the moments in time that I do not understand. I had the greatest urge just to run outside and be by myself. I did not run outside; I stayed and cried what almost seemed to be a forced cry. As we huddled around our mother, I remember thinking to myself that this is a tragic time—why is it so hard to cry? I guess I never had a really close relationship with my father, but I loved, respected, and sometimes feared him. But at the particular moment when I was told of his death, I was almost without feeling, or so it seemed to me.

As the day passed, more relatives and friends made their appearance to pay their respects. The sorrow I felt grew deeper and deeper, but there was still some question within me. What should I do? How should I act? I felt as if I were lost in the woods, not knowing which direction to go in order to escape. It felt like the remaining hours of that day lasted for an eternity. I was completely exhausted when I finally got to bed that night, more confused than anything else.

For the next two days everyone was in a state of shock. In preparation for the viewing and funeral, all the necessary formalities had to be completed. There are two things that stand out vividly in my mind from the events that took place in those two days: buying the casket, and buying a black suit for me. Even at these times, the tragedy and reality of the whole ordeal had not yet been made evident.

The night of the viewing (visitation) was especially difficult for me as, I would imagine, it is for everyone who has gone through this experience. All my classes, the football team, and friends sent flowers to the funeral home. As I walked about the funeral home, reading the cards on the flowers, it gave me a very warm feeling to know that people really cared. People came to pay their last respects. On this occasion, it was very difficult for the family. The one particular moment that stands out in my mind from the night of the viewing is when my sister-in-law brought in her daughter, the only grandchild. My mother completely broke down, which in turn caused everyone else to cry. I think the reason I broke down was seeing my mother crying so violently. My aunt took me to another room to try to console me but her attempts were futile for quite some time. The tears of empathy and sympathy are truly tears of deep feeling.

Later, as we stood around at the viewing greeting people as they made their appearances, it seemed as though every now and then I would catch a glimpse, out of the corner of my eye, of my father moving. Of course, after a more critical glance, it only proved to be my imagination. It was difficult for me to comprehend that my father was lying there dead, and not just sleeping.

The funeral was not as trying an experience for me as the viewing. As we gathered around the burial site, my feelings were somewhat remote, because I was still not fully aware of the meaning of the events that were taking place. My feeling was like that of an outsider because it did not appear that I felt like the majority of the people around me. After the funeral, we returned to the house, and I went about my business much the same as I would have on any other day.

The following Christmas, not much more than a month later, was a traumatic time for my family, especially for me. When I got up Christmas morning and started opening my presents, I found one marked: "From Santa Claus." It really made me stop and think. I had not missed my father a great deal up to this point. It was at this time it hit me; my father would never be around again. I did not cry at this time, but I was very sad.

On Christmas day, as usual, many of our relatives gathered at our house for Christmas dinner. My mother broke down a couple of times that day, which caused me to do the same. It was a difficult day. Although most fourteen-year-old youngsters do not believe in Santa Claus, not having a father at Christmas time can be a very crushing experience.

In conclusion, I would like to say that it has amazed me that I can remember the events that happened in that hectic part of my life as clearly as I do. My point is that because I had a feeling of such insecurity and a sense of disbelief at that time, I was not sure if what I was feeling and doing were right. To a fourteen-year-old boy, this can be very disturbing. As I look back on the situation, I realize that the feelings I had and my actions were right because there are no wrong or right feelings or actions at such a time. But, even to this day, I do not know what to say to people who have had a recent death in the family. Although it may sound insignificant at the time, probably the best thing to say is a simple: "I'm sorry" or "You have my deepest sympathy."

What can you do?

While teaching social studies to a group of seventh and eighth graders, I encountered the worst problem I have ever been confronted with in my twelve years of teaching. This problem developed in my 7-1 class which, for the most part, was one of my better classes. The intelligence quotients in the class of twenty-six ranged between 119 and 130. The subject of this paper, Bill, had an I. Q. of 126.

Bill had many of the outward appearances of a model student. He was very neat in dress, and his work, when it was done, was also very neat. From the onset, however, this boy would always do the opposite of what he was told. If I gave him history to do, he would do math. If I were discussing material in history, he would be doing some other work with the book in full view where I could easily see that he was not paying attention. Many times he would bother the people around him with any antic he could think of. Most of the children in the class disliked him because of his disturbing behavior.

I could see, in no time at all, that Bill had a definite psychological problem. I tried every approach that I knew to get him on the right track. I sent him to the office approximately five times, but each time he would return to class and be worse than before he left. I told the guidance counselor and principal that Bill definitely needed some psychological help, but they just kept passing it off with the idea that he would grow out of it.

I didn't know Bill's family because this was a consolidated school and they lived in another town. One day when I had some trouble with Bill, I called his home and talked to an older sister who had graduated from high school. After I told her of the trouble I had with Bill, she stated that it didn't surprise her a bit because they couldn't do anything with him at home. She said that her parents had all but given up on him. She suggested that the school officials should do anything in their power to correct the situation. Again I advised the administration to seek psychological help for the boy, and again it was ignored.

I started to do some checking of my own about Bill's family. I inquired into the family situation with some people I knew from Bill's home town and also with some teachers who had had Bill the previous years.

It so happened that when Bill was in the fourth grade, he and an older brother who was in the seventh grade took their preschool age brother swimming. The younger brother accidentally drowned. I was informed that the father blamed both boys, especially the older one, for the mishap. The father would bring it up almost every time the family sat down for a meal. I also found out that the father, although a good provider, drank excessively and when under the influence of alcohol would fly into a rage about Bill and his older brother, accusing them of the death of the young one. It seems that the mother would just sit back and not say anything. Either she was afraid of her husband or she agreed with him.

Two years after the mishap Bill's older brother told a couple of his classmates that he was going home after school and hang himself. The boys just laughed, but about five o'clock that evening they found Bill's brother hanging from a tree in the woods near his home. He had done what he said: he committed suicide.

After I learned of this I went to the administration again and asked if they could not get Bill to a psychologist, but apparently nothing could be done immediately. I talked to the other teachers about Bill. They were all having the same problems that I has having, but many stated that, although he could do much better work than he was doing, he was at least doing enough to pass their subjects. I seemed to be the only teacher who was trying to reach the boy; I felt as though he welcomed both the attention and the discipline.

At the end of the school year I changed teaching positions and Bill was promoted to the eighth grade. I saw him occasionally and he was always friendly; however, some of the teachers said he was still a classroom problem.

When Bill was in the ninth grade, his mother accused him of stealing five dollars from her purse. He told her that he had not taken anything from her purse, but she insisted that he did; upset by her disbelief, he shouted that he was going to go into the bathroom and hang himself. His mother was believed to have said to go ahead. Bill went into the bathroom and approximately one-half hour later, they found him hanging by his belt from the shower rod. He was dead!

When I heard the news of his death, I was stunned. I kept thinking to myself that if I had been more persistent in getting this boy help, he might be alive today. I can't help wondering what Bill may have been or what he might have done with his life if he hadn't had this tremendous psychological problem. Ironically, after Bill committed suicide, his sister admitted that she had taken the money.

Reflections on becoming a teen-ager

A teen-ager. It must be rough to be
Tossed to and fro upon life's stormy sea.
Struggling in athletics, music, books;
Relying on abilities and looks.
Developing a knack for winning friends
By being "cool" and following the trends.
Anxieties and doubts are locked inside;
Thus many joys and freedoms are denied.
Acceptance, social status, are the dreams,
And friendships, popularity, the means.
Success, good health, and lots of happiness,
These hopes remove the fear of future stress.
Recapture smiles and wipe away the tears
With faith that life will brighten with the
    years.

Sue Manchey

THINGS TO THINK ABOUT AND DO

1. Visit a junior high school during a class day or attend a junior high school function. What are your observations of the social, emotional, and physical developmental levels of these teenagers? Do they seem awfully young to you? Were you like them when you were that age?
2. What were some of the fads common when you were in junior high school? Why do people follow fads? Do adults follow fads, or do they merely follow fashions? Can there be fads of thoughts, ideas, and views as well as of clothing and material things?
3. Talk to your parents, grandparents, and other adults about what junior high was like when they went to school. Do you detect any similarity of student characteristics? Have things changed much in school in other ways? What about the food in the cafeteria, the rules for walking in the hallways, classroom discipline, and bussing?
4. Do a survey of the problems, concerns, and need for help or information as expressed by junior high school students.
5. Debate or discuss: Junior high school students have it easier today, in all ways, as compared to the time you went to junior high.

6. What kind of problems do junior high school students have to work out with their parents? With their peers? With authority figures?

7. Are vandalism and delinquency more prevalent in junior high than in senior high?

8. How do teenagers determine what is right and what is wrong? Do they need any help with this question? Should they be given any help?

READING SOURCES
Developmental psychology texts

CRM: Developmental psychology today, ed. 2, New York, 1975, CRM/Random House, Inc., chap. 16.

Gesell, A., Ilg, F.L., and Ames, L.B.: Youth: the years ten to sixteen, New York, 1956, Harper & Row, Publishers.

Hurlock, E.: Developmental psychology, ed. 4, New York, 1975, McGraw-Hill Book Co., chap. 7.

Kaluger, G., and Kaluger, M.: Human development: the span of life, St. Louis, 1974, The C.V. Mosby Co., chap. 9.

Mussen, P.H., Conger, J.J., and Kagan, J.: Child development and personality, ed. 4, New York, 1975, Harper & Row, Publishers, chap. 14.

Related readings

Alexander, W.M.: The emergent middle school, New York, 1969, Holt, Rinehart and Winston, Inc.

Ausubel, D.: The peer group and adolescent conformity, Delta 9:50-64, 1971.

Blos, P.: The child analyst looks at the young adolescent, Daedalus 100:961-978, 1971.

Broderick, C. B.: Sexual behavior among preadolescents, J. Soc. Issues 22(7):7-21, 1966.

Collins, J.K., and Thomas, N.T.: Age and susceptibility to same sex peer pressure, Br. J. Ed. Psychol. 42:83-85, 1972.

Gordon, C.: Social characteristics of early adolescence, Daedalus 100:931-960, 1971.

Harper, J.F., and Collins, J.K.: The effects of early or late maturation on the prestige of the adolescent girl, Aust. N. Z. J. Soc. 8:83-88, 1972.

Kagan, J.: A conception of early adolescence, Daedalus 100:997-1012, 1971.

Marshall, W.A., and Tanner, J.M.: Variations in the pattern of pubertal changes in boys, Arch. Dis. Child. 45:13-23, 1970.

Muuss, R.E.: Puberty rites in primitive and modern societies, Adolescence 5:109-128, 1970.

Sullivan, W.: Boys and girls are now maturing earlier, The New York Times, Jan. 24, 1971.

Tanner, J.M.: Sequence, tempo, and individual variation in the growth and development of boys and girls aged twelve to sixteen, Daedalus 100:907-930, 1971.

Tanner, J.M.: Growing up, Sci. Am. 229(3):35-43, 1973.

Wagner. H.: Increasing impact of the peer group during adolescence, Adolescence 2:52-53, 1971.

CHAPTER 7

The varied world of late adolescence

The ages of fifteen to sixteen are turbulent, unsettled years. What should be a period that is rather structured, clear-cut, and undisturbed often becomes muddled or uncertain because of a myriad of conditions that seem to come about all at once. There is always some type of question or problem in the air. There are peer pressures and social conditions that constantly play upon a mind that is just in the process of making a change from childhood adaptations to recognizing and trying to cope with the demands of an adult world. Fortunately for adolescents, they generally live for a day at a time, dealing with the pressure items of that day. Some problems cover a longer period of time, but it is amazing how well adolescent minds and bodies can survive under some very trying conditions. What is quite evident in this period of growth and development is the sense of being just on the edge of maturity but lacking the social, communicative, and cognitive skills to make a breakthrough.

"Going on Sixteen" describes a rather typical, happy, involved young girl who wonders why things have to be as they are. Different forms of adaptive and adjustive behavior are noted in "Brake or Breakaway"; the ages and backgrounds of the teenagers involved are just different enough to lead their social and ethical values into slightly different pathways. This profile reflects the turmoil produced in the lives of adolescents by the rapid and drastic social changes of the 1960's.

Of course, so many experiences occur during this age period, some for the first time. "Being Had" illustrates learning a lesson the hard way; she is not bitter but she knows she's been taken advantage of. It is not difficult to imagine "The Impact of Agnes" as the major hurricane touches the lives of many people, including the person who wrote the profile.

"Case Study of a Delinquent" is an in-depth revelation of a boy who, for all intents and purposes, could have gone either way with the law. Direct action, however, is taken in an eyewitness account in "Murder on the Street." A social welfare worker does a workup on "The Gang Wars of Philadelphia" and has some suggestions to make.

Problems of late adolescence come in all forms, sizes, and shapes. Of a poignant nature is the haunting, sometimes heartrending story of "Pregnant, Unmarried, and Unwanted." In a different vein, "The Change of Marvin" shows what can happen when a person "is found out."

Going on sixteen

Lynn will be sixteen on Saturday. After the turmoil of the junior high years, the picture of the adult Lynn will someday be is starting to emerge. After a growth spurt of four inches and seventeen pounds in one year (sixth grade) and a gradual growth thereafter, Lynn's sixteenth year has seen mostly a rounding out of her boyish figure. Standing five feet, six inches in height and weighing 115 pounds, Lynn is slim and athletic in her build, leggy, and well coordinated. She has long, straight brown hair, pretty dark brown eyes (which she insists are too small), braces on her teeth (which she accepts in good humor), and sporadic bouts with a less than perfect complexion (which she does not accept in good humor).

Lynn's mental abilities have placed her in the honors program in her school, where she maintains A and B grades with an average amount of effort. In the past year, as a result of being involved in activities at school, she has learned to budget her time more wisely; consequently, she accomplishes more in less time than before.

Her moods vary—when she is up, she is euphoric; when she is down, her chin is scraping the pavement. Woe be to the mother who chirps cheerfully at her when she is down or the household that does not buzz happily when she is up. She is, however, becoming a little easier to live with. She seems less intense—or perhaps more self-controlled. Her relationship with her ten-year-old sister has even improved. There are moments in which she seems almost maternal and tender; most times, though, she is more likely to complain: "Mother, you've got to do something about that child!" Understandably, she is most affectionate to her sibling when she is most angry with her mother—a joining of forces, perhaps, to face the adversary.

Lynn's parents were divorced when she was thirteen, and she has made what seems to be a very good adjustment to a major upheaval in these important years. Remaining in the same home with no change in school or friends may have helped. Because her relationship with her father had been a warm and close one, Lynn has always been at ease with boys, and she is on her way to establishing a good rapport with adolescent boys. Although she was interested in boys in junior high, she did not date; this year, as a sophomore in the senior high school, she has been dating occasionally—mostly as part of a group—and enjoying her social life very much. Lately her dates have been limited to one boy who shares her interest in dramatics.

Lynn has become more outgoing and poised this year. In junior high she spent more time on studies than on extracurricular activities; this year the reverse seems true. After an inauspicious beginning in which she announced after the first day of school: "I hate that school—I don't know anybody in my classes—you can't move in the halls—and the food is lousy!" this has turned out to be her best year yet. Making an early decision to get involved in things, she tried out for the school play, became one of the few sophomores to get a part, and her year was underway. In the middle of the year sports took over, and she made a place on the girls' J.V. basketball team. Playing every game with unbounded enthusiasm, she earned her letter, an accomplishment which further bolstered her self-confidence. The spring activity was a tossup between the school musical and softball. The musical won by a slight edge; and although she had only two speaking lines in the entire production, she managed to find herself minor dancing and singing parts in about five scenes.

Lynn has made sporadic attempts at keeping a diary, but she possibly expressed herself best when her class was asked by the English teacher to keep a journal of their day-to-day thoughts and activities. This literary effort ranged from the silly to the serious. Most of it was a casual interpretation of the day's activities—the basketball game to be played, freezing on the corner waiting for the school bus, the orthodontist's "implements of destruction" with which he hammered and pounded on her teeth (are beautiful teeth really worth it? she mused). Occasionally she sounded serious—she reflected on the meaning and worth of a second in time, concluding her writing with the importance of how we spend all those seconds in our lives. Then occasionally a silly unwinding at the end of the day. "I'm so glad, I'm so glad, I'm glad, I'm glad. Today is Thursday, Friday is tomorrow—how do you like that? Anyway I don't have any philosophical thoughts in my head—I usually don't. I feel like talking. I want to talk. Why can't I talk? Because I'm supposed to be writing."

For the most part Lynn's thoughts are not terribly profound, for she is still at a very self-centered stage. She is mildly concerned that she doesn't know what she wants to be, and she is beginning to question the relevancy of much that she studies. Being an inveterate griper, she complains loudly: "Chemistry tomorrow—a double period, and Mr. B. will lecture for two solid hours. He's driving me up the walls. Why should I care about nitrobenzine?" How much is griping and how much searching? She seemed to sum up her feelings in the following poem she wrote:

Poem of the Stuffy Classroom

Through time I sit here pondering,
every second passing, ticking away
with my life. I grow older, but no wiser.
Education teaches us that the Egyptians
invented toilet paper. I know this, but
I still sit here and become no wiser.
I am cramped and squeezed, my mind
is filled with insignificant data that
I will never use. But sit;
everyday I sit here, hoping
that I may learn something valuable
    —like how to live life.

Brake or breakaways

We have had an interesting theory under discussion in our house, from A. L. Kroeber's *Anthropology*. It is about the nature of more primitive cultures, in which he states that mysticism and superstition, concern with bodily functions, and a denial of technological knowledge are characteristics of the less advanced civilizations. We see aspects of these characteristics in our three teenagers, who are, for this profile, Jim, eighteen; Mary, seventeen; Tom, sixteen.

Another theory we consider is that from two to five years is a generation gap. Younger teenagers are more "radical" than their other siblings, although circumstances other than birth also will play an important role.

Tom has just graduated from high school. It was a graduation unknown in the 113 years that this particular boys' school has been in existence. The boys came to graduation in prescribed attire—coat, tie, shirt—but the rule to wear blazer or dark suit was relaxed by a vote of the Student Council. Some wore exaggerated European-type suits, striped, loud shirts, wide neckties. Some wore army fatigue pants with a jacket and tie or other "inappropriate" combinations. Some wore the school blazer and gray flannels. More than half the class had long hair, as long as they could get away with, and some wore beads or other symbolic neck pieces. Tom had been forbidden to dress "improperly" by his father. He chose gray pants from one suit and his other suit jacket, so he was respectable but nonconforming. His hair, too, was long, but groomed. There was the usual form, with the school song in Latin ending the traditional ceremony. As I watched the boys line up to say good-bye, I had to remember Jim's graduation two years before. Jim had said revolution was brewing, but his class had not put its grievances into action. His was the last of the really "old school" graduations, everyone properly attired and groomed. Tom remarked that next year's class would be much more openly defiant than his.

Definitely, two symbols of their revolution were clothes and hair. Why? I can trace Tom's defiance to hair. Just before spring vacation that year he had been extraordinarily busy. He was the president of several clubs on campus, including the largest, known as "The Mish." Its real name is The Missionary Society, and through the school's history it has been one avenue to help others. It had fallen into a shambles of do-nothingness when Tom took it over and, with many others, began several "relevant" activities. One had been the collecting of an entire library which the school then sent to a Mississippi parish for use by a number of segregated schools too isolated for a public library. Then The Mish organized a trip to the parish for spring vacation. They had been invited to help a self-help community build a cooperative grocery store. Also before spring vacation were the last of the college entrance applications to file, and the increasing pressure of waiting for answers. (This is an agonizing time for all teenagers and I feel must be brought back into some proper perspective.) A master told Tom to get his hair cut. It was the master's privilege, and I am sure Tom was too cocky in his response. (Tom can be humble, but he has yet to learn to accept reason in unreasonable dress.) The word went out: "Before you come back from vacation, cut your hair."

Spring vacation was a disaster. The boys went to the parish, only to find after a long and sometimes scary drive that the community was not ready to build the grocery; they hadn't yet gotten the money for the land. The boys came back to our house five days later, feeling *used*. "They took us around to show everyone they had white friends." "They weren't organized." "All we did that was useful was address some old envelopes." It was complete disillusionment, though discussions afterward showed they did understand how complex the difficulties were. It was hard, for they had worried, almost to the point of not going, about how to be accepted as friends who wanted to help, not as Eastern kids on a charity kick.

So Tom, really bruised in his soul, turned to a personal grievance. "Why should they tell me to cut my hair? It's an infringement of my personal liberty." Our discussion centered around the fact: "Agreed, hair is not the important part of a person; therefore, if it is not important, why make such a fuss? If the master and the school want it short, cut it. In any event, you want to graduate, and it is stupid to imperil your future over what is agreed is essentially nonimportant." Shortly after Tom went back, we got a postcard saying: "My hair has been given a light trim. Love, Tom."

It is apparent that Tom "gives in" in a manner which always allows him a tiny, but evident, bit of rebellion. And, for the record, it will be two years this coming April since he has cut his hair, which now means much, much more than its first growth. It is now a symbol which immediately identifies him to friend and foe. I, myself, have felt the hostility and heard the insults: "Thank you, *ma'am*," which he receives—rather like purple hearts in a war.

There were more serious events than hair growing that last year in school. He used a profanity on an exam. He was trying, inelegantly, to say something critically important to him about the teaching of a subject in which he was getting high marks (he was always in the top five to ten percent of his class). The teacher focused on the language, not the message. Fortunately, the master, who was supposedly insulted, and Tom settled the argument; the master did not think it was a word directed at him, and it wasn't. But Tom was again disillusioned. The teacher had always stood for fairness and understanding. Tom was a leader, a scholar, and a very devout Christian. He thought the teacher should be aware of this and believe his explanation. (So do I.)

Tom really tries to live by what he believes. He chose by himself to be confirmed in the Episcopal Church, after a year of serious reading, discussion, and church sessions. (His father, a born Unitarian who does not believe in early confirmation, and his mother, an Episcopalian, have given the boys religious training but have left confirmation to the child, so that his faith will not be an inherited one but an action committed freely by his own decision.) Tom's disillusionments, however they may look to others, were, to Tom, a major source of concern. He has been "shook" by the fact that adults are not always truthful, correct, under-

standing, and right-minded. He has lived his life in black and white (he once got a friend to give up stealing candy for Lent!) and now, as he says, he is trying to "put his head together." He is using long hair, bare feet, and shoddy clothing as an indignant protest. His university permits it and has allowed him a year's leave of absence to play the drums, which he does for his living. He may yet reject our civilization for the less demanding, less conflicting ways of a more primitive society. To outward eyes he has done so.

Mary was a new addition to the family graduation gatherings. She had come to us six months before, rather like a bundle left on the doorstep. She is our niece, a child who has run away from home countless times, dropped out of school twice (always a French-system school), and, in a way, been abandoned as hopeless by her parents; in any event, at this time they were overseas. We had gotten her some new clothes for the big trip to see Tom graduate, which was agony, since she was about 160 pounds and five feet, four inches.

It was then hard to predict how she would act, but she was a perfect lady, even dropping an involuntary curtsey on introduction. (There *is* something to early training—that's one thing the French insist upon!) In spite of our concern for Tom and his behavior (would he make a speech?), Mary was a more likely source of trouble. She showed, instead, glimmers of the charming girl she has become.

Mary's route from childhood to adolescence has been unique. She was away in a French school in Austria during her junior high years, beginning at age ten (she was slated to be the family genius) because her parents were in a country with no schooling provisions after the sixth grade. On coming back to the United States, at age thirteen, she had become mother to her two younger sisters, while all three were attending a school in Washington. At that time, her mother was ill. Her years in Austria with older friends, her limited U.S. neighborhood friendships (everyone went to the nearest public school), and many other facts drove Mary into contact with older, less "regular" friendships. She became intimate with the unhappy adolescents who used pot and drugs—outcasts, as she felt herself to be. Warmth, companionship, exchanged confidences, food, shelter, were given without question in this group. She felt home unbearable and ran away to join this accepting group.

Skipping her years of battle, we got her from an unbelievable detention home for the young, straight out of Dickens, after her last running away, which coincided with her family's leaving for a new assignment. One good sign, the first night we could talk to her in the Home, was her humor. Sullen, miserable, she didn't want to come home with us. She wanted to get married. It was sheer blessing that I didn't rise to the bait but asked: "Has anyone asked you?" It struck her funny. Ready to do battle for her rights, she was caught short and forced to laugh. No one had popped the question. It stood us in good stead to know that her humor was vulnerable; time and time again, it was a force in our conversations.

We took her home and, having been told to have her tested, found out that she was not neurotic or psychotic but socially aged twelve. Her chronological age was just seventeen. It was a terrible worry, but many wonderful and wise people helped.

At first Mary did nothing but eat and sleep. Gradually, we began to insist on things—up for breakfast, peel potatoes, etc. Then she agreed to enroll in a typing school, to which she traveled by herself on the bus. She still needed to be told to take a bath, wash her hands, and comb her hair. The hair obsessed her. She used it to cover her face, hanging her head down, so that we talked to a wall of unkempt strings which were streaked with red from a homedone dye job. She was fascinated by the stars, horoscopes, the *I Ching,* and an old book on Tarot cards. We got her to explain these mysteries and found she really wasn't all that knowledgeable.

Since the boys were away in school, she was alone during the day; gradually movies with us in the evening became a better-than-nothing deal. She stopped sleeping so much, finished typing school, was encouraged to go out with friends. Rules were simple but firm—she must be in at the time set, and she must call us to meet her at the bus stop since walking the rest

of the way home at night was forbidden. She protested but promised. When she makes promises, she keeps them.

The crisis came one night when we were going out. She called to ask to spend the night with friends. The answer was no, for it had to be planned ahead; she was to be home at 9:30 as agreed. Slam went the phone on her end. We went out wondering whether she'd run away again. We found her asleep in her bed when we returned around 10:30. At the time, of course, we didn't know she'd turned the corner.

She did progress; on occasion she'd even get interested in a conversation and talk. Sometimes in the kitchen, she'd talk too, when she was busy and didn't have to look at anyone. She was terribly clumsy, breaking things often. When anything upset her, she'd head for the frig—and then say we shouldn't keep food on hand.

Our trip to New Hampshire to see Tom graduate was her first family outing. Jim was there, and her grandmother, great-grandmother, aunts, uncles, and cousins. Everyone helped, so Mary was seldom without attention from someone; she and the boys became immediate allies.

There is probably nothing so salutary as a peer opinion—the "don't be an idiot, Mary!" comments that summer did what no adult could do. The topics of pot and drugs, sex, morals, and money were often discussed at the dinner table (our family meeting place). Mary put her hair back and became able to argue, less and less often losing her temper. She contributed a good deal of firsthand knowledge to the discussions and volunteered that she'd given up drugs forever—she didn't want split chromosomes! It was dinnertime conversations with adult friends and her peers, plus a Neighborhood Youth Corps job in her old neighborhood, which got Mary firmly on her new track.

Mary finished her two years of school in one year, receiving her baccalaureate degree from a French school in Montreal, and has taught school for an entire year without missing a day. She is now in Vermont, wanting no part of cities, suburbia, or the Establishment. She lives with her friend, Bernadette, in a house with no central heat, only cold running water, no telephone. She eats only "natural" foods, rejects cosmetics and deodorants, and makes her living at odd jobs while she looks for a compatible teaching job. She talks of going to college, at least to get a teaching certificate. She is happiest when she is engaged with children. All the love she craves for herself is evident in her dealings with small children. She comes home for attention and a soft bed occasionally. She has left her Tarot cards untouched in her room. As nearly as we can tell, the back-to-nature living had also relegated astrology to a sometimes hobby.

She is now a 120 pound beauty and delights in being told so. She is emerging into the last phase of her late-blooming adolescence, finally evincing some interest in the opposite sex. Her future, in large measure, will be determined by the kind of man she marries. To outward eyes, she is usually an aimless, sloppy, dirty, sandalled hippie, but is she really?

Jim was our college man at Tom's graduation. He took great pains with his dress. He was torn, as he always is these days, between his natural desire to conform and his desire to be part of "the scene." He would not wear his school tie but decided on his suit with a Carnaby Street tie and black flowered shirt. He looked an exact reproduction of his state of mind. Graduation was difficult for him. Tom is a better student and received recognitions which Jim had wanted but could never permit himself to think about. "If you don't care, it doesn't hurt," I believe he thinks. The recognition he receives he tends to denigrate.

Jim, the easiest of children, has been failed somewhere, resulting in his lack of self-confidence. Mary was an eye-opener for him. He saw his parents permitting action from her that would be unacceptable from him. He understood her background and the reasons, but emotionally he did not accept them. Instead of becoming a more secure member of our enlarged family, he has become less so. He adopted the long hair—but only medium long, and he wears blue jeans with a shirt. He tried to grow a beard. (Fortunately, heredity has kept us from looking like wooly bears; beards are late in the family.)

Even his university disappoints him, though he chose it. The campus protests have been on campus issues, and gentlemanly in conduct.

While sitting out in front of the president's house to indicate displeasure with some issue, an announcement that the president was hospitalized with pneumonia resulted in the students leaving quietly; they could wait until he was better. Jim is both pleased and disappointed not to be part of the news made by the Eastern universities. His ambiguousness extends to the war, too. [AUTHOR'S NOTE: in the late 1960's.] Draft number 67, he wavers between quitting school and being drafted or leaving the country. He doesn't approve of the war; neither does he want to become an exile. He stays in school, half-heartedly, not a member of any side. He rejected fraternity bids and works hard for independent dorms and the Student Union.

He and many of his peers feel most acutely the shifting sands of our times. If he had been a few years older, he would have escaped these doubts, accepted the old established order, and found joy in college years. This has been borne out by my friends' children—the older ones are out of the turmoil and are now establishing families and lifetime occupations. Their siblings of Jim's age are often caught, like Jim, and those of Tom's age are committed to change.

Jim is straddling a line that he must leave—will he choose the old ways or the new? His parents are helpless—he has made it clear he wants no help, no advice. He is kicking off reins which remain invisible to them, but which are very real to him. A guest at dinner when Jim is home sees Jim outwardly composed, a delightful conversationalist, well groomed for the occasion—a young man with a sure and happy future. It is not yet so.

And so, back to Kroeber. Why has youth so unerringly gravitated to the three characteristics of a less cultured society? I don't know. I do know that since becoming parents of teenagers, we have been forced to reexamine every belief, every action, every nonaction of our own. Much is wrong with our society today, with inequities of grave proportions. Much is good. My husband's theory is that unwittingly these young are putting the brakes on the world's pell-mell rush to "somewhere." If they can make society stop, reevaluate, redirect its energies into other channels, they will be, in very fact, the future of the world.

I feel, too, that we must stop, look, and listen. If we can learn from our present teenagers, perhaps we can teach the next ones a little better. However, Kroeber is reassuring to the doomsday prophets; he says: "Recessions in civilizations, in short, either are local or likely to be compensated for elsewhere; or they primarily affect patterns or organizations and the values of their products—cultural qualities."

Being had!!!

It finally happened. After seventeen years, eleven months, and eighteen days of guarding my virginity, I had lost it.

He was tall, dark, and handsome, as the saying goes. I had been wild about him since our sophomore year in high school. He hadn't paid much attention to me until now, our senior year.

We had been dating for about four months. I was going steady with him. I suspected that he was not going steady with me. But that didn't matter. I was just happy to be with him. I was content to look at him and to feel him near me.

When he held me and kissed me, I felt such peace and comfort and, yet, excitement. We did a lot of necking in the beginning. Then we started to have petting sessions. I always managed to call a halt to these sessions before things got out of hand.

My stepmother placed great value on virginity. She was constantly telling me of the dangers of necking and petting. I felt that she knew what she was talking about, since she and my father had gotten carried away. She got pregnant and they had to get married. At the same time, I felt that she should understand how hard it is to control one's emotions. At any rate, whenever the big moment loomed near, her preachings would come to mind and I would again be saved.

So I kept resisting. He kept insisting. He even started insisting that he loved me. He hinted at marriage. And finally came the old argument: "If you love me, prove it."

And because I felt I loved him more than life itself, I proved it!

When I think back on it, it's not a very pleasant memory. Being had in the front seat of a car in a cemetery is not at all romantic. But, at the time, I was very happy. I had pleased him. I had committed myself and felt that he had also committed himself. I was sure that I, as in the fairy tales, would live happily ever after.

Afterward, he was very gentle, reassuring me that he loved me more than ever before. And I believed him. He took me home, walked me to the door, kissed me gently and lovingly, made a date for the following evening, got into his car, and left.

I was deliriously happy. I spent the night dreaming of wedding bells and booties.

The following evening came but my intended did not. I didn't try to make excuses. Somehow I knew I was being stood up. Not only for one night but for the rest of my life.

I had been rejected again. First by my mother in favor of her new lover. Then by my father in favor of his new wife. And now by him in favor of what? I did not know.

I did know that he had gotten what he wanted—and I had lost far more than my virginity!

The impact of Agnes

In the summer of 1972, my city was hit by a major disaster. It was caused by Agnes, the huge hurricane that did tremendous flood damage. The reactions of the people, both before and after, are something that I'll never forget.

In the beginning of the month of June we had heavy rains almost every day. Most people were not aware then of the sorrow that these rains would soon cause them. I, myself, as well as everyone else, was just hoping for a nice day with the sun shining or for at least one day without rain. Each day we would say that maybe tomorrow, or definitely next week, the weather would be nicer. This miserable rain went on for two weeks without much change in the weather. The weather forecasters were predicting the possibility of some flooding in low-lying areas because the ground was saturated with water which would not seep away. Not many people took this warning seriously because it had happened before and only the cellars got wet. Then, quite unexpectedly, Agnes veered into the area and stalled. Major flooding occurred.

The night before the flood, my friends and I walked in the pouring rain to look at the river. We were surprised to see how high the water level was. In some places the water was up to the roadbed of the bridges. While we were there, we wondered if the dikes would hold. By the unconcerned look on everyone's face, it seemed that we really didn't have much to be worried about. We left there laughing and joking about the idea of a flood; no one really seemed to think it would be too bad.

That night was like any other night. Early in the morning, however, we were awakened by police, with their loudspeakers, going up and down the streets telling us to evacuate our homes. My parents told us children not to panic, leave everything at home, and just take clothes to wear for that day. Mother told us that it was nothing serious and that we would probably be back in our home the same night. So I left with my mother and sisters. My father and brother, after moving some of our furniture upstairs, joined us at a relative's house some miles away from the river.

That same morning there were hundreds of people sandbagging the dike trying to contain the flood waters. We were told that a fire siren would go off the minute the water broke through the dike. At around eleven that morning, we heard the siren and everyone and everything around me became ominously silent. I had the strangest feeling. For the first time I suspected that when I did return to my home, it just wouldn't be the same. Still, some people had said that conditions would probably be similar to those in the flood that happened in the thirties. That flood was not too severe in our area. People thought that when they returned home they would have about three feet of water in their basements.

It was not until a week later that we were allowed to return to our homes. No one knew what to expect. From a hilltop, each day we watched the flood water and the river level rise higher and higher until it finally crested and then gradually receded. We could not see our neighborhood from where we were. The only information we had was from reports and pictures given on the daily TV news. From that, we knew that our home would be damaged severely because it was in an area where the water was up to the rooftops.

The day came when we were able to go back to our homes. We walked through streets of mud and destruction. The town looked desolate and damaged as if a war had occurred there. For some people the impact was really bad because they could not find their homes or only found shambles. There were some who had heart attacks. Others became depressed and anxious because they couldn't face the fact that they had lost everything, including their place of employment. The reaction was the same everywhere; everyone was crying.

Once the initial shock was out of their systems, people realized that they had to get to work, if they had anything left to salvage. No one can really imagine the feeling of futility, uncertainty, and loss unless he has experienced something like this. It was hard on the elderly because their home was their whole life, and they didn't have either the strength or the time to rebuild the life or the memories that were there. In a short while, quite a few people moved away and left everything behind, seeking to start a new life somewhere else. Most people stayed, however, and began to rebuild. In that rebuilding process, everyone became closer and more friendly. People were more willing to help one another. People from areas in the East that weren't affected by the flood came into the valley to help clean up our homes, without expecting anything in return. I

was surprised to see how many people came just because they were devoted people who were interested in helping their fellow man.

That summer was spent in trying to get houses and businesses back in use. However, things could never be the same again, because even if you could refurnish your house completely, some sentimental things such as yearbooks, picture albums, and items of that sort were destroyed and could never be replaced. What hurt the most was when you had to throw the damaged memory items out into the street to be picked up as trash or garbage. It seemed that you threw away part of your life when that happened!

After the first year of adjusting to a new life had passed, things began to get back to normal, although they were not quite as they had been before. The flood changed my life completely and made me appreciate more what I now have. I realize that I was lucky, because after the disaster, my house was still standing while my neighbor's house had been washed away.

Murder on the street

Tuesday, June 17, is a day I will never forget. That was the day I witnessed an actual murder. After dinner my brother left the house, my mother went to sit on the porch, and, as usual, I proceeded to clean the kitchen. It was a typical June evening, and the children were playing outside, running up and down the street.

After washing the dishes, I went to the porch with my mother. All of a sudden a man (I'll call him Larry) came running down the street. He was being chased by two teenagers (Sumpter and Al). At first I thought they were just playing with each other, but later Larry came back down the street and collapsed in my neighbor's front yard. There was blood covering his chest. After Larry fell, Sumpter ran up to him and stabbed him several times. Each time the knife plunged into Larry's body, I could feel the sharp pains. As Sumpter and Al began to walk away from Larry's mutilated body, I heard Sumpter shout over his shoulder: "That's what you get for f---king with my mother!"

Mrs. Dexter, the owner of the yard, told me

to call the police, because she was too shocked to move. My mother and I ran inside, called the police, and told them what had happened. By the time I returned outside, Larry was dead.

When the police arrived they pronounced him dead and took him to the morgue. Men from the Crime Lab were sent out later to take pictures of where Larry had lain. Then detectives came around to ask questions.

My brother and his friends had returned from playing basketball; they all were sitting on the front steps. I was the only one who had witnessed the murder. When the detective came to our porch, I wasn't sure if I could answer their questions or not. The one detective asked: "Did anyone here see what happened?" No one answered. Then he explained how nothing would happen to us if we told him what had occurred. Still no one answered. The silence was broken when one of the boys told the detectives that everyone was at the basketball court when Larry was killed, and nobody saw anything. The detectives left and started asking other people in the neighborhood what happened.

The reason I didn't volunteer any information was that I was scared. I feared that some harm would happen to me, because one of Sumpter's friends was sitting on our front steps; he would certainly tell if I told. I knew that Sumpter and his friends would find some way to hurt me. One of our neighbors told the detectives what had happened; she identified Sumpter, and he was arrested the next day.

Later I found out the reason behind Sumpter's act. Larry had been seeing Sumpter's mother for several years, and Sumpter's brothers and sisters never liked him. Earlier Tuesday afternoon, Larry and Sumpter's mother began to argue and Larry started hitting her. Sumpter didn't find out about it until later that evening, but when he did, he began searching for Larry. He found him around the corner from our house and stabbed him three times. Larry tried to run away, but Sumpter and Al caught him and eventually killed him.

This incident had a deep psychological effect on me because, until this day, I am wondering whether or not I should have been the informer. This probably will remain on my conscience for the rest of my life.

Case study of a delinquent

This case is probably unique in that it departs from the usual case study with which a guidance counselor or a teacher in the school setting would normally be confronted. The writer has selected an inmate from a correctional institution for the purpose of a case study.

PRESENT STATUS

Alfred is a nineteen-year-old white male who is serving a sentence of five years for larceny of a motor vehicle. At the present time he is enrolled in the Vocational Machine Shop. The course lasts a period of six months, and upon completion the student is awarded a Certificate of Completion certified by the State Board of Education. The course concerns itself with a broad area of training in the specific trade of machinist. The theoretical "book-learning" is taught by three full-time instructors with programmed texts pertinent to the machinist's trade. Practical experience is accomplished by assignment to a series of projects that the student pursues in the shop. Graduates of the course are eligible for jobs as apprentice machinists on the outside when released.

EARLY CHILDHOOD

Mrs. M., Alfred's mother, stated that her pregnancy was an unwanted one. During the prenatal stage she received extensive medical care due to a kidney malfunction, and, at one point, a therapeutic abortion was considered. However, the doctor thought it best to let the pregnancy run its course. Apparently there were numerous complications in the birth process since Mrs. M. carried the child in a horizontal position. After much deliberation, labor was induced to avoid further complications. The baby was born three weeks prematurely but was healthy and with no imperfections. He was bottle fed and weaned after seventeen months. Likewise, he learned to walk and talk at approximately the same age. Toilet training was delayed until twenty months. According to both parents, the client was an ideal baby who seldom cried. He encountered the usual childhood diseases, but there is no history of any neurological deficit.

Discipline was initiated by both parents and usually consisted of mild spanking until the age of about six. Verbal warnings and deprivations were later used as a mode of discipline. Mrs. M. described her son as being a very active child; from the very beginning of his social development he enjoyed associations with children older than he. Family activities such as hunting, fishing, sailing, and picnicking were planned and enjoyed.

Mrs. M. recalls Alfred as being an intelligent child, but at an early age he began to resent parental authority. He had to be "psyched" in order to assure his obedience. She further related that he was a very talkative child who needed an audience to meet his demands for attention.

EDUCATIONAL STATUS

Born in San Diego, California, Alfred finished the first grades of school at a parochial school. Records are not available from that institution, but apparently Alfred got along fairly well with his classmates and made average progress, both academically and socially.

When Alfred was ten years old, he and his parents moved to another state. He continued to go to Catholic schools through the tenth grade. His last years were spent in a public high school.

After entering the public school system, Alfred's academic and behavioral problems increased markedly. Alfred feels it was because the public schools were too lax. He also says he had a reading problem that may have caused him to fall behind. Reports from schools of last attendance indicate that "he often engaged in fights and was a general nuisance in class." He was often cited as being truant. The school record generally indicates low scholastic averages in the face of a generally high potential in I.Q. Alfred stated that he was doing poorly in school and so he felt it better that he run away and find a job.

HOME AND FAMILY

The client's mother and father were interviewed at the institution. An attempt was made to hold an interview at their home, but they were hostile to this suggestion and insisted upon meeting at the institution. The parents have for the last eight years resided in a six room rambler home. The house is located in a middle-class residential section and reportedly presents a good appearance, both inside and out.

During an interview with the parents, Mrs. M. impressed the case worker as being overly talkative. She frequently interrupted Mr. M. and on one occasion they both began to argue. They feel that they have raised their son in the best possible manner and blame all his difficulties on undesirable associates. They feel that their son is perfectly normal and that he received an unfair trial. They are willing to do everything possible to help make Alfred a better person.

Mr. M., aged fifty-seven, was born in Kansas City, Kansas. He is the youngest of five boys; all his brothers are now deceased. His father was a policeman and reportedly provided adequately for the family. Both parents of Mr. M. are now deceased. Mr. M. quit school at an early age to work but was able to obtain a B.S. degree from the University of Missouri by attending night school. He began working for the Department of Agriculture as a grain inspector. Within the last few months Mr. M. retired from the federal service.

Mrs. M., aged fifty-seven, was also born in Kansas City and was the eldest of a family of three children (two girls and one boy). Her father (eighty-four years of age) is a retired decorating contractor, residing in San Francisco, California. Mrs. M.'s mother died many years ago as a result of a heart attack.

After finishing high school, Mrs. M. attended business school in Chicago and eventually worked for the telephone company as a rate clerk. At the age of seventeen, she met Mr. M. and, after a lengthy courtship of ten years, they were married. Alfred, their only son, was born eleven years after they married. Neither parent was previously married nor have there been any separations.

Mrs. M. was extremely hostile and critical of her husband during the interview sessions. She portrayed him as uninterested in the welfare of the family, a man with a vicious, uncontrollable temper. She described him as obsessed with his hobby of shooting guns and felt that he gave neither time nor attention to Alfred. She impressed the case worker as a very disturbed, neurotic individual who defends herself by compulsive talking. The interview with the parents and Alfred was dominated almost entirely by her tirade against her husband. Similar situations existed in the courtroom where it was necessary for the Court to force her into silence on several occasions. Mrs. M. related to the judge that her husband had, at one time, strangled her, leaving bruises on her throat. This was later admitted by Mr. M. with the addendum that it was the one time in life that he had been able to shut her up. Mrs. M. has a very severe arthritic condition and required the assistance of her husband to rise from the chair.

HOBBIES AND LEISURE TIME ACTIVITIES

Alfred stated that his primary hobby was fooling around with cars and attending drag races. He also enjoyed hunting and target shooting. His spending money was in the form of an allowance; the family provided the necessities from their own purse. His hobby interests developed into a strong interest in the auto mechanic's trade and the machinist's trade.

His leisure time in the institution consisted mainly of listening to the radio intercom, TV, movies, writing letters, and studying technical manuals on the machinist's trade. In the meantime, Alfred expressed interest in the High School Equivalency Program in order to get a high school diploma. No special problems were expected of Alfred during his incarceration.

PSYCHOSEXUAL DEVELOPMENT

Alfred contends that he has a normal heterosexual adjustment. He has gone steady on one occasion; however, he left the girl with whom he was in love because she dated a black man. He denies any homosexual activity; however, he indicates that on a number of occasions—for "fun" or in order to make money—he was engaged in "hustling" homosexuals in a large nearby city.

WORK EXPERIENCE

After withdrawing from school at the age of seventeen, Alfred worked a number of odd jobs including salesman at a tire company, gas station attendant, and construction worker. He never worked regularly at any of these jobs since he lists them as parttime. He has volunteered for the military service on several occasions but has been rejected each time.

Prior to his being placed in detention as a juvenile the first time, he had an argument with his father and left home to live with friends. Mr. M. had become disgusted with Alfred for sleeping late and being tardy for work. According to Mrs. M., his father had told Alfred to get out of the house. Apparently, though, Alfred returned home on several occasions during the day while his father was away at work. Mrs. M. consequently knew of his whereabouts during the time he was gone. Alfred felt that his father rejected him and cared very little what happened to him. He felt he had been disowned by his father, and Mrs. M. supported him in these feelings.

PREVIOUS CRIMINAL RECORD

Officially Alfred came to the attention of the juvenile authorities when he was sixteen, shortly after dropping out of school. However, according to him, he had previously been charged with assault and battery at the age of eleven. Three years later, at the age of fourteen, he was charged with breaking into pay telephones. While attending high school as a tenth grader, he stole $600 from his father and ran away from home to Florida. He stayed away for one month, coming back only as a result of his father's pleading and insistence. It was then that he was officially referred to the juvenile authorities for a series of traffic tickets and being out of parental control.

He was placed on probation but later violated his probation status by being convicted of auto larceny. He was committed to a training school for boys and remained there for six months prior to his release. Later on, in the same year, Alfred was charged with three separate cases of larceny of a motor vehicle. Under questioning concerning the latter named offense, Alfred related quite a "string" of events in which several cars were stolen by him and the group of boys he was hanging around with. Engines, transmissions, differentials, everything salable was stripped from the stolen cars and the different parts were sold. Apparently the group had built quite a reputation and caused a minor crime wave in the area. These offenses accounted for the present incarceration of five years.

RECORD AT FAMILY AGENCIES

After the runaway episode to Florida, the family was referred to Family Services. Mr. M. came in for several interviews, but Mrs. M. refused to participate. Mr. M. was referred to the Consultation and Guidance Center and, after evaluation there, it was recommended that Alfred be placed in one of the adolescent groups for group counseling.

Mrs. M. gave her husband no credit for his efforts to effect any change in the family situation. At the detention hearing the Court advised her that, unless she cooperated with the Family Service Agency, the Court would remove Alfred from the home and place him elsewhere. Mrs. M. finally agreed to cooperate.

Soon after, Alfred was placed under the jurisdiction of the Court and released to the custody of his parents on probation. He was ordered to attend group counseling at the Consultation and Guidance Center with such frequency as they might recommend. He was further ordered to pay $10 per week for room and board at home and not to be away from home without the permission of both parents.

PHYSICAL EXAMINATION AND HEALTH

The client's medical history is essentially negative. He sustained what he calls a "minor concussion" at the age of sixteen; however, he was not unconscious at that time. Physical examination by the staff medical doctors reveals normal limits in all categories except for a substantial decrease in weight during the past few months.

Alfred is a tall, rather thin individual with high cheekbones. He stands slightly stooped, probably due to his rather tall stature. He appears to be a well-nourished, healthy individual with no gross disfigurations.

Further studies, including thyroid function, have been performed; however, the results have not been reported. Electroencephalograph results noted that "because of an abundance of theta range activity during the wake-resting

stage, with some 14/6 pattern in dozing, the implication was of some diffuse brain damage." It was also noted by the electroencephalogram that "the 14/6 pattern carries a fairly high statistical correlation with so-called teenage behavior disorders."

PSYCHOLOGICAL DATA

The psychological examination resulted in the following summary:

> The patient is currently functioning in the bright-normal range of intelligence, with a full scale I.Q. of 110 on the Wechsler Adult Intelligence Scale. His performance was above average in most areas, except in those related to judgment. No evidence of neurological impairment was found. Staff psychologist reports that Alfred is basically a self-centered, manipulative sociopath who relates with others on a superficial level. He seems mildly depressed at present. His controls are poor and he is capable of very impulsive, self-defeating acting out.

During the interviews with the case worker, Alfred presented himself as an affable, cooperative individual. He is a tall, thin, well-kept young man who was responsive and intelligent in answering questions asked during our interviews. He talks quite freely and fluently. His mood is minimally depressed, and his affect was appropriate at all times. He has considerable anxiety toward the present incarceration, stating: "This place has thrown the fear of God into me." He appears to be above average in intelligence, and his insight is fairly dominant; however, he feels at a loss for possible solutions. For the most part, he appeared to be a highly impulsive, hedonistic, self-indulgent young man with little empathy for others, especially in the area of damage to other people's property. He has demonstrated in the past few years an inability to profit from past mistakes. During the first few sessions, Alfred showed little personal direction, although he is at least making verbal efforts to "find himself."

Administration of the Minnesota Multiphasic Personality Inventory (MMPI) by a staff psychologist reveals:

> This inmate has strong feelings of inadequacy, inferiority, and insecurity. He has

strong antisocial tendencies and attitudes and considerable covert hostility. This individual feels unable to tolerate anxiety and may resort to alcohol or narcotics as a means of reducing or escaping from stress. He is submissive and dependent. Under supervision, he can be a productive worker; however, his temptation tolerance is minimal.

Administration of the Otis Quick Scoring Intelligence Test places him at the normal (99) range. The California Achievement Test places him at an average achievement grade level of 11.6; reading at 12.3, math at 10.1, and language at 11.6. The Raven Progressive Matrices-1938, Sets A, B, C, D, and E, places him at the 119 level.

IDENTIFICATION OF PROBLEM: PROBABLE CAUSE

One could probably accurately contend that most of the perplexing problems confronted by Alfred are the result of his unfortunate family structure. From information gathered about the family, the evidence is strong in support of this preliminary identification of the problem.

An unwanted pregnancy in the first place, Alfred was to be raised by a neurotic mother who had already demonstrated a somewhat insecure life herself. This might well be the same conclusion we can set forth in the father's case also. A courtship of ten years and another eleven years before a pregnancy has to indicate something to the effect of instability in both the parents.

It seems then that the plight of Alfred had its basic roots implanted even before birth. It has been pointed out by some psychologists, psychiatrists, and other responsible professionals that the mother's attitude toward her pregnancy can affect the eventual outcome of the personality in subtle if not direct ways. It has not been demonstrated that a direct relationship exists between neurotic expectant mothers and the resultant sibling, but again we can come to some predictive conclusion as to the outcome of the child in such a case. My impression of the mother is that she is a cold, unloving parent who has not given her son the affection or attention he so badly needed in the

developmental stages of his personality structure. Basically, it seems that Mrs. M. is very insecure herself and is in no advantageous position to instill warmth and trust in the personality makeup of Alfred.

Mr. M. is apparently the dominant figure in the home and advocates rugged individualism. On the other hand, Mrs. M. would like to retain Alfred as still a child. Consequently, we find Alfred torn between the two opposing philosophies with few alternatives if he is to retain either parent.

The typical pattern in the home consisted of emotional shouting matches between the parents. This was especially the case when anything was to be decided about the welfare of their child. Alfred was torn between the clashing personalities, with little feeling that either accepted him. As a consequence, Alfred feels that he has been rejected by both parents, is resentful of authority, and has turned to delinquent associates as a means of compensating for dependency strivings.

The case worker feels that this incarceration will provide many positive as well as negative aspects in eventual habilation. Most important, Alfred will have the chance to remove himself from the conflicting, frustrating family environment and develop a "lifestyle" apart from what the parents have so rigidly directed. Hopefully he will develop his vocational interests to a fine point and will be able to count this as a positive achievement when he is eventually released.

On the negative side, we find that it will take quite some time to quiet the traumatic effect the incarceration has produced. Pre-release procedures at the institution will provide in part for an easing-back into the mainstream of society. Work release seems a positive step to be taken at the appropriate time.

ADDITIONAL DATA

Reports from institutional personnel, his vocational instructor, tier officer, and other pertinent information concerning Alfred have been positive during the past seven months. He has not been cited for any type of rule infraction and has been personally observed by the case worker in his vocational choice area.

He appears to be a very sincere person who has set positive goals and has taken every advantage offered at the institution that will help to eventually increase the changes of a favorable prognosis.

He was seen by the State Parole Board after serving one fourth of his sentence. At that hearing, it was decided to rehear his case in seven months. The parole "set-off" was designed for him to finish the machinist's trade training with possible work release considerations.

During the preparole interviews, it was pointed out by the case worker and became apparent to Alfred that a parole request would not have been appropriate at the first hearing. Alfred agreed that returning him home at that time would not serve any useful purpose. He expressed the desire for a new start in life at a different address when released. The family has agreed to move to another state, because of the unfavorable reputation that Alfred has where they now reside.

Institutional progress appears to have been positive during the past seven months. Maximum rehabilitation should have been accomplished in the very near future.

PLAN OF TREATMENT

Alfred has been very cooperative with this case worker in regard to setting goals and attaining them. At present, Alfred has successfully finished the machinist's trade school and recently has been approved for the work release program.

The work release program removes Alfred from the institution complex as a security risk and places him in a separate annex of the campus. He is allowed to go to a nearby community to work on a regular job with regular wages. At the same time he takes on additional responsibilities that are available with the program.

Progress within the context of the institution has steadily been developmental. Alfred will have four to five months on the work release program, plenty of time for him to make the transition from institution life to life on the streets. It is almost guaranteed that he will make parole at his next hearing with success on the work release.

A psychiatric interview conducted just before he entered the work release program reports:

> During the interview, the patient was quite realistic in his approach to the future and showed appreciable insight into his difficulties. He feels that it would be a mistake to parole him in the summer months since he would probably go back to his old hangouts, and the idea of gainful employment would probably disappear; in other words, his good intentions would give way to his temptations. For this reason, it is recommended that he be assigned to the work release program to prepare him for a release in the fall.

SUMMARY AND RECOMMENDATIONS

It will be my duty to represent the case of Alfred before the Board of Parole at his next hearing. At that time everything cumulative will be presented in an effort to provide parole consideration. In the meantime the case worker will continue meeting with Alfred in an effort to provide for a favorable long-range prognosis.

The change of Marvin

My senior year of high school was my big year for friends and good times. Since we seniors had been together in high school for three years, we were fairly secure in our friendships and in our position in the school.

My particular interest stemmed from one field—drama productions. I devoted my time to plays, drama club, and the Thespians, which is the honor society for drama members. Since I spent most of my free time on these activities, my best friends were those who shared similar interests. It wasn't long before we formed our own group or clique.

Our group was very close-knit and, whenever we weren't working in drama together, we were engaged in some other activity outside of school. One particular play we were all involved in was the backbone of our relationships to each other. The play was *Peter Pan*, the first play of the year. In order for you to understand some of the personalities of the gang, it is necessary to describe a few of them.

Randy played the lead role of Peter Pan. He is a "ham" actor in real life, somewhat on the self-centered side. This aspect is easy to overlook because he is a very likable, funny person.

Marvin played Captain Hook, the other major male lead. He is extremely bright, and I guess you could say he is an intellectual. Outwardly he might appear rather shy and quiet, but once you are able to know him, you see how funny he can be and that he is an all-around nice guy.

Winston was not in the play. We came to know him through his personal cheering section in the audience. He was always there to give a laugh and clap for us during the performances. Winston is the type of person that you just can't help liking.

Jo Alice played a minor role in the play. Outwardly she is shy and very inhibited when it comes to showing any emotion; however, once you have a chance to spend some time with her and talk with her, it is plain to see she was fun to be around. She often provided her house and yard to the gang for parties and games.

My role in the play was that of Wendy, the female lead. It was through this role that I was able to work closely with Randy, Marvin, and Jo Alice and came to know them well. The whole experience of performing gave each of us that intimate feeling one has when he has shared something wonderful.

As the year progressed, the group became larger as we worked with different people in other dramatic productions. Winston eventually became involved in them after overcoming his nervous condition at the tryouts. Since the group was larger, it seemed as if someone was always having a birthday. Birthdays were always special, and we had party after party. The gifts we gave were mostly gag gifts. Some examples of our offbeat presents were things like puzzles of "Freddie the Fag-a-la," nude posters of Burt Reynolds, or a picture of two men hugging each other. They were jokes and we thought nothing of them since they were all in fun.

Of course, all good things must come to an end, and graduation ushered in the end for the group as a whole. Summer parties and Winston's swimming pool kept us together for a few final occasions. Jo Alice threw the last party at the end of the summer. A lot of drinking went on, and almost everyone there was drunk. Some of us managed to refrain from becoming inebriated and acted as baby-sitters for those who needed them. Both Randy and Winston were drunk and asleep on the floor. The others were scattered about the room talking or sleeping. Marvin was pretty drunk and his behavior became rather uninhibited. Usually he was careful about his actions and guarded himself against expressing any deep-seated feelings. He let himself go that night and shocked everyone when he made implicit passes at Randy and Winston and tried to get them into the back rooms. He didn't stop his advances until Jo Alice and I tore him away and asked him what he was trying to prove. At that point I guess he didn't care what he said. Marvin told us he was "different"; he didn't know why; all he knew was that he's always felt this way. He admitted he was a homosexual and that he was in love with Winston. He liked Randy but felt he wasn't his type, but that Winston was. Marvin explained that it was through the gag gifts that he first got the impression that Winston was like him.

For Winston's birthday, Jo Alice and I gave him a puzzle of a transvestite, and he also received a poster from Marvin with two men on it hugging each other—the same poster Winston had given Marvin for his birthday. Unfortunately, Marvin didn't take it as a joke; he was dead serious.

Randy and Winston were both too drunk to react one way or another to Marvin's advances, and they really did not realize what he was doing at the time. It wasn't until the next day that Randy and Winston shocked themselves into the realization that a good friend of theirs had actually made passes at them and was a real homosexual.

I was shocked and surprised, to say the least, since I had no clue of his being that type at all. But I was more angry by the entire group's reaction to Marvin's behavior. He was "queer" to them, and it was disgusting. No one wanted anything to do with Marvin because he was sick and abnormal. Now he had no friends to speak of. All of his activities and interests had been centered around the gang, and his friends were only those in our group. Marvin went from being a "big man"—popular, well-liked, and admired—to a sick, grotesque person no one wanted anything to do with.

Since I myself went on a final week's vacation to Denver before entering college, I was not around to call or talk to Marvin during the week that followed the party. When I arrived home I heard no one speak of him. His name was mud as far as anyone was concerned. When I tried to bring his name into the conversations, the subject was immediately changed.

I called him before I left for college, and he seemed to be overjoyed to hear from a friend. I could tell from the sound of his voice that he was very depressed. No mention of the party was made nor of anyone else in the group. I gave him my address and told him to write. He was worried about going to school at the university, but I guess that is natural for anyone to feel. His fear was heightened, I believe, by the fact that he had no one to fall back on when he needed a friend.

Throughout the year we exchanged letters. Marvin wrote quite often and his letters were long and sort of depressing. He became involved in drugs and alcohol. His studies were centered around philosophy, and he was smart enough to receive good grades without opening a book. Whenever I was home for a vacation, I made a point of giving him a call; we would sometimes go out together somewhere. He became more and more confused with life in general, and his appearance had gone from conservative to far-out. His hair was now frizzy, thick, and long, and he was growing a long beard and moustache. His entire face was almost completely covered with hair. I'd see these changes and ask myself why it was happening to such a nice guy, and whose fault it was. The others reacted the only way they knew how; they were taught to think that way. And Marvin couldn't help the way he was. He is different and knows it, but what power does he possess to change himself?

I still see Marvin once in a great while and have a talk with him. He is so completely different from high school years that it is hard to find the real Marvin under all the effects that drugs and alcohol have had on him, as well as the whole unforgettable experience of our last party that summer, for that was the real downfall of his personality. I hear he is into the hard drugs and more confused than ever with himself. He is called a sexual deviate in today's society, but what is so deviant about a sexual preference? I believe that it is not a sickness as so many people think; rather the treatment they receive from others may result in mental sickness. Society treats them as outcasts, and they in turn act their part. Knowing a person like Marvin really opened my eyes to see a person as himself and not as just a crazy weirdo. Under that craziness I know there is someone who needs a friend.

Pregnant, unmarried, and unwanted

When Betty talks of family life and her childhood, she shows little interest or enthusiasm for the subject. She offers basic facts such as her birthplace being in Georgia where her father's vocation was that of a railroad coaler. Her mother was home all the time.

After her father contracted tuberculosis, she remembers that the mother and children moved north to live with her grandparents. Her mother was never home because now she had to work. The grandmother assumed the responsibility of caring for Eric, Betty, and Jane. After Betty turned nine, the father also came north and the family was reunited in a home of their own. The father's lengthy illness restricted the nature of his work activities; he could not do strenuous tasks. He eventually became a truck driver. The mother kept her job as a section manager in a department store and started taking college courses at night. Financially, the family was surviving, but with the mother and father away from the home so often, Betty took over the household chores. She did not mind it until babysitting for Jane interfered with her participation in after-school activities. Betty was thirteen and had just entered junior high school. As a black girl, she met black teenagers from other neighborhoods. Basketball, football, track, and boys came into her life now. She wanted to be a cheerleader, but practice was after school at 3:30 and Jane got out of school at 3:15. Betty had to pick her up and watch her until 6:00 when her mother got home. Betty admits that she began to hate Jane and her family. She could not see why Eric and Jane could do anything or go anywhere they wanted and she couldn't.

Betty started seeing boys by sneaking to the forbidden side of town, the west end, whenever possible. The predominantly black neighborhood had a notorious black gang whose membership was composed mostly of juvenile delinquents. She chose the gang's leader to be her first beau. "He's so wild, carefree, and gay," wrote Betty in her diary. The diary, found by Jane, got into her parents' hands. Her father and mother restricted her permanently to the home, church, and school. Betty, now fifteen, had had enough! After she had run away several times with Henry, her beau, both were committed to the County Juvenile Detention Home. Upon entry, Betty was given an examination. She was not pregnant and responded well to the clinical psychologist but would not converse with anyone else (parents included). During the sessions, the psychologist noticed that Betty used language that she had picked up in the detention home. She had changed considerably from the scared, misled, innocent teenager to a hardened, bitter young woman. He decided to recommend her for probation after a four month stay.

Betty's return home upset the family household. She cursed, smoked, and fought everyone in the family. Her probation officer, an elderly woman who came to see her once, recommended that she be given psychiatric treatment. Betty refused.

Shortly after her beau was released, Betty, then sixteen, ran away again. This time she went alone. However, when she was found three months later in a nearby large city, she was four months pregnant. Her parents had Henry, now eighteen, arrested for rape. Betty would not testify. She withdrew herself completely from the world. She could not face her situation. She would not go to a doctor for medical treatment because he "insulted" her by telling her that she was like all the other black wenches he had to see. In despair, she attempted suicide.

The parents went to the Family Service Bureau for help. The Bureau had a waiting list, but they sent a counselor to talk to Betty and the family. The outcome of the meeting was that Betty was sent to a state mental hospital to recover from a nervous breakdown. Betty was not happy there and kept insisting and pleading to be released. The parents agreed to her release if she would go to a home for unwed mothers. Betty agreed.

Once again, the Family Service Bureau was consulted. The names of three homes were obtained but none could accommodate Betty. The parents were given a number of reasons, but apparently black babies just weren't in great demand.

Medical bills were mounting steadily. Betty decided that she would go to the free clinic "like all the other black wenches." But she couldn't get accepted because she was under parental care and was not a welfare recipient. The clinic offered to take her for a fee. She accepted. For Betty, however, it was a most horrifying experience. Pregnant women and girls were lined up and checked by nurses. There was a two-hour wait for a doctor. She felt "like a cow in a stock-pen."

A social worker who reminded her of a fashion model in a magazine came to see Betty. The embarrassing questions that she asked shocked and upset Betty. No one had asked such personal questions with so little feeling. Betty told her how she felt. The caseworker remarked that it was all routine and that there was nothing said that she hadn't heard before. The questions she asked made Betty feel as if she were the most shameful creature on earth.

However, one situation did arise which made Betty think. What was she going to do with the baby? She knew she couldn't keep it. As a matter of fact, she was ashamed of bringing it into a loveless world. It would have no father. The mother was a child herself. The woman agreed with her. She assured Betty that she could find care for it. She said that Betty and her mother would have to sign a paper stating that Betty was willing to place the baby up for adoption.

As the baby began to move within her, Betty began to think about life. She knew hers was miserable and she did not want it to continue being that way. She decided that maybe her child was a way to start over again. She convinced herself that the baby was a sign from the Supreme Being. He was giving her another chance. Her mother called it nonsense. She asked Betty to speak to her minister. The minister told Betty that the decision was hers. She could keep the child and make it as unhappy as herself, or give it the chance for happiness with a loving family.

Betty went into labor undecided. After she gave her baby girl its first feeding and held her in her arms, she knew she could not relinquish her claim on a part of herself. She would not sign the adoption papers that the caseworker brought. The caseworker did not take the time to reason with Betty. Instead, she told her continuously how foolish her decision was.

The mother, on the verge of hysteria, told Betty that she would not allow her to bring the child home. She said that she could not keep the child herself because of her job. This reasoning did not convince Betty.

But when the mother, the caseworker, and Betty's psychiatrist testified in court that Betty was incapable mentally and physically of taking care of the child, the judge ruled that the baby should be a ward of the state and placed in a foster home until Betty decided what she would do with her life.

Betty was upset. She told the judge that she didn't want the baby because she couldn't care for it. She told her mother that she would not return to her home either. She cosigned the papers to place the child up for adoption. Then she asked the judge if she could get placement for herself. The judge recommended that Betty be placed in the Children's Home for an indefinite amount of time if she agreed to return to school. Betty agreed. The mother was instructed to pay $15 monthly for her room. Her other needs would be cared for by the state.

Betty liked the Home because many girls her age with similar problems were there. The director was nice but very impersonal. There was no parental authority but "house mothers" who were just maids in reality. The older teenagers instructed and advised the younger children.

Her return to school was frightening. She encountered the old gang, but they didn't bother her. The guidance counselor was new and black. She was the only person Betty felt would understand her. Mrs. Wilson gave her a job as her secretary. Often, when they were in the office alone, Mrs. Wilson would have a heart-to-heart talk with Betty. She encouraged Betty to study because she knew that Betty had the potential to go to college and make something of herself. Betty did study and was advanced a grade so that she would graduate with her original class. Mrs. Wilson found friends for Betty and eventually she selected a male friend to help Betty make her debut back into society. Bob was older than Betty. Because he was the high school football star, Betty, as his girl, was accepted anywhere. Everyone treated her kindly. Betty was at last happy.

Betty's world fell in, though. One day Bob's ex-girlfriend approached her with a baby's picture. She told Betty that her friend's aunt had her baby. Cynically, she told Betty that it was a shame about babies who have no mother or father, and other people have to take them. Betty began to have nightmares. She pictured her baby as being tortured by an old witch. The nightmares turned into daydreams. Mrs. Wilson sensed something was wrong with Betty but she didn't press her. Soon the story spread through school until she knew Betty's reason for dismay. Bob and Mrs. Wilson told Betty that now would be the most important test of Betty's character. They advised her to ignore the gossip and conduct herself as the lady that she had become. They helped Betty as much as possible. Bob stayed with Betty a lot. They stopped going out to dances and parties. They spent most of their time at Bob's apartment. Because they were human and in love, it was inevitable that sex would occur.

Betty was pregnant again. Bob insisted that they get married as soon as possible. Betty refused. She said that she loved Bob but she wanted to bear the burden alone. Bob thought Betty was trying to punish herself. Betty explained that if she could bear the burden alone, she knew that she had become a woman.

Bob graduated when Betty was six months

pregnant. He worked at two jobs to save money for the baby, but Betty wouldn't take it. She became a welfare recipient and told Bob to use his money for college.

The stares, gossip, and the indignant remarks did not bother Betty. She held her head high. She was proud of herself. Really, the guidance counselor told Betty, she was trying to right a wrong. Betty always felt ashamed of her past. She felt that since she had neglected the first child, the second would have everything.

The guidance counselor told Betty that a baby could not get much on a welfare roll. This made Betty think. The caseworker came, and Betty refused to see her.

Since Betty's mother saw that her daughter had prospects of a good future with Bob, she decided that Betty should live with the family again until Bob got out of college. Betty refused. She stayed with the family only until the baby was born.

The baby was a girl delivered in a hospital by a professional gynecologist. The delivery and everything went perfectly. Betty was happy. It was quite different from her last time in a hospital. The first thing she saw was the baby in a germ-proof incubator in her own room. She watched it constantly.

Betty's thoughts were of future plans. She knew that the baby was a big responsibility. She felt that she was woman enough to care for her, whether they were alone or with Bob. But, there were still questions to be answered and problems to be solved.

The gang wars of Philadelphia

Street gangs and groups are viewed by developmental psychologists as a natural consequence of the growing-up process of adolescence. When antisocial behavior occurs, it is a product of factors in the community such as family disorganization, discrimination, and emotional maladjustments. Because the gangs do not have specific goals, they can be used to divert individuals to either prosocial or antisocial behavior, depending on the leaders, prevailing conditions, and social, economic, or emotional influences. Sociologists generally agree, however, that repressive reactions against gang members that are punitive fail to change basic attitudes and behavior.

Gangs are usually classified into three basic types: the nonproblem gang that hangs around street corners and whose activities are essentially innocent; the problem gang that includes some members with police records, whose chief threat to the community is the disruptive potentiality of its disturbed and maladjusted behavior patterns; and the conflict gangs that have a reputation for violence and for fighting rival gangs where patterns of disorder emerge full-bloom. The last gangs acquire a delinquent subculture.

My paper will deal with the conflict gangs of Philadelphia in general and specifically with the Moroccans, a gang of northwestern Philadelphia.

I feel that the gangs of Philadelphia are in ways unique when compared with the gangs of New York, Los Angeles, or any other large or small community. There are about 5,000 gang members in Philadelphia. Gang membership ranges from twenty-five to two hundred. The members range in age from twelve to twenty. The greatest proportion of the gang members are fifteen years old. The Moroccans are estimated to have about eighty members. Many of the members, however, are high school dropouts between the ages of sixteen and seventeen. Several of the members are adult "warlords" or "senior runners."

Why are these gangs different? Philadelphia gangs are considerably younger in force when compared with those of other cities. This youthfulness may account for their extreme impulsiveness. The gangs of Philadelphia are more violent. The City of Brotherly Love leads not only the nation, but also the world, in gang wars! There were over thirty gang killings in 1969 as compared to none in New York City. Each year until 1975 there has been an increase in the number of gang killings in Philadelphia. The gang members are generally not copouts from society; most have entered the gang subculture at such an early age that they have never known any other culture. They are not fighting the middle class or the upper class;

they consider themselves to be existing legally in accordance with what they understand to be *their* legal society, whether the rules fit state or federal legal standards or not.

The Philadelphia gangs also show an extremely accurate insight or perception. They know when they are being exploited by social work agencies, city officials, etc. For example, one district attorney hired boys from a gang, the Zulu Nation, to advise him in clearing up gang problems. Eventually, the DA was forced to prosecute some of his advisors from this gang for inappropriate financial dealings. The advisors saw through the DA's front of gaining good publicity for himself in Philadelphia while not really attempting to solve the gangs' problems. They thought they would "hustle" him in return.

The Moroccans, a typical Philadelphia gang, are fairly active in northwestern Philadelphia. The neighborhood that gave birth to the Moroccans is, quite naturally, rundown. The streets are cleaner, however, than those of the central slums. There are few or no graffiti on the buildings in the area; however, on almost any wall are numbers, gang symbols, names, etc. This seems to be one of the ways the adolescents find a channel for identification. The neighborhood junior high school is the only educational institution where gang members are in attendance. In regard to the entire student population, none of them is actually interested in school; at least 10% of the students are mentally retarded and others are slow learners. The teachers are frequently attacked and usually have to leave class immediately at the sound of the bell to avoid confrontations. The Moroccans who are in school act normally in respect to the other students. School itself has little or no value in their lives because they can't see a connection between their future and this education.

Only at night do their violent characteristics become apparent. One of the Moroccans, when asked why he was a gang member, just shrugged his shoulders for lack of a definite answer. When asked if he feared for his own safety, he replied: "That don't do no good. When you gotta beat a dude, then you do it, and if you get copped, then that's all there is. You don't run, though; that don't do no good, cause someone'll only get you in the end. Who cares anyway?"

The Moroccans, as all gangs, are extremely loyal to their fellow members. It is this extreme loyalty to the gang that leads to most killings. The Moroccans have been known to have frequent run-ins with the Zulus; they have been responsible for several killings.

Reasons for the gang wars have been attributed to invasion of territory, insulting remarks, an attack upon one gang member, threats, etc. It is interesting to note what one gang member told my uncle about the "dudes" who investigate gang fights for their own enjoyment. These dudes, better known as policemen, have two basic tactics. Their first tactic is called "dumping." This entails the picking up of a gang member in his own area and then dumping him into enemy turf. When the home gang tries to protect the area from invasion, the "dudes" arrest all of them.

Another police tactic is "sending messages down the pipe." To do this the police pick a member from one gang and tell him that the neighboring gang has been insulting them and that plans are in progress for an all-out attack upon them. Then the police will go to the other gang and tell them the same story, thus setting the stage for a conflict. As to the validity of these reports, I have a comment made by a police officer when the twenty-ninth murder victim (a gang member) was found: "It's too bad that it wasn't the twenty-ninth millionth one," was his reply as reported in a Philadelphia newspaper.

The leaders of the Moroccans are definitely pathologically ill, which is true of almost all other gang warlords in Philadelphia. The reasons are evident: paranoia, mental retardation, fantasy worlds, and other biological disturbances. Almost all of the gang leaders are either alcoholics or drug addicts. Their life expectancy does not reach much past 21 years.

The leaders and members of the Moroccans, as well as the other gangs of Philadelphia, do not place any value upon life. This is one reason for the high murder rate. Why should they place a value on life? All they can see in the future is their eventual decay and death due to alcohol, drugs, poverty, malnutrition, and even their own murder. Their lives have no importance to them; they were never taught to give them any importance. They usually come from socially degenerate homes and disorganized neighborhoods. Most kids, even in the worst slums, do not join gangs. Of course there is pressure in many instances to join, sometimes under threat. Those who do join are the kids who can't relate to their families, teachers, school, work, or even other kids. There is no one, anywhere, who can provide help, counseling, or guidance. So, in recourse, they join the gangs where they receive acceptance by their actions. This is one way by which they gain recognition; it does not matter to them whether their reputation is good or bad.

Now that I have explained why Philadelphia gangs are different and have given some of the characteristics of a certain gang, I must ask myself the questions: What can be done and why must it be done? From the outside looking in, I think that one of the major problems is that the political strategies of the city and the different welfare programs of the city are not coordinated. There appears, at this time, to be no plan or central organization for coping with the problems. At this stage in the game, there is no concerted, positive action to curb gang violence. There has been none other than the "dude" action.

An expert who has been working with gangs for nearly twenty-three years had this to say: "First, the social services are fragmented. There are seven different private agencies as well as the city's Youth Conservation Service in the business. The confusion and incompetence is such that two or more agencies frequently find themselves in competition for the same gang, and the kids play the workers off against each other." This lack of organization and cooperation points to at least one reason for no gains in stopping the bloodshed.

But what should be done when organization finally does reach Philadelphia?

First, action has to be taken out of the office and put into the streets. What sociologists call detached workers must be used. These men, who go out into the streets, must be willing to give their lives for their cause.

They must be with the kids constantly. They must be there when a crisis arises. They must be there on the street corner with the gangs, talking them out of fighting. An ongoing relationship must be established so that once the gang member is free of the gang, he will never return to its violence. One such detached worker says: "It means acting as an intermediary between a boy and his school and trying to talk him into going back. It means helping a boy get a job, or helping him deal with a problem between him and his family or between him and his landlord. The one thing you have to remember is that these kids have no significant adult figures in their lives. They don't have anybody grown up that they can turn to and trust."

Gang kids are failing in school. They are bad athletes and find their only human relationship in the gangs. It is their whole world. The gang takes the place of the father that most of the boys never had, the mother that didn't care, the brothers and sisters whom they hate, and the friends they never had. The job of the gang worker is to open up other options for these kids, to help them make friends outside of the gang and to go back to school, or to help them get a job.

The detached worker continued: "You can break up a vicious gang and turn it into an acceptable social group, but you can never go away and leave the problem. As long as there is deprivation and poverty, gangs will spring up again. The worker has got to be there to fill at least some of the needs."

Philadelphia doesn't need the typical nine-to-five social worker. The usual do-gooders are not enough either. Philadelphia needs people who are willing to live with the gangs day and night. The worker must be there *before* the problem arises. The worker must be willing to die for a kid. Period.

THINGS TO THINK ABOUT AND DO

1. Discussion: Do all adolescents ages fifteen to eighteen go through a period of "stress and storm," a period when so many things are happening at one time that they don't know if they are coming or going? All they know is that it hurts and they are miserable.

2. Who or what helped you the most in making the transition from relative dependency to some semblance of independence? Your parents, your friends, your relatives, your teachers, books you read, your experiences, or your own characteristics?

3. Think of someone who did something especially important or valuable to you at a time when you needed help or were seeking to find yourself. Why not give that person a telephone call, just to inquire how he or she is? Better yet, why not write a nice, short note of appreciation?

4. What was the developmental sequence of dating and dating experiences followed by the majority of adolescents in your junior and senior high school? At what age did the different steps occur?

5. Is there a difference between dating, necking, and petting? Do they all have to occur? Is the question one of "how far can you go before it's too far" or is it one of "a respect for me and my values, just as I respect your values even though I may not agree or abide by them"? Are there other alternatives?

6. Survey a high school class or group to determine what concerns, problems, and need for information and help they may have.

7. What age is old enough to assume legal responsibility for your own actions?

8. Is delinquency a problem? Could it be true that the delinquent of today is the criminal of tomorrow? Is there any solution? What would you suggest?

9. Attend a high school athletic contest, play, or other activity. Notice crowd and individual behavior. Did you and your friends act that way when you were in high school?

10. If you are still in high school, do you think adults are justified in what they seem to be saying about high school youth? What are they saying, anyhow? Why not ask a large cross section, agewise, and find out?

11. What part does or should the development of moral principles and ethical values play in the development of late adolescents?

READING SOURCES
Developmental psychology texts

CRM: Developmental psychology today, ed. 2, New York, 1975, CRM/Random House, Inc., chap. 17.

Hurlock, E.: Adolescent development, ed. 3, New York, 1973, McGraw-Hill Book Co.

Kaluger, G., and Kaluger, M.: Human development: the span of life, St. Louis, 1974, The C. V. Mosby Co. chap. 10.

Mussen, P. H., Conger, J. J., and Kagan, J.: Child development and personality, ed. 4, New York, 1975, Harper & Row, Publishers, chap. 15.

Related readings

Berry, G. W.: Personality patterns and delinquency, Br. J. Ed. Psychol. 41:221-222, 1971.

Bettelheim, B.: The roots of radicalism, Playboy, March, 1971.

Delissovey, V.: High school marriages, J. Marriage Family 35:245-255, 1973.

Horrocks, J. E., and Weinberg, S. A.: Psychological needs and their development during adolescence, J. Psychol. 74:51-69, 1970.

Gold, M.: Juvenile delinquency as a symptom of alienation, J. Soc. Issues 25:130, 1969.

Kang, T. S.: Name and group identification, J. Soc. Psychol. 21:334-336, 1972.

LaVoie, J. C.: Punishment and adolescent self-control, Dev. Psychol. 8:16-24, 1973.

Littrell, M. B., and Eicher, J. B.: Clothing opinions and the social acceptance process among adolescents, Adolescence 8:197-212, 1973.

Thornburg, H. D.: Peers: three distinct groups, Adolescence 6:59-76, 1971.

Zube, M. J.: Changing concepts of morality, Soc. Forces 50:385-393, 1972.

CHAPTER 8

Emerging adulthood: youth

Remember the day you graduated from high school? Remember how you felt afterward? "Well, world, here I am. What next?" During much of the senior year in high school students think about all kinds of ideas as to what to do after they finish high school. Even if they decide on going to college, there is that unsettling feeling of uncertainty as they ask questions such as: What shall I major in? Where should I go to college? Can I (or my parents) really afford it? Do I really want or need a college education? Students going directly into the job market have even greater anxieties: Will I be able to get a job—especially one I will like? How long can I continue to live at home? Should I pay my parents for room and board? Will I be able to compete with older, more experienced workers?

Regardless of the decisions made as to what to do after high school graduation, a stark reality sets in—you are no longer a child and, very soon and very quickly, in many ways you are going to be on your own. It may be rather frightening; certainly there will be anxieties and uncertainties. Most young adults plunge right into the new reality and work at it, a day at a time. They win a few battles and lose a few, but they learn how to handle the next obstacle or decision-making crisis with more finesse.

Of course, some individuals are not ready to cope with the brave, new world. The boy in "Identity Crisis" is still trying to adjust and find himself so he can relate more effectively with adulthood. The girl in "Rebellion or Growth?" thought she was settled in her philosophy of life until she learned of other ways of viewing the world. Then she was caught up in a situation of the moment that completely changed her thoughts and attitudes. The "Image of Self" vignettes are first person accounts of four girls as they see themselves, their personalities, and their identities.

The new world for the emerging adult is not without its problems and challenges. New dimensions of society are revealed and more personal involvements are required. "A Professional Learns to Accept Death" reveals how young people are exposed to situations they have never experienced. In "Boot Camp" a new recruit learns what it is like to be under strict authority. In "Test Shock" a college student reveals her fear of not being able to measure up to expectations. There are trials—some minor and some major. "Inflation Hit More Than Just My Pocketbook" will sound familiar to many readers, while "A Sister's Decision" can be appreciated for what it is. The problems in "How Drugs Affected a Friend" are part of the world, too.

Love and sex will emerge strongly in many forms during this developmental stage. "Falling Out of Love" tells of a dream world falling apart because true love requires the deep responsiveness of two people. Two people are involved in "Will She Ever Learn?" the story of an abortion, and in "Had to Get Married," but apparently more is needed than involvement. "An Open Relationship" seeks a "modern" approach to love before marriage, but "Mental Conflict" illustrates the anxieties that can arise when physical love comes into conflict with personal values.

Identity crisis

A teenager who rebels against his parents and the establishment and ventures out to find his own values is a familiar story. That is, it seems familiar and run-of-the-mill until it happens to someone you know well. Then all at once the little pat answers and simple solutions that should work fall apart.

When I first met Paul, he was a typical fifteen-year-old high school student. He was popular with both boys and girls; he was interested in sports and was an active participant. He didn't particularly enjoy school. Thinking back, I believe he was about the same as I was when I was in school. But I was to see differences occur only two years later.

Most adolescents, as they mature, begin to think about their future. But this is where Paul differed. He did nothing to prepare for his future. He was not thinking of an occupation, considering colleges, or doing any of those things that one normally expects of a high school senior. He also refused to assume any responsibilities at home. He made little contribution to the family and took for granted everything that was done or given to him. He did not try very hard to find a job to help earn spending money. His grades, instead of improving, became steadily worse.

He assumed that he would get to go to college, although he didn't know what his major would be. He could decide that later. As for getting accepted, there was no problem. He was quite good in track—he had even gone to the state championships. Paul figured this would be enough to have a college grab him.

To his dismay, Paul soon learned that more was needed for college than to be good in track and have a recommendation from the coach. He did not get accepted to the schools he had wanted. This unexpected rejection disturbed him and affected his behavior. During his last semester in high school he began to display an open, defiant "I don't care" attitude. He gave up many of his interests and values at this time, even to the extent of quitting the track team. Because the establishment had hurt Paul by saying, in effect, that he wasn't good enough, he took refuge in deviant behavior and ideas. He let his hair grow longer, wore wild clothes, and subscribed to the philosophy of "Peace, Love, and Brotherhood." He began to associate with like-minded individuals.

As his new friends became all-important, his family became increasingly less so. Although he was extremely concerned with showing love for his fellow man, the sincerity of this belief was not apparent from his actions toward his family. He treated them with actions that ranged from indifference to contempt.

Paul claimed to be finding himself as an "individual"; instead, he was becoming more like his friends. He was still too confused and insecure to be actually on his own. He needed others who were like himself to give him a feeling of security and acceptance. So, although he was different from the "establishment," he was just conforming to the ways of his friends.

But even as confused and dejected as he was, the summer after he graduated from high school he decided that he would go to college. Apparently, he still had the desire to do something and to succeed. He also got a summer job, a sports car, and seemed to be becoming a working member of the establishment. Soon, however, he began thinking of working and going to school every day as a "real drag." He changed his mind about attending college. He also thought of his living at home as being unbearable to his independence, although very few restrictions were forced upon him. He made plans to move in with some of his friends.

Also showing his confusion were the many contradictions to his "back-to-nature" philosophy. He kept saying he wanted to do away with luxuries and go back to the simple things. But, on the other hand, he bought a little yellow Triumph sports car, electric guitars and amplifiers, and a good stereo system. When he decided to go to a dance, he bought a flashy knit jump suit.

I don't believe Paul is intentionally being different or difficult, but he is confused. This confusion is manifested in many young people. Most of them have been brought up on traditional values, concepts, and goals, but they cannot see how they can work in today's world. So they claim to disown them while still trying to attain them, although in a different way and under different titles. This, I believe, is what has happened in Paul's case. He has not found himself or a value system he can accept. To keep from having to face this identity problem, he has taken shelter in a new look that seemingly rejects the values of the past while claiming to expound the true "basics" of life.

Paul is still lost.

Rebellion or growth?

Little had I suspected at my high school graduation when I received the Daughter of the American Revolution citizenship award that someday I would be labeled a radical because of my political views. I had always followed a straight Republican line, had never questioned the actions of my country, and had professed equal rights for all people.

Like most of my friends, I was bound for college away from home. In the fall of 1967 I entered a conservative, church-related college. Student life on university campuses in the late sixties was filled with political activity and questioning. Some of this anxiety was beginning to catch on at smaller schools. Students were demanding things: black studies, student rights, abolition of ROTC on campus, and, most dramatically, an end to the war in Vietnam.

For most of my freshman year I remained quite removed from the turmoil taking place around the country. I was absorbed in my studies and new surroundings. I wrote faithfully to a friend stationed at an Air Force base in South Vietnam and never doubted United States involvement in Southeast Asia.

In the spring of 1968 the college scheduled a weekend of workshops and lectures by outside speakers from all political persuasions. This was called "Colloquy." A resource person was assigned to the dorm room next to mine. She was a most unusual and fascinating person. I had never met anyone like her and did not understand how to react to what she was saying to us. Although she herself was white, she represented the Southern Christian Leadership Conference and came primarily to explain the black struggle in America. After her lecture, I became so interested that I continued questioning and talking with her until nearly four in the morning. She succeeded in disputing many of my impressions of blacks, in exposing myths I had held as truths, and in forcing me to confront reality by thinking and reasoning. She introduced me to a number of important books written by blacks. This experience was the metamorphosis of a college student. After such

an intense weekend of dialogue my ideas began to take on new shapes and values. For the first time I viewed the world as a place of difficult struggle for much of mankind. I realized my own naiveté, and saw that I had so much to learn about my own country — not only from books but also from personal experience.

During the summer of 1968 I read books by Dr. Martin Luther King, Jr., James Baldwin, Malcolm X, and, for the first time, books about our involvement in Vietnam. Ideas so contrary to my previous concepts filled my head and thinking that I began to totally reject the beliefs of my parents about the general goodness of our governmental system.

By the time I returned to college the next fall as a sophomore, my strong relationship with my parents had begun to crumble until our intolerant remarks and arguments made my life at home quite unpleasant. We did love each other, yet they recognized that I no longer shared their thinking; therefore I was labeled as an immature, rebellious college student. It was during this time that I became involved in a YMCA tutoring program for Puerto Rican migrant children. This personal contact shattered more myths about minorities. I began to see firsthand the inequalities and unfairness in our American way of life. More and more of what I read and heard I saw as being true. By the age of nineteen, practically nothing that I learned or heard shocked my anymore. The terrible reports about the war and the draft caused deep resentment within me against the opinion of my parents. One day, while I was having a bitter argument with my father, he called me a Communist. From that point on there was no more political discussion in my home. I felt only intolerance and resentment about his unjustified accusation.

In my junior year I decided to actively show my concern about the killing in Vietnam by working at a draft counseling and peace literature table at college. For the first time in my life I was rejected by a large percentage of my peers. It was an unpopular thing to do — to oppose the war.

By the time spring came around there was a general call for peaceful mass demonstrating in Washington. I knew that I had to go, yet I

There is a calculated risk in everything. There has been a calculated risk in every stage of American development. The nation was built by men who took risks — pioneers who were not afraid of failure, scientists who were not afraid of truth, thinkers who were not afraid of progress, dreamers who were not afraid of action.

Brooks Atkinson

wished people I knew could understand the reason I was going: not because I was a radical, but because I was concerned about what was happening to our country when it was destroying lives in a land far away. Finally, after returning from Washington without encountering any serious trouble, I had a long serious talk with my parents, explaining my deep feelings. This discussion began, at least in part, to restore our very important family relationship.

In my senior year, I still attended peace meetings and spoke out on issues I was deeply concerned about. I believed that I developed a more mature, realistic picture of the attitudes of Americans. I understood better why certain segments of the population acted and talked the way they did. By talking with more and more people of age groups other than my own, I saw what experience had taught other people. I found that most individuals who had directly encountered combat in World War II could grasp the motives and reasoning of nonviolent antiwar groups even though these same veterans often did not agree with their tactics.

During the small space of four years my attitudes had shifted from unconcern to active, aggressive involvement and arrogance, then to tolerance and understanding to others. It was a valuable growth experience to be able to stand on my own and, I must say, I am glad I survived the turmoil.

Test shock

Surely, there are few experiences which endanger a person's being that can compare with the agonizing syndrome I find myself so frequently facing. I understand this condition is not fatal, but I fear the authorities are only offering a pitiful excuse for what I am sure will ultimately result in my demise. Why, I had an attack just this month!

I do not feel I can turn to anyone for professional help, because not only do I suffer from "test seizures" but also from "examination neurosis" (of any kind—intellectual or physical). Though they are often diagnosed independently, it is my belief that these two conditions are often present in the same individual at the same time and, most probably, for the same reason.

Let's take a case study. I'll be the subject for two reasons: first, I have a case; second, I know my subject very well. We've spent a great deal of time discussing the problem and attempting to implement a solution.

There are two basic environments in a young person's life: the home situation and the classroom situation. The former is a most difficult place to begin because it is hard to remain objective, but I will try.

Among the many diseases which cripple children, few note one of the most threatening and seemingly least researched—the home life. Our subject was fortunate in that the effects of her type of exposure were not paralytic.

As a child she was faced with what *appeared* to be a typical, (upper) middle-class family background; perhaps some would say she was better off than many. But upon examination of the environmental influences, we find she is confronted with a condition that is most detrimental to the development of a healthy self-image.

Our subject's father is a very intelligent and professionally qualified doctor. He has been endowed with many attributes others admire, respect, and trust. However, having suffered the same childhood disease as our subject, he does not have self-esteem. His wounds manifest themselves through disappointment (openly expressed) of loved ones. Our subject herself had many fine qualities, but her relationship with her father was one of the scholar and the schnook. He could never find anything about her that he could praise or admire. Even his silence was condemning!

The other environment I mentioned also held some unpleasant memories for our subject. She was reared in a fairly large metropolis just outside Los Angeles. Many of the problems of a large city school presented themselves at her junior high school. Besides being socially retarded when compared with seventh graders who wore tight skirts, tighter sweaters, and lipstick and who had bleached or dyed hair, she was made to feel she was intellectually retarded. Before psychologists and educators sought to humanize education, our subject was made to feel inadequate by remarks, such as: "What's the matter, Stupid?" "Can't you pay attention?" "Didn't you do your homework?" as she sat there with her homework paper in plain view, or "How in the world could you ever get an answer like *that*?" The effects of such frequent comments on an introverted late-maturer have been quite damaging.

Unfortunately, these two worlds of criticism overlapped, especially in the area of classroom evaluation (otherwise known as tests). Her father would despair if she failed a test; her teachers weren't surprised. Her father would admonish her if she passed but did not have a perfect paper; her teachers had varying reactions depending on her grade. If she did achieve a perfect score, her father would say it was not much of a test because other students also made a good score (maybe she cheated!). If she had the highest score in the class (but not one hundred percent), it was not a *perfect* paper. However, if she had the *only* perfect paper in the entire class, his comment was: "The test was too easy; no one is perfect; therefore, no one should have a perfect paper." How frustrating! No wonder she felt guilty about letting her father down; she could not achieve any satisfaction no matter what course of action prevailed.

Our subject has outgrown many of the emotional handicaps that occurred during her childhood. She decided to go into teaching because of the traumatic classroom experiences she has faced. Her theory is: "I know firsthand what a teacher should *not* do. Because of my past fear of teachers, shouldn't I become the type of person I would have liked to have had?"

As for her father, he is part of her past. She has only seen him once in the past ten years. Her memories of the bad times for the most part have faded. She realizes he is an emotional cripple, and she is thankful most of her wounds have healed. But she still regresses.

I am a professional employee with a bachelor's degree. I have taken twelve credits towards my masters' degree. I am aware of my strengths and weaknesses, and I like me. But! I still suffer from evaluation phobia. Before a scheduled exam, I don't eat; I fret. I develop all the symptoms of the most recent virus. Whenever I am handed the test, my heart seems to stop beating, and yet it pounds within my chest. My mind is again a tabula rasa, and the fine muscle coordination has been drained from my hand. I frantically search for *one* question to trigger the flow of knowledge I so painstakingly put in chronological, sequential, or alphabetical order. I feel like my body is dying (or is it my self-image?). Numbly, as if I have had a stroke, I work my way to the last question. When the test is over, I feel physically drained.

Ironically, I experience many of the same feelings a day or so before the test and up to the very moment that I see the scored and graded exam.

I am sure I underestimate many of my own capabilities, but I only hope I am also underestimating the personal effects of testing:

OBITUARIES

ELLEN B. BAKER

Date, 19–, Classroom: ELLEN BEAM BAKER, age 21+, passed away today in Course 521 of Main Building at State University. Ms. Baker has been suffering from a cancer of the testing area since childhood. The effects of this disease have led to many minor attacks of the input/output regions. She is donating her body to science. Friends and relatives may make donations to the Department of Education to be designated for research into nongraded classroom situations.

How drugs affected a friend

Judy Williams (fictitious), a white, nineteen-year-old college student, decided to "turn on" during the spring semester of last year. She was brought up in a moderately stable home in a small town. Her father is very active in community affairs. He is on the hospital board and school board, belongs to the country club, and owns an appliance store. Judy's immediate family consists of her parents and three younger brothers, all of whom are in good health. No serious illnesses or disabilities are known in the history of the family, except for a few neck and back ailments that her mother has. This complaint is also characteristic of Judy.

Judy was socially active when she was a child. She was a member of numerous groups, including the Girl Scouts, a horseback riding academy, and cheerleaders, and was also given piano, ballet, art, and riding lessons. Judy enjoyed reading and was fond of dramatics.

Since Judy has been away from home, her interests and values have changed considerably. She no longer participates in extracurricular activities; she would much rather be by herself. Judy has no desire to be a part of society. The change in Judy's social pattern was first noticed last spring. Judy was "curious" about the effects of drugs, so she decided to try some of them. At first, it was only when she was with certain people that she would "turn on." Judy found herself making new acquaintances, but she did not make any new *close* friends. The guys and girls with whom she was now associating were different. "You have to pry if you want to find out anything about them," Judy explained. A common sign found in someone who is going into drugs is a sudden dropping of old friends for new ones.

Some physical characteristics that I now notice in Judy are scorched fingertips, glassy eyes, and a sniffy or running nose. A slight loss of weight is also evident. Once "speeding" Judy lost seven pounds in two days. When asked about that experience, she explained that she was by herself studying and decided to "speed." That night she was involved in this experience with two other girls and a guy. She was studying for tests in two courses. The following day all she could talk about were those two subjects. She just could not relate to anything else. Speeding to her was a very pleasant experience. She was pleased to see that she had a lot of excess energy. The terrifying fact is that speed can kill, but she "loves it."

As yet, I do not think that Judy is totally "hooked." She finds herself resorting to drugs only when she is with certain people. Presently Judy is taking drugs three to four times a week. In Judy's case, her "friends" are quite helpful in maintaining her needs. However, she can also do without them. During the summer, while living at home, Judy "turned on" only once. It was harder to obtain drugs at home than it was at school.

Judy is reluctant to go home. She is continually lectured to "for her own welfare." Her parents question her constantly because they suspect that she might be caught up in the drug world but they refuse to admit or accept the idea. They just will not let themselves believe that it is true.

What is the future like for Judy? It is hard to say. Surprisingly, many drug users do have values and wonder about the future. Judy believes it is morally wrong for people to get so hung up with drugs that they cannot stop. She also believes that it is morally wrong for an individual to use drugs that will leave harmful effects on an unborn child. Other users merely say: "It's my body, so let me do what I want." Judy at least expresses some concern.

Judy's drug problem may be one of psychological addiction. Her mind develops a feeling of immense pleasure and satisfaction that, in turn, creates a drive to continue the use of a drug. She has not experienced withdrawal symptoms. But Judy is socially lost. The only time she has a feeling of belonging is when she is with like-minded companions. These friendships are shallow but she refuses to believe that. Nothing is to be found at home but naive parents who still give her everything she asks for but love and understanding.

What have drugs done to Judy? She has become a chain smoker and she has acquired a cough; she feels she may be allergic to marijuana. She has dropped out of society completely. Not only has her health and social life deteriorated, but her values have become meaningless as has her reason for being. Judy's philosophy of life is that "society is going nowhere so why should I be different?" Her vocational choice in life was changed drastically. Whereas at one time her ambition was to do research, now she just wants to travel (get away from it all?) and bum.

Falling out of love

I don't know why I chose this topic to write about. Perhaps it is because I can't seem to get away from it, and perhaps it is because I think that putting it all down in black and white will make it seem more objective and less personal. It happens to everybody, but it never happened to me before. At the age of twenty-three, it seems almost impossible that I've never been in love. Consequently, I've never felt the need to fall out of love.

He came into my life when, as the axiom states, I least expected it. I was happily going about my own business, just having a good time; then he walked into my life and took over completely. I didn't know I could be so happy. I had somebody besides my family to share with. Every day when we talked, he'd ask me how my day had gone. If I had a problem, he'd listen and advise. I seldom took his advice, but it was comforting knowing that he cared.

When Christmas came, the beautiful snow created a fairyland. He took me to meet his parents—something he does with few girls, as both he and they had assured me. We went to parties, we went dancing, we fell asleep in front of the fire. We wrestled in the snow. We got stuck in the snow. Everything we did, we did together. I baked cookies and he ate them. We weren't going to get serious, he said. We were just going to have fun.

Then, on Valentine's Day, we had our first and, as a matter of fact, our only major argument. This happened on Friday. That weekend was miserable. He didn't call to break our date on Saturday; when I called him and realized that I was being "stood up," I was quite upset. I cried. My mother cried with me. She always loved Brian. "This is one boy I could gladly call 'Son,'" she'd said. Sunday was just as bad. Monday was worse! I could hardly wait to get home from the office so I could let myself "feel." I sobbed.

That night I went to a movie. Really, I only went to get out of the house. While I was gone, Brian called. He called back after I got home. He'd been sick all day and hadn't gone to work. I don't remember the conversation, but I do know that he apologized and that we talked it out. He asked me how I felt and I said: "I felt like you dropped me from the third floor, watched me splatter, and laughed." He said: "I wasn't laughing." Everything, I thought, was back to normal. On Wednesday, his day off, we went out. He assured me that "all was forgiven."

From that time on, however, we saw each other less and less. I didn't go out. I still expected that he'd call. When he went to the hospital for three weeks in March, I visited him every day. Since his parents don't drive, he called me for the things that he needed. I loved doing things for him, and I know he appreciated it. But when he was released from the hospital, it was the same old thing. I thought I had prepared myself not to be hurt, but when he missed calling me, I was miserable all over again.

I began to question myself and my situation. I tried to talk it out with him, but all he managed to do was to criticize me. I wanted to say: "Okay, don't bother me anymore." But I couldn't do it. I didn't want to lose him.

One time when we'd had a minor disagreement, I very coolly stated our problem as I saw it. We happened "to like each other" in spite of everything. This should be a problem? It was for us because neither of us wanted to hurt the other—or ourselves.

Through April and May, Brian called less and less frequently. By the end of May he wasn't calling at all. How did I feel? I hurt all over. It was especially bad, too, because I'd moved into my own apartment on May 19, and I was not yet used to living alone. I felt absolutely empty. I was lonely, unsure, bereft.

All I had to do with my time was to fill it with thinking. Finally he called. He made a date for the next day, and I was elated. He never came. From the heights of ecstasy to the depths of despair in twenty-four hours—that was me! There it was, all over again. All the fresh, new hurt. He called later that week and acted as if nothing at all had happened. He asked about every member of my family, about everything that I was doing. But no date!

So now I'm concentrating on falling out of love. But I find myself daydreaming about him constantly. I have long, involved, imaginary conversations with him that are filled with questions and explanations. Sometimes I quarrel with him. I remember our good times and I become depressed. When I'm shopping and I see a cute greeting card, I have to remind myself that I can't send it to him. I catch myself thinking: "I'll have to remember to tell Brian that joke . . . or this story . . or that comment." When I buy a dress, I wonder if he will like it—then I remember that it doesn't really matter any more. I find his name creeping into conversations that shouldn't relate to him at all. I jump when the phone rings, and I'm sad when it doesn't. Until very recently I've had no desire to see other people socially, and I've turned down more dates than I've accepted. I have so much energy that I don't know what to do with it all—and yet I have no ambition to do anything. I get violently jealous when I see couples our age having a good time with each other. I get angry with myself for feeling this way. Knowing that others have had the same experience is no consolation at all. Even the realization that I am better off without him doesn't help. Logic has absolutely nothing to do with my feelings.

So what is it like to fall out of love? It is hard. It is lonely. It is depressing. It is necessary. I keep telling myself that it gets easier every day, and most days it does. I just hope that I never have to do it again.

Mental conflict

I have a situation to present that consists of a conflict within myself and a great deal of stress between my parents and myself for the past year.

The background is important to give an understanding of the present. The day after I graduated from high school, my parents moved to Ohio, sending me west to be a summer missionary for the Southern Baptist Convention in a city that was the location of a state university. My parents were very proud of me, since their life is based in the Southern Baptist religion.

That summer proved to be a disaster in terms of my beliefs and values. I found myself to be playing the good Christian role on the outside while inwardly rejecting people in general, the other missionaries, the rigidity of our schedule, and even the concept of God. In August I left to visit my parents. I told them of my feelings and they sympathized, as my fellow missionaries had, saying they too had had doubts but to just have faith.

The end of August I returned to that same city to enter the university. Like many freshmen, I was in the process of trying to find myself. Spending many hours by myself, I decided not to allow religion or God to bother me.

One month after school began I took a job as keypuncher for the Sociology Department. Here I met Bill, who was working toward his doctorate in sociology. He was twenty-nine years old, divorced after being married for eight years. He had two children who were with his wife. We developed a strong liking for each other that resulted in my agreeing to move in with him.

Though this arrangement was totally contrary to my upbringing, I felt guilty only when confronted with the concern of my Christian friends or when faced with needing to lie to my parents to avoid hurting them. After only three weeks of living with Bill, I decided to move back to my dormitory.

I always felt that someday I would return to God. However, I was bothered, since I was beginning to love Bill and wanted to be with him. I debated what to do. By the end of the semester, I decided to return home and to go back to the church and God. This way I would be with my parents and they could help keep me away from tempting influences. However, at home I found myself rejecting both God and my parents' lifestyle. I missed Bill and cried day and night, wanting to go back.

This situation only resulted in creating great tension between my parents and me. For hours I talked with my parents, presenting my new views on life, how I wanted to live, how I loved Bill and wanted to return to him. My parents, obviously, were very distressed and tried to talk me out of it. I felt as if I was weighing my love for my parents against my love for Bill. Being at home, feeling that I should try to get back to God, feeling the hurt of my parents, made me decide to stay, try to forget about Bill, and start a new life.

The next seven months, however, saw me move further from my parents' lifestyle and into a philosophy better suited to my personality. The philosophy I developed was similar to the one that Bill had. I felt good about myself and pleased that my parents knew where I stood. I learned, however, that the more my philosophy was like Bill's, the less satisfying were my relationships with other men. I wanted to be with Bill more than ever.

In September I entered an eastern college. This time I went to college with the intention of solidifying and adjusting my philosophy of life and experiencing as many different situations as possible. After one month of college, I realized, for the first time, that I wanted to completely commit myself to Bill. I wrote him a letter and found he felt the same. We decided that I should return west and live with him during the spring semester. Then we could decide where our relationship was to go.

My parents and I have now had nearly two months to think about this decision. The emotions aroused between us have caused much pain on each side. They have felt that I rejected them and, more important to them, that I was rejecting God. They also believe, and perhaps rightly so, that I am wrecking my life, throwing it away. I have felt their despair and grief and it hurts me very deeply, but we both have to open our minds and really listen and try to understand each other.

My parents still completely disapprove of my decision. Surprisingly, this conflict and the stress and anxiety that developed between us has not torn us apart but rather brought us into a very close relationship. I can tell them anything, and though they might disagree, they know I love them and I know they'll always love me.

For once in my life, I have not wavered in making a decision but have become definite and sure. At first I felt the need for them to accept my life-style but their acceptance of me has satisfied this need. I no longer feel under stress.

The conflict within me as to what God is to mean to me I've left unresolved and open-ended. The conflict between my life-style and that of my parents is resolved and needs to be accepted. Perhaps someday I will, as the Bible says, return to the ways of my parents. Perhaps I am unrealistic in feeling I will be open to return. I do not feel I am rebelling, and I do not wish to discuss the right and wrong of religious belief. I will assume that if I am rebelling, it is being done unconsciously. I have not yet seen the signs of repressed guilt.

AUTHOR'S NOTE: This profile was written during the third week in November. One month later, this young lady and I had a chance to talk.

During our conversation, she told me that she had been thinking about her decision. She said she had no pressure from her parents because they had accepted her right to run her own life. Out of the blue, quite unexpectedly, she said she abruptly changed her mind and decided not to go to Bill.

A year has passed since she made that decision, and she is still enrolled at her eastern college.

A sister's decision

In our home, the events preceding Christmas were always exciting and mystifying. I can remember how anticipation kept building from Thanksgiving onward, even though at the age of eight I no longer believed in the proverbial Santa Claus. Little did I know, at that time,

what that particular Christmas would hold in store for me and my family.

Being one of two children, I had always admired my older sister and attempted to copy her even though there was a nine year gap in our ages. Ann Margaret had always been the pretty, popular, and extremely intelligent member of the family. I had always envied her long blonde hair and huge sparkling blue eyes which, combined with her quick-witted bubbling personality, made a sharp contrast to my dark hair, tomboyish appearance, and quiet, thoughtful personality. Since her freshman year in high school, Ann Margaret had attended a private girl's boarding school, which meant that her weekend visits home were always a delight for me. Christmas was especially enjoyable since she would be home for over two weeks. When the day finally arrived for the beginning of the vacation period, I accompanied my father down to the academy to collect my sister and her overwhelming amount of luggage. On the return trip, Ann Margaret seemed rather untalkative and oblivious to what was going on about her. My father attempted, with little success, to keep up a steady flow of conversation. I remember Dad talking about how the following year she would have to travel in from Boston since she would be attending college there. She responded with an unenthusiastic nod of the head. I sensed that something was wrong, but I didn't concentrate on it too long as snowflakes had begun to fall; I was daydreaming about sled riding and having fun now that school had recessed.

That evening at dinner, Ann Margaret remained subdued and disinterested to the point that Mother began to worry about her health in view of her noticeable lack of appetite. As soon as the dessert was completed, Ann Margaret asked me to go play for a while before we started the dishes since she had something to discuss with Mother and Dad. Offended at being shut out from the usual family conversations, I wandered off into the living room that was far enough away not to be seen but close enough to hear the proceedings. After what seemed like an eternity of silence, Ann Margaret finally said: "I've decided that I'm not going to go to Boston next year." Before she could finish, my mother interjected: "But, Honey, why? You just loved the school when we went to visit it last year. You know that we would never interfere in your decisions as long as you believe that what you are doing is right, but I just don't understand!" Ann Margaret's response was slow and soft-spoken as she said: "I hope you meant what you've always said about not interfering in our lives. You see, I've decided that in September I'm going to enter the Convent of the Sisters of Divine Providence."

Silence reigned for what felt like an infinite amount of time; then a barrage of questions followed. I recall my father's voice getting progressively louder and comments flowing, such as: "You're too young—just seventeen." "Get your education first." "Go to college for one year." "I'll buy you a car or anything you want if you'll just wait." "Why? Aren't you happy?" and others too numerous to mention. I heard Ann Margaret's calm voice giving a reply about her ideals and basic philosophy of life.

Finally, I decided that I should make my entrance. As I looked around the dining room, I had never seen such expressions on the faces of my family. My mother's eyes were welling with tears and her flushed expression of hurt made me want to cry. On the other hand, my father's eyes were flashing with rage and his normally ruddy complexion flamed. Meanwhile, Ann Margaret sat looking uncomfortable but none the worse for wear, with a certain stubborn, determined expression pursed on her lips. That was one trait I had learned to recognize well over the past eight years. Eventually, Ann Margaret rose, looked at me, and with a quick "I'll wash, you dry" took me off to the kitchen.

Soon I heard the familiar sounds of my mother's feet on the way to her room with a quick stop at the medicine cabinet for what I'm sure was an aspirin and the heavy tread of my father's steps as he stomped down to the game room (more than likely to the bar). As I gazed up into Ann Margaret's eyes, she looked down and said flatly: "You heard?" I nodded, and, although I had thousands of questions, decided that was not the time to pursue the subject.

The following days leading up to Christmas were busy but somewhat unenthusiastic. I still could not quite comprehend the situation, but I was afraid to ask what was happening for fear of starting another uproar. It appeared that my parents were trying desperately to shut the whole incident out of their minds in the hopes that my sister would soon come to her senses. Finally, Christmas Day dawned bright and sunny over the snow-covered landscape. After the usual rituals such as church, breakfast, and exchange of presents were completed, we began to prepare for the entourage of relatives and friends for Christmas dinner. As the doorbell chimed to announce the first arrivals, Ann Margaret looked at my parents and said flatly: "I hope you won't say anything to anyone just yet." My parents nodded in agreement. To my knowledge this was the first comment that related to my sister's decision since that night almost a week ago. The remainder of the vacation went quickly, and soon it was time for my sister to return to school.

January rapidly merged into June, but during this time lapse there was a noticeable change in the personalities of my usually fun-loving, outgoing, and always understanding parents. Their entertaining habits changed drastically; now they rarely attended parties and hadn't given one since New Year's Eve. Mother's interest in her card club dwindled, and her Saturday shopping excursions into Hartford came to a complete halt. Her normally exuberant personality transformed itself into a quiet, withdrawn manner. On the other hand, my father began to spend considerable amounts of time away from home either working or "out with the boys." His drinking habits, which up to this point had been on a social level, became progressively worse. I noticed a shortness of temper and rising irritability that made life rather difficult. Somehow, home was just not the same.

That summer we planned our normal three week vacation on Cape Cod just as though nothing had happened. However, much of the normal enthusiasm was lacking. My sister quietly confided in me that she really preferred to stay at home but would go to the shore just to "keep peace." I think my parents were attempt-

Education is not something done *to* but something done *by* an individual which is actually self-education. It is a slow, subtle growth entailing a life-time of self-discipline and an unquenchable passion to learn and to grow up to the full stature of one's abilities. The outcome should be competent, self-active, responsible, and socially minded citizens whose lives are predicated on faith, courage, integrity, intelligence and the will to achieve.

F. Earl Williams
BULLETIN, NATIONAL ASSOCIATION OF
SECONDARY SCHOOL PRINCIPALS

ing to show Ann Margaret what she would be giving up because the vacation was the best ever with all types of exciting things to do both day and night. However, underneath the external gaiety, it appeared that everyone was trying just a little bit too hard to please everyone else.

Sometime in the middle of August my parents reluctantly told our relatives the news. I shall never forget that one hot muggy August day—Mother, Ann Margaret, and I were doing the luncheon dishes and talking when my Uncle Bill stormed up the back steps. Such a tirade I had never heard, and the language, although mostly unfamiliar to me at that time, was not the least gentlemanly. Since he was a bachelor, Ann Margaret had always been his favorite niece. He could not accept the decision. When he finally finished what he felt compelled to say, he left the house in a huff and with a slam of the door. The three of us were in tears—Ann Margaret and Mother from being hurt and me from sheer terror and lack of understanding.

Eventually the situation calmed itself, and our relatives half-heartedly accepted the fact that they could not change the inevitable. Ann Margaret and Mother began to busy themselves with shopping and preparing for the departure. Such a strange array of clothing for my normally style-conscious sister. Dull white flannel was everywhere combined with drab gray and mournful black cotton. These seemed so incongruous to Ann Margaret's normal taste for vivid, soft pastels. The worst item purchased was the heavy, ugly pair of black oxford shoes. I can remember sneaking up to our room and trying on the outfit—what a sight!

September arrived and with it the long dreaded day. With only one small black suitcase, my sister emerged from the house dressed in her prettiest blue shirtwaist dress. The color matched her eyes perfectly. We drove over to my grandmother's home where we picked up the remainder of our assemblage and then continued on our way to the Motherhouse. As we drove up the long circular driveway past beautiful landscaped grounds, I remember looking up at the huge white brick building with towering pillars and being reminded of a medieval castle. As we were ushered in the main

doors and down long dark hallways, our footsteps rang out against the eerie silence.

Eventually we arrived at a large room filled with other family groupings, all with uncertain looks on their faces. Soon a kindly little woman appeared and introduced herself as the Mistress of Postulants. She took my sister and a group of about thirty young girls out of the room. As the large brown varnished doors closed behind the girls, chills ran up my spine, for it seemed like an insurmountable wall had just been established. The rest of the people just sat there, some attempting to converse in whispers but for the most part silence abounded. Then the doors opened and the girls returned. My sister walked toward us carrying her blue dress over her arm. She was garbed from head to toe in her new black habit. When she handed my mother her dress, it seemed that she was not only renouncing the outside world but was breaking all links with her family.

The remainder of the time spent at the convent that day is merely a blur in my memory, perhaps something that I prefer not to recall. I do remember wondering that night as I climbed into my bed, looking across at the empty twin bed on the other side of the room, if my sister would ever return to sleep in it. A deep feeling of extreme loneliness came over me.

Within a few months relative normalcy was restored to our home. My parents slowly began to regain their zest for life and the outside world. As visiting days at the convent came and went and we could see the obvious happiness written on my sister's face, everyone seemed to regain their old spirit of living. The emptiness was not gone, but a spirit of acceptance and belief had made it more bearable.

An open relationship

Donna and I had been engaged for about half a year when we decided to live together for a week. We left for college a week early during the summer before my senior year.

We realized life together would be different from our dating and engaged relations but just how much different we didn't know. Two couples whom we knew and whose marriages were "on the rocks" advised us to live together for a while before marriage to be more certain that we could be happy with each other twenty-four hours a day. It's true that seven days might not be enough time to tell anything about our relationship, but I must say, after our experience we both felt that we had gained a great deal of insight about each other and our relationship in general.

We moved into my apartment on a Saturday morning, so we actually had nine days until classes started. The first day was set aside to get everything in some sort of order and to do general cleaning. Our thoughts seemed to be centered on the idea of how wonderful it would be if we were married and this was our first apartment together.

The freedom we had enjoyed the three previous years at college seemed so much sweeter after a summer of being at home under "parental guidance." We were filled with the excitement of returning to this freedom, and especially so because we returned with each other.

During our stay together, we realized how much we didn't know about each other—spiritually, emotionally, physically, and socially. For example, we quickly learned that each other's early morning grumpiness was short-lived and, in a way, humorous. I began to understand why a girl has to start getting ready for a date an hour before her date. Donna in turn was amazed at how I could get ready in the span of five minutes.

Helping each other with everyday routine such as vacuuming and cooking was so much more enjoyable than ever before. Washing the car and shopping also took on added meaning since it was for and by us.

We had a lot of time alone together. We talked about our feelings on different topics to a greater extent than we ever had before. Through these in-depth talks we learned a great deal about each other. Inner feelings we had been reluctant to disclose before now seemed much easier to express. I'm basically quiet and don't talk very much. I often don't express my feelings, but with Donna I felt an urge to let her

know what my feelings were because I felt she was sincerely interested. She also became more open and we grew much closer as a result of our open expression of our feelings.

One area which caused some friction was the pace of each of our lives. I'm very active and have to be doing something or going somewhere. I hate to let anything go until tomorrow and feel that the more I get done today, the more things I can get done tomorrow. I am also impatient in many situations. Donna, on the other hand, is almost my opposite in that she hates to rush or to be hurried. She enjoys taking her time and can't see any sense in hurrying through anything. Trying to find a happy medium where both of us are happy is difficult and we still have some trouble with it occasionally. We both respect each other's position as we try to become more compatible.

We found our ideas on sex, and the human body in general, to be different. We both felt sex was an expression of love and should be given and received as such. This view had not been Donna's original outlook, but through sincere talks and my openness she gradually took on my viewpoint. I come from an extremely uninhibited family. My parents had literature for us children on birth and conception and would answer any of our questions honestly. We were taught that there was nothing sinful about the human body. It was not an uncommon event to see one another nude while dressing or going to or from the bathroom. We would often skinny-dip in the pool before going to bed.

Donna's background was very inhibited, and her sexual knowledge came entirely from a sex education class and her peers. Her parents viewed sex as dirty and sinful and they never talked to her about it.

Our first sexual relations were enjoyable even though she was scared. She thought it was wonderful because we viewed sex as a shared expression of love. We now feel that the best and only way to deal with sex is openly and honestly.

Through our experiences we learned many things, but perhaps the most important thing was that love is sharing—total sharing of mind, body, and soul into a beautiful relationship.

Will she ever learn?

My sister is fifteen months younger than I am. We have gone to school together until I graduated from high school. For one glorious year, I was alone at college; then my sister came and joined me this fall. We live in the same dorm, and I must admit it's convenient (for borrowing clothes, money) but somehow I feel closer to my roomie than to my sister. I really do love her, I even *like* her. She's more intelligent than me, but all she lives for on this campus is the social life—fraternity keggers, drinking with the girls, and goofing off in general. We've had some real fights in the past year. This is all background—now—recently (in February) my sister got pregnant. It was a one night stand and not the first time this could have happened (she had been lucky so far). I can honestly say I hated her—not for what she'd done to herself (I hardly thought of her side) but how it would kill my mother. My parents are quite understanding, but they live in the Dark Ages when it comes to physical relationships among our friends.

Anyway, my sister planned to quit school and tell my parents. Fortunately, a close friend of ours had connections in New York City, so we arranged an abortion. I was all for this idea—by far, it was the easiest way out. My sister pulled through without any great traumatic experiences, except that she's $330 poorer and will be in debt for a long time.

It's been a few months now, and she hasn't changed at all—she's back in the same routine, as careless as ever! Why can't she understand the importance of a *real* relationship with people? I feel so lucky that I am close—very close—to a few kids whom I hope to know the rest of my life. I think I should do something to help her, but whenever I try to talk with her the same subjects always come up—boys, booze, sex. I'm not innocent by any means, but I look for a relationship first. I can honestly say that my sister has no *real* friendships, only kids she hangs around with. There are so many things I could tell her about people's feelings, but how do I begin? I've run out of approaches; not one day goes by that I don't think of things I want to let her in on.

Had to get married

MJ is a twenty-two-year-old divorcee, presently living in her home town with her two-and-a-half-year-old son. A certain amount of background is necessary in order to appreciate and understand the present situation.

Four years ago MJ began college. She had no definite goal except, as many coeds, the hope of finding her mate. Within a year, she became emotionally and, for the first time, physically involved with a fellow. As the relationship progressed, MJ became pregnant. There was no doubt in either of their minds that they would get married. In fact, MJ was happy she was pregnant and relieved to get out of college. The academic atmosphere was boring and frustrating to her.

She adjusted readily to the role of a housewife. Her husband continued to attend classes and began working full time. This schedule left him little time to devote to the marriage, aside from eating and sleeping. MJ started to have doubts about the marriage before the baby was born. She would rationalize that when the pregnancy was over she would be herself physically and emotionally again. She hoped that the baby would bring her husband and her closer. After five short months of marriage, MJ gave birth to a healthy baby boy. The couple now had a new role to play, but they were not quite ready to assume the responsibility of parenthood.

After the baby was brought home, the couple seemed to have less interaction than at any other point in their relationship. MJ now assumed the role of mother and housekeeper twenty-four hours a day, but the role of wife was hard to experience without cooperation from the husband. Because of this lack of communication between husband and wife, emotions were strained. The physical effect of the tension prevented MJ from nursing her baby. She ate constantly as she sought to relieve her anxieties and her depressed state of mind. Her husband commented that she was no longer attractive to him. He was living in his own world and neglecting his family in many ways—financially, emotionally, and physically. In his role as a father, he lacked responsiveness even to his child.

It was easy to see all the weaknesses and frustrations of the situation. The couple had been faced with big decisions and little time to feel out the situations; they were growing further apart. MJ poured all her love and attention into her role as a mother. At the least sound made by the baby she held him; it was too hard on her nerves to hear him cry. She became hypersensitive in her attitude toward people and almost neurotic in caring for the baby. She felt as though everyone looked down on her; she did not trust anyone else to care for the baby. She felt she had no one to rely on and was not in the frame of mind to rely on herself. The ground she walked was unstable, but before the walls crumbled completely, MJ made another big decision.

With the hope that someday her husband would want his family back together and be ready to assume his role, MJ took her baby and went home to live with her parents. It was with utmost concern for her son that she sought peace of mind. Her husband's visits were few and far between. MJ slowly began to realize that it was up to her to get hold of the situation and plan a future for herself and her son. The first step toward independence was a divorce. She paid for the divorce and started to see life in a new light. The marriage lasted only eleven months, but in this time MJ had lost a great deal of self-control and self-respect. She was overweight and under great stress. It was a long, slow process, but eventually a new strength of character and a more positive self-concept was acquired. Her son fulfilled her desire to love and be loved that is so important at all stages of human development. She was beginning to relate to people her own age and taking an interest in her own physical appearance. The next step was to move to a place where she could start living a life of her own. She started working and moved from her parents' house to her own apartment.

With feminine strength, MJ has gone through a maze of disillusionment and seems to have found her way out. There were times when she felt lost in a world of disappointment and confusion; no one really seemed to care. It was not until she stopped waiting for someone to help her and started depending on her own sense of direction that her life had order. She could not respect her own sense of right and wrong until she overcame feeling inadequate and defeated as a woman. She has done remarkably well in establishing a home for her son and a place in society for herself. She is presently involved with another man and believes she is in love again. He helps to restore her sense of being a woman and fills the empty niche in her life for the time being. The future status of this new relationship is uncertain. Presently it is stimulating to MJ and keeps her mind off the past. She has no desire to go back with her ex-husband. She is concerned with making each day as meaningful as possible for herself and her son.

Boot camp

My first trip to talk to the Coast Guard recruiter did not worry me too much because I had not signed anything or been sworn in as a member of the U. S. Coast Guard. However, I was very nervous when my parents were driving me to the recruiting office to take the oath of enlistment and leave for basic training. The whole way there, I kept wondering if I was doing the right thing. When I got out of the car and started to say good-bye to my parents, I could hardly talk. The thought of spending four years in the service had caught up to me! I actually considered turning around and going back home. But I had come this far, so I decided I'd better go through with it. The recruiter gave us one last chance to back out, but nobody did; I took the oath with several others. Immediately after taking the oath, I felt relieved; I had made my decision. However, my next step in the Coast Guard was pretty uncertain; I was far from being relaxed.

On the bus trip to Cape May, New Jersey, I was nervous and couldn't sleep. I kept wondering how bad boot camp was going to be. However tough it was going to be, I was determined to get through it with as little trouble as possible and as quickly as possible.

The bus arrived at the training center about 12:30 the following morning. I got to bed about 1:30 A.M., but I couldn't get to sleep for a long time because I worried about what tomorrow would bring.

Reveille was sounded at 4:30 A.M.; I had hardly gotten to sleep when it was time to get out of bed. The first day we did nothing but eat, get examined, and wait. I got my first look at boot camp in the daylight and I didn't particularly like what I saw—several hundred bald recruits marching around and being harassed by their Company Commanders. Since I still had my hair and civilian clothes, I stood out from the other recruits. After two days, I actually wished that they would shave my head and get it over with. The sooner I started basic training, the sooner it would be over!

After about four days of waiting around and being nervous and bored at the same time, we were finally formed into fifty man companies. Our new Company Commander introduced himself by putting us through some pretty rough exercises, so I knew boot camp wasn't going to be fun. He didn't talk, he yelled! He didn't have to repeat anything—he just punished anyone who didn't react quickly or correctly. I never did like taking orders, and taking them from this guy was a real insult. To add injury to insult, the Company Commander gave several fellow recruits authority to order the rest of us around. This really aggravated me because these guys didn't know any more about the military than I did. But to disobey their orders was to disobey the Company Commander, and that is against military rules.

Once we were formed into companies, basic training really got underway. The first few days they didn't give us a free minute. We didn't have time to think about anything but what we were doing at that particular moment. We were always running, marching, drilling, getting lectured, eating, or cleaning. I was really ready for the few hours that we had off on Saturday and Sunday morning and evening. Even during this free time, we were not allowed to leave the barracks or even sit on our beds. We cleaned our rifles, polished our shoes and brass, and wrote letters.

One of the things that I disliked most about boot camp was the uncertainty about what would happen next. This feeling was especially true concerning physical education class, which I considered to be the worst part of basic training. Gym class consisted of two hours of exercises, harassment, and punishment. I really would have liked to have taken some physical action against our gym instructors, but I held back the urge.

I also disliked marching and drilling with our rifles. Whenever one person blundered, the whole company was punished. An M-1 (rifle) got extremely heavy when I had to hold it above my head while running around the parade grounds. I kept on going no matter how tired I was or how much it hurt because I didn't want to be the one to quit first; I wanted to show the Company Commander that I could take anything that he ordered me to do.

Several times a week our Company Commander would hold a "white tornado" in our barracks. He would turn over the beds and mess up everything possible. This action really irritated me because it was a stupid and needless harassment that taught nothing and only proved to be very frustrating.

At meal time we were treated pretty much like animals. Get in, eat up, and get out. We weren't supposed to talk and we never had much time to eat. As soon as we were finished eating, we had to run back to the barracks. We often got to taste the food twice.

From the beginning of boot camp, I looked forward to getting out for a few hours on our fifth weekend liberty. Never did forty hours go so fast! I was no sooner home that it was time to leave to go back. Probably the worst feeling I have ever experienced was having to walk back through the gate to basic training. I dreaded it so much that I even thought about taking off—going AWOL—but I figured that it would do more harm than good.

The threat that kept me in line throughout boot camp was the possibility of being reverted—going through the same training again. More than anything else in the world, I wanted to get out of boot camp and into a more humane world where I would be treated in a more respectable way. The best and fastest way to do that was to square away—discipline myself to military life.

Basic training was not all bad, however; I did meet a lot of guys and made a few friends. Unfortunately, I knew I'd probably never see most of them again after we got out of boot camp. I also met a few recruits that I was very glad to leave behind. Several arguments took place and a few people pushed each other around, but it never got out of hand. The pressure of basic training can really get to you when you work, eat, and sleep with the same fifty guys for several weeks.

Probably the best time of day was mail call—if you got a letter, that is. After a tiring day, it was really great to hear from someone on the outside. If you didn't get a letter, however, it was very easy to get depressed and really feel low.

The most enjoyable part of boot camp was competing with other companies in track, swimming, and the obstacle course. It gave me a chance to work off some of the excess pressure that I built up every day during basic training. Also, I was pretty proud of my company because we won honor company three weeks in a row—three out of eight was pretty good.

What was supposed to be a highlight of basic training turned out to be a failure. On one of our last weekends, they permitted us to go to the USO. We were all rather excited about seeing girls again, but it turned out that there were three hundred males and twenty-five females. I spent most of the evening reading the current issue of *Playboy*. It was nice, though, just to see civilians and hear music for a change.

Inflation hit more than just my pocketbook

It was almost Thanksgiving, which meant that Christmas was not far off. I decided to do all of my shopping at once by going to the large Valley Mall in a nearby city where I knew I would have a wide variety of merchandise to choose from, thereby doing "one stop" shopping for the people on my Christmas list. I hadn't been shopping for quite a while so I was anxious to see the Christmas decorations and display after display of crisp, new merchandise.

Well, I got one of the biggest shocks of my life that night at the Mall. I knew from grocery shopping that prices were rising, but there at least seemed to be some logical explanation for them doing so. Either it was a bad year and the harvest was small or someone was on strike. Regardless, the quality of the food was still the same. This fact was not to be so with the merchandise I saw at the shopping center.

My first encounter with the Mall was a pleasant one. I went into a fabric shop looking for corduroy material. I have been sewing my own clothes for almost eight years and the price of material has hardly changed. There have been new fabrics made, but always with a price that seemed to fit the quality of the fabric. When I went into the next store I was still unaware of the shock that was to come.

Since I had included something for myself on my shopping list I decided to stop at a shoe store next. That was my first mistake. I was looking for a nice pair of winter boots. In this first shoe store, as was true in all the rest, the boots were priced from $20 to $30, but they were not made of leather and they were not of good quality. Four years ago I bought a beautiful pair of leather boots for $16. They were much fancier than anything I saw that night. Since they are still in fairly good shape, they must have been of good quality. This revelation was just the beginning of my nightmare!

As I was walking into the next store I noticed a display of hairdryers on sale, so I thought I would compare their prices with those in my little home town. I had been considering a new hairdryer so I knew what the prices were. Right then I decided that store would not get any money from me. Their hairdryers were $5 more than the average price asked for them back home. While I walked through the store I noticed other items that were priced much too high.

Whoever thought that there would come a day when knee socks would be too expensive? I never thought about it and maybe that's why I was so shocked. Every year at Christmas I have to buy knee socks because I wear mine out so fast. This was the first year that the price had gone up and the thickness had gone down, almost to nothing. Knee socks aren't any good if they aren't warm, and the knee socks I saw were about as warm as nylon stockings. Knee socks now come in every color imaginable, and every design too. All I wanted was a warm pair of plain navy blue knee socks—but none could be found!

I went into a store to buy a record album. When I saw that the price had gone up over a dollar since last year, I casually looked around and then walked out. Now I have a $300 stereo that I can't afford to buy albums for!

This next experience was not so much my problem as it was that of my friend with whom I was shopping. She was looking at briefcases without really looking at the prices. The one she finally decided on had the price of $30 crossed out, $35 written above it and then crossed out, and the present price was $40. This dilemma was solved by *not* buying the briefcase.

Last but not least were those cute little dried flowers in a glass container. They were four inches tall and cost $4 each. I thought a dollar an inch was a little ridiculous. Of course, I made this judgment, and all the others, strictly on the basis of my own opinion. However, I have watched price and quality changes taking place, so my opinion does have some merit behind it.

Each time I went to a different store I hoped I would find what I wanted, and at a price I could afford. I would have paid a higher price if I could have found something with the quality to match the price.

As the night went on I could feel the stress and anxiety building. I live on a limited budget. I pay my own way through school. I work twenty to twenty-five hours a week as a lab assistant for the Biology Department on campus. I only get paid $1.62 an hour, so it just barely pays my bills. The day I went shopping I had just gotten my tuition bill for the next semester so I knew exactly how much I could spend on Christmas.

As I walked around the Mall that night it became more and more evident that I was not going to be able to buy for everyone on my Christmas list. This bothered me because I had had such good feelings about my shopping trip. In three short hours my spirits went from very high to very low. I didn't know exactly how to cope with this frustration. I knew that the situation would be the same no matter where I went. I would guess that my defense mechanism in the form of withdrawal took over because I left the Mall without buying a single thing. I know that I can't fight inflation by not buying anything, but I still can't convince myself to go out and buy something when I know it will bother me. I think I'm going to wait until the merchandise goes on sale after Christmas, and then maybe the price will be justifiable—in my mind at least!

A professional learns to accept death

I was always told not to become too close to a patient because you will probably end up being really hurt. Everyone working in a hospital has to learn to accept death in a nonchalant way. Some of us have had to learn the hard way. My first experience with this involved a cancer victim who spent most of the summer in the hospital.

Mr. Mallon was admitted to the hospital during the first week I started working. I remember him from the first time I had to draw blood for tests. He wasn't very old. He was a "model" patient, always pleasant, never complaining. I think some of us went to him for consoling.

I saw him practically every day and watched him get progressively worse. He was moved from room to room so he could be closer to the nurses' station. I finally realized how ill he was when one day I went in to see him and he kept asking me where the PX was. He had no idea where he was.

Finally, Mr. Mallon was moved to the Intensive Care Unit. I could tell that he was hanging onto life by a thread. He would just lie there day after day without saying a word. Each day, he seemed a little more detached from reality. I watched him drift farther and farther away.

I hoped he would get better. I thought he just had to. He was getting the best care possible and had constant attention by nurses and doctors. I suppose I always knew he might die but I suppressed this idea and would not even consider it. I think it was then that I became the closest to Mr. Mallon. He was like a child that just wanted to be loved. I couldn't help but love him and silently say a prayer that he would get well.

The last day I saw Mr. Mallon, things were the same as any other day. I was doing early morning collecting. Like any other day, I had to draw blood from him. He seemed about the same as he had been the past few days. Later that day, I heard a code 99 (a signal that means someone's heart has stopped beating and to alert the heart specialist). I didn't think anything about it. Afterward, I found out that the code was sent out for Mr. Mallon. My heart sank when I found out that he didn't make it.

That afternoon, I had to go to the room where he had been. I looked at his bed—it was empty. That's when the full impact of death hit me! Someone whom I had seen every day for two months was now gone. There had been deaths in my family, but none of them affected me like this one did.

I went back to the lab after visiting his room. The other employees could see how I was shaken. I could not believe how they were acting. It made me furious to hear how they talked about him. They talked like he was just some small animal that had been hit by a car. They did not care that a person had just died; he was just one less person that tests had to be run on. To the nurses it was just one less bed that they had to worry about—at least, that is, until the next automobile accident. They really did not care, or so I thought.

As the day progressed I got more and more tied up in myself. The shock of his death left me in a sort of limbo. I could control my actions but I could not think for myself. I could only follow others' directions. I cannot remember what I did during that time span.

The people I worked with could tell something was bothering me because I never was as quiet as I was that afternoon. They probably knew what was wrong with me but did not know what to do about it. They knew it was something I would have to work out by myself.

The next day I went to work in the same state of mind as I had left the day before. I still was not thinking. This could not be tolerated because the job I was doing required precision. In my mental state I could have made many mistakes which very easily could have been fatal to the patients. My supervisor realized how upset I was. She also knew something had to be done. I could not just wander around the lab all day—there was a lot of work to be done. She came over to me and asked what my problem was; I shrugged her off. She then said some very sharp words to me that made me furious. I wanted to scream and ask her if she ever cared for someone who died. Although she reprimanded me and made me very angry, it was the best thing that anyone could have done. It snapped me out of my own little world back into reality. I was hurt for a long time after that, until I realized the big favor she did for me.

This incident was not so dramatic, but it changed my personality for a short time. It was a case of anxiety that I did not know how to cope with so I produced an exaggerated behavior. I dwelled too much on this man's death; it was something that I should have been able to handle. I know that I will never get that close to a patient again. I cannot if I want to make medical technology my career. From this experience I learned that acting nonchalant to death is not "not caring" for the person. We do care about people; if we did not we would not be in the profession. We just have to learn how to accept death, for we cannot let it affect us to the point that it hinders the quality of work we do or hampers our entire life. If we did get that involved with each patient, we would constantly be upset and depressed because we are exposed to death every day in the hospital. I made a big mistake and I know I will never do it again. I just wish I would not have to learn everything the hard way.

Self-image of four girls
THE IMAGE OF SELF: DEBBIE

I. Describe your physical self. How do you see yourself physically—size, shape, attractiveness, etc.? How do you think others see you?

I'm about five feet, six inches with light brown hair and blue eyes. I'm a little bit overweight, but not too much. I feel that I'm fairly attractive. One of the most noticeable things about me is my eyes. They can express a lot, so I try to bring out their expression with my makeup.

I'm fairly certain that others see me about the same way I see myself. They'll tell me if I look good or bad on certain days and in general I feel they approve of my looks.

II. Describe your mental self. How do you see yourself intellectually: how do you think, learn, study, etc.? How do you think others see you?

I find that when it comes to thinking I sometimes have difficulty in applying myself. Usually, I have to be in a proper frame of mind before I can actually "get into" something. I can learn things easily depending upon my interest in them. As far as studying, it's a very static process for me. I can't apply myself when I don't want to—it's a useless function! But when an idea hits me, then I can come right out with it in a very short period of time.

Others have tried to get me to open up, but I think they've tried the wrong way. It takes me a while, but if they just have some patience I feel their wait will be worthwhile.

III. Describe your emotional self. How do you see yourself in terms of your disposition, moods, temperament, etc.? How do you think others see you?

My temperament is passive. I try to understand people by thinking there is a reason why someone does or says different things. When I get in a bad mood, I become quiet and withdrawn rather than releasing it. My parents say I let people walk over me a lot. I guess this is true in some ways because I lack nerve to say "no" or to let people know how I feel about certain things. I tell

myself that in an hour things will look different, so control your temper—and try to rationalize what motivated and made a person the way he is.

IV. Describe your social self. How do you see yourself in a large group, a small group, with individuals of the same sex, the opposite sex, your relatives and family, etc.? How do you think others see you?

Socially, I get along with just about everyone. I can react best in a small group where I can get to know everyone. I like to get to know individuals and I can feel much closer to a guy than another girl. I guess guys are sort of that "big brother" that I never had. Relatives and family are more difficult to communicate with because I feel that they don't understand the world in which I'm living. They see things the way they are around them and often don't consider other possibilities. Others must like me for I feel I have many close friends and many more acquaintances. I try not to forget names and faces for I feel that a friendly "Hi" is always welcome in any situation.

V. Describe your moral or spiritual self. How do you see yourself in terms of values, standards, etc.? How do you think others see you?

Morally, I guess you could say I'm not a naive kid. I see and understand much of what is going on around me. I try as much as I can to be myself although at times this proves to be quite difficult. Spiritually, I feel alienated from the idea of a church at this time. I've come to believe that I want to find myself first and then from there I can believe much more strongly in something. I have a faith that there's someone above me, but I want to learn this on my own. You appreciate something a lot more when you can say that "I did this myself" and not that I had help. I can feel religion slowly coming back into me as the time goes on. All it takes is some time.

VI. How would you like to be different or to change? Or, how did you get that way?

I don't really want to change except maybe to be able to express my emotional feelings in words in an easier manner. My parents helped me very much in the way I grew up.

I am usually permitted to do what I feel is best for myself and in this way I learn at the same time.

THE IMAGE OF SELF: GWEN

I. Describe your physical self.

I am a small person, petite as some would call it. I suppose my shape is what can be expected for as small as I am (five feet, one-half inch). I have small features. Attractiveness—well, I feel there is room for improvement (a big one), but my boyfriend says there isn't, that I'm perfect, so "what to do?" Other people have told me I'm attractive. My one good aspect is my hair, which is usually clean and shines.

II. Describe your mental self.

According to the I.Q. test I took, I'm supposed to be pretty good, but my grades indicate otherwise. My thinking is often incoherent. I have the ability, the potential to learn, but I never developed proper study habits and I don't really know how to study. My parents think of me as very capable of learning and I know sometimes I disappoint them. Subjects like music (especially), art, P.E., I pick up easily, but others like psychology, literature, history are my downfall. I daydream constantly.

III. Describe your emotional self.

Emotionally I am immature and very confused. My disposition is changeable, but generally very good. My moods come fast and furious. I can be a completely different person from one day to the next. I can get angry very easily, depending on the situation. I also can cry very easily, especially in the past six months since I've had problems with my boyfriend and our families. His mother has told me a couple of times that I'm immature.
I am usually happy and love to be with people, especially children.

IV. Describe your social self.

In one word—shy! My social self is probably my poorest aspect. I'm very hard to get to know and sometimes I get the feeling that people are uncomfortable around me. I feel more comfortable in a small group than in face-to-face relationships. I'm much more comfortable with people of my own sex. With the opposite sex I am usually quiet and at a loss for words. I wish I could change and be more outgoing, but I don't know how.

V. Describe your moral or spiritual self.

Morally—wow! I need help but who do I go to? I have good morals; never dreamed of premarital intercourse. But my boyfriend and I have been separated (by *force*) for five months and often I wonder: "Maybe if I have his baby they'll see we love each other." I have high standards, otherwise good morals and values.
I believe in God, attend church every week, and lately have found myself praying—something I rarely do.

VI. How would you like to be different or change?

How do I say it—I'd like to be a little better built and get my face cleared up. I'm tired of looking like a boy. I would like to grow up emotionally and most of all, I'd like to have my boyfriend back. I'm a much more stable person when I'm allowed to see him.

THE IMAGE OF SELF: SANDY

I. Describe your physical self.

I'm tall and thin. Sometimes I think I'm too slender. However, I can wear almost any style of clothing, which is one advantage. I wear my hair fairly short because it's easy to take care of and because shorter hair frames my face better. My glasses bother me. I think I'm more attractive without them and hope to wear contacts as soon as I have the money to buy them. Some people tell me I look pretty without glasses—especially my boyfriend. I can see well enough without them and usually don't wear them on dates. I wish I could gain ten or fifteen pounds because I'm sure others see me as "skinny."

II. Describe your mental self.

I don't mind studying. I feel an accomplishment in learning. I especially enjoy my Spanish courses and my education courses. There's so much I don't know. I'll learn as much as I can so I can become a good teacher. I'm fairly intelligent and through good study habits manage to make very good grades. However, others see me as more intelligent than I really am. I feel as though I don't know enough to teach school. But my friends and classmates usually ask me for help with homework or other problems.

III. Describe your emotional self.

As far as my moods are concerned, I am fairly neutral. I seldom lose my temper, but neither am I usually overjoyous. I get along with everyone as a result. Lately, I have been generally depressed because of a broken engagement. I shouldn't be because I broke it. After a year of being engaged and really in love, I realized that no matter how much I loved John, I couldn't live happily with him. He was bossy and possessive of *everyone*. He didn't listen to his parents or me when he got a notion in his head.

IV. Describe your social self.

I'm much more at ease in a small group than in a large group. If I'm with people I know, it's easy to talk to members of either sex. But if I don't know anyone in the group, I'd rather talk to a member of my sex. I'm at ease with older or younger people. Everyone fascinates me whether a child, a young adult, or a middle-aged person. At first encounter, I feel that people see me as uninteresting. But after a conversation or over a period of time, they seem to like me more. I especially make good impressions with older people.

V. Describe your moral or spiritual self.

I was raised in a religious home. My parents were fairly strict in their discipline. I went to a few parties, but certainly not beer parties. My parents are very concerned about who I date. They controlled almost every aspect of my life until I came to college. My moral values have changed somewhat since then. I can tolerate being around booze and have even enjoyed drinking wine. However, I have never let myself go to the point of getting drunk. After being engaged for a year my ideas about sex have changed completely. I don't feel that a couple has to wait til marriage for intercourse. However, they must be very careful! My parents are shocked by this view!

VI. How would you like to be different or to change?

I would like to weigh more and be able to express my emotions in stronger actions.

THE IMAGE OF SELF: KAREN

I. Describe your physical self.

I have always been tall and "thin," though I've been filling out in the waist since coming to college. My figure is pretty good—tinier girls in my hall call me "Super Bod(y)" when I wear my sexy slip. I'm fairly plain but cute (freckles still!), and active. My clothes vary from mini to conservative to maxi, and my wardrobe is neither extensive nor expensive. I'm now considering changing my appearance by a different hairstyle (cut shorter).

II. Describe your mental self.

I realize from the grades I've received all through school that I am an above average student. I don't find college so very different or even much harder subject and workwise than high school. Rarely do I miss a night of studying during the week, and I usually make up on Sunday night what I neglect Friday and Saturday nights. I copy over neatly into notebooks what notes I sloppily take in class—this takes a lot of extra work and time, but I find I learn the material better that way. I usually study most the night before a test.

III. Describe your emotional self.

I know that recently I've become quieter around others. My interests are limited to working, studying, art, Frank, and home. I just can't see getting "worked up" over little things. I'm usually happy but often nasty and not very nice when I'm neglected or "picked at." I do a lot of "mental planning" and get kind of upset when things don't turn out.

IV. Describe your social self.

I like large groups better than small ones because I'm not "stuck" with dull or irritating people. There is less need to talk to and to include *everyone* in a large group and there's more freedom of thought and talk. Girls are always willing to talk and listen, but when the same old subjects are hashed over, I'd leave. Guys are okay but don't usually want to sit and gab for a long time about hundreds of different things. Frank says I'm *too* friendly.

V. Describe your moral or spiritual self.

I believe in myself, mostly. I talked with a girl we call "Judy Bible" and her thoughts are that prayer is the best thing of all—does wonders. Bull! I got what I have mostly through my own work or through my parents. There may be a God (I don't know) and if there is, fine. But I can't see what all the fuss is about. I do what's best or most pleasurable at the time, hoping that I've learned what's right and wrong.

VI. How would you like to be different or to change? Or, how did you get that way?

I got this way definitely through my entire home setting—the way the house is built, our land, our location, my brothers (no sisters), my *Dad* especially, and the silent guidance of my Mom. Dad is still the director of activities, but Mom is the provider and takes care of the little, needed things. I really am happy I've grown up who and what I *have* grown up to be.

Write about anything...
CONFLICT OF VALUES

I am a girl, 20 years old, and a junior in college. I have a problem that I've had for about a year. I suppose one would call it a conflict of values. The situation is this: I have been going with a guy for about three years now. We plan to be married sometime after I graduate but we have no definite plans. About a year ago or maybe a year and a half, we began sleeping together. I had always been taught that premarital sex was wrong, and before I met this boy there was no doubt in my mind that I would be a virgin until my wedding night. Now I can only rationalize my actions to myself by saying we are in love and this is only a way to express that love. We have talked it over together several times and made several attempts to stop. But neither of us has the strength or willpower. Deep inside I cannot

justify this to myself. If I ever became pregnant it would hurt both our parents very much. I'm not sure I could live with that knowledge. I suppose all I can do is hope it never happens until after we are married.

A FABLE

Once upon a time, not so very long ago, there was a little boy. Not actually a little boy, in fact, he was a big boy, and a very nice boy. This boy was average in that he desired what all little boys want—the freedom to choose what they want to do or what they think would be right. This particular boy's friends liked to drink alcoholic beverages (gasp!) and then do naughty things such as drive their cars very fast or say very bad words to the friendly policeman or do dirty ignorant things with little girls. However, our little boy did not enjoy these things because he didn't like to hurt other people. So, instead of consuming alcohol, he did something else. He began to smoke the dangerous killer-weed marijuana! But, instead of doing bad things and having fun at other people's expense, our brave little boy had fun doing nice things—like smiling at people, and being passive to violence, and just sitting in his little room listening to records. However, our little boy didn't realize that smoking "grass" was a very bad thing to do because "you can become a dope addict (dreadful) and kill and maim and rob to get money for opium and heroin." However, our little boy had no desire for these other nasty things—he only wanted to grow his little plants and smile and hurt no one. His little friends, however, felt sad that their good buddy was so bad. They just criticized him as they got drunk and wrecked their cars and vomited on each other. The next day all of these little boys' girlfriends were pregnant and they were all hung over, but they weren't bad boys, right? After all, the marijuana smokers are all psychotic misfits, the dregs of society, and social deviants, right? Because marijuana is illegal it's very bad, right? So we better lock up our little boy for eleven years so he doesn't poison our system, right? But suddenly there are many more smokers than we realized! What now! Actually there are a hell of a lot of smokers. What now? You got me...

GROWING UP

It is very confusing and frustrating to be an "emerging adult." As has always been true of young adults, I don't really know where I want to go or what I want to do. But today there are so many directions to go and to all extremes. Sometimes I feel like I have to try all the extremes: I've often thought of escaping from my middle-class parents, college, and the whole bit to join a commune just to try it and maybe just to appreciate my life a little more when I return. I've seriously considered being a Vista volunteer in order to feel like I can really accomplish something that *means* something. At other times I feel like I'm just kidding myself with these fantasies and that the only thing I really want is to graduate, get married, refinish furniture, and plant rosebushes. But maybe I won't be satisfied until I try the other extremes.

SOCIAL DRINKING

Should a young adult be a social drinker or not? This is a problem that many youth are faced with today. I myself am confronted with this problem quite often. I am a minor, and this, above all, influences my decision to decline all drinks at parties. Also, I do not believe in alcohol because of the many effects it has. Yet what bothers me in the issue is that the majority of my friends are also minors, and when going to their homes for a party, their parents serve us drinks. It upsets me that the parents go along with this because many of the youth do not stop with one or two drinks; they go to the point of drunkenness. When asked if you want a drink, it is uncomfortable to decline. In all instances, they look at you as if you are odd. I'm not talking about beer parties, because I've never been to one, but parties such as New Year's eve, birthday parties, and get-togethers over term break. You are *expected* to drink. This in itself can start nondrinkers along the wrong path, especially in the late teens. It is important to have your friends and parties are fun for a while, but if you don't drink, you run the risk of being excluded. I think for many youth alcohol is an escape and for others, a show. They make sure everyone sees how much they drink. How can drinking seem wrong to youth when parents O.K. it? The main factor that bothers me is that it drives nondrinkers to social drinkers, and from there . . . ? I can see it happening to many of my classmates and I don't know what to do about it. Also, if I continue my nondrinking policy, will I eventually be ousted by my circle of friends? At the present, I hope to follow my policies and run the risk. But what about the others?

MY CONCERN

Sex is a big hangup with me. I enjoy dating, but I don't feel like I am ready for one person. I'm not a free person with my feelings because I don't want to hurt anyone or be hurt myself. I'm very gullible and believe what people tell me. I learned a little bit about sex from my parents, but mostly I learned from the people I have dated. I do have high morals and sometimes I get teased about it. This bothers me. I feel in order to go all the way with someone you should be in love and married. Is this wrong to believe this way? I don't condemn anyone for having sex before marriage, but I feel it is something that is up to the individual. If society wasn't so hung up on it, maybe people wouldn't feel so guilty if they themselves really felt strong for another individual. I feel there is more to life than just sex. Getting to know people and accepting them for what they are is more important than having a one-night affair with a stranger. Consequently, because of my beliefs, I don't have as many dates as other girls my age. Should I change to meet other people's standards? I don't think I should, but others do.

WHAT'S HAPPENING?

What will happen to the world? Is some Supreme Being trying to tell us something?

As we look into our newspapers daily, all we read about is earthquakes, tornadoes, and other forms of devastation. Why has there been so much trouble placed on man? Maybe we have brought it on ourselves. Man has been ruining the earth since he was placed on it. At the present we are surrounded by all types of pollution, our natural resources are dwindling, and man continues to spoil. The earth is answering back; it is tired of being destroyed by man and therefore has decided to destroy man, little by little, just like man has destroyed earth. I would like to see the end of the world when it occurs to see how the earth finally gets even with man.

EMERGING ADULTHOOD

What it's like to be an "emerging adult"—confusion! This one word expresses the mixed up thoughts and feelings which I have. In a few months I will be twenty—only one year away from supposed adulthood. Does the age twenty-one turn you into an adult overnight?

I feel that college has been, and is, such a worthwhile experience. Here I've been exposed to many different people and problems. I'm at the point now in my life in which I am searching for my identity. Who am I? What am I doing? Where am I going?

When I look out into the world of so-called adults I wonder if I'll become like the majority of them seem to me. War, poverty, and personal strife are very sad realities that still plague us. When will we (all people) learn to live together on this earth?

The United States has so much to offer—but the prejudices are too real. There are just so many things which are here that I don't think should have to be—crime, for instance; I could make a long list.

This might be confusing to you but I'm trying to express how I feel in this time. There are so many thoughts running through my mind. What will I do when I leave this campus and become a part of that competitive world, a world where too few people care about their fellow man?

Many programs, such as welfare, penal systems, and rehabilitation, that our government has set up don't seem to be working. But maybe if we sit down as human beings and work for the common goal of social betterment instead of personal betterment we will be able to accomplish something. There are too many people who have right and wrong attitudes. I don't think that it's necessary to have the whole world democratic or communistic. People should work to coexist on this earth and not have the attitude of being here for one's own self.

SHOE-COLOGY

Studying for two psychology courses at one time can do strange things to one's mind. I find myself categorizing everything into Piaget's stages. (I have read numerous Piaget books in six short weeks.) Today, as I notice people's feet, I find myself wondering if shoes are any indication of one's personality. I wonder if they fit into "categories."

Perhaps this seemingly well-adjusted gal in front of me with the white sneakers is actually very fearful of the criticism of others so she hopes by her shoe choice to sneak into a situation or group of people without arousing notice.

Or perhaps the guy behind me with his big, clunky loafers with the heavy sounding soles actually wants to be noticed and feel important.

I wonder about the many sandaled feet I see. They must belong to "outdoorsy" people who definitely have a claustrophobic tendency and cannot stand closed-in toes.

Big heels for little people, little heels for big people; buckles and ties, straps and laces; you name it.

Finally I wonder how many people like myself would *love* to kick off their shoes and run in the green grass outside, enjoying the liberated feeling of finishing a test.

What is love?

Love
Is
A tender kiss
That awakened in my heart
An ecstasy never before known

Love
Is
The warmth of your embrace
After a leisurely walk
Through autumn leaves or snowy fields

Love
Is
The glow which fills my being
At the sound of your voice
Or the quick nod of your head

Love

Is

The memory of sunlit afternoons

When we watched a puffy white cloud

And listened to the sound of a crow

Love

Is

Laughter, sadness, ecstasy

Sharing our thoughts, our hopes, our
    dreams

Knowing that someone really cares

Love

Is

All of these

Because, my Darling,

Love

Is

You.

Meriem Fair Kaluger

THINGS TO THINK ABOUT AND DO

1. Emerging adulthood means coming out of a cocoon, like a butterfly, spreading your wings, and flying on your own—free. What kinds of butterflies are most eighteen- to twenty-year-olds? How beautiful? How frail?

2. Think back to your high school friends. What are they doing now? What will they probably be doing ten years from now?

3. Think back to your high school graduation class. Can you estimate what percentage went to college, what percentage went directly into the job market (or unemployment), what percentage got married, and what percentage went into the armed forces? Contact your high school counselor to learn whether follow-up figures are available.

4. Debate: Does freedom of sexual discussion and expression mean that a "sexual revolution," in terms of increased permissiveness and promiscuity, has taken place as compared to twenty or thirty years ago when your parents were of your age?

5. Gain a historical perspective concerning human sexual behavior. Find out what you can about sexual behavior and expression in Grecian, Roman, and Biblical times. Compare that with sexual behavior during the Middle Ages and the Renaissance, as expressed in art and in literature. Was sexual behavior, in terms of permissiveness,

any different during the 1700's and 1800's? How does the degree, extent, and value orientation of sexual behavior today compare to its expression in the past?

6. What is love? Survey people of different age levels, married and unmarried, professional and nonprofessional, to see what kind of answers you get.

7. Are the profiles of "An Open Relationship," "Will She Ever Learn?" "Had to Get Married," and "Mental Conflict" typical?

8. What parts, good and/or bad, do drugs play in the lives of emerging adults? Will drugs affect or influence one's future? Future generations?

9. Conduct a study to determine the kinds of problems and concerns that post–high school youth have. Where can they turn for information and help?

10. How do you see the future of today's eighteen- to twenty-year-olds as they approach the year 2000? How old will they be? What part will they play in society, government, and technology? Can we plan for and direct the future, or are we helpless pawns in the chess game of life?

11. What are the sources of values, extrinsic or intrinsic, that dominate moral judgments and decisions of the emerging adulthood age?

READING SOURCES

Developmental psychology texts

CRM: Developmental psychology today, ed. 2, New York, 1975, CRM/Random House, Inc., chaps. 19, 20.

Kaluger, G., and Kaluger, M.: Human development: the span of life, St. Louis, 1974, The C. V. Mosby Co., chap. 11.

Papalia, D. E., and Olds, S. W.: A child's world, New York, 1975, McGraw-Hill Book Co., chap. 14.

Related readings

Bienvenu, M. J.: Kids want more religion, America, p. 252, Oct. 4, 1969.

Eighteen-year-old adults: their unexpected problems, U. S. News & World Report, pp. 40-42, Aug. 1973.

Goethals, G. W., and Klos, D. S.: Experiencing youth, Boston, 1970, Little, Brown & Co.

Horowitz, I. L.: Rock on the rocks, or bubble

gum, anybody? Psychology Today, p. 59, Jan., 1971.

Keniston, K.: The young radicals, New York, 1968, Harcourt, Brace and World.

Keniston, K.: Youth: a new stage of life, American Scholar, Autumn, 1970.

Kohlberg, L., and Turiel, E.: Research in moral development, New York, 1971, Holt, Rinehart and Winston, Inc.

Ohlsen, M. M.: Dissident students, Contemp. Ed. 42:157, 1971.

Yankelovick, D.: The changing values on campus, New York, 1972, Pocket Books.

Part four

PERSONHOOD
Maturity in the offing

CHAPTER 9

The broad horizon years

Primitive societies and tribes of today, as well as those of the past, usually have a ceremony called "puberty rites" by which they induct their young men and women into adult society. The more sophisticated and complex a society becomes, the more difficult it is for that society to delineate the point in time when an adolescent becomes an adult. The substance of adulthood in a complex society requires more than the attainment of a certain age level; it requires a level of cognitive and emotional maturity that is reflected in a capability and a willingness to assume the responsibilities of adulthood.

To define the specific responsibilities of adulthood would be a monumental task. Suffice it to say that these obligations would center around economic, vocational, social, personal, family, emotional, and cultural tasks. The scope of these tasks would seem as broad as the ocean and as high as the sky. At this stage of life, the horizons are unlimited and never-ending. All phases of adulthood are in an expanding, growing state of being. One thing is certain, however. The time has come to put away "childish things"!

The profile "Joe College to Manhood" is a first-person account of how his life after marriage was different from his life before. Marriage is an expectation of most young adults, as are the questions and qualms pertaining thereto. A "his" and "her" account of prewedding anxieties are revealed in "Thoughts of a Bride-to-Be on the Eve of Her Wedding" and "My Wedding Day." It should be noted, however, that these profiles were written by two individuals who did not know each other.

Difficulties do occur early in some marriages. "The Second Time Around" is a story of marriage in haste—because it was the socially acceptable thing to do—then a quick divorce with time to think. After getting to know each other as they really were, they remarried and are now happy.

With so many changes taking place at one time in early adulthood there will be a need to make many kinds of adjustments. "Being Thirty is Not All That Bad" reveals an adjustment to getting older, and "Changes on Hudson Street" presents a readjustment problem that comes as a neighborhood changes it makeup.

After fourteen years of marriage, some degree of stability can be assumed, especially if the couple seemed to get along fairly well. In "The Breakup of a Marriage" the wife raises many questions for which she can find no answers until she learns of an indiscretion on the part of the husband and recognizes his inability to free himself of his guilt feelings.

Serious illness is not just something that happens to older people, as we read in "Lupus Erythematosus." "Thirty-One and Single" reveals another type of illness that can cause maladjusted and maladaptive behavior although it is not incapacitating.

Stress in different situations is part of "After-effects of a Death" and "Crisis of Anguish." Quick sketches of personal problems are presented in "Write About Anything. . ." Some are rather revealing, some are shocking—but they all reflect human concerns.

Joe College to manhood

Recently I have been noticing the changes that have been taking place in my life as my status changed from college student to husband and provider. In the past, changes in my thoughts and actions have been gradual, occurring over a period of several years. They had to be pointed out by my parents or a friend for me to even notice them. But this time, the changes were so rapid and to such an extent that I noticed them as soon as they occurred.

There are two things that have changed in my life; I am no longer a college student but an employed engineer, and I am no longer single but have a wife to support. What I did as a carefree college student last year I can no longer even consider doing.

Even though most college students won't admit it, they live the most protected, cared for, carefree life they ever will have. If a person goes to work after high school, he is usually set free by his parents and considered as being old enough to look after himself and take care of his own responsibilities. But if the person goes on to college, he gets a four year (or more) extension on his time under parental wings. In college, he is responsible to himself and himself only. He is free from direct parental supervision for the very first time in his life and will do some pretty crazy things with some of his new friends just to prove that he really can do whatever he wants. If he gets into trouble of any kind, his parents are still there waiting to run to his aid.

I know I did a lot of things in college I could never do now. Those frequent all-night pinochle games are hard to take when one has to get up for work the next day. And those parties where we could let some of our inhibitions hang loose without worrying about our dates are gone, too. Now that date is my wife, who can't get a ride back with anyone else because she has to go back with me. And if I do "hang loose," she probably won't talk to me for several days! I can honestly say that the four years I spent at college were the most fun years of my life, even though I am now very happily married.

At the ripe old age of twenty-three, only five years older than when I first entered college as a freshman, my life has totally changed from the way it was. I am now officially out of my parents' nest and on my own.

Probably the main thing that has changed my world is not getting out of college but getting into marriage. While I did work summers before I was married, I lived at home, had plenty of money for just myself, and lived fairly well. Right now, only a year later but married, I am making seven thousand dollars more a year but I am living just above the brink of poverty, not knowing if we can make it week by week. I have more bills coming in than I ever

imagined! Due to the unfortunate economic situation, I am forced to get a part-time job. That extra money really does make a difference, but who wants to be limited to a total of about three and one half hours a day with your wife so soon after getting married? It kind of makes both of us suffer. I also have many things I'd like to do and people I'd like to see, but I simply can't because of the lack of time. I feel that the little time I do have should be spent with my wife.

Imagine, one day I was a college playboy with all the wild parties, et cetera, and the next day I was a married man with many responsibilities. Under these conditions, the little boy must become a true man in every sense of the word.

Thoughts of a bride-to-be on the eve of her wedding

Well, tomorrow's the big day. Tomorrow Dick and I will be married. Tomorrow night at this time I'll be Mrs. Richard Walton. I hope everything in the ceremony goes all right. I hope the flowers arrive on time, the cake's all right, the beauticians finish our hair on time, and the food is all ready for the reception. Gee, I sure hope the reception goes off okay. I hope Dad's not too nervous to say his four big words. I hope I don't fall down the aisle or trip up the steps to the altar.

I wonder if Dick will think I look pretty. I wonder if he'll like my wedding gown. I hope he shows up and doesn't chicken out! I wonder what wedding gifts we'll get at the reception. We've already gotten such lovely things— toaster, T.V. tables, blankets, and something I'm going to need, a cookbook. I wonder whether we'll receive any money as gifts. We sure could use it on our honey...

Honeymoon! Tomorrow night at this time we'll be on our honeymoon. We'll be halfway to the Catskills. What will Dick think when he sees me in the sexy nightgown I bought? I wonder if I'll have it on long? Will he be satisfied with me tomorrow night in bed? Will I be able to please him? Will I be a good bed partner? Will he love me as much after we've made love to each other? Oh, I hope so. I love him so very much; I'm sure I'll be completely satisfied with him!

A week in the Catskills and then my job really starts. I'll have to make a lovely apartment for Dick to come home to at night. Will he be happy with my cooking? Will I? I sure wish I had taken the time to learn to cook when my mother wanted me to! I wonder if he'll think my cooking's as good as his mother's. His mother always makes food so sweet; I hope he'll like my food. And what about the apartment! Will I be able to keep it clean enough for him? It'll sure be a job—working as a secretary during the day, coming home and cooking a meal for my husband, doing the dishes, keeping the place clean, doing the washing and ironing and mending. How will I ever get all that finished! I guess I better get used to ironing slacks and shirts all the time because Dick will need to have a neat, clean appearance every day.

I wonder when we'll be able to afford to buy a house. What will it be like? I know it probably won't be as nice as Mom and Dad's house, but I wish it could be. Even if we don't get a house for several years, I'll try to make a warm, comfortable, loving home for Dick wherever we are. How soon will we have children? How many children will we have? Dick and I have decided that we would like to have four children—two boys and two girls. I hope everything will be all right and we will be able to have them. What will we name them? Tammy? Candy? David? Mark? I wonder what they'll want to be when they grow up. Doctor? Lawyer? Dentist? Teacher? Nurse? Secretary? Will they want to go to college? Will they be in the military service?

Will I be a good mother to my children? Will Dick be a good father? Will we do a good job of raising our children? Will we produce good responsible citizens? Will we give them the religious instruction they need? What will the world be like when they are ready to meet it face to face? Will there be a lot of riots and dissension? Will there be wars for them to fight in? Will there be depressions? What will it be like? What will it be like when our children are all grown up and have left us and we're left with a big empty house? Will Dick still love me then? Will I be a good companion to him in our old age?

What about our marriage? Will it be a happy one? Will Dick get tired of me and want to try someone new? Will I get tired of having him around the house every night? Will our marriage last until "death do us part"? I pray to God that our marriage may be a good, healthful relationship between two mature people who love each other very much. . . .

My wedding day

The hour was late, but falling asleep seemed to be an impossible task. Although my body desperately wished for sleep, my mind refused to submit to this condition. My thoughts seemed to run the entire spectrum of emotions. An anxious thought would be followed by a happy one, which in turn would be followed by one of fear. The reason for this turmoil was that in seven more hours I was to be married!

Since sleep still seemed to be impossible, I began to dwell on these thoughts. First, I attempted to speculate as to what marriage was really like. I tried to imagine what the honeymoon would be like; how it would be to come home from work to a wife; whether we would be able to have children. These were only a few of my thoughts as I mentally tried to encompass the lifespan of a marriage.

Next my thoughts turned to ones of anxiety. "Was I really ready to get married" was the foremost one. I began to question myself in relation to this thought. Would I be able to make the transition from being a bachelor to being a married man; could I cope with the responsibilities inherent in marriage; would I resent the loss of my so-called "freedom" that I had heard other married men speak about so often. These were some of the thoughts that raced through my troubled mind. It was with these thoughts that I finally fell asleep.

Again I was awakened. Although I felt as if I had only slept for a few minutes, a glance at my watch showed that three hours had passed. My first thought was "Only four more hours until I'm married!"

I decided to go with my brother and eat breakfast. I thought that having something to do and having someone to talk with would ease the tension that I was starting to feel. However, this proved to be an erroneous assumption on my part. I had little appetite for food and all conversation invariably returned to the subject of my marriage. My brother's attempts to assure me that all men had these last-minute thoughts did little toward alleviating the nervousness that I was feeling. There seemed to be a direct relationship between the passage of time and the intensity of this feeling of nervousness. The closer it came to the hour of eleven, the more nervous I felt!

We returned to my apartment and I started to dress. As I put on my tux, my thoughts took a new and somewhat strange twist. I began to wonder why I had selected this particular woman to be my mate for life. I had dated other girls but had never really considered marriage with any of them. What quality or qualities did this woman possess that made her so different from other women I had known? What was so special about her that I was wanting to change my entire life pattern? She certainly was physically attractive, was interesting to talk with, had a pleasant personality, and was fun to be with. However, I had known other girls who had these same qualities, and I didn't marry any of them. I continued to think along these lines but, try as I did, I couldn't arrive at a concrete solution. My thought process was interrupted by the sound of my brother's voice as he announced it was almost time to leave for the church.

Now I was standing in the sacristy of the chapel. It was now ten minutes before eleven o'clock and the nervousness which began at breakfast had reached a new height. The best man's attempts to ease my tension with some humorous remarks about marriage met with no success. I was again dwelling on the same thoughts that had plagued me since early this morning.

The music started. We left the sacristy and I walked to the center of the chapel. My bride-to-be was walking down the aisle with her father. As I watched her approach, I felt as if a great weight had been lifted from my shoulders.

All of the doubts, fears, tensions, and nervousness disappeared. They were replaced by a feeling of happiness and confidence. She arrived at the place where I was standing. I looked at her and she took my arm; as we approached the altar, I had one thought in my mind. I now knew why I had selected this woman to be my wife. I loved her.

The second time around

Upon graduation from college, I got married. It seemed like the thing to do. Most of the discussions with friends my senior year centered around wedding plans. I had known and dated Keith less than a year, but we were married in spite of objections raised by my parents. This was what I wanted; therefore this was what I did. It took us a long time to adjust to each other and to married life. After only one year, I was sure that I had to be the most unhappy girl in the world. After two years of marriage, we had a baby. I was sure a baby was going to take care of all our problems. Somehow the little fellow compounded our small problems into monumental ones. I didn't know how to care for him, and I resented the fact that I had to stay home day after day caring for a baby and doing daily household chores. Certainly a college graduate should be above washing and ironing, cooking and cleaning. I wanted to go back to work. I wanted to talk to other people. I wanted a better life. My husband just didn't understand me. There seemed to be only one solution to my predicament, so I hastily filed for a divorce. Again my parents tried to talk me out of such a drastic move, but I was old enough to make my own decisions!

Keith didn't object to my divorcing him, so that confirmed my belief that he loved neither our baby nor me. The fact that he was working at two different jobs from six in the morning until midnight to make ends meet didn't concern me. He helped me pack my belongings and furniture and even helped the movers. He followed us to my rented house and helped me settle. Then he moved a bed, some linens, a few

There has been too much talk of what children
owe their parents, too much talk of the tremendous gift we give them when we bring them to
life. Life is a pretty terrific gift for those of us
who get a reasonable number of breaks, but it
is a gift only if it is a free gift. Yet most of us
parents have an irresistible impulse, as soon as
we have given a child the gift of life, to start
tying strings to it.

Hannah Lees
SATURDAY EVENING POST

dishes and pots into a tiny apartment of his own.

It surprised me greatly that he was sitting on my front porch every Sunday morning before I even got up. Why had he come so early? I couldn't understand why he sent me flowers just because I had a cold. Why should it make any difference to him? As the months passed, I began to realize that trying to be a mother and father and a breadwinner while living alone was not fun. It was difficult to try to be so many things at one time. Keith was calling me during the week to see how our son was. He even asked me to have dinner with him. We started to date occasionally and discussed our previous problems. We saw each other more frequently. We had longer talks and began to reconsider our marriage. Both of us had matured a great deal during that year.

I realized my childish haste in obtaining a divorce. It was not the answer. I was both pleased and honored when Keith asked me to marry him again. Since the beginning of our "second time around," we've grown to love each other deeply. Our marriage is solid and happy. We understand each other, and I feel that my husband is also my friend. I like him. We share now and are considerate of each other. He is in my thoughts constantly. I like to do small things for him that I know will please him. We can spend a quiet evening at home together without saying much to each other. A smile seems to communicate so many things that we couldn't have said to each other before. I now know there is much more to marriage than I ever conceived possible. I take pride in my husband and children. The birth of our daughter was a joyful experience for both of us, and I have a feeling of inner contentment as I care for our children. I take pleasure in preparing meals for our family instead of merely cooking. My household chores no longer seem to be the burden they once appeared to be. I realize that these tasks must be accomplished but I derive so much pleasure when Keith comes home to a happy home, children, and wife. Our experience was a painful one but a well-learned lesson. We have profited greatly from it. I, especially, have grown to the extent where I can consider myself well on the road to adulthood.

Being thirty is not all that bad!

"So you're thirty! Better be careful or you'll start falling apart." "Never trust anyone over thirty." I've heard these comments and many more like them since my thirtieth birthday recently. In fact, in today's youth-oriented society so much ridicule and negative statements seem to be directed toward the thirties that I began to wonder if anything was good about being thirty. While my life-style and personality may not be particularly stimulating to a younger person, I think they offer some definite advantages.

Probably the most advantageous characteristic at this point in my life is a developing sense of autonomy. The recent impact of social and technological changes had imposed such great changes on all of us that it is sometimes difficult to think of oneself as self-governing. However, I feel it's crucial to realize that what one says and does can still make a difference. For me, the years spent in school helped me to develop a sense of competence that, in turn, has helped develop within me a positive self-image.

My personal relationships have been particularly affected by this feeling of autonomy. My older friends reflect my own type of life-style and interests; my newer friends are not always so much like myself. No longer do I feel the need to join the "in" crowd and do the "in" thing. Relationships are now built on more honest levels than on society's current idea of being "with it." I feel more free to be me.

Recently, I find myself in that peculiar position of sometimes being the oldest member of a group. I think, by virtue of my "advanced years," I'm often asked personal opinions and advice regarding all sorts of things. My younger friends' confidence in my viewpoints has actually given me greater self-confidence in decision-making. At one time I would have welcomed someone making difficult decisions for me, but now I usually try to approach problems more maturely: gathering all pertinent information, digesting it, consulting knowledgeable people, and making a decision that seems best for all concerned.

Perhaps decision-making is less difficult because I feel I've gained a clearer sense of myself through the development and awareness of values. When a person has a strong sense of values, the task of choosing from the vast range of alternatives offered today is lighter.

Setting one's values can be a very complicated process since changing times appear to bring about changes in values. I suppose those values taught in early life from parental and religious teaching still affect me; however, I feel more knowledgeable in deciding what's relevant for me today.

Perhaps I can illustrate how changing times and life experiences have affected my position concerning abortion. I was always taught, both at home and in school, that abortion under any circumstance was wrong. This was the unwavering view I held until I recognized the problems of overpopulation, poor quality of life, new permissiveness in sexual attitudes, etc. Abortion may or may not be the answer to some very complex problems. However, I've also come to realize that abortion and the high regard I place upon human life are incompatible. After attending conferences and meetings regarding the pros and cons of abortion and reading about human development, I've decided that, for me, abortion is still wrong. Nevertheless, I can be understanding of the views of others.

I've mentioned that autonomy and an awareness of values are an important part of my life today. Goals are also very relevant to my daily routine. Life seems more meaningful when arranged around goals—not only long-term goals but simple, everyday goals, such as stating: "Today I'm going to wash windows."

Ideally, the mature individual constantly sets sights on new aims and achievements. This is important since one must be flexible, willing, and able to change in order to exist in our world. Very often change is a refreshing challenge for me. But not always. More than I would like, I opt for the secure in the conflict of stability versus change. Stability and predictability offer a less frustrating, safer way of life. In time I hope to become "vulnerable" to change as explained by Fromm in *The Revolution of Hope.*

On the whole, my broad goals haven't changed much since first established some time ago. Fortunately, many of them—marriage, family, career—have been realized, and I have

confidence to hope for the achievement of the others. It's comforting to dream; it's even more so when I believe I have the abilities and support of others to see dreams become reality.

Along with becoming surer of my inner self, I've begun to concentrate on maintaining my outer self as well. When friends told me I'd start falling apart at thirty, they were only partially correct. I have noticed some body changes and, consequently, try to take better care of myself through exercise and diet. I'm afraid it's taken thirty years to realize the importance of this!

While I don't always enjoy exercising, I am enjoying other things lately since I've stopped feeling guilty about my inadequacies. Having been raised in a very competitive environment with material rewards the ultimate accomplishment, I constantly strived to compete on the highest level, in sports, in school, and in my work. I've carried this thought with me for a very long time, but, suddenly, last summer, I learned the knack of priorities and self-competition. Having to do two important things adequately always seemed like an impossibility to me until I finally decided that usually one task was more important than the other to my family and me. I did my best work in my first choice and only fulfilled what was necessary for the other. What a relief to let down a little once in a while without feeling I had short-changed someone!

Just being thirty doesn't automatically make all indecisiveness and insecurities disappear, as this profile might suggest. There are two worries or anxieties which concern me from time to time. They pertain mainly to my family. Our life together is good—so good that I sometimes worry about whether I will be able to cope with difficulty if and when something might go wrong. Besides this, I constantly wonder whether I am doing everything I can to bring greater fulfillment to all of us. I would hope that by trying to move away from my egocentricity and toward a keener perception of my family's feelings, I can be of more help.

I'd be less than honest if I said thirty was the perfect age for me, since I still sometimes reflect and say: "I wish I would have done that." But my concern is really not for the past but for the future. At the moment I am experiencing a great impatience to "get on with things." I'm very anxious to resume my career and, perhaps, start a new phase of my life. However, I also realize giving my small son a good start in life is very much more important. In the meantime I'll use my time to spread the word: "Being thirty is not all that bad!"

Changes on Hudson Street

We knew when we moved to our house on Hudson Street six years ago that it was not the house of our dreams. The move was made simply out of necessity and economy. We desperately needed a house, and Hudson Street offered one for an amazingly good price.

The fact that the house was located on the fringe of an inner city never had any influence on my husband's and my decision. Besides, Hudson Street doesn't resemble a typical city street. Although encircled by some fairly busy intersections, the street seems cut off from the inner city atmosphere. Wide, spacious lawns surround older, substantially built two-story homes—the kind constructed prior to World War II. Every spring the older residents and, due to rising food costs, younger residents alike can be seen planting good-sized gardens in the alley directly in back of their homes. Only two blocks away is a playground that used to be filled with fantastic action toys, not just the usual swings, sliding boards, etc. Within walking distance is a school formerly used as an elementary school; since school district reorganization, it has become an early childhood center where the oldest student is a second grader. There are a few presupermarket grocery stores nearby which feature many things I remember from my childhood—penny candy, big soft drink cabinets where one can open the top lid and choose whichever drink suits him. It's a nice city neighborhood with a small town atmosphere. That's the way it was!

Remembering back, I can still hear myself comment while taking our young daughter for walks: "Doesn't anyone under thirty live here? What are you going to do for playmates?" It seemed, and was later substantiated, that most of the residents on the two-block long street were senior citizens. Several had their homes built for them years ago and continue to live in them today. Rarely did a house go on the real estate market. Our own house was put up for sale only after its original inhabitants had both died within a few months of each other. Ironically, that's how several other younger couples got their homes. Little by little, younger couples began to move in, and our daughter was fortunate to become acquainted with a nice group of friends of comparative age.

Characterizing the residents of Hudson Street is not too difficult. The majority, as mentioned previously, are older, middle class, white, and conservative in their viewpoints. The six or seven younger couples are also middle class, white, and, it would be a safe statement to make, they also hold rather conservative opinions. These parents are very conscientious, perhaps a little too protective, and somewhat reluctant to let their children have independence.

Here are a few samplings of some of my neighbors' opinions regarding this question on education: "What do you feel is most important for schools to emphasize?"

> Sandy, age thirty-five, mother of an eight-year-old girl: "I want Lori to listen and learn to respect authority."
>
> Rosemary, age thirty-three, mother of one preschooler and two in elementary school: "Discipline is really the most important thing because then they can fit in almost anywhere."
>
> Mrs. W., age sixty-eight: "Children need more guidance. Teachers should lay the law down more often."

My answer to the above question would be in disagreement with my friends. I think schools need to deemphasize rigid control and help children learn to handle independence more effectively. Many incidents that have happened in our city schools recently make me wonder whether I should look at this question more closely. If I were teaching in a large city school, would I answer it in the same way?

One subject that seems to particularly bring a consensus of opinion is that of civil rights, especially pertaining to blacks.

Mrs. W.: "They're ruining our neighborhood. Just look what they've done to our schools and playground! They should have their own place to live and we should have ours. Due to the bussing law, students are bussed in and out of neighborhoods to achieve a fifty-fifty socioeconomic ratio. Our neighborhood children attend a variety of schools and keeping track of bus locations and schedules is a rigorous task. Our children can no longer walk to school or participate in the 'neighborhood school' concept."

Rosemary: "Mr. and Mrs. Dexter (our black neighbors) are fine, but maybe we won't always be so lucky. You know the reputation some people have for messing up neighborhoods."

Sandy: "Lori is having trouble with two big

Man must work. That is certain as the sun.
But he may work grudgingly or he may work
gratefully; he may work as a man, or he may
work as a machine. There is no work so rude
that he may not exalt it; no work so impassive
that he may not breathe a soul into it; no
work so dull that he may not enliven it.

Henry Giles
GOOD BUSINESS

black kids and the teacher won't do a thing about it. I bet if Lori was bothering someone her teacher would jump all over her."

My personal views are so totally dissimilar. Every so often I manage to get a word in; however, I'm very doubtful that it's really heard.

Hudson Street has members of different ethnic and religious backgrounds. Most adults have high school educations, but only three families have college experience. They're a patriotic group as indicated by flags waving every appropriate holiday. Not overly materialistic, there is no trying to keep up with the Joneses, but they do take an extraordinary pride in the upkeep of their homes. Although not really social, a friendly feeling pervades as expressed by their unspoken axiom: "I'll respect your privacy and I expect you to do the same for me, but if you should need help, I'll be the first to come."

This, then, is a brief background picture of Hudson Street. The picture has changed, and some interesting developments have occurred during the last two years.

The first change began when my neighbor, Mrs. B., started to complain two years ago about the rough treatment her teenage children were receiving in the city schools. "They are both bright and enrolled in advanced classes, but they still come in contact with blacks from time to time," she revealed. The culminating, deciding factor came when her son was attacked by a group of black students after school one afternoon. Within weeks her house was not only put up for sale but sold—to a black couple.

Our neighbors on the other side of us, Mr. and Mrs. W., had known Mrs. B. and her family for years. I thought I knew the W's. fairly well, but I was unprepared for the extent of their deep, emotional feelings regarding blacks. Mrs. W. actually cried every time she contemplated the thought of black neighbors, and Mr. W. on several occasions stood in the middle of his yard and directed some of the strongest language I ever heard him use toward his neighbors who had sold their home to the blacks. In between phone calls from other neighbors inquiring if we planned to move, my husband and I tried to grab a quiet moment to get our own feelings in perspective. First, disgust. The black family paid so much more than the true market value for their new house. Second, doubt. What kind of people would pay so much for that particular house? Perhaps this was really a block-busting move. Third, disappointment. Our new neighbors were older and had no small children. Since that hectic time we have met and made valuable friends of our new neighbors; they have become very much a part of our lives.

Not far from our street is a low-income housing district that has become known as "the projects." In the six years that we have lived here this area (but not our street) has become quite a problem for our city—the center of robbings, rapings, murders, and drug raids. That nice playground mentioned earlier is now completely rundown, and the city had long since stopped replacing play equipment. Many of the grocery stores are closed because of repeated burglaries, and children are warned not to go beyond Hudson Street. It just seems as if the inner city is closing in on us and the question everyone is asking is: "When will all this hit our street?"

We didn't have to wait long. Last October the house next to us was burglarized by two young black boys. Ironically, it was our black friends who were robbed. A few months ago one of our teenage boys was badly beaten by a group of blacks who attacked him not far from his home on Hudson Street. Not long after this incident happened, an elderly couple decided to retire to their vacation home. Within weeks they were gone, and we had new black neighbors who had two albino children. Well, this just proved too much for the W's, who bought a cottage up the river and spend most of their time there.

"Little Joe," as he has come to be known, had a lot against him from the beginning. He is one of the new children who moved in. His looks are a little startling and his eyesight, which is extremely poor, is compounded by crossed eyes. He's clumsy and uncoordinated and looks so much older and bigger than his five years. "Why can't he act his age?" is a comment frequently made by parents thinking that he is actually older than he is. On top of all this, Joseph has a very unpredictable temperament and displays actions and behavior our children are unused to. Consequently, "Little Joe" is not the most popular playmate on Hudson Street. He can be difficult for the adults as well. As an example, during this lovely fall weather my family spent a great deal of time in the yard. I learned to keep the doors locked because once in a while when we were out Joseph came in and left quite a mess. Talking to his parents hasn't been too profitable, since his mother told us she's unable to watch him every minute and if he does anything he shouldn't I should hit him as she does—with a plastic baseball bat.

The "Little Joe" incident has brought knowing "I told you so" glances from some of my neighbors. Rosemary mentioned she warned me long ago that we wouldn't always be so lucky with our new neighbors. Mrs. W. hinted it really was my own fault since I should have insisted from the very beginning that Joseph stay away from our yard and children.

All these physical changes have initiated a lot of emotional changes in the people of Hudson Street. I'm not as trusting or amenable to new ideas of community development after several attempts at trying to secure greater protective measures have failed.

I honestly don't think any of us want to move just because blacks are moving in, even though quite a stir occurs after each new black family moves in. Somehow we'll find a way to "get it together" and learn to live with one another. The real culprit and cause of discontent is to have that ominous question constantly before us: "How long before it will come to our street and to my home and family?"

The breakup of a marriage

Two people have been married for fourteen and a half years. As half of that marriage, I had expected to be a part of the relationship until one of us died. We shared many things—numerous friends, the creation of two children, the stillborn birth of another, the adoption of a third, many and varied sexual experiences, camping vacations in many areas, three different homes, ideas, books, and many other things. Now I wonder if maybe there wasn't a lack of inner sharing and feeling of these things that I thought were so meaningful to both of us; otherwise why would a split occur and a parting of the ways seem necessary?

There was a feeling of utter desolation within me when I realized that someone I still loved had rejected me. I can't sleep at night, and in my nightmares I continually ask: Why? How could I have avoided this? What is wrong with me that I am rejected so? I examine and look at things that have happened during recent years, and many of them I see in a different light. I wonder why I was so naive about some things that seem so obvious now. Or maybe I now understand words that were spoken long ago in a new way. For example, I asked: "Do you love me?" and got the answer: "I'm committed to you." Why didn't I see through that half-hearted reply?

Many, many thoughts go roaring through my mind; in fact I find it difficult to do many of the daily tasks because I think of nothing else. Reading is particularly difficult because my mind continually slips away, but I must read because part of the way back to happiness is to return to school.

First and foremost, I realize how little I knew and understood about him, even though I supposedly lived very close to him. I know, even more now, how we are all truly islands unto ourselves when it comes to knowing what goes on within our minds. Some people apparently seem to prefer to maintain more of that "islandness" than others. Why do some people not want to share what is going on inside? Are they afraid of what other people will see and know about them or don't they know how to share themselves? Who can understand and comprehend the mind?

I instinctively turned to friends and family who loved me to help me share the burden, to unlock the secrets. But he refused to tell anyone how he feels and why. He is willing only to say that he has decided that the break must be made. Why does he keep to himself so much?

He is forty-two, and he has long felt that he is in the wrong profession. There are other things that he would rather be doing. Is he at the crucial stage when he realizes that it is now or never and that an allout move to fulfill himself is the only way? It is almost as if he is possessed by a power beyond himself; he has become a different person. It is as if he has to overturn everything to begin again.

I know that more than anything else I dread the aloneness that is at hand. I wonder about my attractiveness and whether I have the courage to try to build a new relationship. Am I even capable of a satisfying relationship with another human being, especially if that being is male? I know that I don't want to go to bed alone for the next twenty, thirty, or forty years that I might have yet to live. I know that I want to have someone with whom to share ideas, love, laughter, sex, problems, and all that makes up life. Can I ever trust myself to someone again? I ask: "Will someone want me or does my having been rejected mean that I'm not much to be desired?" If someone else never comes along, can I live alone happily? Looking at my marriage through new eyes, I realize that in its present state it could never be very fulfilling and, as much as it pains me to see it end, I somehow know that it may very well be for the good. No matter how I look at it, the pain is excruciating; unless one has experienced it, I doubt that another can understand.

Looking back over the last two years, I have had premonitions that we were pulling apart. I had felt depressed and have often wondered what to do, but no answers came until suddenly it all exploded in my face. One night my husband decided that he wouldn't make love to me, even though I asked him to. He merely said: "What is the use?" The previous few times that we had intercourse he had complained of pain. Does this have anything to do with it? Several evenings later, he said to me, hesitatingly, that he felt we should ultimately be divorced. The words seared into my innermost being like fire. I lost my head and said: "You might as well leave now." He did, and the real break began. Pride, rift, and hurt are now hard to overcome, and I feel that there may be no turning back.

He has indicated that there isn't another woman. For that I am thankful because the hurt would be twice as much to know that someone else had been able to know and to understand and to love where I couldn't. That there isn't anyone else, however, makes it more

difficult to understand and accept. My presence must be so unbearable or such an evil force that he feels the need to get away. What thoughts and feelings are eating away at him? Or is it that my needs are too much for him to try to meet?

A fellow worker of his suggested the best of psychiatric and marriage counseling, but he said "No!" without hesitation. Is he afraid of something—of what he may find out about himself or of possible reconciliation? If so, why? I am determined in my own mind that the one stipulation that I will put on consenting to a divorce is that we both must have counseling—not only so that I can feel that all possible avenues have been tried but also so that I can have some inkling as to why it happened. This might make future relationships a better possibility and more workable.

I can't quite put the puzzle together, but somehow I know that some of what is being said in the women's liberation movement has some logic. Women should have their own identity. What they are should not depend completely on their husbands. Women should not be raised to all fit into one mold type—that of wife and mother. New ways of dealing with marriage have to be tried. What and where are the answers?

He is gone, and he has even refused to communicate with me, so I am completely in the dark and very much alone. My heart aches, my stomach churns, and I wonder each day how I can ever continue to live without falling apart. I watch people around me laugh and carry on life's simplest tasks with contentment and I wonder if ever again I will be able to live as happily.

AUTHOR'S NOTE: A year later, the cause of the breakup came to light. The husband had an affair with his secretary. His feelings of guilt, remorse, and shame were more than he could cope with. He felt that he did not deserve to have his wife and children because he had disgraced himself in their eyes, so he pulled out. He left his job, the secretary, and his family.

Lupus erythematosus

The following profile deals with an event in my life which I will always remember. I was in my late teens when I was told that my oldest sister, Helen, probably had only two days to live.

For about three years following the birth of her daughter, Helen had been having health problems. She had visited various physicians for treatment, but none of them could accurately diagnose her illness. Some said that she had arthritis, and others felt her sickness to be psychosomatic or simply her nerves. After visiting so many doctors who could not help her, I, too, was beginning to wonder if her difficulty was in her mind. But on the other hand, I would ask myself if the mind could cause that much pain for a person. Helen was at a point where she could barely move any part of her body without crying. I can not forget how helpless I felt. I wanted to do something that would comfort her, but nothing seemed to work.

Finally, her family doctor decided to admit her to a medical center. When I learned that she was entering the medical center, I felt somewhat relieved. I thought that now, once and for all, we would know what was wrong. However, after her admittance, Helen did not appear any better. Again when I visited her, I felt helpless. I wanted to aid her in any way—but how? I remember thinking back at the times I had been able to calm her when she would become upset. Helen had always been rather high-strung and would become emotionally upset rather easily.

Once she was in the medical center, all kinds of tests were run. Still the doctors could not pinpoint her problem. I asked myself: "What's wrong with these doctors? They've been testing, jabbing, and poking at her and still don't know the answer." I kept thinking that the doctors had to know why she was ill. They were doctors, weren't they! They had to know!

Several hospital consultations were held to try and ascertain the answer. Finally, the doctors arrived at a conclusion. The doctors told us that Helen had a rare blood disease called lupus erythematosus. They stated that at times it can be fatal. Immediately, my mind flashed to leukemia and its terrible end results. Then I tried to convince myself that Helen could never be in the fatal category. She couldn't be—not my own sister!

The following day, Helen's husband came to my parents' home. My mother, dad, and I were eating lunch when my brother-in-law walked into the room. He had a strange look on his face. My parents didn't say a word, and Jack asked me to go into the other room with him. When I did, he told me that the doctors had said that when lupus is at a critical stage, the patient usually has a weakness of some internal organ. Helen's kidneys had become very bad, and she probably would survive only two days longer. After that, Jack broke down. I had never seen him like that before and tried to think of something to tell him. I put my arm around him and said not to give up hope. I told him that he had to go on, especially for Nikki, their little girl. Immediately, he pulled away and said that he didn't want pity. I felt numb. In the meantime, my parents had guessed what Jack had said to me. My mother began to cry, but my dad just looked into space with a blank expression on his face. Before leaving, Jack gave us a little hope. The doctors were going to try to pull Helen through with massive dosages of cortisone.

Shortly after, my parents and I drove to my aunt's home to tell her the sad news. I did the driving but can hardly remember being behind the wheel. My mind flashed back about four months when Jack had been in a serious automobile accident. I remember Helen being in the emergency room waiting. She didn't appear to be too concerned about Jack, but now I realize that she must have been in so much pain herself that she wasn't capable of thinking about him. I feel guilty because I had thought that she didn't care. When we arrived at my relatives' home, I told my aunt and uncle about Helen. I went through everything that Jack had told us. I couldn't believe that I was the one to be telling them. Why me? I never thought that I could keep my composure in a situation like that, but somehow I did. After hearing the story, my uncle began to sob. Still, my dad just walked around and kept staring into space. I wondered how my dad felt and why he didn't say or do something. He had been much more strict with Helen than with my older sister and me. At times, I think he had been unfair with her. I wondered if he was thinking about that. My mother continued to cry and blurted out that she loved me. I didn't believe it! She hadn't told me that in ages. During the previous five years or so, the two of us hadn't gotten along very well. I remember asking myself why she had waited until now to tell me that.

That evening I felt that I had to talk with someone. I called Mark, who is now my husband, to tell him. Really, I guess I needed someone to comfort me. He talked with me and told me not to give up, but I just wasn't able to think clearly. That night I kept waking up with a sick feeling in my stomach. I felt so frightened and couldn't believe such a thing could be happening. I thought morning would never come.

For the next few days, things continued to be confused and upset. Everything seemed a blur to me. Finally, we received the good news that Helen was improving. She was taking twelve cortisone tablets a day. I wanted to be optimistic, but I was afraid to be. As the days passed, Helen continued to get better. Gradually I began to believe that she would live. Her kidney condition cleared up, and she began to move without pain for the first time in years. I felt like a tremendous load had been lifted from my shoulders. Also, I felt thankful to God and the doctors who had saved her. Simultaneously I wondered how I would have felt about God and the doctors if she had died. From the cortisone, Helen developed purple blotches over most of her body. Her face swelled tremendously and became covered with blemishes. I felt so bad for her, yet I knew it was that or nothing. Eventually her dosage was cut, and her skin started to clear.

Today Helen is no longer taking twelve cortisone tablets per day, only one. Her doctor feels that her health is very good. Still, I wonder if Helen realizes how ill she was and would be without her medication. Recently she mentioned having another child, but her doctor was very much against it. He told her that if she did have another baby, it would probably be retarded or defective in some way because of the medication she was taking. Again my heart went out for her, but I keep telling myself that

she's just lucky to have her precious little girl and I'm especially fortunate to have my sister Helen.

Thirty-one and single

Janet is single at thirty-one, and this fact causes her a great deal of unhappiness. She is not an unattractive woman, but she does not do much to make herself look attractive and more desirable. Janet also has emotional problems and is usually experiencing some physical problem. Some of her physical discomforts are emotionally based, I'm sure, but for some reason she does seem to contract all the contagious viruses that prevail during the fall and winter months. Many people suffer similar illnesses but, combined with her mental state, Janet is in a constant state of hopelessness and despondency.

Janet is one of two daughters in an upper middle-class home. As a child, Janet never wanted for anything material. She had many girl friends, and she played in the band in junior and senior high school. However, Janet was extremely overweight in junior high school, and she was also somewhat masculine in appearance. Her weight created an emotional problem that wasn't helped by the fact that her only sister was a small, petite, popular blonde. Janet lost some weight when she entered senior high school, but she never gained any real self-confidence or sense of self-acceptance. Her attitude at that period was one of self-deprecation.

Janet began to look forward to going away to college as a means of establishing her independence from her parents and meeting a nice young man with whom she could establish a meaningful relationship. She also decided at this time that she would like to enter the field of education because she had always loved children and felt she would be very happy working with them. Unfortunately, in choosing a college, Janet chose to go to the same school where her older sister had gone. Her older sister had been very popular and had gone through two engagements during her four years at this college. Now Janet was again following behind her sister. Although she did date and had joined a sorority where she made many friends, she still felt inadequate because she kept comparing her situation to her sister's.

Her college days completed, Janet and several of her single girl friends rented an apartment and began their teaching careers. During these two years away from home Janet really began to enjoy herself. However, at the end of the second year, due to some dissatisfaction with her teaching assignment and also due to some dissatisfaction with her romantic interests (in comparison with those of her roommates), Janet decided to return home to teach in her home town.

Janet had now returned to a situation where she was dependent upon her parents in every way, except financially. Her older sister had since married and was settled into a beautiful home nearby with her husband. Janet's mother was the typical overprotective mother who welcomed her "baby" home with open arms. She proceeded to do everything for Janet that a mother ordinarily would do for a young daughter—including washing, ironing, packing her lunches, preparing her meals, etc. Janet was required to do nothing around the home; in fact, at times she was asked not to because her mother could do it faster or better without her help.

Janet's father was a very quiet man who seldom offered words of encouragement to her. There were moments when he did manage to let her know that he rather favored her and that he understood how she felt. He was a source of comfort to her. However, he died of cancer within the year after she returned home, and Janet suffered a great deal from the loss.

The following year Janet decided to go to graduate school to begin work on her master's degree. It was at this time that the loss of her father plus all her other concerns took their toll. After being at school for about one month, Janet suffered a total nervous breakdown.

Janet returned home and was under a psychiatrist's care for quite some time. She gradually gained enough confidence to go back to teaching, but every obligation beyond that of the ordinary routine threw her into a frenzy. Just the thought of a PTA meeting created severe stomach pains and nausea for weeks in advance. Any attempt to go out socially produced the same effects, although she always participated in these events.

Janet's sister, at this same time, was divorcing her husband. In a way I think this softened the resentment that Janet felt for her sister and they became somewhat friendly. However, within two years, her sister had met and married another man, hence producing another emotional setback. Her sister had now been engaged four times and married twice while Janet had still met no one.

It was at this time that I met Janet. I had no previous knowledge of her nervous breakdown or her emotional problems. I just found her to be a pleasant, extremely considerate person. She came to my home and introduced herself to me when she knew I was to be teaching in her school the following year. She made every effort to help me begin my new teaching assignment with as few difficulties as possible. As she began to exhibit some of her nervousness about encounters with other people, I tried to build her self-confidence. I pushed her to go places with me, and she began to take an interest in the community civic organizations that I had joined. As the year progressed, she began going to meetings and social gatherings on her own.

We decided that she should do something about her weight and her appearance. We went on a diet together and she has since lost thirty pounds. (Unfortunately, it was my idea and I lost only five!) She half-heartedly bemoans the fact that she has spent a fortune since we became friends having to buy clothes and altering those she had before.

I was really happy to see that she seemed to be coming out of her shell. All of a sudden, for no known reason, she developed a frightening state of depression. She feels that her future is very bleak with no hope of marriage or children that she would desperately like to have. She knows that her chances of meeting someone in her job are very slim, but she lacks the courage and self-confidence to make a break and try something new. She also cites a very true observation, that she had no one to be with socially because all her friends have married and have families of their own to take care of. No one is left to do things that a single girl would like to do. She stated that she has lost weight and changed her appearance but that these things have not really changed her life or broken the vicious circle that keeps her from achieving her goals.

As I sit here typing this profile, I question whether I have written it to complete a course assignment or whether I have written it to find out where I should go next. Any advice that I have ever given this woman I have given as a friend, not as anyone qualified to give real guidance. After she fell into this last state of depression, the only advice that I could give her was to seek the help of a professional who was qualified to examine and analyze her problems. Although I feel that this advice is logical it somehow does not seem adequate. The next step, however, must be hers.

After-effects of a death

My husband was killed in an automobile accident at the age of thirty-three years, six months, no days. His death was instantaneous.

At 1:30 A.M., when I was notified by a local policeman of my husband's death, my physical reaction was externally placid. I did not faint, cry, or show any hysteria, yet I felt trancelike and couldn't think of anything to say. No pain, headache, or other discomfort was experienced except for a numbness and inability to talk. After that night, the emotional outlet that most women seem to savor—crying—became possible and offered a welcome relief. There was a temporary loss of appetite. My silence was temporary also. In fact, I talked incessantly, beginning that day and continuing for the next few days.

Emotionally, I was able to laugh and felt the need to cheer everyone else up. I had, before this time, no conscious awareness of any ability to use laughter as a defense mechanism. Laughter had evidently become habituated and integrated into my personality. Thus it served as an outlet for which people rewarded me with their approval.

Spiritually, I suffered no loss of faith. In fact, I felt more a dependence and need to go to church. While I remain inactive in any church groups, I need the contemplation provided by a Sunday trip to church and a nightly prayer. It is as though I have a reason for going to church not spelled h-a-b-i-t. Call it belief in God or call it rationalization. I believe I had the best years of married life, and that I am now experiencing an independence of life never previously tested. Was this God's reason that I had no children? Well, the best years of marriage, plus a lack of children, combined with the apparent independence of spirit I now feel, give me reason to accept the need for, and belief in, a higher Being.

The experiencing of independence was not evident for at least two years after the event. The time period—two years—brings me to another phase of adjustment, prefaced by a Johnny Carson joke: "What is a widow's peak?" Answer: "About two years." Perhaps my feelings concerning sex should be mentioned in a paragraph dealing with physical reactions. Yet I am unable to separate sex from the emotional and the spiritual. I feel no sexual needs, but I think this may be the result of attitudes ingrained in my personality from premarital days. Unmarried sex is a no-no. I can make this much of a statement: What seemed to be repression of an urge during adolescence doesn't take half as much effort in one's thirties!

Socially, in the months after the event, I went anywhere my friends and relatives invited me. After about six months, the need for forced socialization seemed to subside and I was able to become more selective and enjoy a social event on my own rather than going because duty called. Today, I am fortunate in having a friend to escort me and I feel the need for his companionship. I am relieved to know I still have the capacity to care for someone as part of my personality.

What psychological changes have taken place within me? Before my husband's death I never experienced sudden and permanent forgetting. When the policeman asked me to call my brother, I walked to the telephone and, still not wanting to acknowledge that anything had happened, I forgot his telephone number. For two years thereafter, until he and his family moved and changed their number, I was unable to recall it at will. Today I still find it hard to believe that I could forget this commonly called number.

Another reaction has been that of not feeling that I have to please a husband's friends and family. I cultivate a friendship on the basis of my own likes without that nagging compulsion that I must be nice to everybody and that everyone must like me. This idea of a smaller circle of friends may be an aspect of age also.

Adjustment to the death of my husband has been like going through adolescence all over again. My acne of the heart is clearing up, and the remaining scars can be covered.

Crisis of anguish

It's close to midnight Sunday, March 20. I've been in bed nearly an hour but thoughts of this day, and indeed of the previous six weeks, keep me awake.

Since early February when my husband moved to an apartment, I have found sleeping difficult. I'm constantly searching my heart in an effort to decide if I did the right thing in consenting to that move. I don't believe he would have left without that consent. I'm glad I have begun working again this year. At least during the day I don't think of my personal problems.

As I lay here, I keep reliving all the events that led up to Matthew's request for a divorce. There were so many incidents of which I was unaware that evidently had great importance to him. I know I am much to blame. From the time of our son's birth—six years after our marriage—when I stopped working, I began to let Matthew grow away from me. I was much more anxious to stay home than to go out socially. I gained weight. I encouraged Matthew to continue activities in which I had no interest and took no part. I just didn't work at our marriage; I took everything for granted.

Inevitably Matthew became interested in a woman who built up his ego in ways I was too blind, too stupid, or too unaware to do. When I learned about this, how did I feel? I felt like the

pit of my stomach had dropped! I felt frightened and insecure. I tried desperately to prove my love had never lessened. I guess I felt disbelief that this was happening to me since he and I had been so happy in the past. I know I felt shame that he preferred another woman to me.

We have been going through a very difficult time these few weeks. Usually I am patient because I know so much of the blame is mine. I hope he will come to believe we should try again. Often I get angry, mostly because of frustration at not being able to change the situation. He won't even consider a reconciliation. I feel he is very unfair to want a divorce over incidents that I didn't even know bothered him. Now that I *am* aware, he won't give me another chance.

But Matthew is having an even more difficult time. He feels so guilty at what he is doing to his son, Benji. He hates thinking what he believes people will say about him. His parents are no comfort at all to him. They constantly badger him with the wrongness of his behavior. They not only condemn his actions; they even seem to condemn him. It's one of the things that is tearing him apart. His parents never will admit I have wronged Matthew. In their minds my inattentions were not sinful, but his adultery was—no matter what the provocation.

All these things are going through my mind as I lay here. I think of the amount of weight he has lost, of his extreme nervousness, of his increased drinking which had never been cause for concern before. Mostly I think of the times he has said he'd be better off dead. I know he is serious, but no one else believes me. Our priest doesn't think he is serious, and his parents think it's only a device to get me to grant a divorce. I know better. I can see the real anguish he's going through.

It seemed like the only answer was to agree to a separation. I thought this would give him a chance to see if he really preferred to live without me, and it would give me a chance to decide if I must grant a divorce or not. I don't want to, but I am really concerned about what he will do if I continue to hold back. He can't divorce me because he has no legal grounds.

Today was a horror. Benji was supposed to

spend the day with his daddy. Only five and a half, he misses him. When he hadn't come for him at noon, I called him. It took such a long time for him to answer the phone. He sounded so groggy. He said he had overslept. Since Benji was so anxious to see him, I agreed when he asked me to bring him to his apartment.

As always when I talked to Matthew or knew I was about to see him, nervousness and apprehension started. The drive to the apartment was nervewracking. I love him so and I don't want to lose him. I knew I'd probably beg him to reconsider. I also knew I shouldn't because it had no effect. This in turn would make me angry—that he wouldn't even try to reconcile.

When we went in the apartment I knew I couldn't leave Benji there that day. Matthew had been having more difficulty sleeping than I had. He was not in any condition, even at one o'clock, to care for a little boy. Matthew was very angry when I said Benji couldn't stay. I followed him through his apartment into the bedroom, trying to make him understand. When I saw all the pictures of that other woman in his bedroom, I really lost control of myself. I even tore some up. I shouted at him that he shouldn't want a woman who would knowingly break up a home. Matthew became enraged. He smashed pictures of his family, broke a lamp, and even tore the phone out of the wall. He shouted that he never wanted to see me again. Benji didn't see this, but he heard it all—the first such experience in his life. I was so upset by this time I didn't try to change the situation, even though I knew it was bad for Benji to be exposed.

We left, but the horror, frustration, and shame have been in my mind all day and all night long. I wish I had controlled myself or not gone in that bedroom. Will I ever fall asleep?

Apparently I did, because I waken to hear the phone ringing. Who can it be, it's still dark outside? As I really become conscious, all the events of the day and the threats come rushing to my mind. I feel panicky as I reach for the phone.

It's Matthew, and he's in a terrible state of mind. He's saying he wants me to say good-bye to Benji for him. He says he's decided to kill himself. I'm crying as I tell him Benji needs a live daddy, even if he doesn't live in the same house. I beg him not to hang up. He agrees. Looking at the clock, I see it's only 5:00 A.M. He must have been thinking of this decision all day and all night. He is really at the end of his rope. I feel so guilty at starting that argument. I beg him to wait until I can get to his apartment. He says it won't do any good, he's made up his mind. I plead more, and he agrees to wait but he says he may not let me in.

I throw on a coat over my pajamas, put on sneakers but don't bother to tie them. I scoop up my sleeping child. Down the street I run to my neighbors and pound on the door until I arouse them. I shove Benji into Allan's arms and tell him I must hurry to Matthew.

Things I want to say to Matthew are buzzing in my mind. The fear that I won't get the chance to say them is almost overwhelming. I'm not conscious of traffic lights or direction, but I pull up in front of Matthew's apartment. I am so scared as I get out of the car, scared that I'll be too late or that he won't let me in.

I knock and knock on the door, and finally he opens it. I am so relieved to see him alive I can hardly stand up. I follow him up the stairs to his second floor apartment, and I'm telling him how much I love him, that we can work things out. At the top of the stairs he turns and screams that he hates me worse than the snakes in hell. I have never heard such a tone of voice. I know I'll never forget that phrase, even as I realize he is not himself at all. His voice is hoarse and loud. His face is distorted with anger and loathing. He shakes visibly.

I see all of this and wonder how I'll ever be able to communicate with him. He is completely out of control. I am perspiring with nervousness. Little of what he is saying at first is coherent. But I see the gun cabinet is unlocked. I'm not at all afraid for my own safety. It never even enters my mind. He tries to pull the rod out of the gun cabinet, but I get in the way and won't let him. I follow him all through the apartment. I won't let him alone at all. His bedroom is still a shambles—broken glass all over the floor. The useless telephone still lies there. I wonder where he called from. I remember. There's a phone booth down the block from the apartment.

We say many things, but it really isn't conversation at first. Matthew is too angry to talk. He just shouts obscenities. It is so unlike him. It hurts so much to see the hate on his face and hear the things he says. Gradually he begins to calm down. I think he is under the influence of some kind of pills.

The downstairs door opens and I am overwhelmed with relief to see our friend Baxter. He's on his way to work and has stopped to pick up cigarettes Matthew buys for him at the PX. I don't want to say much aloud because I know it will start Matthew's rage all over again, but I try to mouth to Baxter to send for Matthew's father. I don't think he understands.

I feel very apprehensive and scared of my responsibility after Baxter leaves. Matthew at least seems more rational now. He says he must go call his office to say he won't be in today. I stay in the apartment as he gets in his car. I see that he is headed *away* from the closest phone booth, so I run down the steps, jump in my car, and hurry to the phone booth. I dial his parents, say only that Dad must hurry to Matthew's apartment; I hang up and rush back to the apartment. I couldn't have been gone more than three minutes.

I feel a cold dread as I see Matthew's car already in front of the apartment. I run to the door, but it's locked. As I stand there in indecision, I think I hear a low, dull thud. I run around to the back and up those outside stairs.

The door is unlocked! With the greatest apprehension, I open the door and walk into the bedroom. What do I sense? A complete and absolute stillness as if I were alone. But I smell something I can only describe as acrid. I can't explain how I feel as I walk through the bedroom into the hall. I don't want to go, but I must. I'm afraid what has happened, but I also think Matthew may need me. As I leave the brightness of his bedroom, I enter the dimness of the hall. Some part of me is aware that all the living room drapes are pulled shut—they had been open. And at the same instant I see Matthew's legs. He's stretched out flat on his back at the far end of the hall with his feet nearest me. In the dimness I breathe a prayer of hope that I'm not too late. As I step closer, I can see the shotgun lying at the side of his body. I call to him: "Don't do this, *please* don't do this" as I start closer.

And then I see that horror that I will never stop seeing. The unbelievable and unspeakable mutilation that was a man's head. I know my husband is dead by his own hand.

The rest of that morning really isn't very clear. The kindness of a stranger—the woman next door who let me in—the arrival of my doctor, the priest, my poor father-in-law, the police who questioned me with a gentleness I remember even now. It's hardly worth remembering. Matthew is dead, and the rest doesn't seem to matter.

Write about anything...
ONE OF THOSE DAYS...

My womanly intuition told me it was going to be a bad day when I woke up before the alarm went off. It's bad enough getting up at 5:45 A.M. without waking up before it's time. Then I looked out the window and saw a cloudy, rainy day which will probably mean staying indoors. Getting into the car, somehow I managed to get black gunk all over my hands. The black stuff went from my hands to my books, to my arms, to my face, to my pocketbook, and to my jacket. Now that really made me happy! Before going to class, I zoomed through Franklin Center, heading for the rest room to wash off the black gunk, and didn't bother to read the sign on the door. I went into the men's room!

LOVE

The first thing that came to my mind was the subject of love. Maybe because right now I am very deeply in love, and for the first time I realize that it's "the real thing." Our relationship is based on a number of things. It is a "giving" kind of thing, very unselfish. Then, too, there is honesty and trust. These are very important to me, because previously I wouldn't think anything of telling a lie or two, but I *never* will lie to this man. I used to kind of intellectualize what I thought was love, but now I *feel* more than I've ever felt in my life. I also hold a great respect for him and for the love we share. Simple things are important to us; for example, a walk through a meadow, sharing problems, talking things out, etc. To communicate is the beginning of understanding. You must have faith, too, and even love the faults we all have. There is no idealization where I've set him on a pedestal as "one who can do no wrong." I realize he's fallible, just as I am. Sharing things that are important to him and to me. It's not just a romantic infatuation type of thing. I guess we went through that stage, as all people in love do, but we're at a more mature and realistic level now. There are so many ways of expressing love, from the glance and meeting of eyes to the fuller expression—sexually. Sex is important in love, but there are so *many* other things that are more important or just as important. Too often people base their love on sex and mere physical attraction. This kind of love lasts only so long.

It's just so great for me to be in love that I want to shout it to the whole world. And I hope I haven't bored you telling you about it! I could really go on and on but time won't permit.

BREAKING UP

When you've gone with a guy for two years, you should know whether you love him or not. Even if you haven't had much dating experience before. You're really sunk if the other person is sure and you are not. So you make him wait, and wait, and wait. You know he loves you—you're positively sure. If he loves you so very much, you naturally should love him. You can kind of talk yourself into it. If there are things about the other person you don't like, try to change them. If he loves you so much, he'll change. Finally after a long time, you realize that you were forcing yourself to love that person. You make up your mind that this is the end, the end of a long relationship. Lots of things can happen in two years—and many things cannot. You cannot change a person deep down inside—personality, attitudes, values, and self-concept.

Now you must do the very thing that hurts you most—tell the other person you've finally decided—decided that he is not a part of your future. You had been his whole world and now it has come to an end.

People are the most delicate things in the world. It hurts inside—deep down inside—to hurt them. But you must have enough pride, courage, and faith in yourself to know that what you are about to do is the right thing. It must be done—because what was before can be no more.

UNMARRIED

Since I am twenty-five years old and still unmarried, the stress that is put on me in tremendous. Why should I marry when I really don't want to? Yet I have a feeling that if I don't, I may remain alone the rest of my life. I do date very often and was engaged once; however, I just cannot bring myself to marry. My family at home was never really very happy, and I'm sure my life would be the same. And yet, as I get older, I realize that if I don't go through with it now, I may never be able to later. Believe me, it is really some problem to understand. I really am very indecisive.

I know I want children and everything that goes with a family, and I certainly do admire other people who are married and have children. So why do I still hold off?

Some day I'm sure I'll find someone, the right person, and get married in a hurry. Until that time, I do feel quite inferior and rejected by other people who have obtained part of their goal in life.

If I never marry, I'll always feel that there is a part of me missing—the part that could have meant complete happiness and joy—but whichever way it goes, I'll make the most of it.

MONEY MANAGEMENT

I got married in May and I feel that money management is one of our biggest problems. My husband and I were both used to living rather comfortably with our parents. But after getting married, we realized that our money situation was quite different than when we lived at home. For the first time in my life, I was confronted with living under a budget. This I found was quite difficult to get accustomed to.

We both want things that we really

don't need—for example, a stereo console. We didn't need it, but we *wanted* one, so we got it. We also wanted an air-conditioned car which we didn't need—but we wanted one, so we got it.

It certainly is easy to buy things these days; at times I wish it were more difficult. We want someday to build a home and raise a family. But these things will have to wait—at least until we have formed a sound basis for money management.

MARITAL DISCORD

The problem I am faced with at the moment and which has been pressing heavily on me is my relationship with my husband. I feel as though he's very dissatisfied with me except when we get into bed at night. Little things have been setting him off and I can't believe he actually is getting mad for such ridiculous reasons. We've always tried to resolve our disagreements before going to sleep, but recently our argument lasted for two days where we didn't speak except for common courtesies. I don't discuss this with anyone except him, but often I feel I have to let my frustrations out on someone or something, so I usually end up banging or slamming things. It really made us stop and think this past week when my little girl (two and a half years old) told me to "talk to Daddy." Everything has been fine since then, but I am still frightened about the situation. He also gets very upset when we don't have sex, usually because I'm tired or one of us falls asleep. Things always work themselves out; I guess I've heard the same type of complaints from other people who have been married about four years.

THE OTHER SIDE

Saturday night was really something. My husband and I started out at a faculty banquet and when things there began to slow down— about eleven o'clock—we left and with six other people went to the Rock Top Inn where a "hillbilly" band played. Since we were quite dressed up and "new" at the place, we got many stares when we went in. People there ranged from seventy-year-old men in suits to young girls in their twenties with short skirts and puffy hair—dancing *together* to a "jazzed-up" version of "Cold, Cold Heart." The "hillbilly" band consisted of a big man wearing white socks, a sad looking girl looking about sixteen years old but wearing a wedding band, and two other men who didn't particularly stand out.

Watching the people was the most interesting part. Men, again in white socks, danced with women two heads taller. Women in spike-heeled shoes sat together eying the men in the white socks; a lone man sat all evening, just tapping his hands to the beat.

We didn't sit for long. After some refreshment (Coke at 50¢ a glass to help pay for the "entertainment" we guessed), we decided to try a polka. We soon discovered that what we were dancing to wasn't a polka but a Paul Jones—a dance in which all couples get in a circle, dosey-do when the singer whistles, then dance with the closest partner when he whistles again. With howls of laughter from our friends, we were swept into the Paul Jones against our better judgment. "This the first time ya did this—yore not sa' bad," was a comment to me. "Dontcha drop me!" a buxom woman whom my husband ended up with said to him. The rest of the evening went this way—certainly a change from the stiff, sophisticated faculty dinner—but certainly enjoyable to be with people who are different from you.

We plan to go back to the Rock Top Inn soon—Marie and the Melodies play next week!!!

CONCERNED

What does a person do when a person who was very close becomes involved in the drug culture? The individual has gone from a responsible married man into a situation which becomes more and more involved. At first the involvement was simply the use of marijuana but has progressed to the point where this person is now involved in the buying, selling, and distribution of many types of narcotics.

TWO LOVES

Everyone knows that life has its problems, its ups and downs. But no one knows better than I that life can be pure downright hell. And I suppose the funny thing about this is that it is brought on by love. The unfortunate thing is that this love is not of social acceptance because being a male and loving another male just doesn't seem to turn people on, except for those of us that are supposedly "sick." I don't really know why I'm writing this. Maybe its the fact that during the past four weeks I have found someone who cares for me and loves me beyond my wildest dreams. Great! Well, yes. But considering he is married and has a family, things are a bit tense.

Now, not to leave with a wrong impression, I am in love (?) with a wonderful girl who knows all about me and still wants to marry me. Only, how do you break it to her that there is someone else you care for just a "little" more?

THINGS TO THINK ABOUT AND DO

1. Imagine yourself as being twenty-one years of age. How do you see yourself? In what ways are you ready for the world and in what ways are you not? If you are older than twenty-one, think back to what your life was like at that age. Which age do you prefer—your present age or the age of twenty-one?
2. Marriage is an event many young adults look forward to. What would be an ideal time or age for a woman to get married? Would this be the same time or age for a man? Should the man or woman be the older person?
3. What qualities, characteristics, or attributes do you consider important in someone you would consider marrying?
4. Is love necessary for a happy marriage? Survey a number of married and unmarried people to get their opinions.
5. Does an individual have to be married in order to live a fulfilling, satisfying adult life? Is there an acceptable place in society for the unmarried adult? Why so or why not?
6. What are the characteristics of a mature adult?
7. Early adulthood includes persons who are in their late thirties. Do you agree with this statement? Could someone the age of forty be a grandparent?
8. Look at the Profiles "The Second Time Around" and "The Breakup of a Marriage." What similarities do you note? What do these profiles say in terms of what is needed for a happy, adjusted marriage? Look at the profile "Crisis of Anguish." Is there anything here that relates to the qualities of a happy marriage?
9. Is there a point in time where individuals of early adulthood age reflect on religious and moral values? Can you think of any occasions where these values would assume great importance?
10. In what ways do persons of ages twenty-five and thirty-five differ according to whether they went to college or not? Do you find much difference socially, emotionally, and economically between college and noncollege groups?
11. Do an occupational or career study of your community either by contacting the local Chamber of Commerce or by checking the latest Statistical Abstracts of the Census Bureau as found in the library. What percentage of workers are found in the various job categories? Check women workers and minority group workers. Any surprises?
12. Talk about anything.

READING SOURCES
Developmental psychology texts

Bischof, L. J.: Adult psychology, New York, 1969, Harper & Row, Publishers.

CRM: Developmental psychology today, ed. 2, New York, 1975, CRM/Random House, Inc., chap. 20.

Hurlock, E.: Developmental psychology, ed. 4, New York, 1975, McGraw-Hill Book Co., chaps. 9, 10.

Kaluger, G., and Kaluger, M.: Human development: the span of life, St. Louis, 1974, The C. V. Mosby Co., chap. 12.

Pikunas, J.: Human development: a science of growth, New York, 1969, McGraw-Hill Book Co., chaps. 18-20.

Related readings

Bowman, H. A., Marriage for moderns, New York, 1970, McGraw-Hill Book Co.

Elder, G. H.: Role orientations, marital age, and life patterns in adulthood, Merrill-Palmer Quart. 18:3-4, 1972.

Figley, C. R.: Child density and the marital relationship, J. Marriage Family 35:272-282, 1973.

Glick, P. C., and Norton, A. J.: Frequency, duration, and probability of marriage and divorce, J. Marriage Family **33**:307-317, 1971.

Gornick, V.: Why women fear success, The New York Magazine, Dec. 1971.

Helson, R.: The changing image of the career woman, J. Soc. Issues **28**(2):33-46, 1972.

Reevy, W. R.: Petting experiences and marital success, J. Sex Res. **8**:48-60, 1972.

Rose, V. L., and Price-Bonham, S.: Divorce adjustment: a woman's problem, Family Coordinator **22**:291-297, 1973.

Scott, R. D.: Job expectancy: an important factor in labor turnover, Personnel Psychol. **51**:360-363, 1972.

Scarf, M.: Husbands in crisis, McCalls, June, 1972.

CHAPTER 10

The years of contented encapsulation

When a person becomes twenty years of age, there is just the slightest suggestion of apprehension as the individual ponders the uncertainties of "finally becoming an adult." It appears that even greater anxiety is encountered when the thirtieth birthday has arrived. Could it be that the generation gap syndrome of the late 1960's, with its admonition: "You can't trust anyone over thirty" is creating a mental image suggesting that one is getting old when they reach thirty? The number one villain for "over-the-hill" honors, however, is still the age of forty. Countless women, and men, bemoan the fact that they are now forty and "youth is gone." The optimist says: "Life begins at forty," but the pessimist queries: "Begins what?" Closer to the truth is the fact that prime physical, emotional, and vocational conditions exist about the age of forty. There is no reason why things have to go "downhill" after that age except that an individual may neglect doing those things, healthwise, that continue good body tone and good health.

The youth cult and the urgencies of the environmental movement appear to be getting to the woman in "Middle Age: Are We Condemned?" but she still holds her own. That middle age need not be all bad is seen in "Grad School in Middle Adulthood," in the portrayal of a satisfied middle-aged housewife in "Never a Dull Moment," and in the story of a ballet dancer in "At the Barre" who discovered a use for skills she developed as a teenager.

The middle adult years are a little early for reliving memories and nostalgia, but the present middle age generation has grown up during some tumultuous decades. "How the Great Depression Affected Me" speaks of the not-so-good ol' days. In another vein, most of us would have someone special, a friend, neighbor, or relative, whom we recall fondly, as in the profile of "Aunt Bebe."

No one says that the middle years are not without their problems. "Mastectomy" is an all too familiar story in many families. The need to readjust a life because of a separation or a divorce is not unusual, but it is sad and difficult when it happens close to retirement age. Somehow it doesn't seem fair or right, but how one woman accomplished a readjustment is told in "Sixty but Separated."

Middle age—are we condemned?

It has been said that the lowest status one could hold in the United States today is that of a black, Jewish woman. Maybe so, but it's an unlikely combination. Much less rare is the middle-aged, middle-class, white, suburban mother of teenagers—*she* really has no place in society, except as a target of scorn. Consider one example.

THE PAST

The sketch for the picture is serene—all the brush strokes of the "good life." One can see a busy, happy, outgoing woman, coming and going from a house often filled with guests. She speaks.

Our house is just over the District line in Virginia, in a creative, liberal-minded community. We bought this house because of the good schools, not because of its architecture. We are constantly painting and rearranging for more space. Even when we are posted abroad, it is "home." From the dining room windows, I look out on a twelve foot dogwood which started life in a cottage cheese carton, bought at a church fair for fifty cents. In the backyard is a twenty foot spruce, once our live Christmas tree, the first year we were home from Korea. Perennials given by friends, some far away, grow with love. Almost every tree, bush, and plant has a history, though you might think the yard as ordinary as anybody else's.

Looking back, it is almost possible to see the boys, little, washed and combed, going off to school with their friends. The Cub and Boy Scout meetings in the basement rec room have left visible marks (or would one say badges?) on the walls. There are the childish paintings, framed; toys, discarded in favor of more grown-up interests, not to be thrown out. The signs of former pets are on carpets and furniture; old costumes from plays and Hallowe'ens, drawers still crammed with boys' souvenirs—a mixed bag of marbles, evil eyes, foreign money, baseball cards. Those drawers give silent evidence of the varied interests of two children who, born abroad, consider a good part of the world casually as neighborhoods they lived in. The boys are now away at college.

The house shows the chaotic, sometimes exotic, life of a Foreign Service family. Treasures from other lands lend an air to the early Salvation Army furniture that's banged around the world. Books in other tongues are mixed with mysteries, novels, and histories in the English language. The bedroom study is piled with government documents with which my husband deals till late in the night.

The kitchen shelves are untidily stuffed with cookbooks and clippings for every diet, every occasion. There are menus for parties of officials, foreign and American, for PTA meetings, for neighborhood committees joining in the typical projects and protests of an "enlightened" community, for children's birthdays, for celebrations, for welcomings and good-byes—food for family, friends, relatives, and strangers.

It is history now, but it seemed that life was always opening, filled with roles that gave satisfaction and a sense of achievement, with anticipation for what would come next, how the boys would be in a year, where we would be living, what kind of assignment for my husband. There was a sense of doing, growing!

Organizing the priorities of living was easy: everything flowed from a central core of belief in the ultimate rightness and usefulness of my husband's career. There was a sense of being part of a pattern, needed and wanted, loved and loving.

I was not different from my neighbors, am not now. We spoke truth to our children, gently. We participated in their activities (those dreadful carpools!), seeing they had every need

fulfilled, not accounting for the cost, timewise or moneywise. We used action for setting examples. Among us, we worked for fair housing, beautification, better schooling, the end to discrimination, and international education. We did not sit at home playing bridge or gossiping, or spend our money on "keeping up with the Jones'." We were committed to making life a little nearer to the principles we were taught and, in turn, taught. Maybe we were smug and deserve scorn, but I am not conscious of anyone harboring that sort of feeling.

THE PRESENT

The picture that was to become a little masterpiece got paint spilled on it. Throw it away—it's out of style anyway! Our "Spock-marked" children, grown, find us materialistic, destructive, prejudiced. Our nonprofessional volunteering is not wanted; the city found us laughable. Either it's too little, too late, or we were seeking to bolster our egos at someone else's expense. Our age, too, was held against us. Read any ad, listen to any friend—our husbands are suddenly vulnerable, too, since they most certainly are over thirty! Everything becomes personal when one is unhappy. Every accidental bump in the crowded street becomes a planned assault to the mind in pain. Uncertainty replaces conviction.

For us personally, the picture was abandoned when my husband, tempted by a good job offer, opted for early retirement. The day he became eligible, he left, and we moved.

It is astonishing at a time when life should be coming to a fruition, when the painting should have taken on definite form, to find oneself suddenly adrift, not using one's skills for the purposes they were intended, but to be starting over, hesitantly, with a new canvas. One day I sat down to write out the things I must remember. The words came hurling to the sheet, and I have not edited them. Somehow, they say more than a polished product, which would not be true to life.

Oh, my God!
I do what I see is necessary.
I feed my husband good meals.

Julia Childs and Craig Clairborne are constant companions.

As for economy—don't be fooled. Be educated—figure out if it's 200 napkins for 33¢ or a better buy at fifty for 10¢. That's easy, but is the quality the same?

Worry about the streams, the air. Buy nonleaded gas and save money somewhere else. Wash the clothes in soap, real soap; it leaves deposits on the clothes, but never mind—it's nonpolluting.

Don't throw out the trash. It will be burned, fouling the air. Don't burn the leaves in the fall—divinely delicious smell now turned quite properly to ashes. Don't buy colored paper—the dye is not soluble. Don't spray the poison ivy; if you do, there's no legal way to get rid of the can.

I must not get rid of spiders, flies, moths by chemical means. But what about the cockroaches? How much damage to spray them? Is the damage to them or to us? Impasse.

I must not, I must not. But I am a human, excreting, making trash, taking up space that perhaps I shouldn't. I'm over thirty, ha! over forty.

I fail everyday in every way. Surely I must know how to use up the leftovers nutritiously and beautifully. Surely I must know how to dispose of waste carefully. It reminds me on many cans now. And I must surely know, I am educated, how to entertain a hundred people and still give my money to Save the Children. I want to.

I give my time to causes. Volunteer, nonprofessional—I jerk sodas for the hospital snack bar. I go to school, learning new tricks for an old dog. I must keep my mind alert—being middle-aged, one must suspect atrophy and mind set—guard against it.

And so I love—I love most every kind of people, black, yellow, whatever. I am fortunate, indeed blessed, to have friends of almost every region under the sun; we are friends because we care about each other. What use? Oh, I know—and it is *my* own satisfaction. But do my children care? They'd care only if all this weren't true; any step of mine is a step in the wet sand, where the tide will obliterate it next wave. My children are pure. Their attitudes uncorrupted by practical living. Is this because I

am paying the price in pain and sorrow? Being in Ivy League colleges they are outcasts according to Spiro T. Agnew, and I have failed. *They* care. But they are the effete. The radical destroyers of all good things in our great democracy. Not true, but who am I to say?

Why am I existing in my upper middle class, middle mind, white sort of way?

Violence rocks the cradle. It rocks me too—as angrily as violence can. The bomb! Hiroshima and Nagasaki, millions of wonderful unique human beings perished or lived on in death. Hitler, Jews, Aryans—oh, my God. The very words Viet Nam burn the page. Don't mention JFK, RFK, or MLK!

Must I agonize through life for all these things, most of them out of my control? I went to a psychiatrist. His message, expensive, painful, loving, and involved, was: "I cannot find answers for you. You must do it yourself." An honest man but not helpful.

Anxiety, frustration, the insecureness of a liberally educated average sort of mind. What to do? Eat bitter rue for breakfast. Read Toynbee. Realize that such unbearable pains are nothing in the sweep of history. Joys, desires, aims, achievements even, will be nothing, are nothing now. That's this age. Another might have been, might be, more welcoming, more accepting. Maybe happier, but I am living now. Living is pain.

THE FUTURE

The future is shaped by the past and the present. Yet man has some control over his destiny. Middle age has some of the same problems in any time period—the empty nest syndrome, the menopausal anxieties, the normal aches and pains of growing old. But it is also true that women live longer than men and are better able to bear pain. There must be some reevaluation in our present thinking, or we will have in the near future a country divided not only by race and religious differences but also by age differences. It is not sensible to waste the talents and skills of the middle aged woman—prejudice has wasted too much talent already. I, for one, am fighting for my space in the art class, with a new canvas and a new brush, preparing to start painting a new picture. Wish me luck!

Never a dull moment!

This particular Saturday morning, July 1, started out like all others. Up at six, my husband had breakfast and went to the barn to milk. I scurried around, trying to accomplish as much as possible so I could spend part of the day studying. While the three boys slept a little longer, I cleaned the upstairs. In the meantime, they woke up and got ready for the day. They had breakfast, then started doing their chores. David, at sixteen, is a studious, introverted boy; a slow-moving perfectionist. He is interested in gardening and has a good-sized vegetable garden as a 4-H project. He spent the best part of the morning working there. Fifteen-year-old Allan is an intelligent extrovert, full of nervous energy. He is interested in dairying, so he helped his father milk.

Dale is eleven and just beginning to "emerge." The baby of the family, he has always been quite small, quiet, and timid. He could never compete with his brothers and developed an "I can't" attitude. The older boys tease and ridicule him after the manner of big brothers and call him "Shrimp." Strangely enough, he likes them to call him that and sometimes refers to himself with a comment such as "I'm a tired old Shrimp." So far, his interests haven't manifested themselves, except for baseball. He carries a transistor radio around and listens to the games, even when working. He is quite knowledgeable about the game and the players and reads a lot about baseball. As for work—the other boys complain that they did a lot more at his age than he does, and maybe they did. But he is small, and he does more than most children. He helps with the milking, feeding, and field work and mows the lawn with a ride mower. Since he can ride to do that, his brothers don't consider that work—at least, not when Dale does it!

Our home life does not lend itself to scheduling, so I seldom get out of the kitchen when I am home. There is a constant coming, going, and eating for them and a constant fixing

of food and washing of dishes for me. I like to cook, but I would appreciate regular meal times. These days farmers work in the fields as long as they can and eat at odd times when they come in for something.

This Saturday I planned to be efficient and get most of my work done by early afternoon. But the best-made plans go awry at times.

After the boys left the house, I put some turkey legs in the oven and washed the dishes. Just as I was ready to start cleaning the downstairs, Dale said: "Mom, will you please finish cleaning these onions for me? I have to gather the eggs and feed the peepies for Grandmother while she is at market." His onions were fresh from his little garden but he had no time to clean them.

My husband, Charles, has an egg route on Saturdays. He and Allan have over two hundred customers. Charles grew up on the route. He stays with it, partly because it gives us customers for our produce, but mostly because of the contacts he makes with so many interesting people. He is also an ordained minister and preaches in a little country church. The contacts he makes on the route often provide him with sermon material.

The boys each have a 4-H garden, and Charles sells their produce to customers on the route. So I finished cleaning Dale's onions and put them in bunches. After getting rid of the mud and waste, I again thought I would continue cleaning, but David came in with a lot of garden lettuce. "Mom, will you please wash this lettuce for Dad to sell? I have to pick two pounds of green beans and feed the rabbits." So I cleaned the lettuce and packed it in an ice chest, ready for the truck.

By this time Allan came in to get ready to go on the route. He nosed around the refrigerator, then decided to eat some turkey. Charles came in but didn't have time to eat before leaving. I fixed a thermos of ice water for them, and they left. Then Dale returned from gathering eggs and ate some lunch. "Mom," he asked excitedly, "do you know how to keep fleas off of you?"

"Fleas?"

"Oh, gnats or whatever they are. Some kid told me that if you hold your hand up high they will fly around it and let your face alone. They go to the highest part of your body."

"Well," I replied, "you had better walk around with your hand in the air."

During these morning activities, I swept up the dirt they tracked in, shut cupboard doors they left open, turned off lights they left burning, put milk back in the refrigerator, refilled ice trays, swept up more dirt, closed the bread bag, sprayed ants that discovered a potato chip on the floor, told the dog to let the kitten alone, washed more dishes, and swept more dirt.

I also told Dale three different times to gather the raspberries and twice to practice the piano. There was always some reason why he couldn't do either. So finally I became exasperated and got real cross. "Dale, I'll give you just half an hour to gather all the raspberries you can reach and bring them in." He went out and later came in with about a pint. A very purple boy said: "If you wonder why there aren't more berries, I ate a lot of them." Adding these to some we had picked before, I cooked them for jelly. While the berries simmered, David and I had lunch. Then I strained the juice, made a turn of jelly, and cleaned up the mess. By that time Dale's piano teacher arrived to give him a lesson. I still had hopes of studying.

Soon Charles and Allan came back from delivering eggs to get something else they needed. This time Charles ate his lunch. Then they left again.

After Dale's lesson, I talked to his piano teacher for a few minutes, and then cleaned the downstairs. The front porch was littered with rose petals from the red rambler, so I swept them off and cleaned the porch. I noticed that the kittens had gotten the windows dirty on the outside and made a mental note to wash windows when I had time.

The house was now as clean as it ever is in the summer, but I was far from being through. The phone rang, and a neighbor's voice said: "There are a lot of black and white milk cows on the road at the foot of the hill. Are they yours?" I replied that I hardly thought so but would check. Finding Dale at the barn, I told him what was wrong and asked him to count the cows and see if ours were all there. In the meantime, I went down the hill to keep the cows off the road. When I arrived, I almost had heart failure. Five of the cows had gotten on the railroad tracks, and a fast freight was coming. There wasn't time to do anything, so I clasped my hands over my mouth and watched in horror. As the train drew nearer, those cows looked up from their grazing and took off. They really moved and just missed becoming instant hamburger. I breathed a big sigh of relief as the cows crossed the road and went into a field. I didn't think they were ours, although two of them had chains around their necks like David's and Allan's registered 4-H cows wear. By this time, another farmer arrived on the scene, but the cows were not his either. Then the owner came. He had a farm down the tracks, so he drove them back that way. David and Dale had bicycled down, so we all went home again, and they came in for a snack.

David went with his grandfather to make hay that afternoon, and Dale went to the milk house to wash the milkers. I decided to wash my hair and then study. I went upstairs to the bathroom and had a good lather worked up when I heard a car pull into the driveway. Rinsing off most of the suds, I grabbed a towel and went to the window. Getting out of the car were Linda, a young woman from our church, and Lynn, her two-and-a-half-year-old daughter. I called out the window: "Linda, I'm washing my hair. Come on up." So they came upstairs while I finished shampooing.

When we went downstairs I asked Linda if she would like something to eat, but she said no, they had just come from a family picnic. She did accept a glass of iced tea. I asked Lynn if she wanted a fudgesicle, and she said: "Want orange."

I said: "I don't have any orange popsicles, Lynn. All I have is chocolate fudgesicles."

"Want orange."

Linda said: "Lynn, Mary doesn't have any orange. Do you want a fudgesicle?"

"Want orange."

Just as I was returning the fudgesicle to the freezer, Lynn said: "Want chocolate." She ate just a little of it, and we gave the rest to the dog.

While my visitors were still here, the phone

rang twice. The first time, a woman wanted a minister's address from the ministers' directory and I had to look it up. The second time, Dale's music teacher called to say that she passed by when I was watching the cows and had been concerned. After she hung up, Linda and I talked and Lynn played with the kitten. Finally the little girl became tired and sleepy, so they left about 8:45.

Still hoping to study, I decided to take my bath before everyone came home and made a run on the bath tub. I hoped the phone wouldn't ring, and fortunately it didn't. I dressed and put up my hair so I could study until bedtime, but when I went downstairs the phone rang. David and Dale wanted me to go for them, since they had finished the evening milking. It was dark, and I don't like them to walk up the road after dark or to come up on a tractor at night, so I drove down to their grandmother's house for them. Grandmother and I talked for a few minutes. I got some lard and potatoes, and we came home. I gave Dale some supper and he took a bath and went to bed. By that time, Charles and Allan came home from the route. It was late: Charles had to study for his sermon, and David had to tend the rabbits. I knew that I would do no studying that night, so I went to bed, hopeful that Sunday afternoon would not be so eventful. It wasn't—so on Sunday afternoon I wrote this paper.

NOTE: Sometimes I complain about our lack of routine, but I really am happy. We are all busy, and our boys are good boys, occupied with worthwhile activities. We never have to wonder where they are or what they are doing.

Everyone feels the pressure of modern life, and I sometimes wish life were more simple. I am torn between school and home activities and wonder if I neglect one for the other.

My house is seldom in company shape, but it is our home and we live in it. Sometimes I resent having to pick up after the boys when they are so big, but they do work hard, and they cause us no real trouble. I try to "accentuate the positive and eliminate the negative," realizing that before long they will be grown and on their own.

Grad school in middle adulthood

What would it be like—going back to classes after almost twenty years? This is what I asked myself when I was contemplating the idea of returning to college. Upon completion of undergraduate studies, I was married and subsequently began to raise a family. During the years that followed, my family was my main concern; I felt that my place was in the home. As time passed and the children grew older, my life did not seem fulfilled. There was a desire to do something more than I was doing. Thoughts of the future when the children would have families of their own and the awareness of a need for security in later years compelled me to seek a vocation. Knowing from past associations with young people that I enjoyed working with them and was interested in their future, I considered the teaching profession. Starting a program to work for teacher certification and a Master of Education degree in the middle years produced feelings of uncertainty and apprehension. Could I maintain the B average required of graduate students? Would I feel out of place?

My anticipated feelings of not belonging became a reality. Most of the students in the classes were either much younger or had years of teaching experience. Here I was—a middle-aged housewife! It appeared to me that some of the professors looked at me with the question: What is she doing here? I felt that many of the students were asking the same question as I sat in class, walked on the campus, or worked in the library. This feeling was most evident when I was among young adults who filled the Student Union Snack Bar. There were never any incidents to substantiate this feeling of being an "outsider." In fact, professors and college personnel have always been very amicable and cooperative. New acquaintances with classmates were acquired in each course. I realize that the condition was only imaginary; nevertheless, the feeling was real. After two years, this feeling of not being part of the group has subsided to a great extent, but it has not completely dissipated.

I knew that I not only had to attain a B average required by the college, but I also sensed that my family, relatives, and friends were watching to see if I could "make the grade." It was different than it had been in undergraduate studies when mainly my parents were concerned. Now I had a husband and children of my own. The first course was the real test. After successfully completing it and with each following success, I became more confident that I could satisfactorily complete my program.

When I was in undergraduate school, it was necessary for me to study a great deal in order to learn the content of my subjects. This is still the case; however, learning is much more meaningful for me now. I feel as if a void is being filled. New concepts have been developed and previous concepts have been deepened and expanded.

During each course, my thoughts and time are devoted to the work required. The amount of attention given to my family and the house decreases. The Sunday visits with my parents become fewer. Although no one suffers any noticeable ill effects, I sense the feeling of neglect and wonder whether I am placing too much importance in the wrong place.

The strain of completing required assignments and the anxiety resulting from anticipating grades produce physical effects. The desire for food is diminished. Sleep is disturbed, and my eyes become very tired at times. Throughout the duration of each course I somehow have sufficient energy to keep going; however, when the course is completed, I am usually mentally and physically fatigued. I once again become conscious of my environment.

Anxiety is at its peak when a test is forthcoming. No matter how much preparation has been done, I feel disturbed before a test; I cannot completely relax during a test. I usually require more time than others to answer the questions. If time is limited, or if students begin to leave before I have nearly finished, my uneasiness becomes greater. This uneasiness interferes with my thinking processes. My experiences in taking tests have made me aware of the tension that some of my future students will undergo. I am also conscious of the fact that tests cannot adequately measure how much has been learned in a period of time.

If anyone my age would ask if I recommend going back to college, I would answer affirmatively. There has been enjoyment and satisfaction from every class attended. All the time and work required has been rewarded with the feeling of accomplishment. I have found the old adage: "It's never too late to learn" to be true. The pride that my family and parents have expressed has made me feel that I have measured up to their expectations. Being hired to enter a profession at an age when some are thinking about retirement has demonstrated that others have confidence in me. The end result of reentering college is a better self-concept.

At the barre

"Oh, who would want a fifty-year-old trained ballet dancer!" I said, in despair.

"Kindergartens, that's who, and nursery schools," said my older sister, a kindergarten teacher herself. To my surprise, she was right. On the strength of past experiences and with no certification, I was hired by the owner of a private school. She was convinced of the need for purposeful controlled exercises under the leadership of someone trained in body mechanics as well as in child development. She was following Piaget and others who stressed the awareness of sensations, of large muscles, of direction, and of rhythm.

With three- and four-year-olds, I tapped, clapped, circled with hand or foot, counting as we did it, or saying "right, right, right." We hopped, skipped, or tried the jumping jack. We rolled, somersaulted, made a table, or touched our toes to our heads while bellied down to the floor. We also had "free composition" to recorded or piano music, singing games, and folk dances. It was not dancing school. I knew each child was learning and having lots of fun. I was, too.

I had come full circle from when, as a three-year-old, I was requested to dance for admiring relatives: the beginning of self-display. Mother said I danced almost before I walked and never went through an awkward age. As far back as I can remember, I gained pleasure from bodily motions and satisfaction from the applause of those watching. Later I produced "shows" to which the neighborhood was urged to come.

When I was seven, my older sister and I were sent to dancing school. My sister suffered and was allowed to stop. How good I felt to be able to compete with her and my older brother and in this skill surpass them! After three years in which I shone, having solos in dance recitals and on programs at our school, the ballet mistress urged that I be sent in to the city to her teacher for advanced training.

I entered a class of "baby professionals" and soon appeared in productions on the stage of the Academy of Music, Irvine Auditorium,

and at the dedication of the Art Museum. From lesser periods of once a week, I was soon going in to the studio four afternoons a week and performing in ballet and opera several times a month during the season. This meant not getting to bed until midnight. Mother sat out front and stayed until the end. Dress rehearsal, costume fitting, photograph sessions, people swearing in foreign languages, stagehands, and college students who filled in as spear-carriers, these were all new and enjoyable experiences.

Of course I modeled myself on my teacher. I daydreamed about myself as the star, receiving the bouquets and applause. I picked up tap-dancing and really felt there was no limit to what I could do, yet I accepted the fact that I

I used to think that forty years
Would make me wiser than my peers,
But now that I have reached the age,
I find I'm anything but sage.

was not as talented as Stella, Heidi, and Myra. I knew I was better than Dorothy and Bernice. All of these girls continued in the profession as adults.

The daily practice at the barre took concentration. The master or mistress whacked our legs or back with a little springy cane. I remember the muscle cramps and bleeding toes that were the inevitable result of a summer away from regular lessons. I loved it all: the delight of commanding one's body; working together with others to make something lovely; being praised by them and by the audience; the wonderful world of make-believe, great singers, and symphony orchestra music. This was a period of only five years, but the ability to appear in front of large groups has never left me.

When I was fifteen, my family moved to a town where the nearest studio was simply too far away from lessons. I was asked to dance for clubs, community, and school programs. Family groups went to the square dances where all ages joined in following the caller's commands. There were some quadrilles and reels and some "round dances." Boys met girls there, and soon I learned ballroom dancing. Later, when we lived in Colorado, I learned a different type of square-dancing, and in Girl Scouting there were many folk dances to learn and to teach.

Formal ballet was abandoned. There never was any direct confrontation, but I understood that my father objected. It didn't matter as long as dancing class was in the category of piano lessons, but no daughter of his was going to dedicate her life to the performing arts. I was to go to college.

At college, as a major in Dance, I gained an entirely new vocabulary of the dance according to the (then) modern school of Mary Wigman. We composed our own dances to poetry or rhythm patterns. Besides giving recitals and participating in dramatic events at the college, we went on concert tour. But the idea that I would support myself as a dancer had disappeared. In my senior year I was engaged and was married that summer. I continued to enjoy taking part in college productions; only the stage was now that of the men's university where my husband was a graduate assistant.

Through the years of raising our family,

wherever we lived, I danced. I served as dancing counselor for Girl Scouts, led folk-dancing at an International House, and coached PTA and other community programs. I am sure the training I received between the ages of seven and fourteen has given me many more moments of joy than one could have ever believed possible.

How the Great Depression affected me

The Great Depression encompassed the period from 1929 to 1939. I was born in 1927, so it can be easily deduced that my preadolescent years were spent in the middle of the Depression. I was the fourth child in a family that would eventually have eight children. In my mind, not only should the first letter of the word Depression be capitalized, but every letter should be capitalized and the whole word underlined: DEPRESSION.

My father and mother had invested all his savings and all her inheritance in a bank that failed. They lost all of their money. They never recovered one cent.

My father was a "poor preacher" at a time when the free ministry was the only kind there was for small country churches. He worked at any unskilled labor job he could find to make a living and preached on Sunday "for free." Usually, the arrangement was for the preacher to get whatever was left over from the "collections" after other expenses were paid. More times than not, the other expenses were greater than the total collection and he was faced with the choice of either helping pay the expenses or closing the church. Being the kind of man he was, he chose to pay church expenses with money sorely needed by his own family to eat and keep clothed.

As I recall, I accepted my lot mostly with resignation because I saw nothing I could do about it. However, I do not deny a certain amount of bitterness in these recollections. For some years, although it may not have been as often as it seems, we had oatmeal for breakfast and cornbread and beans for supper every day. My father always kept one cow to supply the family with milk and butter and occasionally raised a pig and some chickens for the family larder. We children always became emotionally attached to any animal we raised. After all, we did feed it and saw that it was in its shelter every night. When butchering time came we usually raised a small furor. My father always butchered when we were at school to avoid having to put up with our screams and tears while he was doing his job. We always insisted that we would not eat one bite of our pet pig, but the smell of frying pork chops usually convinced us that, since the horrible deed was already done, we might as well give in.

The leanest time I remember is the period of time when our school lunches consisted of one piece of cornbread and butter per child per day—that's all. I developed a strong hatred for oatmeal and cornbread that lasted many years. I remember that I was especially fond of bananas and can easily recall, with anguish, watching a classmate across from me peel and eat one. I could smell its fragrant, delicious aroma. I wanted some of it so badly, but I did not dare ask for even one bite. I decided then that when I grew up and got a job, I was going to buy a bag full of bananas every week so the whole family would have all they wanted. Just think—all the bananas you could eat—what a Utopia!

Another bane of my childhood was being forced to wear long underwear, long, baggy, cotton stockings, and harness-type garters to hold them up. My father insisted that we girls had to wear those grossly ugly long stockings over lumpy long underwear every day to school during cold weather. I cannot remember one other girl in the school having to wear those horrible things—only my sisters and me. I don't suppose I would have felt nearly as strong an aversion as I did had I not been the brunt of teasing by some of the other children. There is no need to explain to me how cruel children are when they wish to make fun of another child. I know. But my uncomfortable feelings subsided one day when I saw a boy in fourth grade come to school wearing his sister's skirt. His pants were worn out beyond repair and that was all he had to wear. That sight made such an impression on me that I never again complained about my clothes.

Since I was the fourth girl in the family, I do not recall ever having had any new clothes

except shoes. After I wore corns on my toes from wearing ill-fitting "hand-me-down" shoes, my father finally gave in to my mother's pleas to buy me correctly sized shoes. As far as I was concerned, there was no advantage to this arrangement, as he always insisted on buying "practical" rather than "pretty" shoes. Therefore, I never really did object to wearing "hand-me-down" clothes, because I realized he would not buy the pretty clothes I wanted anyway. I had a much greater variety than I would have had if I had had to depend on his buying me new ones. I was especially delighted every time my two aunts from Indiana packed up the outgrown clothes of their girls and sent them to us. I always got some good quality, pretty clothes from those packages, and sometimes they were even "almost new."

It was when I compared my own toys, clothes, and lunches with those of other children that I realized that we were much more "depressed" than were many other families who were living through the depression. What I did not realize was that my father was so proud that even though we were barely surviving, he refused to apply for "relief" or a WPA job. There is something good to be said for that kind of pride, but I am sure that at the time, had I been asked, I would not have been able to think of anything.

Percentage-wise, I am sure that the good times we had as a family outnumbered the bad by far, but the bad ones stick out in my mind much more clearly than the good. As I try to analyze how these incidents colored my life, I have come to these conclusions. I am afraid to go into debt very deeply. I get a feeling of panic when I consider the question of what I would do if something would happen to render my husband an invalid—incapable of bringing in an income. I have seen it happen to other families and I know some of the dire results of an incapacitating accident or illness. I know intellectually that I would be able to figure something out to survive, but the feeling of panic comes first. I believe it is because of a somewhat insecure childhood, monetarily speaking. I hated getting along on nothing and doing without the things I needed and wanted. I still do. It is very frustrating to me to live a hand-to-mouth existence. I learned to sew, primarily so that I could wear a better quality of clothing than I could afford to buy ready-made. The memory of wearing patched and worn clothes and of being scorned by my peers because of them is too poignant to have no emotional effect when I consider the possibility of having to return to such an existence.

I have probably gone overboard in trying to provide all my children's needs and most of their wants, even when I had to go without things I wanted in order to fulfill their desires. Perhaps I have harmed them in their psychological development by overprotecting them from the distress I experienced. How does a person know how to rear children in such a way as to never harm them physically or psychologically? No matter how hard I have tried, I probably have made many mistakes along the way.

Mastectomy

At the age of fifty-two, my mother is very young looking and still very active. My youngest sister and only brother are still at home, so this probably helps to keep Mother young in appearance and attitude. She loves to golf and enjoys caring for her three grandchildren. Recently, however, Mother had to face a crisis many women have had to face who are near her age.

This past December, Mother discovered a lump in her left breast. She did not become alarmed because during the past four years she had four benign cysts removed from both breasts. She did not worry about the lump until it began to grow and pain her, and even then she pushed it out of her mind because she dreaded going to the hospital. Four times in four years was enough. Finally, after her arm started to become stiff and she began dropping things, she decided to go to the doctor. In fact, my father threatened to call the doctor if she didn't make an appointment.

Mother is now able to reveal many of her feelings and innermost thoughts. She wrote some of her feelings down instead of telling me directly because she felt she could think better if alone and because some of her emotions were

still unstable. I think she felt if she became upset I, too, would be upset.

Mother's surgeon is very kind and understanding. The day he examined her, she said he kept reassuring her that everything would be all right. Mother had other suspicions. This examination was not like the others she had encountered because the doctor x-rayed her this time. It was because of the x-ray that Mother began to feel very nervous and frightened. Although her doctor kept reassuring her, she knew he was going to want her to enter the hospital. He felt she should be admitted as soon as possible. This statement did not help her growing anxiety. The few days before her admission to the hospital, she kept very busy and tried to push the haunting thoughts of dreaded cancer out of her mind.

On the way to the hospital, I had tried to reassure her, but Mother, feeling very scared, didn't want to talk. She kept thinking: what if she'd have to have her breast removed? What would her family think? How would her husband feel toward her? When they arrived, Mother remembers Dad being very gentle and considerate. He reminded her not to worry and that he loved her very much. Mother didn't realize that Dad had heard from the doctor that the x-ray showed malignancy. He was having a very difficult time himself. He kept everything to himself until after Mother came through the operation. I can't help feeling some of the torture he must have gone through trying to act normally in order to save us all from a few days of tormenting speculation.

Mother says now that her weakest, yet strongest, moment came the night before her operation. Her roommate, an eighty-seven-year-old woman, was suffering great pain. She seemed very kind and very religious. Mother had never been around anyone with such great faith, and she could see it brought great comfort to the old woman. That evening the woman asked Mother to get her a drink of water. Mother gave it to her and then proceeded to the shower. While she was showering, she was trying to calm herself. Earlier she was asked to sign papers in case they needed to do a mastectomy. She was feeling very nervous, with all sorts of thoughts running through her mind, especially the thought of death. When she returned from the shower the curtain was pulled around her roommate's bed. The nurses all had strained looks on their faces. Mother knew that the old woman had passed away. She began to cry, and then she remembered the woman's many prayers. Thinking of these prayers and of the wonderful faith the woman had, Mother suddenly felt a calming presence in the room. Surprisingly, she was able to sleep fairly well after this experience.

The second day after the operation, Mother felt pretty well and was able to think clearly. She was not sure what the doctor had done, however, because of the thick bandages. She says now that she really knew, but she didn't want anybody telling her for sure just yet. When Dad and I visited her, neither of us mentioned what the doctor had done. Daddy said he couldn't tell her and I knew I couldn't. So on the third day the doctor explained the results of the operation. Mother's first thoughts after the doctors news were for her family. She wondered if we knew, and she prayed she would survive this until they were safely settled in their careers. She wondered if her mother-in-law would be upset since her husband had died from cancer. She wondered if Dad would think her ugly and turn to someone else. Was this going to be the end of her life? She cried until she became sick at her stomach. The nurse gave her a shot which made her sleep for awhile. When she awoke, she decided that being upset wasn't going to get her anywhere and that she was going to have to tell Dad. Of course, when she told Dad, he assured her that all that counted was that she was going to be all right.

After Mother came home, the hardest adjustment was facing friends and neighbors. Most of them were too sympathetic, and this upset her. She felt it necessary to stay away from groups of people until she felt emotionally stronger.

It has been seven months since Mother's operation, and I think she is adjusting very well. She has started to golf again and is very proud of being able to golf four holes. She looks very well and can talk about her operation calmly most of the time. She reads all she can find on the subject of cancer. I do hope that Mother can continue on the road to good adjustments even though we all know it is a long road to a clean bill of health.

Aunt Bebe

The subject of this profile is my very dear friend and aunt. Aunt Bebe, as she is affectionately called, has impressed me so much by her outlook on life and general stamina that I have used her as a pattern or model for my own life. I can only hope that twenty years hence I may be able to function in all areas of life as well as she does.

Aunt Bebe was born to an Alabama farm couple of very limited means; she was the seventh of ten children. By necessity, she assumed household responsibilities at an early age and worked in the farm fields beside her father and other family members. If ever she had leisure time, she enjoyed being outdoors and, particularly, wading in the creek—as the seasons allowed. If she had indoor leisure time, she enjoyed sewing for and playing with dolls.

When her mother died, Aunt Bebe was forced to leave school in the ninth grade and assume complete housekeeping responsibility. Since she was the oldest daughter still at home, she assumed these duties for the next four years. When her youngest sister was able to assume housekeeping duties, Aunt Bebe married a young man who had "courted" her for several years.

The early part of her married life was spent in the home of her husband's parents. There she enjoyed the love of a mother which had been denied her to some extent by the death of her own mother. Several years prior to World War II, she and her husband established their own home. At first, she lived in a house next to her mother-in-law, but after a few years her mother-in-law died. She and her husband moved to an apartment in a city about one hundred miles away. For about three years during World War II while her husband was in the Army, Aunt Bebe worked outside the home—first as a salesclerk in a dress shop and later as a stamp clerk in a wholesale tobacco store. When her husband returned from service, she stopped working and henceforth devoted herself to being a homemaker.

But her talents were not confined to this role alone; she and her husband spent many happy hours planning and building their own home which was partially ready for occupancy after one year. During the building period, Aunt Bebe became an expert carpenter and bricklayer. For many years afterward, they have continued to enlarge and improve their home as they wished. Today their beautiful brick home stands as a symbol of love, patience, and hard work and seems to bid welcome to all who pass that way.

Aunt Bebe never had children of her own, but over the years she has "adopted" many nieces and nephews (first *and* second generation!). She has heard the patter of many little feet: some because they just loved Aunt Bebe and wanted to be there, and some because their mothers were sick or working. Aunt Bebe and her husband also gave refuge and love to older nieces and nephews during times of crisis or efforts to attain advanced schooling. Not many days have ever passed without someone's "staying at Aunt Bebe's house." Life has not always been easy for Aunt Bebe, but she has been willing to share all she has with those about her. In March, Aunt Bebe will be sixty years *young.*

I am convinced that a person's "frame of mind," the general outlook on life, can sustain him far beyond the limits at which the physical mechanism would otherwise function. I have known no person who illustrates this with a more positive and accepting attitude toward life than Aunt Bebe. By no means does she attempt to convince others that she is young and still capable of doing all the things that she once did. But neither does she make the subject of any physical infirmities the focal point of her conversations. Her own feelings are always of second precedence. Perhaps her philosophy could best be summarized as: "Accept each day as it comes, appreciate all its beauties, face all its hardships, and maintain a youthful spirit."

Aunt Bebe has always enjoyed and taken great pride in her home responsibilities. She keeps her home clean and tidy, outside and inside. Although she prefers outdoor activities, she never neglects her indoor duties. Her home

certainly reflects her personality. One can always expect to see a bouquet of flowers on the kitchen table or find "goodies" in the refrigerator. She can turn a simple luncheon snack into a special occasion with the atmosphere she creates at her kitchen table. It is always a special treat to sleep in one of Aunt Bebe's beds because the crisp, ironed sheets have a particular fragrance. Aunt Bebe's furniture and room settings are in good taste, yet each room in her house seems "homey," inviting, and meant for living. Her home is certainly her castle!

Aunt Bebe's great enjoyments are working in her flower and vegetable gardens and doing her yard work. She mows her own lawns, operates a power garden plow, prunes trees and bushes, and tends various upkeep functions around her house. The fruits of her labor—beautiful flowers, nuts, fresh fruits and vegetables—are enjoyed by her many friends and neighbors. Her canned and frozen foods are always shared and enjoyed by those who visit. She is an excellent cook. Whenever there is a "bring a covered dish party," Aunt Bebe's specialties, such as chicken pot pie or cake, are always in demand.

At the local garden club meeting, one might not recognize the Aunt Bebe earlier seen attired in overalls, a battered sun hat, and scuffed shoes working in her gardens. *This* Aunt Bebe, with snow-white hair, will be as stylish and well groomed as a lady in a picture from the society page of the *Washington Post!* Aunt Bebe takes an active part in church activities. She is well known for her cooking and room and table decorating ability. Consequently, she is usually appointed to the social committee of any activity. For the past few years, she has helped direct a monthly social club for senior citizens of the church and surrounding community. The senior citizens all know, love, and admire Aunt Bebe; it is easy to understand why when one sees her patiently giving time and attention to each old person in her vicinity. Each week she drives an older friend to the grocery store for shopping, and many others have known her personal favors.

Aunt Bebe loves children of all ages and has always given them special treatment and attention, such as sewing for them, cooking their favorite foods when they visit, and sending them "care" packages by mail. My children look upon her as an extra and special "Grandmother." My young son remembers her with pleasure because she let him "work" in the garden with her and pulled him in his wagon. Once when my son wanted to take turns and pull *her* in the wagon, she let him try to do so! She is very patient with children, but they soon learn that she insists on discipline and obedience. They readily respond to her direction and guidance.

This past year Aunt Bebe's husband was forced to accept an early retirement because of several heart attacks. Both of them are making good adjustment to the new routine of their life. Their common interests and appreciation of nature and the "simple things of life" sustain them. They have no delusions of grandeur; thus they enjoy and accept life as it is.

One cannot help wondering what course Aunt Bebe's life might have taken if she had been given formal, advanced training in some specialty. She would probably have been very adept in several occupations—home economics, horticulture, or interior decorating. I have known specialists who had formal training in these fields and knew less about their specialties than Aunt Bebe. One needs only to sit and listen while she explains a grafting procedure for a particular plant to know that she is talented and self-trained.

Perhaps sentiment and romance are passe for this time and generation. Nevertheless, I venture to say that if one of the developmental tasks of late adulthood were to make the world a better place for having lived in it, Aunt Bebe would have accomplished just that!

Sixty and separated

The subject is a sixty-year-old female who exhibits some characteristics of late adulthood and some characteristics of early senescence. Her particular developmental trend is at least partially due to resistance to the aging process, which is evidenced by her use of hair coloring for the past ten years, by her constant attention

to figure and diet, and by her increased interest in clothes. Her particular pattern of development is also influenced by family structure which includes a "second family." There are three sons—aged forty-three, forty-one, and thirty-nine—and two daughters—aged twenty-seven and twenty-five. She often expresses regret that she doesn't have a "third family" to rear!

She has been married for forty-four years to a man five years her senior. Although she is still legally married, she has in fact been completely separated from her husband for the past two years. Marital difficulties began about fifteen years ago. This was shortly after the time that she experienced menopause, which was a very abrupt change for her. Conflicts became progressively more frequent and more intense over the next five to eight years. It was at about this time that sexual relations were severed.

In another year, differences reached the point that conflict occurred at any time that the two were together. Since the husband was able to control how often he could be home, his presence at home became limited to one or two weekends per month.

Both the subject and the husband began to have interests in the opposite sex outside of marriage. Contacts with each other became minimal except for a period about three years ago when the husband was hospitalized for appendicitis and recuperated in the home. About two years ago the husband removed all personal belongings from the home, although he still lists this as his legal address.

The subject lives alone in the family home. The house was rented for twenty years before it and a neighboring rental property were purchased. The subject collects the income from the rental property. She also receives a $60 per week household allowance from her husband. She is employed nine months of the year as the manager of a small elementary school cafeteria and receives about $50 per week income from this source. She has been employed in this line of work for seventeen years. She was offered a promotion to manager of the entire school system's cafeterias several years ago, but she felt the increase in responsibility was far greater than the increase in pay. Two years ago she supplemented her summer income by working at a cannery. Last summer she worked as a maid in a hospital, and she is currently helping out there on weekends as she is needed. She also works occasionally as a waitress at a Foreman's Club. Election Day finds her at her post as Inspector of Elections, a position she has held for many years.

Although she spends many hours working, she is also very active in clubs and social organizations. She is a member of a winter bowling league in which her team recently won the championship. She is active in a ladies' card club, American Legion Auxiliary, VFW Auxiliary, Forty and Eight, and Business and Professional Women's Club. She also belongs to women's auxiliaries of the Moose, the Elks, and the hospital. She teaches a Sunday School class of second graders but does not attend church services. She has given up some activities over the past ten years such as most volunteer soliciting for charitable organizations, scouting, Bible school teaching, and other activities associated with her children's activities. She has increased the time spent in reading books and in making her own clothes.

Physically, she appears to be rather better preserved than the average sixty-year-old, but there are signs of aging. Her face shows many lines and wrinkles, and her eyes appear tired when she engages in strenuous activity, when she does not wear makeup, or when she does not get enough sleep. Her knuckles are knotted by arthritis, and she is slightly stooped. She has worn trifocals for several years now. Although not especially noticeable in casual conversation, her hearing may be somewhat impaired since she often speaks louder than necessary and plays both radio and television at a louder volume than would be normal. She is five feet, six inches tall and maintains a fairly steady weight at one hundred thirty pounds.

She prides herself on never having been a patient in a hospital, but she has been under treatment for high blood pressure for a number of years. This condition was aggravated by disregard for proper type and amount of diet, drink, activity, and medication. She was troubled by headaches and dizziness, nosebleeds, and loss of memory of immediate information or events. She has, however, become more concerned for her own welfare in the last year and a half; she has shown marked improvement, since she now keeps her monthly appointments with her doctor and follows his advice.

She takes pride in being able to work harder, longer, and more efficiently than most other women of any age. She was the oldest girl and the second oldest child in a family into which nine children were born; thus she was used to hard work even before she left school at the completion of eighth grade to take a job and contribute to the family support. She now finds it difficult to slow the pace she has set for herself over the years. She is also proud of being an early riser even when it is unnecessary, but she has made some adjustment as she is often found napping in the late afternoon or early evening.

Since the subject and her husband completed only the eighth grade in school, she is especially proud of her children, all of whom have received degrees in higher education courses—three in business administration, one in nursing, and one in education. She sometimes mentions the accomplishments of her children too often or too emphatically.

Her sons have become more involved with their own lives. She feels hurt when they fail to remember her on Easter, Mother's Day, or her birthday. Due to these feelings, she initiates fewer contacts with her sons.

The last of her children left home more than three years ago, but she still has some difficulty adjusting to their independence. She takes offense if her help, which is sometimes excessive, is rejected.

Her nine grandchildren range in age from two years to twenty years of age. She does not always approve of their behavior or of her children's methods of child rearing.

She has become somewhat less tolerant and less patient with others. Unexpected guests are sometimes upsetting to her. She is also less willing to do more than "her share" in social activities.

Although weaknesses of earlier years are more pronounced, her overall adjustment to the aging process is good. She functions well in her environment. Especially over the past year, she seems to have become more calm in her reactions to present situations and more realistic in planning for her future years. A deeper understanding of her by persons with whom she comes in contact (especially family members) would reduce tensions; however, not all these people have the capacity for such empathy and understanding.

Prayer of a seventeenth century nun

Keep me from getting talkative and particularly from the fatal habit of thinking that I must say something on every subject and on every occasion.

Release me from the craving to straighten out everybody's affairs.

Keep my mind free from the recital of endless details: give me wings to get to the point.

Seal my lips when inclined to tell of my aches and pains; they are increasing with the years and my love of rehearsing them grows sweeter as the years go by.

Teach me the glorious lesson that occasionally it is possible that I may be mistaken.

Keep me reasonably sweet; I do not want to be a Saint. Some of them are hard to live with, but a sour old woman is one of the crowning works of the Devil.

Help me to extract all possible fun out of life. There are many funny things around us, and I do not want to miss any of them.

Make me thoughtful but not moody, helpful but not bossy. With my vast store of wisdom it seems a pity not to use it all, but Thou, my Lord, knoweth that I want a few friends left at the end.

THINGS TO THINK ABOUT AND DO

1. Imagine what it would be like to be an adult of forty-five or fifty-five. What are the sociological, psychological, and physiological factors involved? In what ways are these age levels different from that of a thirty-five-year-old or a twenty-five-year-old?

2. Let's take a look at your future. Take your present age and quickly review your family circumstances, your career or educational conditions, and your life in general. Add ten years to your life and to the lives of those in your family circle, including parents, brothers, sisters, grandparents, friends, husband or wife, and children, if any. What might things be like then? How do you see yourself and your circumstances? Add ten more years to your life; what will your family, home, and vocational circumstances likely be? Add ten or twenty more years. How do you see yourself now? Are your efforts and planning of today sufficient to meet the challenges of tomorrow and get you where you want to be?

3. Menopause and climacteric are conditions of life in the late forties and early fifties. What relationship might these physiological circumstances of middle age have with an increased occurrence of health problems? Does the metabolic energy have anything to do with it?

4. Survey or interview a number of people between the ages of forty and sixty as to what they like about their age group and what they don't like about it. Would they suggest an age level that they liked better? If so, ask what makes the suggested age level better than the present one.

5. Do a study to determine the ages of individuals who are in leadership or "command" positions. Seek out leaders in government, in education, in business and industry. You may limit the study to your community, or you may include the entire state. If you hesitate to ask people their ages, consult books such as "Who's Who in Government," "Who's Who in Education," "Outstanding Men and Women in Business and Industry," and similar books.

6. Ask your parents, if they are in this age bracket, what lessons they have learned from their past lives that have been of some help to them or what they know now that they wish they would have known when they were much younger. Any surprises? Any ideas for you?

7. Read "Middle Age—Are We Condemned?" What really concerns this woman? Is she realistic? Is she typical?

8. Mastectomy is a concern for many women. What personal knowledge do you have of

women who have had this operation? Have you ever heard of a man having this operation?

READING SOURCES
Developmental psychology texts

CRM: Developmental psychology today, ed. 2, New York, 1975, CRM/Random House, Inc., chap. 21.

Hurlock, E. B.: Developmental psychology, ed. 4, New York, 1975, McGraw-Hill Book Co., chaps. 11, 12.

Kaluger, G., and Kaluger, M.: Human development: the span of life, St. Louis, 1974, The C. V. Mosby Co., chap. 13.

Related readings

Bracken, P.: Middle age: for adults only, Reader's Digest 95:86, 1966.

Brozan, N.: Middle-age needn't be like dark ages, The New York Times, Mar. 29, 1972.

Eisdorfer, C. and Lawton, M. P., editors: The psychology of adult development and aging, Washington, 1973, American Physiological Association.

Franzblau, R. N.: The middle generation, New York, 1971, Holt, Rinehart, & Winston.

Lear, M. W.: Is there a male menopause? The New York Times, Jan. 28, 1973.

Lynes, R.: A cool cheer for middle-aged, Look 31:46, 1967.

Neurgarten, B., editor: Middle age and aging, Chicago, 1968, University of Chicago Press.

Rogers, C. R.: Freedom to learn, Columbus, Ohio, 1969, Charles E. Merrill Publishing Co.

Vedder, C. B.: Problems of the middle aged, Springfield, Ill., 1965, Charles C Thomas, Publisher.

Winokur, G.: Depression in the menopause, Am. J. Psychiatry 130 :92-93, 1973.

CHAPTER 11

The years of retirement, change, and acceptance

To young people in their late teens, their parents may seem "kind of old but not *real* old" and their grandparents are definitely "elderly." The truth of the matter may be that their parents are in their late thirties or early forties and their grandparents in their fifties or early sixties. To a person in their fifties, the late teens seem "so young with so much to learn," but looking ahead, the sixties "don't seem all that old and even in the seventies, it is possible to get around pretty well." Old, in terms of age, is relative to the age and understanding of the one doing the defining. It comes as quite a shock to young people to realize that many first-time grandparents are in their early forties. In fact it is not unusual to occasionally find a great-grandparent in their fifties. To someone who is sixty, fifty is still the prime of life!

There is no question that major changes occur, sometimes rather suddenly, in the years after the age of sixty-five. Nature never intended for man to live forever. Adjustments to changing physical, mental, social, and vocational conditions must be made. The advent of retirement with its accompanying readjustment of daily living patterns is usually one of the first tasks to be encountered in "old age." The letter to "Dear John and Ellen" reveals rather poignantly the adjustment required both before and after the retirement becomes a reality. Another painful adjustment that most couples have to make occurs when one spouse precedes the other in death, as in the profile of "Grandmother's Adjustment."

Personality changes in old age may or may not occur, depending on (1) how well an individual can adapt, psychologically, to the changes that are occurring and (2) the strengths, philosophy, or purposeful activities that an individual has for living. "Unforgettable Mary Grace" may not be what you expect, or want, in an old maid, but her beliefs form the basis for a determination to continue to be herself and to assert herself. In "Ninety-Five

and All's Well" another basis of determination to live is found.

Not all people in old age have sad or pessimistic views of life. "The Gardener" still enjoys humor and sociability; the woman in "Youth at Old Age" finds her interests and activities very helpful. "A Matter of Time" illustrates, in a pleasant way, how memories—good memories—can add a happy dimension to the later life.

Of course there can be some grief and despondency when decline comes too rapidly or is irreversible. The account of "My Old Age is Getting to Me" reveals an almost helpless feeling of being caught up in changes that cannot be controlled. "The Sadness of Senility" and "The Geriatrics Ward" tell of the somber, disconsolate realities of old age for some people. Too often, these are the type of conditions that are magnified in the minds of younger people when they think of the characteristics of old age. Fortunately, although these situations do exist—and they are painful—they are not the ultimate end results for the majority of people who reach the later years of life, the seventies and beyond.

Dear John and Ellen

It certainly was wonderful to see you again. I only wish you hadn't moved to sunny California so that we could get together more often. I do hope that you enjoyed the visit as much as we did. It has done wonders for Dad to see you two and his first grandson again.

Actually, I've been meaning to write to you about Dad for some time. I'm sure you have noticed the changes since you have been separated from him for several years. Little things go unnoticed around here until all at once something happens, and we become aware of still another change.

It all started, I think, when Dad was forced

to retire from the bank a little more than a year ago. And it's no wonder. After all, he has been working for almost fifty years. During the war he worked an evening shift at the steel mill in addition to his position at the bank. As a child, I cannot remember seeing him much, even after the war, because he was also working as a salesman at the garage at night for a number of years. It's no wonder that retirement poses some problems for him!

The bank put him down a number of times. I especially remember, as I'm sure you do, John, that time he should have become the head of his department but instead some college graduate received the promotion. It's not surprising that Dad was disturbed, particularly when he had to spend the next month showing the younger man how to keep the records, how to handle the clients, and most of the other things about which the college graduate had no idea. The guy did, of course, have a degree and that makes one an expert, right?

Dad saw this same put-down happening to many of his friends as well, and I'm sure these were some of the things that started his deterioration. Perhaps deterioration is too strong a word. Maybe it is simply a personality change. Even when Dad was working, there were pressures—particularly about money. His job was demanding and the pay not exactly adequate, as you know. With the Women's Lib movement swelling, the idea of working mothers is not often questioned. I think, though, that Dad has always blamed himself that Mother had to work all these years. Certainly you and I would not be where we are, John, if they hadn't both been working. Even with our scholarships and loans, we would not have made it without them. And I never heard Dad toss it up to us.

Anyway, about a month before his retirement, Dad started elaborating on all the things he was going to do, places he was going to visit. He really *seemed* quite happy about retirement. However, I do remember how we remarked among ourselves that he seemed "frightened" and was trying to keep us from worrying. Of course, he had the two perfect examples of retired men enjoying their leisure in Uncle Bob and Uncle Lee. It's really difficult to understand how they can do so little and still be alive. But that's another story!

After the party they had for Dad at the bank, the changes started to take place. That was about a year ago. Instead of using the tools he had been talking about and building that workshop in the basement, he sat in the living room or on the back porch. Occasionally he played with the new puppy. You remember how he said he would help Mother with housework (like doing the dishes and running the sweeper, etc.)—well, he could think up some beautiful excuses! One day he said he just had to sit because every time he went to use the vacuum, Skipper barked and carried on. So, he sat! When Skipper went to sleep, Dad started the sweeper but Skipper would wake up and begin his antics. Of course, he never thought to put Skipper outside or even to shut him in the kitchen!

Another time, Dad had been complaining about the dog's nails needing clipped. Dad's skin is delicate and a simple scratch from the dog tore it open. One day, the dog got sick, and Dad took him to the veterinarian. Mother had written a note about the dog's actions and symptoms. When they got home, I asked Dad if he had Skipper's nails clipped while they were there. He really blew his stack. He said it wasn't on the note and he couldn't read minds. I had only asked for his sake, since the nails really didn't bother anyone else. He often takes harmless remarks and treats them as personal attacks.

I thought I could kill two birds with one stone, so I asked Dad to paint my room. You remember how he has always loved to paint. (And what a perfectionist!) Well, it took him almost three weeks to paint my ten by twelve room. I don't know what he was doing. At least it kept him busy, and he really did seem in better spirits.

You mentioned that his hearing seemed worse, but actually he just doesn't pay as much attention as he used to. He often accuses us of not telling him anything only minutes after we have. I think maybe he "tunes" us out because many times we are talking about work and activities in which he cannot participate. Before his retirement he listened to everything we said.

I guess it bothered him that you two and the baby moved so far away. I really don't like to think how he will feel when I leave next summer . . .

All in all, Dad is less active, more quickly irritated, often confused, and worried about money. We try to reassure him without his knowing, but I don't know if it helps. I love having him home all day and not seeing him frustrated by problems at work. I guess, though, that he feels frustrated by a whole new set of problems. I hope he can adjust and shake that feeling of inadequacy that seems to be at the root of all this. We all love him and that's all that counts. It has helped me to get all of this off my chest and I certainly hope it hasn't caused you to worry needlessly. I guess many men go through a period like this. Pray that the period ends quickly and that he can be happy with his new freedom.

Love,
Cindy

Unforgettable Mary Grace

The term "old maid" when applied to a seventy-one-year-old woman may bring to mind the picture of a little old lady with white hair piled high, knitting needles clicking merrily as she rocks to and fro. Or one might be inclined to think of a spinster in a library hidden from sight by stacks and stacks of books. Still another possibility might be that of a dowager, content in a world of antiques and other old "stuff."

The person I would like you to meet is best described by the third option. Miss Mary Grace Sanders is a very versatile person, with interests ranging from sitting-room reading to international travel. A well-educated person with degrees from Goucher and Hartford Colleges, she was formerly a physics teacher on the college level, music teacher, director of religious education for a church, and a writer of worship material for children. As a result of her travels and various experiences in numerous states, Mary Grace has many friends and acquaintances all over the United States.

The home in which Mary Grace grew up was one of much wealth, but the outward appearance of the place would have given one just the opposite impression. The money of the family had been handed down from previous generations, and it was being tightly conserved in every way possible. The furniture was reminiscent of years gone by. Some of it was shabby, and the number of items in evidence were fewer than many poorer people of the period might have had. Her father was an engineering consultant who was constantly on the move from one company to another. Her mother was extremely overprotective of "little Mary Grace" from the very beginning. As Mary Grace grew to womanhood, her mother did not release her grip even slightly: it was too dangerous for a girl to ride a bicycle, too warm to play out in the hot sun, not good for a person to engage in active play, and not healthy to have friends who were too "different." Boys who showed even the slightest interest in Mary Grace were firmly discouraged by Mrs. Sanders. She was afraid that she might lose her daughter to one of these boys.

Mary Grace's parents had passed away by the time of my birth and, since I have known her, she had lived alone in a nearby town in part of an old house that also had apartments that she rented. Since my family knew her quite well, she would often visit in my home for several days or a week. As a rule I enjoyed company in my home. But the visits of Mary Grace did present some unique problems. Since she had been in children's work for many years and had taken many courses on the rearing of children, she considered herself an authority on the subject. However, one critical item had been overlooked—she had never had any children of her own and had very little first-hand experience in dealing with children in the home on a day-to-day basis. Since she was very outspoken on the way a child should behave, I was frequently admonished to act "grownup" and "behave" myself especially well when Mary Grace would visit.

When I was in my second year of college and home for Christmas vacation, Mary Grace again spent a holiday with my family. Deciding to make some eggnog, I proceeded to collect the needed ingredients. Among these items was a tiny bottle of rum extract, purchased from the spice shelf of the local grocery store. Mary Grace immediately objected to the rum extract. I ignored her pointed remarks concerning the use of this small item and continued with my task. She, however, could not let a thing like this go by. Taking the bottle in hand, and summoning my mother from her work, she proceeded to tell her what I was doing and explain in no masked terms or tones how I was going astray. After all, she stated, this was the way alcoholics got started and once a person so much as started to drink, there was no turning back. But somehow I could not fathom how the eggnog her father had made, with an egg in a glass of milk, would be something a person could enjoy drinking!

From a very tender age to this day, Mary Grace has first and foremost in her mind the idea of saving money. In her home, she was taught to conserve and hoard everything humanly possible. Some of these saving methods are quite unique and unusual in nature. At Christmas time, in order to save on greeting cards, she makes her own by cutting pictures from ones she has previously received and pasting them on other sheets of paper. Where she can find old envelopes to fit these cards has always remained a mystery! Then, to save stamps, she delivers personally every card possible, sometimes walking all over town. Any gifts—Christmas, birthday, wedding—are not things she has purchased for the occasion, but things from her vast collection of belongings. Her entire philosophy is to reuse anything possible. Who else would save paper napkins, folded carefully, for use at another meal, or reread, year after year, the articles of the September, 1948, *Reader's Digest?* In the realm of clothing, it should not be washed every week because this causes the material to wear out. Items of clothing are kept for twenty years, until they will come into style again. And if a show window is in the process of changing a display, she is the first to ask for that which is being discarded.

Some years ago, Mary Grace was forced to change cars because her 1938 model had breathed its last. Presently, she is the owner of a 1956 Chevrolet with the unbelievable mileage of 12,000 to its credit. Somehow it's always easier to request a ride with someone else than to drive herself!

Everything connected with this remarkable woman has a long history that she loves to tell, and any events of today lead her to relate her comparable experiences of long ago. Because of these and other idiosyncrasies, I find her truly the most unforgettable person I've ever met.

Grandmother's adjustment

After my grandfather's death two years ago, my grandmother had quite an adjustment to make. They had raised five boys on a three acre farm, and she hated to leave the place which brought her many fond memories. They had lived here for forty-eight years, and my grandmother's whole life revolved about her home. During that time, she had always planted a large garden which contained a variety of vegetables and beautiful flowers. Also, they had a "truck patch" in which she raised corn, onions, potatoes, and pumpkins. She spent a lot of time pulling weeds, picking vegetables, and canning different varieties of fruits and vegetables. Besides this, she raised chickens and had several customers who usually came to the home to buy eggs. She seemed to enjoy hard work, and she liked to work outdoors.

After my grandfather had passed away, my uncle thought it would be best for her to move into an apartment. Much to her disappointment, she moved to an apartment in the city. My grandmother refused to live with any of her sons and was determined to adjust to her new environment.

During the first few months, my grandmother had difficulty adjusting to the confines of an apartment. She seemed very depressed but decided to pursue some of her previous hobbies. She started gathering many varieties of flowers and placed them on every windowsill and table top. Another hobby in which she took an active interest was cooking and baking. Twenty years ago, she received an award for her homemade raisin-filled cookies, and her recipe was printed in a magazine. Since then, she has always made literally thousands of these cookies at Christmas.

This past spring her old home was advertised as being for sale. It was mentioned in the paper at a much higher price than she had sold it two years previous. The advertisement had also listed the acreage of the farm as being greater than it had actually been. My grandmother was infuriated by this false advertisement and proceeded to telephone the real estate agent. She gave him a verbal scolding that he will never forget. I wondered why she did such a thing but I realized that she wanted to move back to the farm.

I am sure she realized that going back to the farm would be impossible, yet this brought about a change in her daily routine. She started to complain about the appearance of the yard and flower beds around her apartment. Since my grandmother liked to work outdoors, she began to weed the flower beds and pull crab grass out of the lawn. She then began pulling weeds along the sidewalk in front of the other apartment buildings. She started to complain to the landlord about the upkeep of her backyard. There were clotheslines hung all around, and the lawnkeeper would miss several places when mowing the grass. On her initiative, she planted several beds of flowers where weeds had been growing. In fact, she proceeded to plant a vegetable garden from one end of the apartment building to the next. She planted seventy stalks of tomatoes, many rows of sweet peas, onions, basil, squash, peppers, lima beans, pumpkins, and radishes. The lawnkeeper was perturbed by her actions and reported them to the landlord. After seeing that my grandmother had worked hard to plant the garden neatly next to the building, the landlord thought that her endeavors improved the appearance of the land. Unfortunately, a few of the tenants did complain to the landlord about the cans which my grandmother had placed over the tomato plants to protect them. One tenant wasn't used to country living and felt that the cans made the view of the backyard hideous. This tenant had overlooked my grandmother's hard work and other efforts to beautify the yard. Because of these complaints, the landlord notified my grandmother that she will not be able to plant a garden next year. She was greatly disappointed because she had always enjoyed working outdoors and watching things grow. She received great satisfaction from this garden project.

My grandmother has adjusted to her new environment somewhat. At first, she was depressed and thought that life was not worth living any more. As she began to expand her activities, she gained a purpose in life, and at the age of seventy-seven, she seemed happy once again. The many thoughtful things that she does for other people have brought meaning to her life. I hope that her landlord will reconsider his decision concerning her garden; otherwise, she may have another difficult adjustment to make next spring.

The gardener

Charlie, an octogenarian, is a retired streetcar conductor and a retired farmer, but he is far from retired from life. Slight of build and rather thin, Charlie has gray curly hair and wears black-rimmed glasses.

On meeting Charlie for the first time, two characteristics would probably be more noticeable than any others: his posture and his voice. His posture could be compared to a stick; both are straight and rather stiff and rigid. This posture is even noticeable when he is driving his car, which is frequently. His voice, the second noticeable characteristic, is always just a little raised—like a quiet shout; this is because Charlie is hard of hearing.

If, after meeting Charlie, one were to talk with him a while, several more characteristics would soon be apparent. For one thing, Charlie's vitality is unmistakable. At eighty-five, he is still working three days a week at his regular job, cleaning airport hangars and small planes at a nearby airfield, not a lazy man's job at all.

Another of Charlie's outstanding traits is his pride in his garden. He plants, cultivates, and harvests several rows of any number of vegetables. Besides freezing some of this produce for his own use, he delivers many of his home-grown vegetables to friends in the area who are not able to grow their own. In fact, Charlie not only enjoys taking care of his own garden, but he also plants a garden for an old friend of his while she works. A "must" when visiting Charlie is a visit to his garden, where he will quite proudly point out his latest plants.

Charlie has been a widower for fifteen years, during which time he has chosen to live alone in his farmhouse, although his son and grandchildren would have been happy to have him live with them. Charlie does his own cooking and housecleaning, and in the evenings he enjoys watching programs on his new color television.

But Charlie hardly sits at home alone. He is more often found visiting his somewhat younger friends who cannot move around quite so well; he even takes these friends to visit some of their friends. At Easter, Charlie is found out around the countryside delivering Easter baskets to all the children who live nearby. In short, Charlie likes to be doing as much as possible for his friends and neighbors and dislikes "being a bother" to anyone.

The fact is, Charlie is not a bother to anyone; he is very self-sufficient and resourceful. Recently when planning to visit his family who live some distance from here, Charlie resourcefully decided to pack some of his frozen vegetables in dry ice, so he could safely take some to his family.

Charlie is not self-centered or contrary as many older people tend to be, but on occasion he will disagree with others and follow his own experience-based reasoning. For instance, a couple of years ago, his family wanted him to buy a new car, but Charlie insisted that his present car was "just right for him," and he seems to have been correct.

Perhaps Charlie's most outstanding quality is his sense of humor. He is frequently found teasing, being teased, laughing, or playing practical jokes on his friends. For instance, after "looking over" a neighbor's garden while the neighbor was working, Charlie pulled a thistle from the garden and stuck it in a pair of dirt-covered garden shoes which were lying on the neighbor's porch—just as if it had grown there. What a practical joke between gardeners!

When asked to what does he attribute his health, Charlie quickly answers: "Clean living." He neither smokes, drinks, nor swears, and he can be seen in church every Sunday. If "clean living" is responsible for this alert, happy, and useful octogenarian, more people should try it; Charlie is certainly a "good neighbor"!

Youth at old age

Grandmother is eighty-four-years-old. To some, without question, she would probably be considered old and very frail. However, on the contrary, I find that she is capable of doing things my own peer group of twenty-six-year-olds finds difficult.

Her early life was really no different from that of anyone else born in 1892. The only thing that might have influenced her chances for longevity was that, as a widow at an early age, she was forced to work and at the same time raise a family. Looking at photographs taken during her early adulthood, one gets the impression that she was eighty-four years old fifty years ago and has reversed the process of growing old physically. One must consider the appearance of modern clothes and cosmetics that could possibly cause her to look younger today. But as far as attitude is concerned, from the beginning she has never really thought about getting old. In fact, until a year ago she held a full time job six days a week as a baker in a college dining hall. She decided to quit because she had too many other things to do! For her, there just weren't enough hours in each day.

She is constantly busy, getting around by way of her own car which she is still capable of handling quite well. Her resource of energy is unbelievable. Her days now consist of many hobbies and social events. Friday and Saturday nights she is an avid bingo fan, going to bed around 11:00 P.M. She is a heavy sleeper and very seldom has insomnia. She has excellent eating habits of regular and balanced meals.

Her mental processes are just as sharp as they ever were. Physically she is possibly an exception of old age in that she has never been disabled or injured or had any serious illnesses. This in itself could greatly affect her youthful outlook.

She is always eager to learn a new handicraft such as pottery or painting and is fortunate to be living in a college town that has many college and adult education classes available. All these interests keep her young in thought and actions. Little or no mention is ever made of slowing down because of age. As a matter of fact, I doubt whether she has ever admitted her age to anyone other than her daughter; when she was working full time, I know for a fact that the records listed her as somewhere in her early sixties in age. If they would have known her true age, they would have asked her to retire a long time ago.

Another favorite pastime which my grandmother greatly enjoys is caring for her flowers. She grows many varieties and is well informed about each type. Along with her flower garden and house plants, she grows grapes from which she makes jam, jelly, and wine each year. I often find myself amazed to see all that she manages to squeeze into a twenty-four hour day, and yet, somehow, she never seems to be in a hurry or too busy to sit and chat when anyone drops in to pay her a visit. And she even finds time to do some visiting of her own.

In conclusion, although she is an active member of the senior citizens group, she is far from being old in actions and thoughts; she is the first person to remind one of that fact if it is suggested otherwise.

Life itself can't give you joy,
Unless you really will it;
Life just gives you time and space
It's up to you to fill it.

Optimist

A matter of time

"Dad had a nice time last night at the auction."

"What time did he get home?"

"Oh, I guess about one o'clock."

"In the morning! My son?"

"Yes, Grandma."

"What time did your brother get home from his date?"

"If you want to know, ask him yourself. And besides, Grandpa, what time did you get home when you dated Grandma?"

"The latest was two o'clock."

"Two o'clock! Wasn't that a little late for those da. . ."

"That was because it was raining and I didn't want to get my horse all wet. So I waited till it was over. Usually I got home at eleven o'clock, and that was only once a week."

"That's right, Karen. He only came on Saturday nights."

"Why just once a week? Didn't you two want to be together more often than that?"

"Karen, your grandmother lived fourteen miles away! It was too much to ask my horse to work all day and then take me all that distance to see Nettie."

"Oh, Grandpa. I drive that far to school each day—that's nothing."

"That is far!"

"He thought more of his horse than he did of me. Didn't you, Dave?"

"Yes, I did, because horses cost a lot."

"How did you two ever get together anyhow if you lived so far apart?"

"My sister and I would always go to the Kutztown Park on Sunday afternoons."

"Where's that?"

"In Kutztown! You know where!"

"I've been through Kutztown many times, and I've never seen it."

"I hear it's all grown shut now because no one cared for it, Nettie. At least that's what they tell me."

"That's a shame, Dave. It was so nice there. Remember the big crowds it always drew. We used to pack a big lunch and load up the buggy. Becky, the gray horse, never liked to go, so we always took Susie. My sister and I knew there would be lots of boys there, and the boys knew there'd be lots of girls. The older men played horseshoes, and there were games for the children. But, you say it's all grown shut! Wonder where the people go now?"

"We've got other places, Grandma."

"Well, anyway, your grandpa and Charlie Davis were there a lot. Charlie said he wanted the tallest of my sisters, and Dave said he'd take me, a little rascal. So we went for walks."

"How long did you two date?"

"Three years."

"Two and a half years."

"Around three years, I guess."

"Yep, and one day while her father was in the barn, I asked him in Dutch if I could have her."

"What did he say?"

"Yes, if I could take care of her. And when I told Nettie, she said: 'You didn't!' "

"Well, he never said he was gonna ask."

"Guess you must have had some other guys you were dating, Grandma."

"Oh, a few. I remember Samuel Wintermyer. I thought he was a real dandy, a real good boy, because he always put flowers on his mother's grave. She was dead, you know. He lived with an aunt on the first white farm in Hametown."

"I don't know where that's at."

"Sure you do, right down from Krout's schoolhouse."

"I don't know where that schoolhouse is either."

"Sure. Go down the old road over the hill and cross the little creek. There's a pretty white house with black shutters on your left. It has a whitewashed fence around the yard. The barn is on your right side and was always painted a neat white with green trim. A little creek flows to the right of the house with three willow trees hanging over it. As you come out of the kitchen door of the house, a grape arbor tickles your head. All kinds of fruit trees are behind the house, along with a well-kept garden."

"Well, you know, Grandma, they extended the impounding dam so most of that area is under water."

"Really! That's a pity! I bet that farm is, too. It was such a pretty farm, too."

"We have to make changes, Grandma."

"Yes, well. So, anyway, Sammy came one night and we were in the parlor on the lounge. It's the last time I'd take a boy there. He tried to get me to sit on the floor and I wouldn't let him, that little sneaker. I fired him!"

"Fired him?"

"Got rid of him, wouldn't see him again. He's dead now."

"What about you, Grandpa? Did you see many girls?"

"Huh! I didn't have time. You can't farm and be thinkin' about girls at the same time. Remember that!"

"I guess you two knew what you were doing. After all, you're married how many years?"

"Sixty till January."

"That made you twenty-seven, Grandpa, and you twenty-four, Grandma."

"Don't wait too long, Karen. You want to get a good picking."

"I've got plenty of time, yet."

"Say, what time did you say your Dad got home last night from the auction?"

"One o'clock, Grandpa."

"Yeh, that's right. I forgot."

My old age is getting to me

Old age can become very frustrating and depressing when one increasingly realizes a growing dependence on others accompanied by a feeling of failure in oneself. I am eighty-five years old, and I have observed a gradual decline in my physical and mental alertness over the past few years. This age reminds me greatly of the young child who needs someone to guide his actions and make his decisions. To me it seems like a sad and difficult period of life.

At the age of eighty, just five short years ago, I lived a very full, patterned, and contented life. My wife and I were both in good health, owned our home, and were able to care for ourselves. I enjoyed gardening in my double lot of ground while my wife busied herself cooking delicious foods and cleaning house. We passed the evenings watching television and reading the newspaper. We had daily visits from our three children and their families who lived in the same community. Yes, life was pleasant then, with few upsets in the routine.

Two years later my beloved wife died suddenly, and that pleasant way of living came to an abrupt end. Henceforth, life was rather lonely in that big house, even though friends and family visited regularly and tried to brighten each day. Oh, there were still things to do: garden to tend, furnace to fire, and house to clean; but somehow life was empty. The children bought me a little house dog, and he became my main concern and constant companion. Here was someone who needed me and shared my day from sunrise to sunset. Summer days became enjoyable with gardening in the morning, a nice nap with my pup curled at my feet through the afternoon, and a relaxing evening on the back porch under the stars. Winter days found me more restless since I could not get outside. The children were wonderful to me, always visiting, cooking my meals, doing my laundry, and helping in countless other ways. I had life better than many at my age. Then, one by one, my old friends died off, leaving me more and more alone. But my dog and I carried on.

Gradually, almost unnoticed by me, I became a little less responsible. A few times I forgot to turn down the furnace thermostat before retiring for the night, and then I misplaced my phone bill once or twice. My memory grew shorter and I misplaced things continually. They tell me I asked the same questions five or six times within an hour, and still I couldn't recall the answer. Yes, I was going downhill, but never would I leave my home; it was my life.

Then one day I did a foolish thing but it was very important at the time. I was eighty-four and, as always, the spring housecleaning had to be done. There was a hired lady to help, but washing windows was no job for a woman. That had always been my department, and this year was no exception. We began upstairs and although I had been warned not to do the windows this year, I positively could not surrender my duties! Well, you can picture the rest. I climbed out on the porch roof and two minutes later was on the cement floor below, unable to move. It was a miracle that my injuries were light—a few broken ribs and a concussion. A few weeks in the hospital and I would be as good as new, or so I thought.

I demanded to go back home, but the family seemed to have full say now and I soon found myself in an old folks home. I've been here now for several months and I suppose you'd say I've adjusted well. I can't walk on my own any more, but I have a walker and a wheelchair to help me get around. The aches and pains are more prominent these days, and I get so bored with myself. Neither television nor the newspaper is of any interest to me. People keep trying to interest me in something, but my mind can't concentrate on any one thing for longer than a few minutes. That is, unless it is something that worries me. For instance, some days all I want to talk about is getting new pants or needing socks. About every five minutes I bring it up again, even though others keep trying to change the subject.

The other people at this home are so irritating. I declare they're always stealing my clothes, although my family insists I just misplace them. But they can't fool me; they're stealing them! When I get new things, I hide them under my pillow or behind the dresser. You just can't trust these folks at their old age.

My family is rather disgusting these days. They never agree with me and always try to change my mind. They tell me my bedroom is on the first floor, but I've gone upstairs to bed all my life, and I want to go upstairs to my room. Why can't they understand these facts?

I guess I can put up with this kind of life until spring, but then I'm going to get a trailer and live alone again. I could do everything I used to do if I were in my own home. I'll get my dog back from the farm where he is now, and we'll have a good life together again. I'll put the trailer on my son's lot, have a little garden to tend, and have a back porch to sit on during those nice summer evenings. All those friends will come to visit again and life will be nice.

The sadness of senility

My step-grandfather is eighty-seven years old. He lived a happy and fruitful life until about four years ago when, following a prostate operation, he entered the stage of life known as senility. Looking back on a life filled with hard-earned success, it seems somehow unfair that such a man should have to complete his life in such an undignified way.

It took him nearly a year to recover from this operation. Possibly due to the lack of physical movement and the loss of mobility during recovery, he began to show signs of senility soon after the operation.

The first obvious signs of a change could be seen physically. The operation had taken its toll. He had lost a good deal of weight, and his big appetite never fully returned. His sense of balance began to leave him, and he started to fall and stumble often. His eyesight, always superb, was to be affected by the onset of cataracts.

Along with his physical decline, Amos lost a great deal of strength and coordination and was now unable to do many of his former routine activities. He became more and more reliant on my grandmother. Due to this partial loss of independence and usefulness, he began to lose his pride and, along with this, his vitality.

He could no longer carry on his church and civic duties, nor could he work in his garden or at his workbench. He couldn't even enjoy reading or watching television due to his cataracts. He now had very little to do during the days, and time began to weigh heavily on his hands.

Along with his physical losses, Amos slowly but steadily began to show mental regression after his operation. He began to have occasional lapses of memory, even to the point of forgetting the names and faces of members of his family. At times he would forget where he was or think that he was somewhere else. Sometimes he would have memory flashbacks. It became hard for him to carry on a long conversation because he would get tired quickly. His mind would wander, or he would on occasion even fall asleep when talking with someone.

As time went on Amos' problems became compounded, and he grew steadily worse. He began to lose his appetite, thus he continued to lose weight. His eyes grew worse and his coordination regressed. He became more and more helpless and more dependent on my grandmother. Unfortunately, she suffered a heart attack not long after his operation.

It was a very difficult situation. My grandmother wanted to continue to take care of Amos, but the family felt that it wasn't a good idea. They decided that Amos should be placed in a nursing home, where he could get the full attention of nurses and doctors, and at the same time lessen the burden on my grandmother. This didn't work out, however. Amos was pitifully unhappy at the nursing home and a very bad patient. He would insist on standing at the entrance of the home waiting for my grandmother to come to pick him up. Due to the fact that he was so homesick and because he was so much trouble for the nursing home, it was necessary to bring him home.

For the past year Amos has continued to grow worse and his situation at present is rather pathetic. My grandmother has had a twenty-four hour job taking care of Amos. It has been necessary for members of the family to offer assistance at times to ease the burden on her. My sixteen-year-old brother has probably done the most to help my grandmother care for Amos.

The schedule that follows presents an average day for Amos during this, his eighty-seventh year.

Early morning:	Gets up before his wife and stalks around the house until she wakes up. When his wife wakes up she takes him to the bathroom. Before getting dressed and eating breakfast he is given a glass of very warm water and a glass of prune juice (to clean out his system).
Breakfast:	He usually has a standard breakfast of cornflakes mixed with 100% bran and fresh fruit, a piece of toast, and one-half cup of coffee.
After breakfast:	He is taken into the living room and sits on his favorite chair and rests. He rests until the morning dishes are done; then he shaves with an electric razor while sitting in his chair. When he is finished shaving, he is ready to take a nap. He is taken to the couch and covered with a blanket. The nap usually is for only a short duration. He spends the rest of the morning following his wife as she does her chores.
Lunch:	At lunch he usually eats soup, a glass of juice, and coffee. (He has, for the most part, lost his enjoyment for food. He also has trouble eating his food because he has trouble seeing it due to his cataracts, and because he can no longer coordinate his eating movements well.)
After lunch:	Most afternoons Amos takes a long nap, but if he doesn't, his wife has to read to him or take him for a ride in the car.
Insert:	Sometimes during the day he cries because he realizes his helplessness. He keeps thinking there is work for him to do.
Supper:	He eats a small meal. He prefers milk and mush over meat. He very rarely cleans up his plate. He often just gets tired of chewing his food.
Evening:	He spends the evening in the living room. The television bothers him a great deal since he can't make out the picture. When it is turned on, he complains about the noise. He enjoys having the paper read to him. Sometimes he makes comments on news items read to him and seems very attentive. Other times he loses interest or falls asleep.

Bedtime: Amos gets very sleepy at about 8:00 P.M. and by 8:30 he is in bed.

During the night: He gets up many times throughout the night to go to the bathroom. He doesn't always make it to the bathroom in time. Bedding has to be changed almost daily.

This schedule indicates just how sad life can be when senility sets in. It's very depressing to see old people like Amos stricken down in such a way. It makes one wonder if it's really worth it to grow old. It's only too bad that each person can't at least keep his pride and dignity during the final years of life.

The geriatrics ward

This paper is based upon a series of observations made in the geriatrics section of a general hospital. In the summer and on weekends, I am employed there as a nurse's aide on the night shift. In particular, my observations are those of people in various stages of paralysis and senility. Geriatrics is a very depressing place to work, and, I think, even more depressing for those patients who know why they are there. But my concern now is those people who do not know.

Third Floor West doesn't really look any different than any of the other wings. When I get off the elevator and look down the hall, I see the same cream colored walls and green floors with signal lights about each of the doors. The nurses' station is to my right and to my left is a long, dark, lonely hall. Those of us working night shift sit around the desk and listen to the nurse going off duty as she describes the patients' conditions and major activities during her shift.

After the report, I start to make rounds. In geriatrics, making rounds mostly consists of checking to see whether everyone is still breathing. The first room is 312. There are two ladies in this room, and neither of them has any knowledge of where she is or what is going on around her. In the first bed is Maude. She is seventy-four years old, blind, and completely paralyzed by a stroke, except for her left arm which shakes if someone touches her. As of this writing, Maude has been in that room for one hundred and fifty-nine days. Twice every day she is lifted onto a cardiac chair and put in the hall to sit. She has to be strapped in the chair in order to do so. Maude is fed through a permanent tube in her nose that leads to her stomach and she has a catheter. She has no control over any of her physical processes and, as far as we know, no control over her mental processes. When I change the sheets on her bed at night and rub her back with alcohol, I often wonder if she hears what I say and if maybe somewhere behind those cloudy eyes there is a spark of awareness that she cannot convey. Maude is a vegetable and will remain that way until the day she dies.

In the bed on the other side of the room is Beatrice. Beatrice is seventy-eight and, like Maude, does not know where she is or why she is there. Unlike Maude, Beatrice can move and has some use of her vocal facilities. During the day she is fairly calm, but at night she thrashes around in her bed and several times has crawled out over the end. To keep Beatrice from hurting herself, she must be kept in a harness tied to her bed. It seems as though she is trying to compensate for not being able to move by screaming and moaning. She emits a loud, steady moan almost all night. I have often wondered how she is able to moan like that for such a long period of time. Beatrice is being sent to a nursing home soon. Her Medicare has run out and her family cannot afford to pay for the care she gets in the hospital.

Having checked 312, I move down the hall to 316. There is only one patient in the room at this time. His name is Albert, and he came to the hospital from one of the local nursing homes. He is eighty-three and in very serious condition. He was not given adequate care at the nursing home and as a result has very bad bedsores. Bedsores are a breakdown of the skin tissue caused by staying in one position for too long a time. Evidently, Albert was never turned. On his one hip, the skin has eroded to the bone. He has no heels; they too have atrophied as a result of not being moved. There are several other large sores on his back and legs. Albert also has epileptic seizures at short intervals. There is nothing to do except to use the padded tongue depressor to see that he does not swallow his tongue. He will never get any better, and he may even be gone the next time I go into the room. I wonder if it is right to let a human being suffer to this extreme.

Across the hall in 317 is Lillian. She is sixty-nine and has had a stroke. Her speech is impaired, and the right side of her body is paralyzed. Lillian usually knows what is going on around her, but she is stubborn when she wants to be. I ask her to raise her left arm, and she just lays there without moving an inch. The next time I look at her, she winks at me and lifts her arm. She usually likes people to talk to her even though she cannot answer. If she is interested in what I say or do, she half grins and winks and almost looks like she's going to laugh out loud. I tell her she's "my buddy" and she winks then too. Lillian is going to a nursing home soon. Her family is burdened by the hospital bills. I'm going to miss her; I hope she is given good care.

On down the hall there are other patients in other rooms, each one different yet each one very similar. How long they will be here, no one really knows. To most of them it does not matter. There are many people like the four I described. They come for a while and then are gone, only to be replaced by someone else like them. Just in the few days that I have been writing this paper, one of the four has died. Maude expired during the day shift, and by the time I went to work that night there was another patient in her bed. Room 312 will always seem sort of empty. Maude was like a permanent fixture; she had become part of the room. The idea of liking someone who never knew me seems a little hard to understand, but I really liked her. I don't know why. Maybe it's because she seemed so helpless and innocent. Whatever it was, there are a lot of faces that have come and gone but I don't think I will ever forget Maude.

Working in geriatrics has taught me a great deal. Many times the experiences have been unpleasant and sometimes gruesome, but if I have been able to provide some comfort for any one of these people, it has been worth every minute.

Ninety-five and all's well

I am of the opinion that many people in our society today consider an individual in the later phases of life as a person who has lived his life fully, grown old gracefully, and is now biding his time here on earth. They feel these individuals should be content with being given a comfortable place in which to live, food to eat, and their monthly retirement or welfare checks to buy their necessities. Many people fail to see the tremendous adjustment these older individuals have to make and how totally alone they are in a world that offers so much to the younger generations.

Aunt Byrd was ninety-five on June 13 of this year, which definitely places her in a later phase of life. Upon meeting her, everyone will invariably say: "Isn't she marvelous for her age?" and I agree. Just to be ninety-five is an accomplishment in itself!

Aging, in the physical or biological aspect, can be seen quite readily, but Aunt Byrd still possesses many characteristics that enable her to get along in this world. She is almost deaf but, through the use of a hearing aid, she can function quite adequately. Her eyesight is very good; she reads two newspapers daily and *Time* and *Newsweek* each week. She has difficulty walking and must constantly use a cane to aid her. This presents a mobility problem; therefore, she can never go far from home. Her sense of taste is deficient, because she complains of never being able to tell whether things are too salty or too sweet.

Her biological or physical aging is not as great as it would be for most ninety-five-year-old individuals, due to the fact that her diet has always been and still is quite adequate and substantial. She eats everything, even at this age. Also, she has not suffered from any major illnesses for the past thirty years; she has always led a very healthy life. She was a nurse at one time.

Since her ability to move about is curtailed but she still has the desire to get about, she has

Anyone who stops learning is old, whether this happens at twenty or at eighty. Anyone who keeps on learning not only remains young but becomes constantly more valuable, regardless of physical capacity.

Henry Ford

taken quite a number of spills in her adventures. She has bruised herself quite badly at times but still has not learned her lesson. She feels she is being a burden by asking others to get things for her and wants to get these things for herself. It is difficult for her to accept the fact that she must now depend on others to do even simple things for her.

In memory ability, Aunt Byrd has declined greatly in some aspects. She can vividly remember days and can relate them in detail, but she can't remember such things as where she placed her pocketbook or what happened to her the previous day. I think she realizes that she is declining in cognitive ability because she admits her memory isn't as good as it used to be. This must be a difficult adjustment to make as she was always very alert and interested in world events and affairs.

She is interested in politics and is staunch, even stubborn, in her beliefs. She follows the role: "I have always been a _____ and I will always remain so." Her stubborn trait shows in other aspects of her personality as well as in her politics. Of course, in her younger days, she was remarkably well known in her family for stubbornness. This aspect of her personality has remained even where others have declined.

Social adjustment has probably been the most difficult for Aunt Byrd. Her husband passed away thirty years ago, and she has no children of her own. She lives with her nephew and his family. All her friends have passed away, and she really has no one to communicate with or reminisce about old times. Every chance she gets, she likes to talk about how things used to be when she was young. She wants desperately to talk with someone but only about her time. She can't communicate about the "now" or present age.

Her chief source of interest is television. She sits for hours watching the television and enjoys this medium thoroughly. The only other interest she has is reading.

As I think about the social aspect of adjustment in old age, I can't help but feel sorry for people at this stage of life. They are so very much alone because of their lack of communication with the younger generation. Aunt Byrd is content, though, to be considered a part of the family with whom she lives. They help reduce some of her needs for companionship. It would be of such great help to elderly people if others could realize this difficult adjustment to loneliness and the desire to relate to someone.

Perhaps Aunt Byrd's greatest strength is in her spiritual and religious commitments. She has much faith and her beliefs are strong. It very well may be that her life has been so full and rewarding because of her beliefs and her tenacity in following them. No doubt her faith has helped her through her period of adjustment.

I have always wondered how she compares life of now to life as it was during her childhood. She has seen so many changes in her lifetime that it must be both rewarding and yet bewildering. I envy her the fact that she has seen and experienced so much in her lifetime. Imagine living in an age that started before the invention of the automobile and eventually saw man walking on the moon. It is no wonder she regrets that we all couldn't have lived "back then." Perhaps if I had lived back then, I would feel the same way.

THINGS TO THINK ABOUT AND DO

1. What is it like to be an adult of seventy-five to eighty years of age? What are the physiological, psychological, and sociological factors and features involved?

2. What "identity" problems are faced by the elderly? What causes some of these problems? Can some of them be avoided? If so, how?

3. Do you know of anyone over the age of ninety? Over eighty-five? Over eighty? Over seventy-five? Do they need any help of any kind? What can society, or the government, do to be of more help to them? What could you or your friends do to be of more help?

4. Debate: To what extent should the government be involved in the care and welfare of elderly people?

5. Interview several persons who are about to retire from their positions of employment, interview several who have been retired for about one year, and interview several who have been retired for two years or more. What kind of responses do you get from

these different retirement levels as to "how life is in retirement"?

6. Do a study or project on death and dying. There are a variety of approaches you might take. In general, consider a sociological approach, economic approach, psychological approach, or religious approach.

7. In the letter "Dear John and Ellen" the pains of retirement for one man are presented. Are his experiences common or typical? What are some of the attitudes, behaviors, and concerns of retired people that you have noticed?

8. In what ways are the people in the profiles "Youth at Old Age" and "Ninety-Five and All's Well" similar?

READING SOURCES
Developmental psychology texts

CRM: Developmental psychology today, ed. 2, New York, 1975, CRM/Random House, Inc., chap. 22.

Hurlock, E. B.: Developmental psychology, ed. 4, New York, 1975, McGraw-Hill Book Co., chaps. 13, 14.

Kaluger, G. and Kaluger, M.: Human development: the span of life, St. Louis, 1974, The C. V. Mosby Co., chap. 14.

Related readings

Alpert, H.: World scientists analyze aging, Harvest Years 9:33, 1969.

Birren, J. E.: The psychology of aging, Englewood Cliffs, N. J., 1964, Prentice-Hall, Inc.

Bromley, D. C.: The psychology of human aging, Baltimore, 1966, Penguin Books, Inc.

Butler, R. N., and Lewis, M. I.: Aging and mental health: positive psychosocial approaches, St. Louis, 1973, The C. V. Mosby Co.

Kastenbaum, R., and Weisman, A. D.: The psychological autopsy: a reconstruction of deathbed attitudes and behavior in old age, Geriatr. Focus 6:2, 1971.

Kuebler-Ross, E.: On death and dying, New York, 1969, The Macmillan Co.

Snyder, A. J.: Why do we grow old? Today's Health 41:51, 1963.

Sundown, D.: Passing on: the social organization of dying, Englewood Cliffs, N.J., 1967, Prentice-Hall, Inc.

Taub, H. A.: Memory span, practice and aging, J. Gerontol. 28:335-338, 1973.

White, K. L.: Life and death and medicine, Sci. Am. 229(3):23-33, 1973.

Youmans, E. G.: Age stratification and value orientations, Int. J. Aging Hum. Dev. 4:53-65, 1973.

Instructions for special projects

A. Profiles or vignettes

A profile is a short narrative that relates to a meaningful event, experience, or aspect of growth, development, or behavior in life. It is a cameo, a vignette, a poignant look at something or someone. The purpose of the profile is to present an in-depth look at some event or experience of life that will give the writer and the reader a deeper insight into the nature of development, behavior, and emotional feeling of life. The topics can be as varied as the whole realm of human experiences. There are no restrictions except that the purpose, stated above, be satisfied. A profile is about four or five pages, double-spaced, in length. One paper should be written on infancy or childhood, another on adolescence or youth, and a third on adulthood or aging. You may use yourself as the subject or you may write about someone else. In some cases, it may be necessary for you to visit and talk with someone to get material for a profile.

B. Short, personal papers

1. Write about a personal concern or problem that has been on your mind.
2. Write about how you feel and what you think about yourself.
3. Write about a particular obstacle or frustration that you have had to overcome.
4. Write on one of the following topics or headings:
   a. What it's like to be an "emerging adult"
   b. How it was
   c. How I learned about sex
   d. My experience(s) with . . .
   e. I think . . .
   f. Make up your own title

C. Open-ended response

Pass out a blank sheet of paper and give these instructions: "The topic is: Write about anything . . . . Do not use your name unless you want to. Please do not write about the course or the teacher unless this is what you really want to do."

D. Age level characteristics

Choose an age level that you would like to know more about. Do some library research and write about such things as the characteristics, the developmental tasks, the theories (if any), and the type of research done (including findings) on this age level.

E. Review of literature

Review the literature in the library on a specific topic. Hand in either an extensive, annotated bibliography or write a critical analysis of what you have read.

F. Related readings

Do a series of readings related to human development, human behavior, or human experiences. A reading is defined as being one chapter from a book or an appropriate article written by a professional person. List each reading on a separate index card with the following information: (1) the title of the article or the chapter, (2) a short summary, not to exceed the space of one card, and (3) a complete documentation of the article or book. About twenty readings would be appropriate.

G. Research

Select a research problem that investigates some aspect of human development or human behavior and set up a research design. A study that has already been done may be replicated or original research may be conducted. Suggested approaches include surveys; interviews; checklists; rating forms; experiments; observations; or measures of values, attitudes, or characteristics. Standard research procedures for collecting, interpreting, and reporting the findings must be followed.

H. Feeling paper

Write about your feelings on any experience, situation, or event about which you have some strong concerns, attitudes, or emotions. This is a very personal type of paper that permits the expression of how you feel inside. Before writing such a paper, make sure the instructor or reader is receptive to such a paper and will treat you and your feelings with respect and care.

Some of the contributors are...

Marianna S. Baker	Sharon Herr	Kenneth W. Mowen
Violet D. Banks	Bonnie Hiles	Carla Pennell
Connie Black	Anna Marie Hogbin	Mary C. Reed
Patricia Blake	Suzanne K. Hollinger	Kay Rhoad
Juliet Bliss	Thomas Holtzman	Nancy Richards
Mary E. Bock	Carol Hozman	Rachel E. Robinson
Dianne W. Carricato	Marilyn J. Imhof	Bruce B. Rost, Jr.
William Chegwin	Susan S. Kahwajy	Michael K. Ruby
Debra Christansen	Mary Kenny	Carol Ruggles
Charles Coomb	Dawn King	Phyllis J. Shelley
Joan Coultas	Nancy Kozeilski	Harold E. Shenk
Stephen Davis	Patricia Linn	Sheri Simonic
James Deihl	Mary Louise Lucas	Linda Snyder
Barbara Desher	Rosemary Lyon	Ruth Sprenkle
Barbara Dick	Jean MacDonald	Marilyn Stewart
Patricia D. Erhard	Sue Manchey	Thomas C. Stohler
Andrew Eschenmann	Carol Mansell	James W. Stoops
Jan Everetts	Kathy Martson	Elizabeth Tarner
Ann Falatovich	Karen E. Martson	Mildred Thompson
Serna A. Frost	Arthur Martynuska	Susan Tshudy
Alice Funk	Carl E. Matson	Ann Walker
Susan Gardner	Barbara McDannel	J. David Weikert
Melodie Gervin	Shirley M. McLaren	Patricia A. Wert
Ted Gilbert	Elizabeth M. Miller	Larry Wichterman
Mary T. Green	Glenn O. Miller	Joan R. Wolf
Patrice E. Grove	Joyce Miller	John Yaccino
Jane S. Guyton	Karen Miller	John Yuda
Hayes A. Hatcher	Thomas E. Miller	Carolyn Zimmerman
Kathleen Heierbacher	Edward J. Monahar	Kim Zimmerman